South Sideboards

COMPILED BY

Junior League of Jackson, Mississippi

featuring

TESTED RECIPES   COOKING BASICS

PREPARING FOOD FOR GIFTS

INSTRUCTION IN SPECIAL TECHNIQUES

HOMEMADE RAINY DAY ENTERTAINMENT FOR CHILDREN

The purpose of the Junior League is exclusively educational and charitable and is to promote voluntarism; to develop the potential of its members for voluntary participation in community affairs; and to demonstrate the effectiveness of trained volunteers.

Copies of Southern Sideboards may be obtained from
Junior League of Jackson
P.O. Box 4553
Jackson, MS 39216

ISBN 0-9606886-0-9

First Printing	June 1978	15,000 copies
Second Printing	November 1978	15,000 copies
Third Printing	December 1978	30,000 copies
Fourth Printing	October 1979	40,000 copies
Fifth Printing	July 1980	60,000 copies
Sixth Printing	July 1982	50,000 copies

Printed by
Hederman Brothers Printing Company
Jackson, Mississippi

All recipes herein have been tested and represent favorite recipes of Junior League members, their relatives and friends. Brand names of ingredients have been used only when necessary.

Editor

Mrs. Clyde X. Copeland, Jr.

Co-Editors

Mrs. Patrick H. Scanlon   Mrs. Ancel C. Tipton, Jr.

The editors take the liberty of expanding the theme of the title SOUTHERN SIDEBOARDS to include any type of meal in this region from the picnic spread on the ground to that meticulously arranged in silver dome-shaped covered dishes on the Sheraton sideboard. It includes the kitchen buffet (served from the stove), the meal served from the charcoal grill, the informal buffet dining from the pine hunt board in the family room and even today's popular tailgate picnic. Wherever spread, the Southern meal represents the cook's best for any particular category of food, and as versatile as she is hospitable, she concentrates mainly on her diners' satiation.

Cover Watercolor by Emmitt Thames

Emmitt Thames is a Mississippi born painter of rural Americana and is acclaimed as being a master of "realism," not only in technique but in recalling time, place and feeling. Watercolor is the medium in which he has received the most recognition. He employs techniques ranging from loose impressions to detailed dry brush treatment, the latter of which may become studies for his egg tempera paintings. He pays attention to immaculate detail and infuses warmth and significance into the most humble of subjects. He is the recipient of many awards including Watercolor USA and was featured on ETV on a syndicated program in 18 states.

Introductory Article by Wyatt Cooper

Wyatt Cooper, native of Quitman, Mississippi, is the author of FAMILIES: A MEMOIR AND A CELEBRATION, published in 1976. His book reflects his pride in his home state, his heritage and his large family. He tells of his battle to keep the sense of home alive in the big city. Cooper believes in man's built-in sense of family. A writer, actor and lecturer, Mr. Cooper was the husband of Gloria Vanderbilt and the father of two sons. He died in January, 1978, shortly after submitting the manuscript for this article.

Cookery is become an art,
a noble science; cooks are
gentlemen.

—Robert Burton
   (1577-1640)

Of Food and Fellowship
by Wyatt Cooper

Speak to me of food and what springs readily to my mind is not so much a recall of particular dishes I've relished, but a succession of images, sad and funny, sweet and tender, of people and places and happy occasions from the recent or long-gone past, a procession of dear, lost, familiar faces and voices, with the echo of laughter from other years. One remembers all those tables, some grand and richly laden, some humble and bearing simple fare, over which have flowed the talk, the tales, the exchanges that have made up the histories of our lives; the tables across which loving eyes have looked into loving eyes, and across which we have reached, friend to friend and spirit to spirit, to touch each other in precious communion. I think of vanished loved ones and of absent friends and simpler times, of youth and joy and wonder, of those early seasons of first discoveries, the seasons in which we were blessed with Heaven's gift for finding all the world's delight in one bright Easter egg, all the world's affection in one home-decorated birthday cake with our own particular name written bright upon it.

At those tables, a child, and later, the child in the adult, could watch and listen and learn. It was and would remain a place of adventure and exploration, a place where the curious eye and ear could partake of the rich store of other people's experience, their adventures in the vast and mysterious world that waited and waits, beckoning but intimidating, outside the window; adventures, also, in those other, interior worlds of the mind, where thoughts, opinions, ideas were and are the exhilarating sustenance of the hungry brain.

Since our associations scurry quickly back to our beginnings, I find myself breathing deeply and knowing once again the romance and allure of the smells emanating from the kitchen of my first home, the warm, comforting aroma of biscuits baking or of coffee and bacon on cold mornings, with Mama beside the stove calling out that we must hurry.

I remember the family reunions with the piling on of food, an abundance and variety of offerings that represented God only knows how many accumulated hours of planning and preparing and packing, a feast to which more than twice our number could not have done justice. I remember the buzzing and bustling of the women crowded into Grandma's kitchen, all full of importance and pride in marvels about to be revealed, each with her own specialty for which she was celebrated within the family — this one's banana pudding, that one's pineapple-upside-down cake. I think of Christmas with the smell of apples and oranges and fruit cakes and with turkeys and stuffing that make the mouth water forty years later.

I was born country, so I know all about frying just the right chickens because the preacher was coming to dinner and about all-day-sings-with-dinner-on-the-ground where heavy baskets and cardboard boxes were hauled out of the back end of family cars or even horse drawn wagons or buggies. The contents were spread proudly out, displayed like the golden wedding presents of princesses, set out upon glistening, freshly starched and sun-dried linen cloths. There would be much calling out to each other from families inviting others to try this or that from their bounty, while grabbing loose strays, especially bachelors, and there would be a scampering about of colt-legged boys, impatient and giggly while overly devout deacons went on too long at asking the blessing, when any sort of mumbled " . . . bless this food to the nourishment of our bodies . . ." would have done just as well.

I know about hog-killing time in the first sharp cool of fall, when the children were allowed to help with the scraping if they were careful to stay away from the scalding water. I know about the way molasses was made, when you took turns feeding the cane into the grinder and remembered to duck each time the pole, pulled bumpily around and around by dull, plodding mules, made its way overhead again.

These activities were co-operative efforts; we didn't do them by ourselves. Neighbors came together to help each other. We worked out the dates — Tuesday for the Longs, Thursday was the Timmses' turn, and Monday week was for us. The doing of it was all mixed up with community feeling, with jokes and gossip and catching up on news and horseplay and grown-up talk.

What I've been talking about, when you come down to it, is friendship, sharing, caring. I'm talking about love. To show our love for one another we devise little rituals. We beg the passing traveler to eat. We toast brides. We drink each other's health. We give dinners for those we seek to honor. There is a particular bond between friends who prepare food together, between friends who dine with each other. The breaking of bread together has, for many centuries, held something of a ceremonial significance for us.

It seems as if it were always so. It was in the Bible and in the earliest Greek plays and in the writings of Homer. Obviously it goes way back. I should think that it must have been soon after they first came down from the trees and began improving their manners that one of our hairy ancestors must accidently have dropped onto the cave hearth the baby brontosaurus leg on which he'd been gnawing, or stumbled onto a succulent pig just roasted by a recent forest fire, and made the revolutionary discovery that the raw and natural stuff with which he'd been sustaining his life could be improved upon. On that distant red letter day a new art form was born and man took a giant step in the direction of Julia Child.

It seems to me that the invention of cooking must have made a considerable contribution toward the very process of civilization. Surely, Mr. and Mrs. Piltdown Erectus and their children, having found the new way of dining an enrichment of the cultural tone of their own household, must certainly have hastened to call in their neighbors to share the benefits of the revelation so happily and so accidently bestowed upon them. Thus, on that evening of joyous and primitive grunting that then served as conversation, undoubtedly began the ancient and inseparable association between eating and hospitality, the eternal connection between food and fellowship.

I should mention somewhere along here that I was not invited to set down the few words of this preface because I can claim to be a passable practitioner of that noble science. The truth is I can't cook. Anything. My instant coffee is barely acceptable even to me, and my peanut butter and jelly sandwiches have repeatedly been rejected by my sons. "No thanks, Daddy," they say with wistful politeness, "We'll make our own." Alan Campbell once told me that before his wife, Dorothy Parker, would cook anything she'd go into the kitchen and eat raw bacon. In that category at least, Dottie and I were in the same league.

One of the saddest failures of my life was the time I tried to delight my little family, those underprivileged citizens of the pre-packaged, machine-made, and mass-produced age, with the home-made ice cream that is such a treasured memory from my youth. For years I'd tried to impart to them some idea of the magical creation of that frozen treat by describing how you break up the block of ice by putting it into a croker sack and beating it with the back of an ax, pack the crushed ice tightly around the metal can inside the wooden freezer, argue over who gets to turn the crank first, (several children should be involved; the making of ice cream calls for company; in a one-child family only the presence of grandparents could compensate for the absence of other children) and finally how everybody crowds around for the miraculous moment when the lid is reverently lifted off, and the creamy, vanilla colored, heavenly swirl of pure pleasure is revealed.

My sons were skeptical but willing, and so, one summer in Southampton, having consulted by long distance with my sister in Hartford, Connecticut, I bought a freezer, assembled the ingredients, and, while she instructed over the telephone, began mixing, stirring, and beating. I suspected early on that I was in trouble when it became perfectly clear to me that while Marie makes great ice cream herself, she has no very clear idea of how she does it, " . . . just put in some sugar; you'll know when it's enough . . ." — that kind of direction doesn't help at all. Honest, it doesn't. Not unless you can already do it. Or have talent. At one point I was cooking the mixture and it started turning into something that looked suspiciously like an omelet. "I hope you didn't use too many eggs . . ." she said encouragingly. "Does it look too yellow?" Along about then I had more than a premonition of disaster. Also, for some reason, it overflowed while we were turning the crank, the yellow seeping out the sides and mixing with the ice. That wasn't promising.

There's no point in pretending there's any suspense to this story or in prolonging it, so I'll go straight to the finish. It looked beautiful, actually. The result of all my labor looked very clean and very pretty, but it had no taste at all so far as I could tell and I could not expect those little boys, however polite and loving they are, to pretend that it was worth bothering with. Oddly enough, my wife, who has a very discerning palate, liked my ice cream. She thought it tasted like real yogurt made with goat's milk. Maybe if my sister has a recipe for yogurt I might end up with ice cream.

Recipes, anyway, have to be fleshed out, I suspect, with the cook's own taste, personality, and inspiration. Ethel Barrymore was once rehearsing a new play with an over-eager young director who kept instructing her with details, "Move to that table. Lift the book, pause, and then look at it." She endured this for a while, then she turned to him and said sweetly, "I know just what you mean. I lift the book, pause, look at it, and it is then that I do that special, unexplainable thing that causes audiences to come to see me and enables me to earn a thousand dollars a week." She made her point. With great cooks, as with great stars, there is that "special, unexplainable thing" that has to do with taste, authority, and uniqueness of personality, and the beginner, I should think, should be encouraged to trust his or her own particular instincts and exercise his or her own creativity.

In Saki's short story, "The Blind Spot," one character says, "The man is a common murderer," and another replies, "A common murderer, possibly, but a very uncommon cook." This book contains the secrets of many very uncommon cooks, great stars, splendid artists of the kitchen; secrets, many of them, that have considerable histories, having been handed down, generation to generation, from one famous cook to another.

I am fascinated by the great variety of cooking styles assembled here, representing many different traditions and widely varying national origins. Some recipes remain pretty much as they were when Great-Grandma was finally persuaded to write them down, or when Cousin Jessica spied on some selfish and secretive cook and wrote down each step she took, each pinch of salt, each wave of the hand in the direction of the pot. Others have evolved through adaptation, experiments, and happy accidents. A few of them doubtless traveled south with the earliest settlers, moving along the Natchez Trace from Virginia, the Carolinas or Kentucky, personally watched over by the woman of the family, along with a treasured set of china, an ancestral portrait, a silver candlestick, or some other heirloom.

Outsiders tend to think of the South as all one thing, when, of course, *we* know that our extraordinary diversity is one of our most attractive features. We have absorbed many things from many sources, and have made them our own. Take grits. Grits has, of late, been mentioned in the news somewhat frequently as a native southern specialty, which it is. It is very native, indeed, since it was given to us by the Indians, along with corn bread and many other things. Blacks have made a contribution that is hard to measure, for many black cooks have been among the nameless geniuses who've left the culinary art a better one for their having participated in it. The French and Spanish influence on cooking is very important in the South, and though New Orleans is most famous for it, excellent French and Creole restaurants are strung along the Mississippi Gulf Coast all the way to Mobile.

In the past couple of years I've traveled around my native Mississippi a great deal, and I've enjoyed everything from baked dove at the Governor's Mansion to fried catfish and hush puppies in Vicksburg and stuffed breast of chicken in Natchez, from ham hocks and turnip greens in Meridian to sirloin steak in Columbus, hot tamales in Greenville, and Creole gumbo and soft shelled crabs in Biloxi. In West Point, Mayor Kenny Dill went out and picked blackberries and Mrs. Dill made them into a pie for me. Who wouldn't choose a blackberry pie over a key to the city?

Which brings me full circle and back to hospitality. My children are startled by the extraordinary lengths that Southerners go to in order to make the visitor feel at home among them. Very often, when we have been guests in someone's home, neighbors have rushed in to leave off (or sometimes simply leave outside the door) a basket of yard eggs or fresh butter or vegetables taken from their gardens that morning.

How many times it has happened that after a speech I've found someone thrusting into my hands a container of home-made fudge or a jar of fig preserves, saying "Take these to Carter and Anderson," or "I bet Gloria's never had watermelon rind preserves," and slipping away before I could get the names? I've even been presented with chitlin's (or chitterlings, as the dictionary spells it) and though anybody who knows me can testify that I've always been proud of my farm background, in the matter of chitlin's, born country or not, I didn't know what they were and wasn't too curious to find out. I guess some things are just meant to be forgotten, but I did appreciate the thought. (Though not enough, you understand, to confront my wife with chitlin's.)

Oh, just one more thing. A story about one of my great uncles — one of the Campbells, I think. Having lost his wife (by death, I mean; she wasn't simply misplaced) he was looking around for a replacement and in mentioning the most desired qualification, he made the following observation:

"The huggin' and kissin' don't last forever. The cookin' do."

Contents

Acknowledgments

Mr. and Mrs. John Connolle of New Orleans, owners of the Thames watercolor, for allowing its reproduction on the cover

Mr. and Mrs. James L. Brown of Brown's Frame Shoppe and Little Gallery for assistance in securing and handling the painting

Tom Howe of Graphic Concepts for the special photographic treatments

Chip Bowman, Images Unlimited, for the photography

Mrs. John Bookhart for arrangements for introductory article

Mr. and Mrs. Donald Lutken for the use of their home, Sub Rosa

Junior League Actives and Sustainers for submitting and soliciting recipes, testing, editing, proofing and promoting

COMMITTEE CHAIRMEN

Mrs. Gary G. Mazzaferro
Mrs. Louis Lyell
Mrs. Dick B. Mason, III
Marketing and Promotion

Mrs. Virgil L. Bigham
Mrs. Louis Lyell
Art

Mrs. John Cossar
Mrs. Richard C. Turner, III
Mrs. W. Thad McLaurin
Proofing

Mrs. Julius Collum
Typing

Mrs. David Ross
Mrs. William F. Crosby, Jr.
Compiling

Mrs. James Kelly Wallace
Literary Introduction

Mrs. James P. McKeown
Basics

Mrs. Ed. J. Peters
Mrs. John Thomas Noblin
Mrs. John A. Jenkins, Jr.
Food Editors' Party

Mrs. W. R. Newman, III
Mrs. Jack R. Gibson
Mrs. James L. Teague
Testing

Mrs. William P. Furr, Jr.
Mrs. Daniel H. Draughn
Editing

Mrs. William F. Sistrunk
Mrs. Richard Redmont, Jr.
Mrs. H. A. Kroeze, Jr.
Special Sections

Mrs. John Crawford
Index

Mrs. Robert A. Carroll
Mrs. Boyd Shaw
Printing Research

Mrs. E. Ronald McAnally
Theme

Mrs. Reuel May, Jr.
Editorial Assistant

Mrs. Harrison Russell
Sustainer Solicitation

Our sincere appreciation to all who submitted recipes. We regret we were unable to include all of them due to similarity and lack of space.

Appetizers and Beverages

Cherry Bounce

2 quarts ripe wild cherries
3 fifths vodka or bourbon

Simple syrup

Stem and wash cherries. Be careful to avoid crushing cherries as the pulp can be bitter. Pour cherries into a wide-mouth gallon jar and fill to the top with vodka or bourbon. (For a crisper cherry taste, vodka is preferred.) Apply jar top tightly and let fruit sit for 90 days. Carefully decant liquor from the cherries. Sweeten the liquor to taste preference with simple syrup. Bottle. Yields 3 fifths.

Richard Jaubert, New Orleans, Louisiana

Basic Simple Syrup

1 cup sugar

1 cup water

Combine sugar and water in saucepan. Stir over medium heat about 1 minute to dissolve sugar. Store syrup in refrigerator indefinitely. For gifts pour simple syrup into decorative bottles. Makes 1½ cups syrup.

Rum Punch

3 ounces pineapple juice
3 ounces orange juice
3 ounces lime juice

8 dashes Angostura bitters
6 ounces rum
2 ounces simple syrup

Combine ingredients and shake well with ice. Serve in tall glasses. Serves 4.

Richard L. Redmont, Jr.

Mt. Vernon Punch

3 cups lemon juice
Grated rind of 2 lemons
2 quarts water

1½ cups each of brandy and rum
2 pounds sugar

Combine all ingredients and mix thoroughly to dissolve sugar. Set in freezer compartment of refrigerator for 3 hours before serving. Stir every 30 minutes until punch is the consistency of loose sherbet. Garnish with lemon wedges. Makes 1 gallon of punch.

Mrs. John Bookhart

It is as satisfying today as when George Washington drank it!

Milk Punch

1 gallon milk
1 (1 pound) box powdered
  sugar

3 to 4 Tablespoons vanilla
1 fifth bourbon
Ground nutmeg

Mix together the milk, sugar and vanilla. Add bourbon. Chill or put in freezer overnight and serve partially frozen. Sprinkle each serving with nutmeg. Serves 32 (6 ounce) cups.

Mrs. Robert B. Mims

Strawberry Soup

1 cup fresh strawberries
¼ cup honey
¼ cup sour cream

¾ cup cold water
½ cup dry red wine

Place all ingredients in blender. Liquefy. There will be tiny seeds visible, but straining is not necessary. Chill. Stir well before serving. Serve in wine glasses. Serves 3 or 4.

Mrs. James Kelly Wallace

Wine Punch

Cranberry juice
Chablis wine

Ginger ale

Use equal parts of the 3 ingredients listed. Chill the juices and wine. Pour into punch bowl as needed, adding chilled ginger ale at last minute.

Mrs. James P. McKeown

Very light and tart. Pretty at Christmas.

Bull Shot

Serves 4:
1 (10½ ounce) can beef broth
  (bouillon)
½ soup can vodka
Juice of 1 lemon
Celery salt
Worcestershire sauce
Tabasco

Serves 20:
5 (10½ ounce) cans beef broth
  (bouillon)
1 fifth vodka
Juice of 5 lemons
Celery salt
Worcestershire sauce
Tabasco

Mix ingredients well. Chill, shake and serve over ice. The amount of celery salt, Worcestershire sauce and Tabasco depends upon the individual taste.

F. Coleman Lowery, Jr.

Champagne Punch

Ice ring
1 magnum pink champagne
1 fifth Rosé wine

1 pint vodka
1 (28 ounce) bottle soda

Place frozen lemon juice ring (or any ice ring) in bottom of punch bowl and pour chilled liquors and soda over. (A moderately strong punch can be made by using only ½ pint vodka.) Serves 15.

Mrs. Chick Warner, Vicksburg, Mississippi

Daiquiri Slush

3 (6 ounce) cans frozen
   lemonade
1 (6 ounce) can frozen limeade

8 cups water
1 fifth light rum (or vodka)

Mix ingredients. Pour into plastic containers and freeze. Stir occasionally. Daiquiri is always "mushy frozen" and ready to serve topped with a cherry. Serves 16.

Mrs. Harold Whitley

Summer Sangría

1 lemon, sliced
1 or 2 oranges, sliced
½ cup sugar
Juice of 1 lemon

½ cup orange juice
1 quart Chianti wine
½ (28 ounce) bottle club soda

Place lemon and orange slices in a pitcher. Add sugar and juices and stir to dissolve sugar. Stir in wine. Refrigerate for several hours. Pour in club soda at last minute before serving in ice-filled glasses. Serves 6-8.

Mrs. Ancel C. Tipton, Jr.

Strawberry Daiquiri

1 (6 ounce) can frozen limeade
1 (10 ounce) package frozen
   strawberries

1 (6 ounce) can light rum
8 to 10 ice cubes (or until blender
   is full)

Place limeade, strawberries and rum in blender. Add ice cubes, a few at a time, until blender is full. Blend until slushy. Serves 4.

Mrs. Dred Porter

Vary the drink by substituting for the strawberries either 6 mint leaves, 1 ripe banana or 3 small peaches, peeled and sliced.

Blond Sangría

1 fifth dry white wine
1 cup unsweetened pineapple
    juice
⅓ cup orange juice

3 Tablespoons lemon juice
1 Tablespoon lime juice
¼ cup sugar
1 (7 ounce) bottle soda or 7-Up

Mix all ingredients and chill thoroughly, adding the soda or 7-Up just before serving. Garnish each glass with a cherry, pineapple chunk and orange slice on a toothpick. May be prepared ahead and stored in refrigerator, but do not add soda or 7-Up until serving. Serves 6.

Mrs. Bryan M. Barry

Holiday Eggnog

4 ounces bourbon
4 ounces brandy
4 ounces Tia Maria
1 dozen eggs, separated

½ pound powdered sugar
1 quart whipping cream
1 quart half and half cream
Grated nutmeg, as needed

Add bourbon, brandy and Tia Maria to egg yolks. Add powdered sugar and beat thoroughly. Refrigerate at least 24 hours. Reserve egg whites. When yolk mixture is ready, whip the whipping cream until thick but not stiff, and add half and half. Add yolk mixture and mix. Whip egg whites and add; mix thoroughly. Serve with nutmeg sprinkled on top. Yields an average punch bowl full.

Miss Lisa Reynolds

My father's famous Christmas specialty, served every year without fail.

Wassail

6 sticks cinnamon
16 whole cloves
1 teaspoon ground allspice
¼ cup sugar
2 cups cranberry juice

1 large or 2 small cans frozen
    apple juice concentrate,
    diluted (6 cups)
1 teaspoon bitters
¼ cup rum (optional)

Tie spices together in cloth bag. Combine sugar, juices and bitters. Simmer together 10 minutes and remove spice bag. Serve hot. May add rum before serving. This can be made for a large group in a 30-cup electric percolator with the spices placed in the basket. Use the same amount of spices and multiply the recipe times four. Serves 8.

Mrs. J. Elmer Nix

Velvet Hammer

1 blender vanilla ice cream
2 ounces brandy

1 ounce Cointreau
½ ounce banana liqueur

Place ingredients in blender. Turn to medium speed. Mix to pouring consistency. Serve immediately in champagne glasses. Serves 4-6.

Frank M. Duke

Marie Antoinette

Lemon slice
Sugar
Hot strong black coffee

Brandy
Kahlúa
Whipping cream, whipped

Using stemmed glasses, circle rims with lemon and dip moistened edge in sugar. Fill glasses ⅓ full of coffee. Add to each 1 jigger brandy and 1 jigger Kahlúa. Flame. Top with whipped cream. Serve immediately.

Mrs. Cleve Brown

Hot Buttered Tomato Juice

1 (46 ounce) can tomato juice
2 (10½ ounce) cans consommé
1 soup can water
¼ teaspoon Tabasco

2 teaspoons Worcestershire sauce
1 teaspoon prepared mustard
2 Tablespoons butter
Lemon wedges

Combine above ingredients except lemon wedges and heat until all are dissolved. Let the liquid come to a boil, then remove from heat. Pour into mugs and garnish with lemon wedges. May be prepared the same day and heated for serving. Serves 10.

Mrs. Sam Farrington, Jr.

Piqué Punch

½ gallon raspberry sherbet
½ gallon lime sherbet
4 (28 ounce) bottles ginger
ale, chilled
1 (28 ounce) bottle soda,
chilled

1 (46 ounce) can pineapple juice,
chilled
1 (6 ounce) bottle maraschino
cherries
Fresh strawberries

Mix all ingredients together in large punch bowl. Stir and serve. Yields 2 large punch bowls full.

Mrs. Clay L. Bartlett

Ella's Delta Mint Tea

7 tea bags
12 sprigs mint
Rind of 3 lemons
8 cups boiling water

Juice of 7 lemons
2 cups sugar
8 cups water

Steep tea, mint and lemon rind in boiling water for 12 minutes. Remove from water. Add juice and sugar. Strain. Add water. Makes 1 gallon.

Mrs. Ken P. Toler

Hot Weather Punch

8 tea bags
3 quarts boiling water
¾ cup sugar

1 (32 ounce) bottle ginger ale
1 (12 ounce) can frozen lemonade

Steep tea in water for 10 minutes. Remove tea bags and mix tea with remaining ingredients. Chill. Ginger ale may be chilled and added just before serving if a more carbonated punch is desired. Serves 15.

Mrs. Harold Graham, Crystal Springs, Mississippi

Appetizers

Curried Chicken Cheese Pie

2 envelopes unflavored
  gelatin
1 cup milk
2 chicken bouillon cubes
2 eggs, separated
½ teaspoon Accent
2 teaspoons curry powder
3 cups creamed cottage cheese

2 Tablespoons lemon juice
2 cups finely chopped cooked
  chicken
¼ cup chutney
¼ cup diced pimiento
2 Tablespoons minced onion
1 cup whipping cream, whipped
Radishes and scallions

Sprinkle gelatin over milk in saucepan; add bouillon cubes and egg yolks, mixing well. Place over low heat and stir constantly until gelatin and bouillon cubes dissolve and mixture thickens slightly (about 5 minutes). Remove from heat; stir in Accent and curry powder. Sieve or beat cottage cheese at high speed of electric mixer until smooth; stir into gelatin mixture. Stir in lemon juice, chicken, chutney, pimiento and onion. Chill, if necessary, until mixture mounds slightly when dropped from a spoon. Beat egg whites until stiff but not dry; fold into gelatin mixture. Fold in whipped cream. Spoon into an 8-inch springform pan. Chill until firm. Remove sides of pan and garnish with radishes and scallions. May be made 2 days in advance. Serve with Melba toast rounds or any favorite cracker. Serves 24.

Mrs. John Black, Jr.

Chicken with Lemon and Mustard

3 whole chicken breasts
3 Tablespoons butter
1 Tablespoon flour
¾ teaspoon monosodium
   glutamate
¼ teaspoon salt

1 teaspoon dried tarragon
1 chicken bouillon cube
½ cup hot water
1 Tablespoon Dijon mustard
3 thin lemon slices, halved
1 teaspoon finely chopped parsley

Bone chicken breasts; remove skin and cut breasts in half. Cut each half into 6-8 bite-size squares. Melt butter in a large skillet over high heat. Add chicken and sprinkle with flour, monosodium glutamate, salt and tarragon. Cook 5 minutes, stirring constantly. Dissolve bouillon cube in hot water and add to chicken along with mustard and lemon slices. Stir to loosen any browned particles. Cover and cook 2 or 3 minutes. Sprinkle with chopped parsley. Serve with cocktail picks. Makes 36 appetizers.

Mrs. Richard L. Redmont, Jr.

Chicken Liver Appetizers

⅓ cup enriched corn meal
¼ cup sifted flour
½ teaspoon salt
½ teaspoon garlic powder
1/8 teaspoon pepper

7 chicken livers, cut into ½-inch
   pieces
1 egg
2 Tablespoons milk
Oil for frying

Combine corn meal, flour, salt, garlic powder and pepper. Sprinkle livers with additional salt and pepper. Mix egg with the milk in separate bowl. Dip each piece of liver into corn meal mixture, then into egg mixture and into corn meal mixture again, coating well each time. Fry in hot, deep fat (375 °F) until golden brown (about 2 minutes). Serve hot on toothpicks with SOUR CREAM DIP. Note: Appetizers can be prepared in advance, then cooled, covered and refrigerated. Just before serving, place in ungreased shallow baking pan. Heat in preheated 350 °F oven about 10 minutes. Yields about 30 appetizers.

SOUR CREAM DIP

1 cup sour cream
2 Tablespoons grated onion
4 drops liquid red pepper
   seasoning

¼ teaspoon Worcestershire sauce
1/8 teaspoon dry mustard
½ teaspoon salt

Combine above ingredients in small bowl. Cover; refrigerate until ready to use. Makes 1 cup dip.

Mrs. T. Arnold Turner, Jr.

———

Use miniature muffin tins or styrofoam egg cartons in which to mold individual appetizers.

Chicken Wing'ums

⅓ cup soy sauce
1 cup Sake
2 Tablespoons water
2 Tablespoons brown sugar

1 large clove garlic,
  pressed, or garlic powder
3 pounds chicken winglets
  (drumstick part)

Combine and heat the first five ingredients. Pour over chicken wings and marinate several hours. Turn once. Place in preheated 350°F oven for 1 hour or until all juices are absorbed and wing'ums are brown. Yields about 25 wing'ums.

Mrs. Morris Lewis, Jr., Indianola, Mississippi

Chicken Curry Balls

¼ pound cream cheese,
  softened
2 Tablespoons mayonnaise
1 cup chopped cooked chicken
1 Tablespoon curry powder

1 Tablespoon chopped chutney
½ teaspoon salt
1 cup blanched slivered almonds
½ cup grated coconut, or more

Mash cream cheese. Add mayonnaise, chicken, curry, chutney, salt and almonds. Mix well and roll into walnut size balls. Roll in coconut. Chill. May be prepared a day in advance. Freezes well. Makes 3 dozen balls.

Mrs. Eleanor H. Collums

Oriental Chicken Puffs

1 (7 ounce) package chicken-
  flavored rice mix
2 eggs, beaten
1½ Tablespoons horseradish
1 teaspoon Worcestershire sauce
½ teaspoon dry mustard
¼ teaspoon salt

1 (5½ ounce) can chicken,
  finely chopped
⅔ cup shredded sharp Cheddar
  cheese
1 cup finely crushed Rice Chex
Vegetable oil
Bottled oriental duck sauce

Prepare rice mix as directed. Cool to lukewarm. Combine eggs, horseradish, Worcestershire sauce, mustard and salt in bowl. Add rice, chicken and cheese. Mix thoroughly. Chill 2 hours or until mixture handles easily. Shape into 1-inch balls and roll each ball in crushed cereal. Pour vegetable oil 3 inches deep into heavy saucepan and heat to 375°F (or use electric frypan). Fry puffs until they are golden brown. Drain. Heat duck sauce in small saucepan over moderate heat about 5 minutes, stirring occasionally. Serve as warm dip. May be prepared 2 days in advance. To reheat, place puffs on lightly buttered shallow pan in 400°F oven for 15 minutes. Yields 5 dozen.

Mrs. Robert H. Thompson, Jr.

Selma's Chicken Liver Pâté

½ cup finely chopped onion
½ cup plus 2 Tablespoons
    butter or margarine, divided
¼ pound fresh mushrooms,
    sliced
¼ pound chicken livers
1½ teaspoons seasoned salt

1 teaspoon lemon juice
Dash pepper
Dash cayenne pepper
2 hard-cooked eggs,
    quartered
¼ cup halved shelled
    pistachio nuts

Sauté onion in ½ cup butter until golden (about 5 minutes). Add mushrooms and chicken livers; cook, stirring occasionally, until chicken livers are tender (about 5 minutes). Remove from heat. Add rest of butter, seasoned salt, lemon juice, pepper and cayenne. Stir until butter melts. Then divide mixture into 4 parts. In electric blender at high speed, purée the chicken liver mixture, one part at a time, adding 2 of the hard-cooked egg quarters to each part. Turn into bowl. Add nuts, mixing well. Refrigerate 30 minutes. On sheet of wax paper or foil, shape pâté mixture into a mound. Wrap the pâté mound and refrigerate it overnight. Serve pâté on platter surrounded by salted crackers. Makes 2¼ cups or enough to spread 54 crackers.

Mrs. Charles W. Campbell, Plainfield, Indiana

Venison Meat Balls

8 slices stale bread
¾ cup milk
4 pounds ground venison
2 pounds hot sausage (or
    1 pound ground pork plus
    1 pound hot sausage)
5 whole eggs, beaten
Garlic salt
Salt and pepper

½ cup finely chopped parsley
2 medium onions, finely chopped
4 ribs celery, finely chopped
Oil
6 (10½ ounce) cans cream of
    mushroom soup
1 (8 ounce) jar "Woody's"
    Cook-in' sauce

Soak bread in milk to soften. Mix all ingredients except oil, soup and barbecue sauce together with hands. Roll into bite-size balls. Brown in small amount of oil and remove to drain. Pour off excess fat. Mix soup and barbecue sauce together in remaining drippings. Pour over meat balls, which have been placed in a large baking pan. Place in 350°F oven and simmer for about 40 minutes. Cover with aluminum foil, if sauce does not cover meat balls. Serve in chafing dish with toothpicks. Freezes. Yields 450 meat balls.

Mrs. Henry H. Mounger

The meat balls and sauce may be frozen together in plastic baking bags, then heated in a saucepan of boiling water.

Duck or Chicken Liver Pâté

¾ pound chicken or duck livers
   (Long Island Ducklings)
1 teaspoon salt
Dash cayenne pepper
¾ cup butter, softened
¼ teaspoon ground nutmeg

1 teaspoon dry mustard
1/8 teaspoon ground cloves
3 Tablespoons grated onion
Dash freshly ground black pepper
1½ Tablespoons Cognac

Simmer livers in water to cover for 20 minutes. Drain; put through meat grinder or purée in food processor. Mix livers with remaining ingredients until smooth. Correct seasonings. Pack into 2-cup mold and chill in refrigerator until firm. Unmold and serve as spread with crackers. Serves 8.

Mrs. James Savage, Jr.

This is an exceptionally delicious pâté.

Smoked Rare Duck

2 mallard ducks (or ducks
   of equivalent size)
1 Tablespoon baking soda

2 teaspoons salt
Lemon-pepper seasoning

Wash ducks in pan of water containing soda and salt. Rinse ducks in clear water and pat dry with paper towel. Sprinkle generously with lemon-pepper seasoning inside and out. Using barbecue grill with cover, cook over hot charcoal embers but not directly over flame unless using spit. Cook covered 20 minutes to 1 hour (depending on size of ducks and size of fire) in order to serve rare. Turn occasionally. Remove ducks from fire and place on cutting board. Cut off legs (they are rarely tender). Remove whole breasts and cut into bite size chunks. Salt lightly and serve on warm platter with dipping SAUCES. The carcass may be reserved and frozen with legs for making duck gumbo. Serves 6-8.

HORSERADISH SAUCE

1 cup mayonnaise
Juice of 1 lemon
1 Tablespoon grated onion
2 Tablespoons horseradish

½ teaspoon salt
Dash Tabasco
Paprika

Mix ingredients together and sprinkle with paprika. Makes 1 cup sauce.

WINE SAUCE

1 (10 ounce) jar currant jelly
½ cup red wine

1 Tablespoon orange juice
1 Tablespoon grated orange rind

Melt currant jelly over low heat, stirring often. Add red wine, orange juice and orange rind. Makes 3 cups sauce.

Sherwood Wise

21

Dove Breasts in Cream Sauce

15 dove breasts
Salt and pepper
1 rib celery, quartered
2 slices onion
½ cup water
2 Tablespoons butter or
  margarine, melted
2 Tablespoons flour
1 cup milk, warm
½ cup broth from doves

½ teaspoon Worcestershire
  sauce
Garlic salt
Seasoned salt
Paprika
Pinch dry mustard
Pinch thyme
1 Tablespoon dried green parsley
1 (3 ounce) can sliced mushrooms,
  drained

Cook dove breasts, which have been salted and peppered, in pressure cooker with celery, onion and water for 15 minutes. (Dove can be cooked in covered casserole, breast down, with same seasonings and ½ inch of water in 325°F oven for 1½-2 hours.) Let dove cool in liquid. Make cream sauce by combining melted butter and flour in heavy saucepan, stirring 1 minute. Add milk and dove broth and stir until thickened. Add Worcestershire sauce, generous sprinklings of garlic salt, seasoned salt, paprika, mustard, thyme and parsley. Remove dove from bone and cut into bite-size pieces. Stir into cream sauce. Add mushrooms. If a thinner sauce is desired, add more dove broth. Serve from chafing dish on Melba rounds or thin-sliced toast squares. This dish also makes a nice luncheon entrée, served on toast points. Serves 15.

Mrs. Rod Russ, Jr.

Note: Wild duck can be substituted for the dove.

Sweet and Sour Sausages

8 ounces little "smokies"
  sausages
½ cup vinegar
½ cup sugar
¼ cup sherry wine
1 Tablespoon soy sauce
1 teaspoon grated fresh ginger
  root

2 teaspoons cornstarch
1 Tablespoon water
1 (10 ounce) can pineapple
  chunks, drained
1 green pepper, cut in 1-inch
  squares
½ cup maraschino cherries,
  drained

Brown sausages. Drain on paper towels. Boil together briefly vinegar, sugar, sherry, soy sauce and ginger. Blend cornstarch and water together and add to above mixture. Cook until transparent. Add sausages, pineapple, green pepper and cherries and slowly heat. May be prepared 2 days in advance. Serve in a chafing dish. Serves 6.

Mrs. William C. Norris, Jr.

Teriyaki Beef Strips

1½ pounds top sirloin steak,
    cut in thin ¼-inch strips
½ cup soy sauce
¼ cup brown sugar
½ teaspoon Accent

¼ teaspoon pepper
1 teaspoon ground ginger
2 cloves garlic, minced
2 Tablespoons Wesson oil

Thread meat strips accordion-style on wooden skewers. Place in large Pyrex dish. Combine remaining ingredients for sauce; stir and pour over beef strips. Marinate covered in refrigerator 6 hours or longer, stirring occasionally. Allow meat to marinate at room temperature 1 hour before cooking. Drain and save sauce. Broil over hot coals 5-6 minutes, basting with sauce. Turn once. Serve immediately. Serves 6-8.

Mrs. James J. Hudgins

Hot Chipped Beef Dip

½ cup coarsely chopped pecans
2 Tablespoons butter
½ teaspoon salt
11 ounces cream cheese,
    softened
2 Tablespoons milk

1 (2½ ounce) jar dried beef,
    cut in pieces
¼ cup chopped green pepper
1 small onion, grated
Pepper
1 cup sour cream

Oven toast pecans in butter and salt. Mix cream cheese, milk, beef, green pepper, onion and pepper. Fold in sour cream and half the nuts. Place in baking dish and sprinkle remaining nuts on top. Bake at 350°F for 20 minutes. Serve in chafing dish with Melba rounds. Serves 8-10.

Mrs. James P. McGaughy

Meat Pies

1 pound ground meat
1 medium onion, chopped
2 Tablespoons tomato paste
Juice of 1 lemon
1 (8 ounce) carton sour cream

Ground cinnamon to taste
Salt and pepper
2 (10 ounce) cans flaky
    refrigerator biscuits
Oil for deep fat frying

Brown meat and onion. Add next 5 ingredients. Break up meat while browning. The meat does not have to be cooked; just stir until all ingredients are mixed. Place in refrigerator until cold. Pull apart flaky biscuits to make two. Roll each one out on a floured board. Place a heaping teaspoon of cold filling on each biscuit round. Fold over and crimp edges to seal. Place on tray in freezer. When frozen take out and drop in hot oil to fry. Drain and serve or return to freezer. Will freeze up to 3 months. Yields 40.

Mrs. Kaleel Salloum, Gulfport, Mississippi

Tiny Quiches

½ cup butter, softened
1 (3 ounce) package cream
   cheese, softened
1 cup flour

FILLING:
1 cup grated Swiss cheese
1 large egg, slightly beaten
½ cup milk
¼ teaspoon salt
Paprika

Cream butter and cream cheese. Work in flour. Roll into a dough ball. Chill. When ready to bake, divide ball of dough into 24 tiny balls and press into lightly greased miniature muffin tins, forming small pastry shells. *FILLING:* Divide the cheese evenly and place in the unbaked pastry shells. (A few bits of crumbled bacon, Canadian bacon or ham may be added to each quiche with the cheese.) Beat egg, milk and salt together and drizzle over the cheese. Sprinkle each with paprika. Bake at 350°F for about 30 minutes. Serve warm. Quiches freeze well up to one week. To serve, allow quiches to come to room temperature and warm in a 325°F oven. Makes 24 quiches.

Mrs. William F. Goodman, Jr.

Hot Spicy Meat Balls

SAUCE:
¾ cup ketchup
½ cup water
¼ cup cider vinegar
2 Tablespoons brown sugar
1 Tablespoon minced onion
2 teaspoons Worcestershire
   sauce
1½ teaspoons salt
1 teaspoon dry mustard
¼ teaspoon pepper
3 drops Tabasco
Few grains cayenne pepper

MEAT BALLS:
¾ pound ground beef
¾ cup fine bread crumbs
¾ teaspoon salt
½ teaspoon pepper
½ teaspoon Accent
1½ Tablespoons minced onion
½ teaspoon horseradish
3 drops Tabasco
2 eggs, beaten

1 Tablespoon butter or
   margarine

Mix *SAUCE* ingredients together in bowl and set aside. Mix all *MEAT BALLS* ingredients and shape into ¾-inch balls. Melt butter or margarine in chafing dish brazier over direct heat. Add meat balls and brown, shaking brazier frequently to produce even browning and to keep balls round. Pour off fat, pour sauce over meat balls and cover. Cook 10 minutes, shaking occasionally. Place over pan of simmering water to keep hot. Provide wooden picks to spear meat balls. Meat balls may be frozen. Yields 3 dozen meat balls.

Mrs. Charles O. Jones

Mock Liver Pâté

1 pound liverwurst
1½ teaspoons garlic juice
1½ teaspoons minced onion

1 teaspoon basil
Sour cream
Parsley for garnish

Mix first 4 ingredients and form into a mound. Refrigerate until firm. When ready to serve, "ice" with sour cream and garnish with parsley. Serve with crackers. May be prepared 1 day ahead. Serves 8-10 or more.

Mrs. Leigh B. Allen, III

Monroe Pizza Appetizers

1 pound ground beef
1 pound hot bulk sausage
1 pound Velveeta cheese
½ teaspoon Worcestershire
   sauce
½ teaspoon garlic salt

1 teaspoon oregano
2 loaves party rye with seeds
Sliced or whole green olives
   with pimiento, pitted ripe
   olives or small button
   mushrooms

Cook beef and sausage in heavy skillet until done; drain off fat. Add cheese, Worcestershire sauce, garlic salt and oregano. Stir over low heat until cheese is melted. Spread mixture on party rye slices and garnish with green olives, ripe olives or mushrooms. Place on cookie sheets and heat in 350°F oven until hot. May be frozen on cookie sheets until firm and stored in container. May be prepared in advance. Yields 50 slices.

Mrs. Joseph L. Speed

Popular with teenagers and easy for them to prepare.

Olive Pecan Rolls

1½ cups flour
¾ teaspoon salt
½ teaspoon paprika
½ cup butter or margarine
½ cup sour cream

¾ cup chopped pecans
¾ cup grated Cheddar cheese
¾ cup chopped pimiento-stuffed
   green olives
2 Tablespoons mayonnaise

Sift flour with salt and paprika into mixing bowl. Cut in butter or margarine. Add sour cream and mix well. Cover and chill dough ½ hour. Mix pecans, cheese, olives and mayonnaise. Divide dough into 2 balls. Roll each into an 8 x 15-inch rectangle, then cut into two 4-inch wide strips. Spread olive filling down the center of each strip. Bring long sides together and pinch to seal. Pinch ends together. Place on baking sheet, seam side down. Bake in 400°F oven for 20 minutes or until brown and crisp. Cool and slice. Yields about 3 dozen slices.

Mrs. J. T. Noblin

Cream Cheese Turnovers with Fillings

CREAM CHEESE PASTRY

1 cup butter, softened
1 (8 ounce) package cream
   cheese, softened
½ teaspoon salt

2 cups flour
1 egg yolk
2 teaspoons milk

Mix butter, cream cheese, salt and flour to form soft dough. Chill overnight. Break off part of dough (keeping remainder chilled until time to roll it out) and roll it paper thin on a floured surface. With cookie cutter cut into 2 or 3-inch circles and fill with one of the following fillings. When ready to cook, brush tops with egg yolk, beaten with the milk. Place on ungreased baking sheet and cook at 350°F for 20 minutes. The unbaked pastries may be frozen and baked frozen or thawed slightly.

MUSHROOM TURNOVERS

½ pound fresh mushrooms,
   chopped fine
2 Tablespoons butter
½ cup chopped onion
½ teaspoon salt
Dash pepper

Dash ground nutmeg
1 teaspoon lemon juice
2 teaspoons flour
½ cup sour cream
1 teaspoon dill weed
1 recipe Cream Cheese Pastry

Sauté mushrooms in butter with the onion until limp. Add salt, pepper, nutmeg and lemon juice. Blend in flour until smooth and slightly thickened. Stir in sour cream and dill weed. Cool filling. Place small amount of filling (scant teaspoon) on one side of pastry round. Fold over and crimp edges with fork tines. Bake according to pastry instructions. Yields 4 dozen.

PORK GINGER ROLL

1 pound ground lean pork
½ cup flaked crab meat or
   finely chopped shrimp
1 teaspoon salt
½ cup water chestnuts,
   chopped
2 green onions, minced

½ teaspoon ground ginger
2 Tablespoons soy sauce
1 small clove garlic, crushed
1 egg
¼ cup fine dry bread crumbs
1 recipe Cream Cheese Pastry

Cook pork until whitish but not dry. Mix with other filling ingredients and cool. Roll pastry into four 12 x 9-inch rectangles. Spread each with ¼ filling and roll up, beginning with long side. Moisten to seal edges. Chill. Bake on ungreased baking sheet 30-35 minutes at 375°F. Cool slightly. Cut into 1-inch slices to serve. Yields 4 dozen slices.

Soak wooden skewers in water an hour before using to prevent scorching.

SHRIMP TARTLETS

½ cup mashed cooked shrimp
2 green onions, chopped
1 teaspoon Dijon mustard
¼ teaspoon tarragon

1 teaspoon lemon juice
2 Tablespoons mayonnaise
Salt to taste
½ recipe Cream Cheese Pastry

Mix filling ingredients well. Place small amount on side of a 2 or 3-inch pastry round. Fold over and crimp edges with fork tines. Chill 1 hour, then bake according to pastry instructions. Yields 2 dozen.

OLD CALIFORNIA EMPANADITOS

½ cup shredded sharp
   Cheddar cheese
2 Tablespoons butter, melted
2 green onions, chopped
1 clove garlic, crushed

¼ cup chopped ripe olives
Dash oregano
¼ cup canned chopped green
   chilies, blotted dry
½ recipe Cream Cheese Pastry

Mix filling ingredients thoroughly. Place small amount on one side of a 2 or 3-inch pastry round. Fold over and crimp edges with fork tines. Bake according to pastry instructions. Yields 2 dozen.

SPICY EMPANADAS

1 pound ground lean beef
1 (1½ ounce) package spaghetti
   sauce mix
¼ cup minced onion
2 medium tomatoes, peeled and
   chopped

Salt to taste
½ cup water
¼ cup grated Parmesan cheese
½ cup grated sharp cheese
1½ recipes Cream Cheese
   Pastry

Brown beef. Stir in next 5 ingredients. Simmer 15-20 minutes. Remove from heat and stir in cheese. Cool mixture. Place small amount on one side of 2 or 3-inch pastry round and cook according to pastry instructions. Yields 6 dozen.

Mrs. McWillie Robinson, Jr.

Pepper Jelly Turnovers

1 (5 ounce) jar Old
   English cheese
½ cup butter

1 cup flour
2 Tablespoons water
1 (4 ounce) jar hot pepper jelly

Cut cheese and butter into flour. Quickly stir in water and shape into a ball. Refrigerate overnight. Roll out dough very thin and cut with a biscuit cutter into 2-inch circles. Place ½ teaspoon of pepper jelly in center of each circle. Fold over and crimp edges with a fork. Bake at 375°F for 10 minutes. Turnovers may be frozen before or after baking. Reheat before serving. Makes 2-3 dozen.

Mrs. G. G. Mazzaferro

Turnovers may be filled with orange marmalade and dusted with powdered sugar for serving with morning coffee.

Chinese Egg Rolls

STUFFING:
1 (16 ounce) can La Choy
  fancy mixed Chinese
  vegetables, drained
1 bunch green onions,
  finely chopped
4 ribs celery, finely chopped
½ pound shrimp, cooked,
  peeled, finely chopped
½ pound ground pork,
  cooked and drained
1 small can water chestnuts,
  chopped
1 egg, slightly beaten

1 Tablespoon oil
2 Tablespoons soy sauce
1 teaspoon sugar
½ teaspoon salt
¼ teaspoon red pepper

EGG ROLL WRAPPINGS:
2⅔ cups sifted flour
1⅓ cups cornstarch
2 teaspoons salt
4 eggs, beaten
3 cups water

Oil for deep frying

Combine *STUFFING* ingredients. Refrigerate overnight, preferably. To make *EGG ROLL WRAPPINGS,* sift together the flour, cornstarch and salt. Combine eggs and water; blend into the flour mixture. Beat until smooth. Pour about 3 Tablespoons of the batter into a lightly greased 6-inch iron skillet and turn to cover the edges of the skillet. Cook on medium heat until the edges begin to curl. *Do not flip over.* Stack these as they are made. They will feel like rubber. Place a generous amount of stuffing in the center of each pancake. Brush the edges of the pancake with some of the remaining batter. Fold two sides in and then turn the other side over. Place sealed side on wax paper. Freeze on a cookie sheet until hard and place in a baggie. Deep-fat fry egg rolls at 375°F for about 6 minutes. Do not thaw before frying. Serve hot with SWEET AND SOUR SAUCE and/or a hot mustard. Yields 25 egg rolls.

SWEET AND SOUR SAUCE

1 Tablespoon cornstarch
1 Tablespoon water
½ cup vinegar

½ cup sugar
¼ cup sherry wine
1 Tablespoon soy sauce

Make a paste of the cornstarch and water. Combine with the remaining ingredients in a saucepan and bring to a boil. Stir until mixture is thick and transparent. Serve at room temperature.

Mrs. Joe Dehmer, Jr.

A QUICK SWEET AND SOUR SAUCE can be made by melting over low heat 1 (12 ounce) jar apricot preserves and adding to it 1 (2 ounce) jar pimientos, finely chopped, and 2-3 Tablespoons red wine vinegar.

Wrap a quarter slice bacon around 2 pecan halves which have been bound back-to-back with Roquefort cheese spread; broil until browned, turning once.

Texas Torte

2 eggs, beaten
2 Tablespoons flour
½ teaspoon salt
⅓ cup milk
1 (4 ounce) can chopped
  green chilies

½ pound sharp Cheddar cheese,
  grated
½ pound Monterey Jack cheese,
  grated

To eggs add flour, salt and milk; beat well. Add remaining ingredients and mix well. Pour into a flat well-greased 8 x 12-inch Pyrex baking dish and bake at 350°F for about 35 minutes. Cut into tiny squares and serve as a hot hors d'oeuvre. Makes 96 squares.

Mrs. Edward C. Nichols

Appetizer Puffs

1½ cups flour
1 teaspoon salt
1 cup margarine
½ cup sour cream
2 Tablespoons grated Parmesan
  cheese

2 Tablespoons chopped green
  onion
2 Tablespoons chopped
  mushrooms
2 Tablespoons chopped ripe olives

Mix flour and salt and cut margarine into this until mixture begins to form a ball. Blend in sour cream. Divide dough into 4 parts. Wrap each part and chill several hours. Heat oven to 350°F. On floured board, roll each section into a 12 x 6-inch rectangle. Sprinkle one-half of each rectangle with either cheese, onion, mushrooms or olives. Fold dough over to make a 6-inch square. Cut the 6-inch square into 2-inch squares, pressing edges. Continue until all dough is prepared. Bake on ungreased cookie sheet at 350°F for 20-25 minutes. May be prepared in advance and refrigerated, then baked for 30 minutes. Makes 36 appetizers.

Mrs. T. Arnold Turner, Jr.

Dell's Cheese Straws

½ cup margarine or
  butter, softened
1 (8 ounce) stick Cracker Barrel
  cheese, grated

½ teaspoon salt
½ teaspoon red pepper
1½ cups plus 1 Tablespoon
  flour, sifted

Mix butter with cheese and seasonings. Add flour and form into dough. If available use cookie press with ridged line opening. Otherwise roll out and score with fork. Cut into straws and bake on greased cookie sheet for 25 minutes at 350°F. Yields 5 dozen.

Mrs. L. H. Dunham, Canton, Mississippi

Curry Almond Spread

1 pound cream cheese
½ cup chopped Major Grey's
  chutney
2 teaspoons curry powder

½ teaspoon dry mustard
½ cup chopped almonds,
  toasted

Bring cream cheese to room temperature in mixing bowl. Sprinkle in other ingredients and mix well with hands. Shape into a round ball. Refrigerate. Will keep for a month in refrigerator, if well covered. Take out of refrigerator 15-20 minutes before serving. Place on tray and serve with crackers. Yields 2 cups.

Mrs. Dan Morse

At Christmas time, sprinkle generously with paprika and stick a sprig of holly on top.

Decorative Cheese Mold

1 pound cream cheese,
  softened
1 pound sharp cheese, grated
Garlic salt to taste

6 drops Tabasco
1 teaspoon Worcestershire
  sauce
Salt to taste

Beat ingredients together until smooth. Spoon into 4-cup mold and chill. Freeze and remove from mold while frozen (dip in very warm water). Serve as spread for crackers. Serves 15.

Mrs. Tom B. Scott, Jr.

Especially attractive molded because of its light, golden color!

Mrs. Rhyne's Cheese Boxes

½ pound sharp or American
  cheese, grated
½ pint mayonnaise
1 Tablespoon Durkee sauce
1 teaspoon prepared mustard

1 Tablespoon Worcestershire
  sauce
Onion or garlic juice to taste
Salt and pepper to taste
Regular thin-sliced bread

Blend cheese and mayonnaise; then add remaining sauces and seasonings. Trim crust from bread. Spread 2 slices with the cheese mixture, place one atop the other, then cut into 4 squares. Repeat until desired number of "2-story boxes" are formed. Ice sides of boxes lightly with cheese mixture. Toast at 400°F immediately before serving. Yields 1 pint cheese spread, sufficient to spread 2 loaves of bread.

Mrs. George R. Day

Mrs. Rhyne was the Chi Omega housemother at Ole Miss during the late 1950's.

Cream Cheese-Onion Canapés

White sandwich bread
1 (8 ounce) package
   cream cheese, softened
1 teaspoon Worcestershire
   sauce
Seasoned salt

Black and red pepper
Paprika
Small white onions,
   cut into thin rings
Hellmann's mayonnaise

Cut bread into 1½ or 2-inch rounds, using a biscuit cutter or fruit juice glass. Toast one side only. Season cream cheese with Worcestershire sauce, seasoned salt, black and red pepper and paprika. Spread cream cheese mixture on toasted side of bread rounds. Top with onion ring slightly smaller than bread round. Cover generously with mayonnaise and sprinkle lightly with paprika. Bake at 400°F until toasted and bubbly. Makes about 4 dozen rounds.

Mrs. Charles C. Taylor, Jr.

Bleu Cheese Mold

1 envelope unflavored gelatin
⅓ cup white wine
1 (6 ounce) package bleu
   cheese, crumbled
1 Tablespoon lemon juice
½ cup mayonnaise
2 Tablespoons finely
   chopped parsley
½ teaspoon paprika

1 to 1½ Tablespoons finely
   chopped green onion
1 cup whipping cream
3 Washington red apples,
   sliced in wedges
3 Golden Delicious apples,
   sliced in wedges
Lemon-water bath
Powdered sugar

Soften gelatin in wine. Set over hot water and heat until gelatin is completely dissolved. Mix cheese with lemon juice. Gradually blend in mayonnaise, mixing until smooth. Stir in gelatin and blend well. Add parsley, paprika and onion. Cool until mixture begins to thicken. Beat cream to soft peaks and fold into gelatin mixture. Turn into 1-quart mold. Chill overnight. Unmold, and serve with crisp apples that have been dipped in fresh lemon-water bath. After the apples have been drained from the bath, sprinkle them with powdered sugar and arrange around the cheese mold. This can be made in a pineapple mold with apples placed around it in alternating colors. May be prepared 1 day in advance. Serves 20.

Mrs. Alvin E. Brent, Jr.

Slices of fresh fruit will not turn dark if dipped in a lemon-water bath before serving. Water bath is made by combining 4 cups water with juice and rind of 2 lemons.

———

To facilitate flattening bread slices for rolled party sandwiches, steam slices of bread in a colander over boiling water for a minute or two. The bread will then roll easily.

Cheese Biscuits

½ pound sharp Cheddar
  cheese, grated
½ pound butter, softened
2 cups flour

Paprika
Powdered sugar
Almond slivers

Mix cheese and butter; mash, then cream thoroughly. Add flour to mixture and mix well. Add paprika for color. Shape into logs and chill. Slice thin and place on a lightly greased cookie sheet. Sprinkle with powdered sugar and center with almond slivers. Bake at 375°F for 8 minutes. May be prepared in advance. Yields 5 dozen.

Mrs. Roger Friou

Coleman's Favorite Cheese Ball

1 pound sharp Cheddar cheese
1 pound cream cheese
1 pound bacon, fried crisp
  and crumbled

1 small onion, grated
½ pound Roquefort cheese
Pinch garlic salt
Worcestershire sauce (optional)

With all ingredients at room temperature, mix well. Shape into 2 medium balls or 4 logs. Serves 20.

Mrs. Coleman Frye

Mushroom Appetizer

1 large onion, chopped
¾ pound fresh mushrooms,
  chopped
1 Tablespoon butter
¼ teaspoon salt
1/8 teaspoon pepper
12 ounces cream cheese

½ teaspoon Worcestershire
  sauce, or more
¼ teaspoon garlic powder,
  or more
Tabasco, if desired
1 loaf thin-sliced white bread
Melted butter

Sauté onion and mushrooms in butter for about 2 minutes. Remove from heat. Season with salt and pepper. Add cream cheese, stirring until mixture is smooth. Add next 3 ingredients to mixture and let sit about 1 hour. Trim crust from bread and flatten with rolling pin. Spread mushroom mixture on bread and roll up. Chill and slice in bite-size pieces. Place slices on cookie sheet. Dab butter on each slice and bake in 350°F oven for 15 minutes. Turn and continue to cook until light brown. Serve hot. Can be made ahead and placed in refrigerator until ready to bake. Freezes well. Makes at least 100 bites.

Mrs. Tommy L. Weems

Brandied Bleu Cheese

1 (8 ounce) package cream
  cheese, softened
⅓ cup brandy

2 (4 ounce) packages Kraft
  bleu cheese, crumbled
Dash ground nutmeg

Whip ingredients together. Serve with cocktail wafers. Makes 2 cups.

Mrs. Julius Collum

Celery Crunch Swirls

1 whole bunch celery
1 (8 ounce) package cream
  cheese, softened
½ cup grated American cheese

1 Tablespoon minced onion
1 clove garlic, minced
Salt and pepper to taste
1 Tablespoon milk

Separate celery into ribs; trim and wash. Combine cheeses and blend until smooth. Add remaining ingredients and thoroughly blend. Spread mixture in center of each rib. Press 3 ribs together with cheese facing the center. This results in a center of cheese with celery completely surrounding it. Secure bundles with rubber bands. Chill for at least 1 hour. Remove bands and slice ½ inch thick. Serves 12-16.

Mrs. G. G. Mazzaferro

Marinated Sliced Mushrooms

3 pounds fresh mushrooms,
  sliced
⅓ cup olive oil
Juice of 1 lemon
2 onions, sliced
2 cloves garlic, crushed
¼ cup olive oil
½ teaspoon each thyme,
  marjoram, pepper
3 bay leaves
1 cup red wine vinegar

3 cups Italian tomatoes,
  drained and chopped,
  plus ½ cup reserved
  juice
1 teaspoon sugar
Dash hot sauce
Salt
Party rye bread,
  buttered and sprinkled
  with chopped parsley

Sauté fresh mushrooms in ⅓ cup olive oil (in 2 batches, if necessary). Transfer to a bowl and toss with lemon juice. In skillet sauté onions and garlic in ¼ cup olive oil until soft. Add thyme, marjoram, pepper and bay leaves and sauté 1 minute more. Stir in wine vinegar, Italian tomatoes with juice, sugar and hot sauce. Bring to a boil; then simmer for 20 minutes. Add to mushrooms and salt to taste. Cool, cover; let marinated mushrooms chill 12 hours. Serve on buttered, parsleyed rye bread. Yields 4 cups.

Mrs. Richard L. Redmont, Jr.

Mushrooms Stuffed with Snails

½ cup butter, softened
2 Tablespoons minced
  shallots
1 to 2 cloves garlic, minced
2 Tablespoons minced parsley

Salt and pepper
20 to 30 mushrooms,
  medium to large
1 (4½ ounce) can large
  snails

Cream butter with all of the ingredients except mushrooms and snails. Wash, wipe dry and remove stems from mushrooms. Place ¼ teaspoon butter mixture in cap, add a snail (cut snail in half or thirds for smaller mushrooms) and top with another ½ teaspoon butter mixture. Place in shallow pan and bake at 375 °F for 15 minutes. Serve hot or warm. Makes 20-30 appetizers.

Mrs. William B. Wilson

Spinach-Stuffed Mushrooms

1 (10 ounce) package frozen
  chopped spinach, cooked
  and drained
½ cup sour cream
¼ cup tomato sauce

Dash wine vinegar
1 cup grated sharp cheese
1 pound fresh mushrooms
4 Tablespoons butter

Combine all ingredients except mushrooms and butter. This may be done a day ahead. Wash mushrooms, dry on paper towels and remove stems. Melt butter and dip each mushroom in butter before placing on cookie sheet. Spoon about a teaspoon of spinach mixture into each mushroom cap, or pipe mixture on with large pastry tube. Bake at 350 °F for 15 minutes. If possible, serve on a tray set over a warmer. Makes 30 stuffed mushrooms.

Mrs. F. John Wade, III

Mushrooms with Caviar Cream

2 to 3 dozen small to
  medium fresh mushrooms
Lemon juice
1 (2 ounce) jar red caviar

2 (3 ounce) packages cream
  cheese, softened
1 teaspoon grated onion
Salt and white pepper to taste

Clean mushrooms by wiping with damp cloth. Remove stems. Dip the caps in lemon juice. Combine caviar, cream cheese, onion, salt and pepper. Fill mushroom caps. Serve chilled. Reserve stems for another use. Caviar cream may be made 1 day ahead, but do not stuff mushrooms until day to be used. Yields 2-3 dozen mushrooms.

Mrs. Larry D. Patterson

Care of mushrooms: Clean by wiping with a dampened towel. Store uncleaned in refrigerator until ready to use. Never wash or peel. If stem is dry or brown, cut small slice off end.

Artichoke Squares

2 (6 ounce) jars
   marinated artichokes
1 onion, chopped
1 clove garlic, minced
4 eggs
¼ cup bread crumbs

Dash Tabasco
½ teaspoon oregano
Salt and pepper
2 cups shredded Cheddar
   cheese

Drain the juice from 1 jar of artichokes into a skillet. Sauté the onion and garlic in the juice. Drain the other jar and chop all artichokes. In a bowl, beat the eggs, then add the bread crumbs, Tabasco, oregano, salt and pepper. Stir in the onion, garlic, cheese and artichokes. Mix well. Bake in a 9 x 13-inch pan for ½ hour at 325°F. Cut into squares and serve hot. These squares can be made in advance and then rewarmed on a cookie sheet. Makes about 30 squares.

Mrs. James P. McGaughy, Jr.

Variation: Substitute for the Cheddar cheese ⅔ cup shredded Swiss cheese, ⅔ cup grated Parmesan cheese and ⅔ cup shredded Cheddar cheese. For a thicker square, use a 7 x 11-inch pan.

Eggplant Dip

1 large onion
2 cloves garlic
2 medium green peppers
½ cup olive oil
3 medium eggplants
   (8 cups diced)
1½ (10 ounce) cans Rotel
   tomatoes, drained

1 Tablespoon sugar
½ cup ketchup
1 Tablespoon Worcestershire
   sauce
2½ teaspoons salt
3 Tablespoons dry white wine
1 (2¼ ounce) bottle small
   capers, drained

Peel onion and garlic. Remove seeds and tough white part of green peppers. Mince onion, garlic and green peppers. In very large, heavy skillet, cook these in olive oil over medium heat until onion is golden, stirring constantly. Peel and dice eggplants. Add eggplants to onion mixture and cook for 20 minutes, stirring constantly. Add Rotel tomatoes, sugar, ketchup, Worcestershire sauce, salt and wine; allow mixture to cook slowly until fairly thick and eggplant is tender. Cooking time is about 30-40 minutes longer. Stir occasionally. Taste and add more salt if needed. Cool and add well-drained capers. Refrigerate or freeze until used. Yields 3 pints, making about 65-70 servings.

Mrs. Reynolds Cheney

Serve this zesty dip warm from a chafing dish or at room temperature on toasted rye rounds.

Artichoke and Rye Crisps

2 (14 ounce) cans artichoke
   hearts, well drained
2 (6 ounce) jars marinated
   artichoke hearts, well
   drained
4 Tablespoons mayonnaise
2 teaspoons Worcestershire
   sauce
¼ teaspoon garlic powder
1 teaspoon Cavender's Greek
   seasoning

Salt to taste
1½ cups dry bread crumbs
1 to 2 drops Tabasco
2 Tablespoons lemon juice
4 Tablespoons butter, melted
1 (5 ounce) package fresh
   Romano cheese, finely
   shredded, divided
Party rye bread, cut in
   halves (or fourths)

Mix all ingredients except cheese and bread in food processor or blender. Stir in 3 Tablespoons of the cheese. Spread about a teaspoon of the mixture on the cut bread. Sprinkle cheese on top or place cheese in a saucer and dip the spread side of the bread into the cheese. Bake on a cookie sheet at 350°F for 10 minutes, or until rye bread is lightly browned and cheese melted. Freezes well. Thaw before using. Serves 50.

Mrs. Elton S. Thomas, Columbus, Mississippi

Water Chestnut Dip

1 (8 ounce) carton sour cream
1 cup Hellmann's mayonnaise
1 (8 ounce) can water chestnuts,
   drained and chopped

2 Tablespoons soy sauce
½ cup chopped parsley
3 green onions, chopped
2 or 3 drops Tabasco

Mix ingredients well and serve as a dip. Makes 3 cups dip.

Mrs. Ken Toler

Marinated Brussels Sprouts

2 (8 ounce) boxes frozen
   Brussels sprouts
½ cup tarragon vinegar
½ cup salad oil
1 clove garlic, crushed

1 Tablespoon sugar
1 teaspoon salt
Dash Tabasco
2 Tablespoons dried minced
   onion

Cook Brussels sprouts until slightly under-done. Drain. Make a marinade with remaining ingredients. Mix well and pour over Brussels sprouts while hot. Marinate 3-4 days before serving. Drain and serve. Serves 12.

Mrs. Daniel H. Draughn

Hot Artichoke Dip

1 (14 ounce) can artichoke
  hearts, drained
1 cup grated fresh
  Parmesan cheese

1 cup mayonnaise
1/8 teaspoon garlic salt
Dash lemon juice

Mash artichoke hearts and mix with remaining ingredients. Heat at 350°F for about 10 minutes until warm throughout and cheese is melted. Serve in chafing dish with Triscuits. Serves 6.

Mrs. F. Dean Copeland, Atlanta, Georgia

Ground Jerusalem Artichoke Dip

4 cups ground, boiled,
  well-drained Jerusalem
  artichokes
1 (8 ounce) package cream
  cheese, softened

2 Tablespoons sour cream, or
  more
Lemon juice
Salt and pepper
Worcestershire sauce
Tabasco

Mash the ground artichokes with a potato masher (do not blend) and mix well with the cream cheese and sour cream. Season to taste with the remaining ingredients. Serve with plain crackers. Serves 15.

Mrs. Charles Morris

Spinach Squares

2 (10 ounce) packages
  frozen chopped spinach
3 Tablespoons butter
1 medium onion, chopped
¼ pound mushrooms, sliced
4 eggs, beaten
¼ cup fine bread crumbs

1 (10½ ounce) can cream
  of mushroom soup
¼ cup grated Parmesan cheese
1/8 teaspoon pepper
1/8 teaspoon oregano
1/8 teaspoon basil

Place spinach in strainer and rinse under hot water to thaw. Press out all water. Melt butter in frying pan; add onion and mushrooms, stirring over medium heat until onion is limp. Combine eggs with bread crumbs, mushroom soup, 2 Tablespoons cheese, seasonings and spinach. Blend with onion mixture. Turn into greased 9-inch square pan and sprinkle with remaining cheese. Bake uncovered at 325°F oven for 35 minutes or until set. Cool slightly and refrigerate. Cut into 1-inch squares. Serve cold. May be reheated in 325°F oven for hot hors d'oeuvres. Makes 80.

Mrs. John Augis, San Jose, California

Spinach Balls

2 (10 ounce) boxes frozen
chopped spinach, cooked
and drained well
2 cups herb bread stuffing mix
2 onions, finely chopped
6 eggs, beaten

¾ cup butter, melted
½ cup grated Parmesan
cheese
1 Tablespoon garlic salt
½ teaspoon thyme
1 teaspoon monosodium glutamate

Mix ingredients well. Form balls, using 1 teaspoon mixture for each, and bake on lightly greased baking sheet 20 minutes at 350°F. May be frozen either before or after baking. Yields 4-5 dozen.

Mrs. Robert W. Crowell, Sr.

Spanakopita
(Spinach and Feta Cheese Pie)

2 pounds fresh spinach, or 2
(10 ounce) packages frozen
spinach
1 cup minced onion
⅓ cup olive oil
Ground nutmeg
12 ounces cream cheese,
softened

2 eggs, beaten
7 ounces feta cheese
(more to taste)
½ cup pine nuts, chopped
Salt and pepper
½ to ¾ pound butter, melted
½ pound filo pastry

Blanch fresh spinach or thaw frozen spinach, squeeze out as much moisture as possible and chop fine. Sauté onion in oil until transparent. Add spinach, raise heat and cook for several minutes to evaporate moisture. Season with nutmeg. In a mixing bowl beat cream cheese until smooth. Beat in eggs, then add crumbled feta cheese, the spinach mixture and pine nuts. Blend together well by hand. Season to taste with salt and pepper. To form pie, brush pie pan with melted butter and line with 5 sheets of filo, brushing each with butter and letting the ends fall over the sides of the pan. Pour in filling, place 3 more sheets of buttered pastry on top, then fold all overhanging edges toward the middle, making as neat a package as possible. Brush with butter and bake 40 minutes at 350°F or until brown. Serves 8-12.

Mrs. William B. Wilson

Variations: The method above creates a thick filling. If thinner slices are desired for hors d'oeuvre service, divide filling between two pies, making the second pie pastry with another ½ pound filo and another ¾ pound butter. If individual pastries are desired, cut sheets of filo into 2-inch strips and brush with melted butter. Place ½ teaspoon filling on a corner of each strip; then fold over to cover filling and make a triangle. Keep folding and making triangles to the end of the strip. Brush with butter and bake 20-25 minutes or until brown. Serve warm. These freeze well. Reheat gently.

Broccoli and Carrot Crudités

CARROTS:
8 small carrots
3 Tablespoons vinegar
3 Tablespoons oil
1 clove garlic, crushed
1 teaspoon seasoned salt
Fresh parsley, minced

BROCCOLI:
1 large head fresh broccoli
¼ cup olive oil
1 teaspoon garlic salt
½ cup sliced stuffed
olives
¼ cup lemon juice

To prepare CARROTS, cut in small sticks. Mix other ingredients and pour over carrots. Cover and refrigerate overnight. To prepare BROCCOLI, wash and cut in bite-size flowerets. Toss in oil, sprinkle with garlic salt and toss again. Add remaining ingredients and toss. Cover and refrigerate overnight. To serve, drain carrots and broccoli. Pile broccoli in center of platter and surround with carrots. Serve cold. May be prepared 2 days in advance. Serves 12.

Mrs. G. G. Mazzaferro

Herb Dip

1 cup mayonnaise
½ Tablespoon lemon juice
½ teaspoon salt
¼ teaspoon paprika
¼ cup chopped (or
dried) parsley
1 Tablespoon grated (or
dried) onion

1 Tablespoon chopped
(or dried) chives
1/8 teaspoon curry powder
½ teaspoon Worcestershire
sauce
Garlic salt to taste
1 Tablespoon capers
½ cup sour cream

Mix all ingredients, folding in sour cream last. Serve as dip for raw vegetables. May be prepared 1-2 days ahead. Makes 1½ cups dip.

Mrs. James T. Morris, Jr.

Caraway Celery Sticks

1 whole bunch celery
1 white onion, finely sliced
½ cup chopped parsley
⅓ cup salad oil
¼ cup white vinegar

1 Tablespoon caraway seed
1½ teaspoons salt
1 teaspoon sugar
½ teaspoon white pepper

Trim tops from celery. Separate celery into ribs. Cut ribs into 3-inch lengths; cut each length into four ¼-inch wide sticks. In a large bowl place celery. Add onion and parsley. Combine oil, vinegar, caraway seed, salt, sugar and white pepper; mix well. Pour over celery mixture; toss well to coat. Cover and refrigerate *overnight*. May be prepared several days in advance. Keeps well in refrigerator for about 1 month. Yields 1½ quarts.

Mrs. C. Chunn Sneed, Gulfport, Mississippi

Marinated Squash

⅔ cup wine vinegar
⅓ cup sugar
¼ teaspoon celery salt
¼ teaspoon pepper
⅔ teaspoon onion salt

½ teaspoon McCormick's salt 'n spice
½ teaspoon oregano or ¾ teaspoon
   Cavender's Greek seasoning
1 small onion, sliced thin
9 small squash, sliced thin

Make dressing by mixing together the first 7 ingredients and stir until sugar dissolves. Pour over onion and squash slices. Marinate overnight or at least 10 hours. May be prepared 3 days in advance. Serves 12.

Mrs. Sydney A. Smith

Cherry Tomatoes Stuffed with Avocado

30 large cherry tomatoes
Salt
Sugar
2 ripe medium avocados
2 Tablespoons sour cream
2 Tablespoons minced parsley

4 teaspoons lime juice
2 teaspoons lemon juice
2 teaspoons minced chives
½ teaspoon salt
¼ teaspoon Tabasco
¼ teaspoon sugar

Cut thin slices from the tops of cherry tomatoes and with a small melon ball cutter scoop out and discard the seeds and pulp. Sprinkle the insides of the shells lightly with salt and sugar and invert the shells on paper towels to drain for at least 30 minutes. In a bowl mash avocados and combine with remaining ingredients. Blend the mixture well. Fill the shells with the avocado mixture with a small knife, arrange the tomatoes on a serving dish and serve them chilled. Serves 6.

Mrs. Richard L. Redmont, Jr.

Chafing Dish Pastry Shells

1¼ cups flour
6 Tablespoons cold butter,
   cut into bits

2 Tablespoons Crisco
¼ teaspoon salt
3 Tablespoons ice water

In a large bowl combine the flour, butter, Crisco and salt. Blend until well combined and add the ice water. Toss the mixture until the water is incorporated and form the dough into a ball. Knead the dough lightly with the heel of the hand against a smooth surface for a few seconds to distribute the fat evenly and reform it into a ball. Dust the dough with flour, wrap it in wax paper and chill it for 1 hour. Roll out thin. Cut into rounds. Fit into miniature muffin tins. Prick bottom. Bake at 350°F for 12-15 minutes. Freeze or store in cookie tins. Makes 4 dozen.

Mrs. W. H. Howard, Jr.

Chafing Dish Toast Cups

Thin-sliced bread   *Melted butter*

Trim crust off thin-sliced bread. Cut each slice into 4 squares. Spread with melted butter and press into miniature muffin tins with fingers. Toast in moderate oven until browned. Fill with fillings from chafing dish.

Oyster Patties

4 dozen oysters, chopped
2 Tablespoons butter
1 small onion, grated
1 Tablespoon flour
1 (4 ounce) can sliced mushrooms, chopped (reserve juice)

2 Tablespoons chopped parsley
Salt and pepper to taste
Dash cayenne pepper
¼ teaspoon lemon juice
4 dozen miniature puff patty shells

Cook oysters in their own liquid; bring to a boil and simmer for 10 minutes. Melt butter in saucepan; add onion. Blend in flour until smooth. Add ½ cup mushroom juice, parsley, salt, pepper, cayenne pepper and chopped mushrooms. Then add undrained oysters and lemon juice. Cook 5 minutes. Pour into patty shells. Bake at 425 °F for 15 minutes. Yields 4 dozen.

Mrs. Charles M. Head

Chafing Dish Pastry Shells or Chafing Dish Toast Cups recipes may be used for making individual shells if puff patty shells are unavailable.

Hot Seafood Dip

2 (10½ ounce) cans cream of mushroom soup
1 (10½ ounce) can cream of shrimp soup
1 (8 ounce) package cream cheese
3 (4½ ounce) cans small shrimp, drained and rinsed well
3 (8 ounce) cans sliced mushrooms, drained

1 pound lump crab meat
2 (8 ounce) cans water chestnuts, sliced
2 teaspoons lemon-pepper seasoning
3 Tablespoons Worcestershire sauce
3 Tablespoons white wine or sherry (optional)
Salt and red pepper to taste
2 teaspoons dry mustard

Heat soups. Stir in cream cheese until melted. Add remaining ingredients. Serve hot in chafing dish with Melba rounds. Serves 45-50.

Mrs. William B. McCarty, Jr.

Creamed Crab Meat Dip

½ small onion, chopped
4 Tablespoons butter (do
  not substitute)
2 Tablespoons flour
1½ cups half and half cream
1 egg yolk, beaten
1 teaspoon lemon juice

1 teaspoon Worcestershire
  sauce
Dash cayenne pepper
1 teaspoon chopped parsley
¼ teaspoon celery salt
¼ teaspoon salt
1 pound lump crab meat

Sauté onion in butter. Add flour and then cream. Cook until thick. Stir in egg yolk, then all seasonings. Fold in crab meat. Serve from chafing dish on thin-sliced bread squares or in tiny bread cups. Serves 15.

Mrs. L. B. Pitts, Terry, Mississippi

Shrimp Dip

1 (8 ounce) carton sour cream
1 (8 ounce) package
  cream cheese, softened
½ cup chopped celery
½ cup chopped onion

Salt and pepper
Red pepper to taste
Juice of 1 lemon
2 (4½ ounce) cans shrimp

Blend sour cream and cream cheese until smooth. Fold in celery and onion. Add salt, pepper and lemon juice. Mash shrimp with a fork and add to mixture. Refrigerate several hours before serving. May be served with Fritos, Doritos or crackers. May be prepared 2 days in advance. Makes 1 quart.

Mrs. Timothy Smith

Oyster Bisque

4 white onions, minced
½ bunch parsley, minced
1 green pepper, minced
1 clove garlic, minced
2 Tablespoons Kitchen
  Bouquet
Dash Worcestershire sauce

1 quart oysters, reserving
  liquid
1 cup butter, divided
2 Tablespoons flour
2 cups milk
2 egg yolks, beaten
½ pint whipping cream

Cook vegetables and seasonings in oyster liquid and ½ cup butter until tender. To make a cream sauce, melt remaining butter in saucepan and stir in flour. Add milk, which has been warmed, and stir over medium heat until thickened. Combine egg yolks and cream and add to cream sauce. Cook over low heat several minutes, stirring, to thicken. Chop oysters fine. Blend together the oysters, vegetable mixture and cream sauce and cook in top of double boiler until oysters curl. Never let mixture boil. Serve in a chafing dish with Melba toast. Serves 20.

Mrs. Alvin E. Fagan, Jr.

Crab Dip

1 pound Velveeta cheese
½ pound butter
1 pound crab meat
(fresh or frozen)

3 Tablespoons sherry wine
1 teaspoon Worcestershire
sauce
Tabasco to taste

Melt cheese and butter in top of double boiler. Stir in crab meat, sherry, Worcestershire and Tabasco. Serve in chafing dish with Fritos. Also good for ladies' luncheon served over white or wild rice. Serves 6.

Mrs. Jeff Hirsch, Mobile, Alabama

Cold Curried Shrimp

½ cup chopped onion
½ cup chopped apple
1 clove garlic, crushed
4 Tablespoons butter
2 Tablespoons flour
1 (16 ounce) can stewed
tomatoes

2 teaspoons curry powder
or to taste
Salt and pepper
Mayonnaise
1 Tablespoon lemon juice
3 pounds shrimp, cooked and
cleaned

Sauté onion, apple and garlic in butter until golden. Remove garlic. Stir in flour and cook 1 minute. Add tomatoes, curry powder and salt and pepper to taste. Simmer for few minutes. Strain sauce through fine sieve and cool. Add an equal amount of mayonnaise and the lemon juice. Refrigerate. Will keep up to 2 weeks. To serve, mix cooked shrimp with sauce and chill up to 3 hours. Arrange on a glass plate, surround by thinly sliced unpeeled cucumbers and sprinkle with toasted slivered almonds. Serves 12.

Mrs. William B. Wilson

Hot Clam and Cheese Spread

3 Tablespoons butter
1 small onion, finely chopped
½ green or red sweet pepper,
finely chopped
1 (8 ounce) can minced clams,
drained
4 Tablespoons ketchup

¼ pound processed cheese, cut in
small pieces
1 Tablespoon Worcestershire
sauce
1 Tablespoon sherry wine
¼ teaspoon cayenne pepper

In top of double boiler melt butter; add onion and green pepper and sauté 3 minutes. Add remaining ingredients. Cook in double boiler until cheese is melted. Serve with Melba toast or squares of buttered pumpernickle. Have some thin slices of dill pickle to place on toast or bread before hot spread is added. Serves 15.

Mrs. L. B. Pitts, Terry, Mississippi

Shrimp and Artichoke Vinaigrette

1 egg
½ cup vegetable oil
½ cup olive oil
½ cup wine vinegar
2 Tablespoons Dijon mustard
2 Tablespoons chopped chives
2 Tablespoons minced scallions

½ teaspoon salt
½ teaspoon sugar
Dash pepper
1½ pounds cooked, peeled
  medium shrimp
2 (15 ounce) cans artichoke
  hearts, drained and halved

To make dressing, beat all ingredients except artichokes and shrimp in blender. Marinate shrimp and artichokes in dressing at least 6 hours. When ready to serve, drain off marinating sauce. Let guests spear a shrimp and artichoke heart on a toothpick. May be prepared 2 days in advance. Recipe may be tripled to use as a salad (on lettuce) for a luncheon for 12 ladies. Yields 36 appetizers.

Mrs. Robert B. Mims

Marinated Shrimp

10 pounds raw shrimp, peeled
1 (5 ounce) bottle soy sauce

1 (16 ounce) bottle Wishbone
  Italian dressing

Marinate shrimp overnight in soy sauce and Italian dressing mixed. When ready to serve, spread shrimp on cookie sheet and cook in 350°F oven about 15 minutes. Serve on platter over warmer, if possible. May be prepared a day ahead. Serves 40.

Mrs. Sherwood Wise

Crab Mousse

2 envelopes unflavored
  gelatin
¼ cup cold water
½ cup boiling water
1 (8 ounce) package cream
  cheese, softened
1 (10½ ounce) can cream
  of mushroom soup
1 cup mayonnaise
1 cup chopped green onion

1 cup chopped celery
Juice of 1 lemon
1 Tablespoon Worcestershire
  sauce
Dash Tabasco
½ cup stuffed olives, sliced
2 (6½ ounce) cans Harris white
  crab meat (or 1 pound fresh
  crab meat)

Soak gelatin in the cold water. Add boiling water. In mixing bowl mix cream cheese with mushroom soup. Add remaining ingredients. Add gelatin, mix all together, and place in molds. (May be molded in loaf pan and sliced for a luncheon.) Makes 6 dozen tiny muffin pan molds for canapés or two 4-cup molds.

Mrs. Edwin DeWeese, Philadelphia, Mississippi

Marinated Crab Fingers

¾ (5¼ ounce) jar
  Zatarain's mustard
½ cup wine vinegar
¾ cup salad oil
2 teaspoons paprika

½ teaspoon sugar
3 green onions, chopped
Salt and pepper to taste
1 pound fresh crab fingers

Mix well all ingredients except crab. Place crab fingers in shallow pan. Pour marinade over them; then cover and refrigerate overnight. Before serving, drain. Yields about 25 crab fingers.

Mrs. Daniel H. Draughn

Shrimp on Crackers

1 cup mayonnaise
½ cup parsley, chopped
  very fine
½ cup finely chopped chives
  or green onion
2 Tablespoons horseradish

1 (5¼ ounce) jar Zatarain's
  mustard
Dash Tabasco or red pepper
Lemon juice to taste
2 pounds medium shrimp,
  boiled and deveined

Mix all ingredients except the shrimp. Fold shrimp in gently to prevent breaking. Marinate for 24 hours. Serve on Ritz crackers, one shrimp to a cracker. Serves 20.

Mrs. Alvin E. Fagan, Jr.

Molded Puréed Eggs with Crab Meat

10 to 12 hard-cooked eggs,
  shelled
1 teaspoon garlic salt
1 teaspoon Accent
1 teaspoon Maggi's seasoning
1 drop Tabasco

1 Tablespoon Dijon mustard
½ cup heavy mayonnaise
2 cups sour cream, beaten
2 cups lump crab meat,
  caviar or small shrimp

Put eggs through a fine wire sieve or a potato ricer. To the eggs add garlic salt, Accent, Maggi's seasoning, Tabasco, Dijon mustard and mayonnaise; mix until well blended. This should have a thick consistency. Put into a well-oiled, 1-quart ring mold, cover with plastic wrap and refrigerate several hours or overnight until firm or set. When ready to serve, dip the mold quickly into warm water and run a knife around the edges. Turn out onto a glass plate. Ice the outside of the eggs carefully with sour cream. Fill the center of the mold with lump crab meat, caviar or shrimp. (If using caviar squeeze a little lemon juice over it.) Garnish with chopped parsley and sprigs of watercress. Serve with thin crisp rye bread or rye crackers. Serves 30.

Mrs. Robert W. King

Dede's Shrimp New Orleans

1 cup ketchup
1 (5 ounce) jar horseradish
1 (5¼ ounce) jar
   Zatarain's Creole mustard
¼ cup olive oil
Salt and pepper to taste

1 (24 ounce) package frozen,
   peeled and deveined shrimp,
   cooked according to package
   directions (or fresh equivalent)
Small onion rings, as many as
   desired

Combine all ingredients. Refrigerate in a tightly covered dish. Serve on crackers or with toothpicks. Serves 8 generously.

Mrs. Julius Collum

Maryland Crab Cakes

1 pound lump crab meat,
   cleaned
1½ Tablespoons finely
   crumbled Escort cracker
   crumbs
1 egg, beaten
2 Tablespoons mayonnaise

½ teaspoon salt
½ teaspoon mustard
1 Tablespoon chopped parsley
½ teaspoon cayenne pepper
Dash Tabasco
1 teaspoon white pepper
Oil for frying

Place crab meat in mixing bowl. Sprinkle crumbs over crab lightly. In another bowl mix egg, mayonnaise, salt, mustard, parsley, cayenne, Tabasco and white pepper. Mix together and add to crab meat mixture. Shape into small cakes. Fry in hot fat at 350°F until brown on both sides. Makes about 50 small balls.

Mrs. T. Arnold Turner, Jr.

Shrimp Mold

1 (8 ounce) package cream
   cheese, softened
1½ envelopes unflavored
   gelatin
½ cup cold water
¾ cup finely chopped celery
1 Tablespoon chopped parsley

1 cup mayonnaise
2 teaspoons grated onion
2 cups minced cooked shrimp
1 Tablespoon lemon juice
Salt and white pepper
Seasoned salt to taste
Dash Worcestershire sauce

Beat cream cheese with mixer until smooth. Soften gelatin in water; then dissolve it over low heat. Fold into cream cheese. Fold in remaining ingredients and pour into a lightly oiled 5-cup mold. Chill. This will set in minutes. Serve as a spread for crackers. Serves 25.

Mrs. Harry Watson, Charlotte, North Carolina

This spread looks nice in a lamb mold (for a christening party) or a fish mold for any occasion.

Jellied Crab Meat or Anchovy Hors d'Oeuvre

1 (10½ ounce) can beef
   consommé
2 Tablespoons lemon juice
Dash Tabasco

½ teaspoon Worcestershire
   sauce
1 envelope unflavored gelatin,
   softened in ¼ cup cold water

Heat consommé and season with lemon juice, Tabasco and Worcestershire sauce. Add softened gelatin and stir to dissolve. Pour into a 4-cup mold (preferably a fish mold) and refrigerate to harden. When congealed, scoop out center with a hot spoon, leaving ¼ inch or more around the edges and bottom. Reserve consommé mixture. Fill cavity with CRAB MEAT FILLING or ANCHOVY FILLING and return to refrigerator to set. Melt the reserved consommé, cool and pour over stuffed gelatin to cover. Chill. When ready to serve, unmold on a platter and serve as a spread for crackers. Serves 12.

CRAB MEAT FILLING

1 (8 ounce) package cream
   cheese
1 Tablespoon lemon juice
Dash Tabasco
Salt to taste
2 Tablespoons mayonnaise

1 cup white crab meat
1 envelope unflavored gelatin,
   softened in ¼ cup
   cold water and dissolved
   over low heat

Soften cream cheese and beat in seasonings and mayonnaise. Stir in crab meat and gelatin.

ANCHOVY FILLING

1 (8 ounce) package cream
   cheese
1 tube anchovy paste
2 teaspoons lemon juice
2 Tablespoons mayonnaise
1 Tablespoon half and half
   cream

Salt to taste
Dash bourbon
1 envelope unflavored gelatin,
   softened in ¼ cup
   cold water and dissolved
   over low heat

Soften cream cheese and beat in remaining ingredients until smooth.

Mrs. Sherwood Wise

Marinated Oysters

Simmer oysters in quantity desired in their juices until edges begin to curl; then drain. Mix three parts oil to one part lemon juice in an amount sufficient to cover the drained oysters. Season the oil and lemon juice to taste with minced parsley, minced garlic, pepper and salt. Place oysters in glass dish and coat with marinade mixture. Marinate in refrigerator for at least 12 hours. Serve with saltine crackers.

Mrs. Charles R. Davis

Oysters Rockefeller

ROCKEFELLER SAUCE:
3 bags fresh spinach
Tops only from 2 bunches green
    onions
2 bunches parsley
1 (10 ounce) bottle
    Worcestershire sauce
1 or 2 cloves garlic, grated
2 pounds soft butter, creamed

1 (10 ounce) box bread crumbs
1 (14 ounce) bottle ketchup
1 tube anchovy paste
Salt and pepper to taste
Dash red pepper
Dash Tabasco

Rock salt
Oysters and oyster shells

Purée spinach, onions and parsley in blender or food processor, adding enough Worcestershire sauce to allow blender to work easily. Add puréed mixture to remaining ingredients in large mixing bowl and beat until smooth. Cover a large cookie sheet with foil and spread with a layer of rock salt. Place drained oysters on oyster shells, then on bed of salt. Top oysters with *ROCKEFELLER SAUCE* (about 1 or 2 Tablespoons on each). Bake at 400°F for 15 minutes. This sauce may be stored in jars in the refrigerator for several months or in the freezer for a year. Spoon out as needed. Makes 6 pints sauce.

Mrs. McWillie Robinson

Marinated Anchovies

2 (2 ounce) cans flat
    anchovies in olive oil
1 Tablespoon lemon juice
1 Tablespoon olive oil
1 Tablespoon finely chopped
    shallots
¼ teaspoon finely chopped
    garlic
Freshly ground pepper
    to taste

1 Tablespoon finely chopped
    fresh dill (or 1 teaspoon
    dried dill weed)
1 Tablespoon finely chopped
    parsley
1 teaspoon finely chopped
    chives
1 (4 ounce) can whole pimientos
12 black olives (Greek or
    Italian)
Buttered toast squares

Drain oil from anchovies into small bowl. Add to it the lemon juice, olive oil, shallots, garlic and a little freshly ground pepper. Beat together thoroughly with a fork. Then stir in the dill, parsley and chives. Mixture should be thick but fluid. Place a whole pimiento in center of platter. Cut rest into narrow 2-inch long strips. Separate anchovies and alternate with pimientos around center to form wheel. Garnish the edge with black olives. Spread marinade over all. Cover with wax paper and marinate for 1 hour at room temperature. Serve with hot buttered toast squares. Serves 8.

Mrs. Sherwood Wise, Jr., Tallahassee, Florida

Tuna Pâté

1 (8 ounce) package cream
   cheese, softened
2 Tablespoons chili sauce
2 Tablespoons dried parsley

1 teaspoon minced onion
½ teaspoon Tabasco
2 (7 ounce) cans white tuna,
   drained and flaked

Blend first 5 ingredients. Add tuna and mix well. Pack firmly in 4-cup serving bowl lined with plastic wrap. Chill 4 hours. Unmold and serve with crackers. Decorate with parsley. Makes 4 cups.

Mrs. Robert H. Thompson, Jr.

Aspic Appetizers

36 shrimp, boiled and peeled
1 package unflavored gelatin
1½ cups tomato juice
1 teaspoon grated onion
1 Tablespoon Worcestershire
   sauce

Dash celery salt
Dash garlic powder
Dash Tabasco
Salt and pepper
Juice of ½ lemon

Grease small molds or muffin tins and place shrimp in bottom of each. Soften gelatin in tomato juice for 5 minutes; then heat to dissolve. Add seasonings. Fill molds. Place in refrigerator to congeal. Unmold and serve on crackers or toast rounds topped with a little mayonnaise. May be prepared 2 days in advance. Yields 3 dozen.

Mrs. J. T. Noblin

Salmon Ball

1 (15½ ounce) can Red Alaskan
   salmon, well-drained, boned,
   and skinned
1 (8 ounce) package cream
   cheese, softened
¼ teaspoon liquid smoke

1 Tablespoon lemon juice
2 teaspoons grated onion
1 teaspoon horseradish
Chopped parsley or chopped
   pecans

Blend first 6 ingredients well. Shape into a ball or pack into a mold lined with plastic wrap. Chill several hours or overnight. Unmold. Before serving, coat with chopped nuts or parsley. Serve with crackers and garnish, if desired, with parsley, lemon wedges, black olives and SALMON PINWHEELS. May be frozen. Yields 1½ cups and serves 24.

SMOKED SALMON PINWHEELS

Spread sliced smoked salmon with cream cheese seasoned with lemon juice, salt and white pepper. Place a row of capers at one end and roll up like a jelly roll. Chill. Cut crosswise in ½-inch pieces to make pinwheels.

Mrs. Edwin B. Woodworth, Los Altos, California

Company Coming, No Time to Cook

Fill large green olives with smoked oysters.

Saturate a cake of cream cheese with Pickapeppa sauce.

Top a cracker spread with cream cheese with a slice of sweet pickle.

Use Cheddar cheese and hot pepper jelly as a cracker spread.

Place a smoked oyster on a small, toasted, thin-sliced bread square; paint with butter, sprinkle with chopped parsley and warm in the oven.

Wedge a partially split cherry tomato with a slice of mushroom.

Wrap a Waverly cracker with a thin slice of bacon; bake at 250°F for 50 minutes. Store in airtight tin.

Form seasoned cream cheese in a ball around drained smoked oysters.

Surround balls of sauerkraut with wafer-thin slices of corned beef and serve chilled.

Remove crust from slices of sandwich bread, cut each slice into 2 triangles and spread with mushroom soup. Roll up point to point and wrap each with ⅓ slice of thin-sliced bacon. Fasten with toothpick and bake at 375°F for 25-30 minutes.

In a double boiler melt a roll of Jalapeño cheese with a can of chili with beans; serve in a chafing dish as a dip.

Saturate a block of cream cheese with soy sauce and roll in sesame seeds.

Top Triscuits with melted butter and lemon-pepper seasoning; bake at 350°F until hot.

Spear toothpicks with browned sausage rounds and cubes of Cheddar cheese; serve with dipping sauce made from ½ cup mild taco sauce and ¼ cup picante sauce.

Top an artichoke heart with cream cheese-chive spread; serve chilled.

Over low heat melt a pound Velveeta with a pound of hot sausage which has been browned and drained; place a teaspoon on a slice of party rye bread and heat at 350°F until brown and crisp (tops 2 loaves).

Cover a tostado or Dorito chip with a small slice of Cheddar cheese and sliver of Jalapeño pepper; broil to melt cheese and serve hot.

Thread skewers with bacon, mushrooms and chicken livers; broil until bacon is done on each side, turning once.

Soak 2 cups pecans in 2 cups water and ¼ cup salt for 3 hours; drain and bake at 300°F until done.

Mash a 4½ ounce can of shrimp with 6 ounces of cream cheese, 1 Tablespoon chives, ½ teaspoon Tabasco and 1 Tablespoon lemon juice; serve as a spread on Triscuits.

Soups

Basic Roux Making Methods

STANDARD METHOD   A roux is a mixture of fat and flour browned to a deep golden color (similar to dark peanut butter). Measure solid fat, oil or bacon drippings called for in recipe into a heavy pan. Cast iron works best as the heat is more evenly distributed. Stir in the specified amount of flour. Proportions for roux are usually 1 to 2 (½ cup fat to 1 cup flour). Smaller amounts of roux are easily made with 1 Tablespoon fat to 2 Tablespoons flour. Cook roux slowly over moderate heat, stirring constantly until it becomes a glossy golden brown. To prevent flour from burning, keep it moving all the time, pushing it off the bottom of the skillet and making a circle. The flavor of the roux will be impaired if the flour is allowed to burn, in which case, throw out and start over. Have vegetables chopped and ready to add. When vegetables are added to roux, it ceases to brown. Always add hot stock, never cold, to a hot roux; otherwise it will separate.

OVEN METHOD   Combine fat and flour in amounts specified in recipe and place in heavy skillet in a 350°F oven. Bake for at least 30 minutes, stirring occasionally. Roux can be refrigerated or frozen for later use.

Mississippi Seafood Gumbo

4 Tablespoons oil
⅔ cup flour
2 large onions, chopped
2 cloves garlic, minced
1½ cups chopped ham
6 cups chopped okra
4 quarts water
3 Tablespoons Worcestershire
 sauce

3 (16 ounce) cans tomatoes
Dash Tabasco
Salt and pepper to taste
2 to 4 pounds peeled, raw shrimp
1 pound crab meat
4 to 5 bay leaves (optional)
Cooked crab bodies (optional)
Cooked rice

Heat oil in heavy pot. Add flour and brown slowly until a very dark roux has been made. Add onions and garlic and brown; then add ham and brown. Add okra. Continue to brown mixture very slowly for about an hour or more. Bring to a boil in large pot the water, Worcestershire sauce, tomatoes, Tabasco, salt and pepper. Add browned mixture and cook slowly for 4 hours. Add shrimp and crab meat. Cook slowly 2 hours. If desired, add bay leaves 1 hour before serving. Floured and browned crab bodies may be added shortly before serving. Serve over 2 Tablespoons rice in large bowl. May be prepared several days ahead. Freezes well. Serves 6-8.

Mrs. Gibbs J. Fowler

Duck and Sausage Gumbo

2 pounds smoked sausage
½ cup strained bacon
   drippings
1 cup flour
7 to 8 wild ducks
4 Tablespoons salt, divided
1 bay leaf
2 ribs celery, quartered

1 onion, quartered
2 cups chopped onion
2 cups chopped celery
2 cups chopped green pepper
1½ teaspoons pepper
Red pepper to taste
Tabasco to taste
Cooked rice

Cut sausage into rounds and cook briefly to render grease. Drain. Make a very dark roux with bacon drippings and flour. Boil ducks in about 4 quarts water seasoned with 1 Tablespoon salt, bay leaf, quartered celery and onion. Remove meat from bones and cut into bite-size pieces. Reserve strained stock. Cook chopped vegetables slowly in roux. Add 3 quarts duck stock and cook to consistency of thick gumbo. Add pepper, duck meat and sausage. Simmer 3 hours. Season to taste with red pepper and Tabasco. Freezes well. Serve over rice with salad and French bread. Serves 20.

Mrs. G. Richard Greenlee

Chicken Gumbo

1 (3 pound) chicken fryer
2 whole cloves
1 carrot, sliced
4 to 8 sprigs parsley
1 bay leaf
1 large onion, sliced
1 rib celery
½ cup white wine
6 to 8 peppercorns
Salt and pepper to taste
¼ cup oil
1 Tablespoon flour
2 large onions, chopped
¼ cup chopped celery

¼ cup chopped green pepper
1 cup chopped, peeled
   tomatoes
2 teaspoons chopped parsley
3 cloves garlic, minced
4 Tablespoons Worcestershire
   sauce
½ teaspoon salt
½ teaspoon pepper
½ teaspoon thyme
4 bay leaves
1 cup sliced okra
Cooked rice

Cook fryer in water to cover, seasoned with next 9 ingredients, until done. Remove meat from bone and cut into pieces. Reserve strained stock. Make a rich, dark roux of the oil and flour. Add onions, celery and green pepper and stir until soft. Add 1½ cups reserved chicken stock and the tomatoes, then all remaining ingredients except the okra. Simmer for 30 minutes. Add okra and chicken meat and simmer 2-3 hours, stirring occasionally. Serve in bowls over a mound of rice. Recipe can easily be doubled and freezes well. Makes 1 quart.

Mrs. Michael T. McRee

Duck Gumbo Original

3 wild ducks
3 quarts hot chicken stock
1 cup flour
½ cup bacon drippings
3 yellow onions, chopped
4 ribs celery, chopped with
    leaves
¼ cup chopped parsley

2 green peppers, chopped
8 cloves garlic, pressed
2 (10 ounce) packages frozen cut
    okra or 3 cups chopped fresh
½ bunch green onions,
    chopped (set tops aside)
Cooked rice

Boil ducks in chicken stock until tender; cool and pull meat off bones. Cut into small pieces and place back in stock to keep moist. In heavy black skillet, make dark brown roux with flour and drippings over medium high heat. Stir constantly with wooden paddle to keep from sticking until roux is dark and glossy like chocolate. Add chopped vegetables to roux and cook until okra stops stringing. Add hot stock (1 pint at first) and incorporate into roux. Add duck meat and cover. Simmer slowly 2 hours. Serve over a scoop of cooked rice in bowl. Sprinkle with green onion tops. Note: never add anything cold to a roux, even if it means placing chopped ingredients in a warm oven. Makes 2 gallons.

Mrs. J. George Smith

Cajuns never serve a salad with gumbo, just French bread!

Onion Soup

6 large onions, sliced
3 Tablespoons butter
1 Tablespoon oil
1 teaspoon salt
¼ teaspoon sugar
3 Tablespoons flour
4 cups homemade chicken stock
3½ cups homemade beef stock

Salt and pepper to taste
3 Tablespoons Madeira wine
6 pieces French bread, sliced ½
    inch thick, dried in oven
¾ cup grated Gruyère or Swiss
    cheese
¼ cup freshly grated Parmesan
    cheese

Cook onions slowly in butter and oil in covered pot for 15 minutes. Uncover and raise heat to moderate. Add salt and sugar. Stir frequently until deep golden brown. Sprinkle with flour and stir for 3 minutes. Remove from heat and add boiling stocks, salt and pepper. Return to heat and simmer for 45 minutes. Add Madeira. Serve with a slice of French bread covered with cheese. Brown this under the broiler, if desired. Serves 6.

Mrs. Clarence H. Webb, Jr.

To degrease soup, spread a paper towel across the surface of the soup to absorb some of the grease or refrigerate the soup. The fat will harden at the surface and can be lifted off easily.

Cream of Chicken Soup Lorraine

2 Tablespoons chopped onion
2 Tablespoons chopped green
　pepper
2 Tablespoons chopped celery
1 Tablespoon butter
1 quart chicken stock

1 Tablespoon chicken stock base
2 Tablespoons flour
1 Tablespoon cornstarch
½ cup water
1½ cups diced chicken
½ cup evaporated milk

Sauté onion, green pepper and celery in butter until soft but not brown. Add chicken stock combined with chicken base. Cook at a slow boil for 30 minutes. Make a smooth paste of the flour, cornstarch and water. Add to chicken stock. Simmer for 5 minutes, remove from heat and add chicken and evaporated milk. Do not boil, but warm chicken in hot mixture and serve. Serves 6.

From the recipes of John B. Mason

Seafood Gumbo

4 to 5 pounds headless medium
　shrimp in shells (may use
　equivalent in frozen
　shrimp)
1 center slice ham (about .85
　pound)
3 to 4 Tablespoons Wesson
　oil, divided
5 medium white onions, finely
　chopped
6 cloves garlic, minced

1 whole bunch celery, finely
　chopped
2½ pounds fresh okra, sliced
1 (46 ounce) can tomato juice
1 teaspoon salt
½ teaspoon cayenne pepper
Freshly ground black pepper
1 pound fresh lump (or claw)
　crab meat, drained
Cooked rice

Cook shrimp in seasoned water until they turn pink. Remove from heat and let stand 5 minutes. Drain, reserving about 2 cups shrimp stock. When cool, peel and devein. Place shrimp in refrigerator. Trim ham well and chop into *fine* pieces. Fry ham in 1 Tablespoon oil in skillet over medium heat. Set aside. Sauté onions and garlic in 2-3 Tablespoons oil until onions are tender. Set aside. In a 3-quart saucepan, steam celery and okra in a little water. Pour tomato juice into a 10 or 12-quart stockpot and add salt, peppers, ham and vegetables. Stir to mix well. Cover, place on low heat and cook for 2 hours, stirring frequently. Add shrimp and cleaned crab meat and cook for another 30 minutes. If extra liquid is needed, use the reserved shrimp stock (about 1 cup should suffice). Serve steaming hot gumbo in bowls with 1-2 Tablespoons cooked rice placed in center. Freezes well. Makes 5 quarts.

Mrs. Reuel May, Sr.

An excellent gumbo which does not require making a roux!

55

Brunswick Stew

6 (5 to 6 pound) hens or heavy fryers

10 to 12 pounds lean beef, cubed

2 pounds center cut ham, cubed

1 pound bacon, chopped

1 pound cubed salt meat with skin removed

5 to 6 pounds potatoes, peeled and chopped

18 large white onions, peeled and quartered

5 whole bunches celery, chopped

2 bunches parsley, chopped

10 pounds frozen whole okra

4 to 5 (17 ounce) cans lima beans, drained

4 to 5 (16 ounce) cans cut green beans, drained

18 (16 ounce) cans stewed tomatoes

6 (17 ounce) cans white cream-style corn

1 pound butter

3 (15 ounce) bottles Worcestershire sauce

1 (8 ounce) can black pepper

1 (1 1/8 ounce) can red pepper

1 (2 ounce) bottle Tabasco

4 to 5 (14 ounce) bottles ketchup

Juice of 4 lemons

4 (4 ounce) cans mushrooms, stems and pieces, drained

Boil chicken in water to cover until meat separates from the bone. Take out, discard all skin and bones from chicken, and chop meat. Strain stock through colander and reserve. Cut beef, ham, bacon and salt meat into small pieces and place in large pot with potatoes, onions, celery and parsley. Boil in water to cover 1 hour, stirring infrequently. If there is a large quantity of stock, start the meat mixture with stock instead of water. Add chicken, remaining stock, okra and other vegetables except tomatoes, corn and mushrooms. Boil for 1 hour; add tomatoes. (To keep tomatoes from curdling when added to the hot mixture, place in pan with 1 Tablespoon soda and let stand for 5 minutes.) Boil for another hour; add corn. Add butter and next 6 ingredients to stew about 1 hour before cooking is completed, adding drained mushrooms thirty minutes before serving. Simmer well. Recipe can be reduced for individual use. Serves 40-50.

From the recipes of W. H. Montjoy

This recipe has been cut down from the original recipe calling for 350 pounds of chicken to feed hundreds of people at the annual Billups Dove Hunt at the Billups Plantation in Indianola, Mississippi, cooked each year by Billy Montjoy. The stew would be started by 6:00 a.m., cooked in an old black iron cauldron and stirred with a boat paddle off and on until serving after the hunt. It has been enjoyed for years by many Mississippians, as well as people from all over the country, and has been written about in newspapers in several Southern cities.

To enhance flavor of homemade vegetable soup add chicken or beef bouillon cubes to the stock.

Mrs. McCarty's Minestrone Soup

1 cup dried navy beans
2 (13¾ ounce) cans clear
 chicken broth
2 teaspoons salt
1 small head cabbage, shredded
4 carrots, skinned and sliced
2 medium potatoes, peeled and
 diced
1 (28 ounce) can Italian-style
 tomatoes, chopped

2 medium onions, chopped
1 rib celery, chopped
1 large fresh tomato, skinned
 and chopped
1 clove garlic, minced
¼ cup olive oil
1 cup broken thin spaghetti
Chopped parsley
¼ teaspoon pepper

Soak beans overnight in water to cover. Measure chicken broth and add water to measure 3 quarts. Add salt and cook beans in broth mixture until almost tender. Add cabbage, carrots, potatoes and tomatoes. Sauté onions, celery, fresh tomato and garlic in olive oil and add to soup. Add spaghetti, parsley and pepper. Simmer until spaghetti is tender. Serve with a spoonful of PESTO SAUCE per bowl. May be prepared ahead. Serves 10.

PESTO SAUCE

¼ cup butter, softened
¼ cup grated Parmesan cheese
½ cup chopped parsley
1 clove garlic, minced
1 teaspoon basil leaves

½ teaspoon marjoram leaves
¼ cup olive oil
¼ cup chopped pine nuts or
 walnuts

Mix ingredients together.

Mrs. Ben McCarty

Black Bean Soup

1 pound dried black beans
1 pound spicy stuffed sausage
3 large onions, chopped
3 cloves garlic, chopped
3 green peppers, chopped
1 or 2 hot peppers, chopped
½ cup olive oil

3 bay leaves
Pinch basil
1 Tablespoon wine vinegar
Salt
Freshly ground black pepper
Cooked rice

Wash beans thoroughly. Place in large pot and cover with cold water. Add sausage cut into 1-inch slices and bring to a boil. Reduce heat to a simmer. Sauté vegetables in olive oil. Add to beans. Add bay leaves and basil. Cook until beans are tender. Remove 1½ cups drained beans and place in blender with vinegar. Blend until it forms a paste. Add paste to soup with salt and pepper to taste. Serve over *1 teaspoon* cooked rice. May be prepared 2 days ahead. Freezes well. Serves 8-10.

Mrs. Leigh B. Allen, III

Mushroom Soup with Parmesan

1 medium onion, grated
1 clove garlic, split
1 Tablespoon olive oil
1 Tablespoon butter
1 pound fresh mushrooms,
   thinly sliced
3 Tablespoons tomato paste
3 cups chicken stock

2 Tablespoons sweet Italian
   vermouth
Salt and pepper to taste
4 egg yolks
2 Tablespoons minced fresh
   parsley
3 Tablespoons grated fresh
   Parmesan cheese

In heavy pot sauté onion and garlic in oil and butter until lightly browned. Remove garlic. Stir in mushrooms and sauté 5 minutes. Stir in tomato paste and mix well. Add the chicken stock, vermouth, salt and pepper. Simmer 10 minutes. Beat together egg yolks, parsley and Parmesan cheese. With a wire whisk beat this into the boiling soup. Serve at once plain or over slices of buttered, toasted Italian bread. Serves 4.

Mrs. William B. Wilson

Shrimp Bisque

2 Tablespoons butter
2 green onions, chopped
2 Tablespoons flour
2 cups milk
1 (3½ ounce) can creamed corn

1 (4½ ounce) can shrimp (rinse,
   soak 20 minutes in ice water)
Dash Worcestershire sauce
Red pepper to taste

Melt butter and sauté onions. Add flour and mix. Add milk, stirring over heat until thickened. Add corn, shrimp, Worcestershire sauce and pepper. Let bubble up and serve with salad and hot French bread. Serves 4.

Mrs. Dean Shuttleworth

Lobster Bisque

1 (8 ounce) can lobster
Sherry wine
3 to 4 green onions, chopped
2 Tablespoons butter
1 (10¾ ounce) can tomato soup
1 soup can milk

1 (10½ ounce) can cream of
   mushroom soup
1 soup can whipping cream
Pinch thyme
Chopped parsley

Finely mince all lobster meat. Marinate lobster in about 2 Tablespoons sherry. Sauté onions in butter until soft. Add lobster meat and cook over low heat a few minutes. Combine tomato soup with milk; blend mushroom soup and cream. Combine soups, lobster and thyme and simmer over low heat for a few minutes. Add more sherry to taste. Cool then blend in blender. To serve, reheat in double boiler and add parsley and more sherry, if desired. Serves 6.

Mrs. Richard L. Redmont, Jr.

Bouillabaisse

1 cup chopped onion
1 cup chopped green pepper
1 cup chopped celery
3 cloves garlic, crushed
½ cup olive oil, divided
3 to 4 pounds turbot, or other bland white fish, cut in small pieces
1 bunch parsley, tied in cheesecloth
1 (16 ounce) can peeled tomatoes

2 cups dry white wine
2 cups water
Salt and pepper
Cayenne red pepper
Saffron (optional)
2 bay leaves
1 pound peeled raw shrimp, or more
1 pound white crab meat
1 (12 ounce) jar raw oysters
Any other shellfish desired, such as lobster, scallops or clams

Sauté the first 4 vegetables in ¼ cup olive oil until tender. Lightly sauté the turbot in the remaining olive oil. In a large pot, combine the vegetables and fish with all the remaining ingredients, except the seafood. Bring to a boil and simmer gently for about 30 minutes. Adjust seasonings and add more wine if more liquid is needed. Add seafood and simmer until fish is cooked (about 10 minutes). To serve, replace parsley with fresh sprigs and top each serving with thin slices of French bread toasted with Parmesan cheese. Serves 20.

Mrs. Betty Nell St. Clair

Shrimp and Crab Soup with Mushrooms

2 (10¾ ounce) cans cream of shrimp soup
1½ soup cans half and half cream

½ soup can dry white wine or sherry
½ pound fresh or frozen crab meat

Heat soup with cream and wine until hot but not boiling. Add crab meat. Garnish with SAUTÉED MUSHROOMS. Serves 4.

SAUTÉED MUSHROOMS

1 clove garlic, minced
1 Tablespoon oil
2 Tablespoons butter
¼ pound fresh mushrooms, sliced
Juice of ½ lemon

2 Tablespoons bread crumbs
2 Tablespoons grated Parmesan cheese
1 Tablespoon chopped parsley
Salt and pepper to taste

Sauté garlic in oil and butter for 1 minute. Remove garlic. Add mushrooms and cook over medium heat 6-7 minutes. Add lemon juice; cook for 1 minute. Add bread crumbs, cheese, parsley, salt and pepper. Spoon on hot soup.

Mrs. William H. Wallace

Oyster Soup

3 dozen oysters with liquid or 2 (12 ounce) jars
2 Tablespoons plus 1 teaspoon butter or margarine, divided
1 Tablespoon flour
2 Tablespoons chopped green onion
1 pint half and half cream, at room temperature
½ teaspoon salt, or more
1/8 teaspoon Tabasco, or more
Paprika

Heat oysters in their liquid until edges begin to curl; then set aside to keep warm. Melt 2 Tablespoons butter or margarine in saucepan; blend in flour until smooth. Stir in green onion and simmer a few minutes. Place this in a blender with the oyster liquid and 1 dozen of the oysters. Blend first on low, then on high for about a minute. While blending, add cream slowly. Melt 1 teaspoon butter or margarine in a double boiler. Add blended mixture and stir until well heated and thickened. Add salt and Tabasco. Add remaining oysters or place 4-6 oysters in each warmed soup bowl and pour soup over them. Garnish with paprika. Serves 4.

Mrs. John A. Jenkins, Jr.

Artichoke and Oyster Soup

½ cup chopped onion
⅓ cup chopped celery
3 Tablespoons butter
4 cups chicken broth
¼ cup lemon juice
1 bay leaf
1 teaspoon salt
¼ teaspoon pepper
¼ teaspoon thyme
1½ cups chopped artichoke hearts (canned or fresh cooked)
1 (12 ounce) jar raw oysters, drained
2 egg yolks
1 cup half and half cream

Sauté onion and celery in butter until tender. Add broth, lemon juice, bay leaf, salt, pepper and thyme. Simmer 20 minutes. Add artichoke hearts, reserving ⅓ cup. Remove bay leaf, add raw oysters and purée mixture in blender. Return to saucepan. Add egg yolks and cream. Add reserved artichoke hearts. Cook over moderate heat 5-10 minutes. Correct seasonings. Garnish with parsley or a thin lemon slice. Will keep 1-2 days. Serves 6-8.

Mrs. W. R. Newman, III

The oysters dilute the color of the artichokes, so green food coloring may be added for eye appeal.

EASY, THICK OYSTER STEW

Heat slowly 2 (10½ ounce) cans cream of potato soup and ½ cup milk. Add 1 (12 ounce) jar oysters, drained, and heat until edges of oysters curl. Season with parsley, Tabasco, salt, lemon-pepper seasoning and 1 Tablespoon butter.

Nova Scotia Clam Chowder

1 medium potato, peeled and
    diced
½ cup water
1 (8 ounce) can minced clams
    (reserve liquid)

1 medium onion, chopped
3 Tablespoons butter
1 pint half and half cream
Salt and pepper to taste
2 teaspoons chopped parsley

Place potato in saucepan with water and liquid from clams. Cook for 4 minutes and add onion. Cook another 2 minutes. Add clams, butter, cream, salt, pepper and parsley. Do not overboil but simmer for 30 minutes. Serves 2-3.

Ronald Cook

Rumanian Fish Soup

2 to 3 pounds red snapper
12 cups water
Salt
6 white peppercorns
1 bay leaf
4 large onions, thinly sliced
¼ pound butter, divided
¾ pound fresh mushrooms,
    diced
6 Tablespoons flour

2 (10¾ ounce) cans tomato soup
4 pickles (non-garlic fresh pack),
    diced
¼ to ⅓ (5 ounce) jar Kraft
    horseradish
1 Tablespoon sweet Hungarian
    paprika
Lemon juice
Sour cream

Place red snapper, cleaned and scaled but with head and tail on, in a large oval pot. Add water, 2 Tablespoons salt, peppercorns and bay leaf and bring to a boil. Simmer for 10 minutes, then strain the liquid and reserve. Remove the fish from bones and skin and break up into 1 or 2-inch hunks. Set aside. Rinse the cooking pan and in it sauté the onions in 6 Tablespoons butter for 15 minutes, until soft but not browned. In another pan sauté mushrooms in 2 Tablespoons butter. Blend the flour with the onions and cook for a minute. Off heat blend in half of the liquid, then the tomato soup, stirring to blend it well. Add the remaining liquid. Return to heat. Add the mushrooms, pickles, horseradish, paprika and fish. Simmer for 20 minutes. Correct seasoning with salt, more horseradish, paprika or lemon juice. It should have a slightly tart flavor. Cool; then refrigerate. Reheat gently but do not boil, as the fish will become mushy. Serve with a dollop of sour cream, and toast buttered on both sides. Serves 20.

Mrs. William B. Wilson

To further thicken soup, cornstarch mixed with a little wine may be added. A cup each of carrots and white turnips, cut in attractive shapes and cooked separately in salted water until tender, may also be added. Simmer in the soup for 30 minutes.

61

Vichyssoise

6 green onions
2 medium onions
6 medium Idaho potatoes,
    cooked, peeled and sliced
1½ quarts chicken broth

Salt
White pepper
½ to 1 cup whipping cream
Chopped chives

Discard tough, dark part of green onions and cut remaining stalks lengthwise; wash thoroughly. Chop onions and green onions. Add onions and potatoes to the chicken broth. Bring to a boil and simmer until vegetables are tender (about 40 minutes). Liquefy in a blender and season to taste, oversalting slightly as salt loses its savor in a cold dish. Add cream and chill. Garnish with chives. Serves 6-8.

Miss Betsy Nicholson

Quick Vichyssoise

2 (10½ ounce) cans cream
    of potato soup
1 soup can half and
    half cream
1 soup can chicken broth

Dash ground nutmeg
Dash thyme
Dash Tabasco
1 teaspoon salt
1 Tablespoon chopped chives

Mix all ingredients except chives in blender. Chill overnight. Serve in chilled bowls or mugs. Sprinkle chives on top. Serves 6.

Mrs. Robert L. Abney

Gazpacho

1 cup chopped, peeled tomatoes
½ cup finely chopped green
    pepper
½ cup finely chopped celery
½ cup finely chopped cucumber
¼ cup finely chopped onion
2 teaspoons chopped parsley
1 teaspoon snipped chives

1 small clove garlic, minced
2 to 3 Tablespoons wine vinegar
2 Tablespoons olive oil
1 teaspoon salt
¼ teaspoon pepper
½ teaspoon Worcestershire sauce
2 cups tomato juice

Mix ingredients, cover and chill thoroughly. Serves 8-10.

Mrs. G. Richard Greenlee

This is very good and low in calories. Especially good in the summer with the fresh vegetables in season.

———

Canned consommé, chicken broth, beef broth and clam juice may be used in place of basic stocks or consommés.

Lentil Bean Soup

1 (1 pound) package lentil beans
1 teaspoon salt
1 large onion, finely chopped
1 green pepper, finely chopped
⅓ cup olive oil
2 cloves garlic, finely chopped
4 pounds smoked sausage, cut
  into bite-size rounds

Salt to taste
½ teaspoon Greek seasoning
Lemon-pepper seasoning to taste
¼ cup lemon juice
½ cup chopped parsley
Lemon slices

Wash lentil beans thoroughly. Cover beans with water until water is 1 inch above beans. Add salt and simmer about 1 hour until beans are soft. Sauté onion and green pepper in olive oil until soft. Add these vegetables and the garlic to soup. Brown sausage in skillet. Add water to cover bottom of skillet. Cover and cook 20 minutes on low heat. Add sausage to soup. Add salt, Greek seasoning and lemon-pepper seasoning. Continue simmering, adding water if necessary. Soup will be very thick. Continue to cook 45 minutes. Just before serving add lemon juice. To serve, cover with chopped parsley and lemon slices. May be reheated or frozen. Serves 6-8.

Mrs. John D. Fournet

Cucumber Soup

2 medium cucumbers, peeled
  and sliced
3 cups canned chicken stock,
  divided
2 teaspoons salt
1/8 teaspoon white pepper

4 Tablespoons flour
¾ cup whipping cream or half
  and half cream
1 Tablespoon chopped chives
Sour cream
Grated lemon rind

Cook cucumbers until tender in 1 cup chicken stock with salt and pepper added. Drain off most of liquid and purée cucumbers in blender with flour dissolved in ½ cup chicken stock. Combine cucumber mixture with remaining chicken stock. Cook over medium heat until boiling, stirring constantly. Boil 2 minutes. Chill. Immediately before serving add cream and chives. Serve ice cold garnished with 1 Tablespoon sour cream and a sprinkling of lemon rind. May be prepared 1 day ahead. Serves 4.

Mrs. Alvin E. Brent, Jr.

Variation: Make a quick FROSTED CUCUMBER SOUP by puréeing in a blender 2 cucumbers, peeled and chopped, 1 envelope leek soup mix, ¾ cup milk, 1 teaspoon lemon juice, ¾ cup sour cream and a few drops green food coloring. Chill soup until icy cold. Serve with a spoonful sour cream and a sprinkling of chopped chives or chopped mint over each. Serves 4-6.

Mrs. Woods B. Cavett

Split Green Pea Soup With Sausage

1 (16 ounce) package split green
  peas
1 ham hock
3 or 4 carrots, sliced
1 onion, chopped
2 cups chopped celery

1 green pepper, chopped (optional)
2 Tablespoons chopped parsley
3 or 4 beef bouillon cubes
3 or 4 links hot Louisiana
  sausage, sliced
Salt to taste

Wash peas and soak in water to cover overnight. Add more water if needed to cover peas and bring to boil. Add other ingredients and simmer 3 hours or more. May be prepared 1 day in advance and reheated. Makes 3½ quarts.

Mrs. Norman Stevens, Mt. Olive, Mississippi

Cold Curry Cheese Soup

1 chicken bouillon cube
2 cups boiling water
2 cups fresh broccoli florets
4 (10½ ounce) cans beef
  consommé

3 (8 ounce) packages cream
  cheese, softened
1 teaspoon curry powder
½ clove garlic, minced

Dissolve the bouillon cube in the boiling water; add the broccoli and cook for 5 minutes. Drain and chill. Place the consommé, cream cheese, curry powder and garlic in the blender and blend until smooth. Chill. Serve soup chilled, placing several broccoli florets in the center of each serving to garnish. Serves 12.

Mrs. G. G. Mazzaferro

Low Calorie Vegetable Soup

1½ cups tomato juice
2 cups water
3 cups shredded cabbage
½ cup dehydrated onion flakes
2 Tablespoons parsley flakes
2 beef bouillon cubes or 2
  packets instant beef broth
2 onion cubes or 2 packets
  instant onion broth

Dash artificial sweetener
½ teaspoon garlic salt
Dash Tabasco
1 (4 ounce) can sliced mushrooms
  and liquid
1 (16 ounce) can French-style
  green beans and liquid
1 teaspoon salt

Combine tomato juice, water and cabbage in heavy sauce pan. Bring to boil, then simmer uncovered until cabbage is tender. Add remaining ingredients and heat. Keeps for a week in refrigerator. Serves 6.

Mrs. Louis J. Lyell

Cream of Carrot Soup

6 medium carrots, skinned and
   chopped
1 small onion, chopped
1 small bay leaf
2 Tablespoons butter or
   margarine

3 cups chicken stock, divided
2 teaspoons sugar
Salt and pepper to taste
1 Tablespoon grated lemon rind
1 Tablespoon chopped parsley

Combine carrots, onion, bay leaf and butter in heavy pan with a lid. Cook over low heat until carrots are tender, keeping the lid on to create condensation. The moisture will help to prevent burning, but a little stock may be added if it looks as if it may be burning. Cook approximately 8 minutes. Cool slightly and remove bay leaf; add 1 cup chicken stock. Pour into an electric blender; turn to low and then high. Blend 1 minute. Return to pan in which the carrots were cooked. Add remaining stock and sugar. Season with salt and pepper. Serve hot and garnish with a little grated lemon rind and parsley. Serves 6.

Mrs. J. M. Wingate

If using homemade chicken stock, make it deleting the chicken liver. If using canned chicken stock, do not dilute it. Chicken bouillon may be used.

Mimi's Old Fashioned Vegetable Soup

1 soup bone
¾ pound cubed lean beef
Oil
1 (16 ounce) can whole
   tomatoes
1 large white onion, halved
2 to 3 carrots, skinned and
   sliced
2 white onions, quartered
1 teaspoon Accent

2 cups sliced celery
¾ cup barley
1½ cups uncooked egg noodles
2 Tablespoons soy sauce
½ (10 ounce) package frozen cut
   okra
1 (17 ounce) can whole kernel
   corn, drained
2½ (13¾ ounce) cans
   chicken broth

In large skillet brown soup bone and meat in a little oil. Remove from skillet and drain on paper. Fill 6-quart pot with about 4 quarts hot water and add meat, soup bone, tomatoes and onion. Cover and cook on *low* heat for 2-2½ hours. Add remaining ingredients except chicken broth. Cook another hour, adding hot water if necessary. Add chicken broth during last 30 minutes of cooking. May be prepared several days ahead and is better if not served immediately. Makes 2½ quarts. Serves 10.

Mrs. James H. Knowles

A pint of frozen home-grown tomatoes substituted for the canned tomatoes will enhance the flavor greatly. To freeze, leave out chicken broth when making soup. Freeze soup in quart containers. When ready to use, thaw and heat, adding 1 can chicken broth per quart.

Cream of Zucchini Soup

2 Tablespoons finely chopped
   green onion
1 clove garlic, minced
1 pound young zucchini,
   cleaned, sliced thin

2 Tablespoons butter
1 teaspoon curry powder
½ teaspoon salt
½ cup whipping cream
1¾ cups chicken broth

In tightly covered pan simmer green onion, garlic and zucchini in the butter for about 10 minutes, until barely tender. Shake the pan occasionally to prevent the vegetables from burning. Place mixture and remaining ingredients in blender for ½ minute. Serve either hot or cold. Freezes well, but if frozen omit the addition of the cream until serving time. Serves 4.

Mrs. John C. Vaughey

Emerald Soup

4 cups clarified chicken broth
1 package leek (or onion) soup
   mix
4 sprigs parsley

1 (10 ounce) package frozen
   broccoli florets
Dash Tabasco
½ cup whipping cream

Combine chicken broth and leek soup mix. Bring to a boil. Add parsley, broccoli and Tabasco. Cover and boil until broccoli is just tender. Purée in blender. Cool. Stir in cream. Chill. Serve cold. May be prepared ahead. Serves 6.

Mrs. William H. FitzHugh

White Gazpacho

3 medium cucumbers, peeled
   and cut in chunks
3 cups chicken broth (canned
   may be used)
3 cups sour cream (yogurt may
   be substituted or 2 cups
   yogurt and 1 cup sour cream)

3 Tablespoons white vinegar
2 teaspoons garlic salt
2 tomatoes, peeled and chopped
¾ cup toasted almonds
½ cup sliced green onion
½ cup chopped parsley

Whirl cucumber chunks in blender a very short time with a little chicken broth. Combine with remaining chicken broth, sour cream, vinegar and garlic salt. Stir just enough to mix. Chill. Sprinkle tomatoes, almonds, onion and parsley on top. Serves 6.

Mrs. Charles R. Davis

Salads

Salad Basics

BASIC HANDLING OF SALAD GREENS   Remove core from iceberg lettuce by rapping sharply all around the core on edge of sink. Core can then be easily removed. Run water into head of lettuce and turn right side up to drain. Other lettuces and spinach should be washed under cold water, tough ends and stems removed, and drained in colander or dried on paper towels. Wrap in clean tea towel and refrigerate until crisp. Never cut lettuce with a knife; always tear lettuce into pieces by hand. When making large amount of salad, tear lettuce and store dry in a pillow case in refrigerator. All salad greens should be dry when preparing salad to allow oil in salad dressing to cling to leaves. Add a minimum of dressing; salad greens should be barely coated with dressing, not drenched. It is best not to toss the salad until just before serving, as it will go limp quite quickly when it comes in contact with the oil. If salad must be prepared ahead, mix dressing in serving bowl, cross serving utensils over it, loosely pile the dried lettuce leaves on top and refrigerate, covered with a paper towel, for an hour until ready to toss.

HANDLING MOLDED SALADS   In using unflavored powdered gelatin sprinkle 1 envelope into ¼ or ½ cup of cold liquid and let soften for 3-4 minutes. Gelatin must then be dissolved by stirring over low heat or by adding it to a very hot liquid and stirring until liquid is free of granules. It is preferable to unmold a gelatin dish several hours before using. To unmold, loosen gelatin from mold by running a knife or spatula around the top edge. Set mold in hot water for 20 seconds. Invert on wet serving platter and slide mold to desired position. Remove mold. If salad will not unmold readily, set in hot water for 10 seconds more. Refrigerate to reset until needed.

Paella Salad

1 (7 ounce) package yellow
   rice, cooked
2 Tablespoons tarragon vinegar
⅓ cup oil
1/8 teaspoon salt
1/8 teaspoon dry mustard
¼ teaspoon Accent
2 cups diced cooked chicken

1 cup shelled, boiled shrimp
1 large tomato, chopped
1 green pepper, chopped
½ cup minced onion
⅓ cup thinly sliced celery
1 Tablespoon chopped pimiento
1 teaspoon salt

Mix rice, vinegar, oil, salt, mustard and Accent. Cool to room temperature. Add remaining ingredients. Toss lightly and chill. May be prepared the night before. Serves 6-8.

Mrs. G. G. Mazzaferro

Neapolitan Chicken

1 (5 or 6 pound) hen
Salt
½ bunch parsley
3 bay leaves
1 large onion, quartered
3 ribs celery
6 peppercorns

1 dozen hard-boiled eggs
1½ Tablespoons unflavored
   gelatin
Tabasco
Worcestershire sauce
Lemon juice

Cook hen in water seasoned with salt, parsley, bay leaves, onion, celery and peppercorns until tender. Reserve stock. Remove meat from bones. Grind, using coarse blade of meat grinder, or chop finely the white and dark meat separately. Mash separately the whites and yellows of the hard-boiled eggs or sieve each with a ricer. Arrange in a loaf pan or ring mold layers in this order: white meat of chicken, yellows of eggs, dark meat of chicken, whites of eggs. Make an aspic by combining 3 cups cool, strained chicken stock with the gelatin, then heating mixture to dissolve the gelatin. Season aspic with salt, Tabasco, Worcestershire sauce and lemon juice to taste. Pour aspic over the chicken and egg layers. Chill in the refrigerator overnight. Slice or cut in squares. Serve on lettuce with homemade mayonnaise as a luncheon main course. Serves 12.

Mrs. Sherwood Wise

Beef Salad Français

2 cups sliced, boiled new
   potatoes
1 cup finely sliced scallions
2 cups coarsely chopped celery
   with tops
3 cups sliced, lean boiled beef,
   cut in 1½-inch squares
12 to 14 slices sour pickles
1 cup cherry tomatoes
¼ cup capers
½ cup green pepper strips

Salad greens
6 hard-cooked eggs
3 Tablespoons Dijon mustard
1 cup olive oil
1 clove garlic rubbed into 1½
   teaspoons salt
1 teaspoon black pepper
⅓ cup vinegar
Dash Tabasco
Diced walnuts

Combine potatoes, scallions, celery, beef, pickles, tomatoes, capers and green pepper. Toss and arrange on bed of greens. Shell 3 eggs, reserve whites and mash yolks with fork. Combine yolks with mustard. Stir in olive oil, salt (discard garlic), pepper and vinegar. Add Tabasco and pour dressing over beef. Garnish with 3 remaining eggs, quartered, walnuts and chopped egg whites. Serves 12.

Mrs. William H. Kessler, Jr.

Hawaiian Chicken Salad

3 whole fryer breasts
2 onions
3 carrots
1 teaspoon salt
¼ teaspoon pepper
1 cup chopped celery
1 cup white raisins, soaked in
 hot water and drained
2 (13½ ounce) cans pineapple
 tidbits, well-drained
2 cups flaked coconut

SAUCE:
¼ cup curry powder, or less
1 cup mayonnaise
¼ cup chicken broth
Juice of 1 lemon
Salt and pepper to taste

½ pound bacon, fried and
 crumbled
1 bunch watercress

Boil chicken with onions, carrots, salt and pepper until tender. Cool chicken in the broth. Cut chicken into bite-size pieces, discarding all skin and gristle. Add celery, raisins, pineapple and coconut. To make SAUCE, stir curry powder into mayonnaise and taste as it is added. Add broth, lemon juice, salt and pepper. Add sauce to chicken mixture. When ready to serve, arrange on platter, sprinkle crumbled bacon over top and garnish with watercress. Serves 4-6.

Mrs. William H. Hight, Louisville, Mississippi

Mexican Chef's Salad

1 medium onion, chopped
4 medium tomatoes, sliced
1 head lettuce, shredded
4 ounces sharp Cheddar
 cheese, grated
1 (8 ounce) bottle Thousand
 Island dressing
Tabasco to taste

1 (6¼ ounce) bag Doritos
1 large avocado, sliced
1 pound ground beef
1 (15 ounce) can kidney beans,
 drained
¼ teaspoon salt
Chili powder to taste (optional)

Place onion, tomatoes and lettuce in large salad bowl. Toss in cheese. Toss again with dressing and Tabasco. Remove 10 to 12 whole Dorito chips from bag and crush remaining chips into small pieces. Add crushed chips to salad. Reserve a few slices of avocado and add remaining slices to salad. Brown meat, drain off grease and toss with beans, salt, and chili powder. Simmer 10 minutes; then add, hot, to salad and toss. Decorate top of salad with whole Dorito chips and avocado slices. Some large tomato slices may also be used. Serve immediately. Good for supper as a main dish. Serve with hot buttered flour tortillas, rolled into tubes to be eaten like rolls. Serves 6 as main dish salad or 12 as salad course.

Mrs. Robert H. Thompson, Jr.

To peel tomatoes plunge in boiling water for 10 seconds. Slip off skins.

Chicken Salad

1 (5 or 6 pound) hen
1 carrot, cut into 3 sections
1 rib celery, cut into 3 sections
1 medium onion, quartered
1½ to 2 cups finely chopped
    celery

1½ to 2 cups finely chopped
    blanched almonds
Mayonnaise
Salt

Simmer hen with carrot, celery and onion until meat falls from bone. Cut meat with scissors into small pieces. Combine the COOKED DRESSING and the chicken the night before or several hours before serving. Add the celery and almonds last. Add extra mayonnaise and salt to taste. Serve on lettuce leaves or use for stuffing tomatoes. Makes 12-14 servings.

COOKED DRESSING

3 Tablespoons sugar
1 teaspoon salt
1 teaspoon prepared mustard
1½ Tablespoons flour

1 egg, beaten
¾ cup milk
4 Tablespoons vinegar
1 Tablespoon butter

Blend the first 7 ingredients in the order given and cook over hot water in a double boiler, stirring constantly, until thick. Add the butter and blend thoroughly. Cool before using.

Mrs. Noel C. Womack, Jr.

Tuna Salad Molds

1 envelope unflavored gelatin
¼ cup cold water
¾ cup hot water
2 Tablespoons lemon juice
1 teaspoon prepared mustard
¼ teaspoon salt
¼ teaspoon paprika
1 (7 ounce) can tuna, drained
    and flaked
1 cup chopped celery
½ cup mayonnaise

CUCUMBER DRESSING:
½ cup mayonnaise
¼ cup finely chopped cucumber
1 Tablespoon finely chopped
    green pepper
1 teaspoon tarragon vinegar
¼ teaspoon salt
Dash red pepper
Stuffed green olives, sliced

Soften gelatin in cold water, then dissolve it in hot water. Add lemon juice and seasonings. Chill until partially set, then add tuna and celery. Fold in the mayonnaise, pour into 6 individual salad molds and chill until set. Prepare *CUCUMBER DRESSING* by thoroughly mixing dressing ingredients. Un-mold salads, place on lettuce leaf, top with dressing and garnish with olive slices. Best made 1 day ahead. Serves 6.

Mrs. W. V. Westbrook, Jr.

Chicken-Almond Salad

1 envelope unflavored gelatin
¼ cup cold water
1 cup mayonnaise
1 cup whipping cream,
  whipped

1 teaspoon salt
1½ cups diced cooked chicken
¾ cup almonds, chopped
¾ cup green seedless grapes,
  halved

Soften gelatin in cold water and dissolve over hot water. Cool slightly and combine with mayonnaise, cream and salt. Fold in chicken, almonds and grapes. Chill until firm in mold or 2-quart Pyrex dish. Delicious luncheon dish with sliced tomatoes, pickled peaches and toasted cheese roll-ups. Serves 6.

Mrs. William B. McCarty, Jr.

Salmon Mousse

1 envelope unflavored gelatin
¼ cup cold water
½ cup boiling water
½ cup mayonnaise
2 Tablespoons lemon juice
1½ Tablespoons grated onion
½ teaspoon Tabasco

1½ teaspoons salt
2 Tablespoons finely chopped
  capers
½ teaspoon paprika
2 cups canned salmon, well
  drained and mashed
½ cup whipping cream, whipped

Soften gelatin in cold water. Add hot water and stir to dissolve. Cool. Fold remaining ingredients, except cream, together. Add gelatin and mix well. Fold in whipped cream. Pour mixture into an oiled fish mold or individual molds. Refrigerate until set. Unmold and top with DILL DRESSING or SAUCE VERDE. Serve with crackers. Serves 8.

DILL DRESSING

¾ teaspoon salt
¼ teaspoon white pepper
1 teaspoon grated lemon rind
2 cups sour cream

3 Tablespoons finely chopped
  fresh dill or 1 Tablespoon
  dill weed

Combine ingredients and blend well. Chill for several hours before using.

Mrs. Robert Powell, Jr., Canton, Mississippi

SAUCE VERDE

1 cup mayonnaise, divided
1 teaspoon dry mustard
1 cup sour cream
1 drop green food coloring

2 Tablespoons chopped chives
2 Tablespoons chopped parsley
2 cucumbers, peeled and
  chopped

Thoroughly blend 2 Tablespoons mayonnaise with the dry mustard. Add remaining mayonnaise and all other ingredients. Chill.

Mrs. William B. Fontaine

Curried Shrimp-Rice Salad

1 cup cooked shrimp,
  preferably fresh
1 cup cooked rice
1 cup finely chopped raw
  cauliflower
2 hard-boiled eggs, chopped
1 (2 ounce) jar stuffed olives,
  drained and chopped

DRESSING:
1 cup mayonnaise
1 teaspoon horseradish
  mustard
2 teaspoons lemon juice
1 teaspoon grated onion
½ teaspoon curry powder
Dash Worcestershire sauce

Toss together first 5 ingredients. Stir *DRESSING* ingredients together and pour over shrimp mixture. Toss. Serves 6.

Mrs. Paul Moore, Pascagoula, Mississippi

Variation: Add ½ (14 ounce) can artichoke hearts, drained and diced, to shrimp mixture.

Amelia's Stuffed Eggs in Parsley Jelly

2 envelopes unflavored gelatin
½ cup cold water
½ cup sugar
1 teaspoon salt
2 cups hot water

½ cup white vinegar
2 Tablespoons lemon juice
6 deviled eggs
½ cup finely chopped parsley
1 teaspoon chopped chives

Soften gelatin in cold water. Add sugar, salt and hot water. Stir until dissolved. Add vinegar and lemon juice. Chill until slightly thickened. Pour about 1 Tablespoon of this clear mixture into the bottom of 6 individual salad molds holding about ⅔ cup each. Place deviled eggs, cut side down, in the clear gelatin. Pour another Tablespoon of clear gelatin around eggs. Fold parsley and chives into remaining gelatin. Top the molds with this parsley mixture and chill until firm. Unmold on lettuce. Serves 6.

Mrs. Frank R. Briggs

DEVILED EGGS   Halve and remove yolks from 4 hard-cooked eggs. Push yolks through a sieve. Add to yolks 3 ounces soft cream cheese, 1 Tablespoon mayonnaise, 1 Tablespoon prepared mustard, ¼ teaspoon salt, dash red pepper and 1/8 teaspoon dry mustard. Blend until smooth. Correct seasoning. Stuff mixture into egg white halves. Makes 8 deviled eggs.

———

Watercress and parsley keep fresh longer if stored in a covered jar in the refrigerator.

1½ pounds raw shrimp in the shell equals 2 cups shelled, cooked shrimp; or for 1 cup shelled, cooked shrimp, buy ¾ pound raw shrimp in the shell or 8 ounces frozen shelled, cooked shrimp or 1 (5 ounce) can shrimp.

Caribbean Crab Salad

1 pound fresh lump crab meat
1 large white onion, finely
   chopped
1 Tablespoon finely minced
   fresh parsley
1 Tablespoon Worcestershire
   sauce

Dash Tabasco
Salt and white pepper to taste
½ cup salad oil
½ cup white wine vinegar
Bibb lettuce leaves
Tomato or avocado slices

Pick over crab meat carefully to remove shells. Place crab meat into a bowl and cover with onion and parsley. Add seasonings to oil and vinegar, mix well and pour over crab, tossing gently. Cover and refrigerate for at least 5 hours. Serve on lettuce surrounded with tomato or avocado slices. Serves 6.

Mrs. Wallace V. Mann, Jr.

Congealed Asparagus Salad

1 (14½ ounce) can cut green
   asparagus (reserve liquid)
1 (3 ounce) package lime gelatin
1 cup mayonnaise
½ teaspoon salt
½ teaspoon Worcestershire
   sauce
½ teaspoon dry mustard

½ cup grated Cheddar cheese
½ Tablespoon grated onion
1 Tablespoon vinegar or lemon
   juice
¾ cup chopped almonds
½ cup half and half cream
Dash Tabasco

Measure liquid from asparagus and add water to make 1 cup. Heat liquid. Dissolve gelatin in hot asparagus liquid. Refrigerate until almost set. Mix in asparagus and remaining ingredients and chill until firm. May be prepared the day before. Serves 8.

Mrs. Gibbs J. Fowler

Molded Beet Salad

1 (16 ounce) can diced beets
1 (3 ounce) package lemon
   gelatin
1 cup hot water
3 Tablespoons cider vinegar

¼ teaspoon salt
½ cup diced celery
2 Tablespoons grated onion
1 Tablespoon prepared
   horseradish

Drain beets, reserving liquid. Dissolve gelatin in hot water. Stir in reserved beet liquid, vinegar and salt. Cool. Chill until slightly thickened. Lightly grease a 1-quart mold or individual molds. Add beets and other ingredients to chilled gelatin mixture. Pour into molds and chill until set. Serves 8.

Mrs. Robert Ratelle

Spinach Mold

2 envelopes unflavored gelatin
1 (10½ ounce) can beef broth
¼ cup water
½ teaspoon salt
2 Tablespoons lemon juice
1 cup Miracle Whip salad
  dressing
4 eggs, hard-cooked and sliced

1 (10 ounce) package frozen
  chopped spinach, cooked
  and drained
¼ cup chopped green onion
½ pound bacon, fried crisp and
  crumbled
Dash Tabasco (optional)
Whole canned pimiento, cut
  into strips

Soften gelatin in beef broth; then stir over low heat until dissolved. Stir in water, salt and lemon juice. Cool. Gradually add mixture to Miracle Whip, mixing until blended. Chill until slightly thickened. Spray mold with non-grease spray, if desired. Place eggs on bottom. Fold spinach, onion, bacon and Tabasco into gelatin mixture. Pour over eggs and refrigerate until ready to serve. Unmold and garnish with pimiento strips. Serves 6-8.

Mrs. Don R. Bush

Cucumber Aspic

2 cups boiling water
1 (6 ounce) package lemon
  gelatin
⅓ cup white wine vinegar
¼ teaspoon salt
Green food coloring
2 medium cucumbers, pared
  and grated (2 cups)

½ cup finely chopped celery
2 Tablespoons horseradish
1 Tablespoon grated onion
¼ teaspoon dill seed
20 paper-thin slices unpeeled
  cucumber
2 pints cherry tomatoes
½ pint sour cream

In a medium bowl, pour boiling water over gelatin. Stir until dissolved. Stir in vinegar, salt and a few drops of food coloring. Set bowl in ice or freezer, stirring occasionally until mixture is consistency of unbeaten egg whites (35 minutes). Fold in cucumbers, celery, horseradish, onion and dill seed until well blended. Turn into 6-cup ring mold that has been rinsed in cold water and lined with thin cucumber slices. Refrigerate at least 3 hours. Run spatula around edges of mold, invert on platter, place a hot damp cloth on mold and shake gently to release. Fill center with cherry tomatoes and pass sour cream for topping. Serves 8-10.

Mrs. Albert Meena

This salad is very tart and goes well with roast or seafood dishes with sauces. It is easily made with a food processor.

Fresh spinach, red onion rings and orange slices tossed with Italian dressing create an attractive, tasty salad.

Congealed Broccoli

2 envelopes unflavored gelatin
½ cup cold water
1 cup consommé
1 teaspoon beef stock base
1¾ teaspoons salt
5 teaspoons Worcestershire
　sauce
6 teaspoons lemon juice

Dash Tabasco
¾ cup mayonnaise
2 (10 ounce) packages frozen
　broccoli florets, cooked,
　drained, buttered and
　seasoned
4 hard-boiled eggs, chopped

Dissolve gelatin in cold water. Boil consommé and add to gelatin. Add beef stock, salt, Worcestershire sauce, lemon juice and Tabasco. Cool gelatin mixture until it begins to thicken. Fold in mayonnaise and mix thoroughly. Add broccoli and eggs. Pour into mold and refrigerate to set. Serves 8.

Mrs. Wade Creekmore, Jr.

Congealed Vegetable Salad

2 envelopes unflavored gelatin
½ cup cold water
1 cup hot water
1 (16 ounce) can tiny, whole,
　sliced, or shoestring beets
　(reserve juice)
½ cup vinegar
1/8 teaspoon Tabasco
½ teaspoon Worcestershire
　sauce
1 teaspoon lemon juice, or
　more
4 hard-boiled eggs, sliced or
　sieved

1 (3½ ounce) jar cocktail
　onions
1 (17 ounce) can early green
　peas
1 cup chopped celery
1 (16 ounce) can French-style
　green beans

DRESSING:
½ cup mayonnaise
2 Tablespoons sieved
　Roquefort cheese
Lemon juice to taste

Oil a 12-cup ring mold or 12 individual molds. Soften gelatin in cold water; add hot water and stir to dissolve. Measure beet juice and add enough water to make 2 cups liquid. Add beet liquid, vinegar, Tabasco, Worcestershire sauce and lemon juice to the gelatin and chill until slightly thickened. Place eggs and drained vegetables in mold in the order named. Pour liquid over all and place in refrigerator to congeal. Serve on lettuce leaves or shredded lettuce topped with *DRESSING* prepared by mixing the mayonnaise, cheese and lemon juice. May be prepared several days in advance. Serves 12-16.

Mrs. Sherwood Wise

Note: If individual molds are used, the eggs should be put through a sieve, yolks separately from whites. Place sieved yolks in mold first, then sieved whites. The beet juice gives a pink cast to the liquid, but too much will darken the liquid and hide the layered vegetables.

Tomato-Avocado Ribbon Salad

AVOCADO LAYER

1 package unflavored gelatin
½ cup water, divided
1 teaspoon salt
3 Tablespoons lemon juice

5 drops Tabasco
1½ cups sieved avocado
Few drops green food coloring

Soften gelatin in ¼ cup cold water. Add ¼ cup boiling water. Add salt, lemon juice and Tabasco. Cool until thickened. Add avocado and food coloring. Pour into a 9 x 5-inch loaf pan and chill until almost firm.

CHEESE LAYER

2 teaspoons unflavored gelatin
¼ cup cold water
4 (3 ounce) packages cream
   cheese, softened
½ cup milk

1 teaspoon salt
⅔ cup mayonnaise
¼ teaspoon Worcestershire sauce
½ teaspoon dried, chopped
   green onion

Soften gelatin in cold water and dissolve over boiling water. Beat together the cheese and milk. Stir in other ingredients. Stir in gelatin. Pour over the AVOCADO LAYER and chill until almost firm.

TOMATO LAYER

3 cups tomato juice
½ bay leaf
2 whole cloves
2 sprigs parsley
2 ribs celery
¾ teaspoon salt

Dash cayenne pepper
1½ packages unflavored
   gelatin
⅓ cup cold water
1½ Tablespoons vinegar
1½ teaspoons grated onion

Bring tomato juice, bay leaf, cloves, parsley, celery, salt and pepper to a boil and simmer 10 minutes. Strain. Soften gelatin in cold water, then add to hot tomato juice. Add vinegar and onion. Pour over CHEESE LAYER and chill until set. To serve, unmold on platter. To garnish, sieve the whites and yellows of 2 hard-boiled eggs separately. Place sieved eggs on top of loaf in stripes of yellow and white. Separate stripes with strips of green pepper or pimiento. Slice in ½-inch slices to serve. Serves 12-14 people as a salad or 6 as a luncheon main dish.

Mrs. G. G. Mazzaferro

Common kitchen utensils make good salad molds: muffin pans, custard cups, an ice cube tray and even empty tin cans. Mold salad in a 28-ounce can. When ready, cut around the bottom half of the can, push the salad out of the bottom, slice and serve on a bed of lettuce.

77

Tomato Aspic

3 (16 ounce) cans tomatoes
2 medium onions, chopped
4 large ribs celery, chopped
Handful of parsley
1 teaspoon basil
1 Tablespoon salt

1 (12 ounce) can V-8 juice
3 packages unflavored gelatin
⅓ to ½ cup water
1 teaspoon wine vinegar
1 teaspoon Worcestershire sauce
Freshly ground pepper to taste

Press tomatoes through a strainer, mashing to extract all juice. In a boiler with a tight-fitting top place tomato juice, onions, celery and parsley and simmer until the vegetables are very soft (about 2 hours). During the last 15 minutes add basil and salt. Strain and add V-8 juice (there should be about 6 cups of liquid). For every 2 cups of liquid, use 1 package gelatin. Soften the gelatin in the water; then add it to the hot liquid, stirring until completely dissolved. Add remaining seasonings and pour into a ring mold or individual molds. Refrigerate to set. When unmolded, the center of the ring may be filled with artichoke hearts, minced spring onions, fresh crab meat or cream cheese. Serves 8.

Mrs. Battle Barksdale

This recipe has been used in the family for generations and makes a clear, light aspic.

Marinated Vegetable Platter

¼ cup wine vinegar
¼ cup salad oil
½ cup mayonnaise
1½ teaspoons prepared mustard
¼ teaspoon salt
¼ teaspoon garlic powder
1 hard-cooked egg, grated or
  sieved

4 Tablespoons chopped chives
1 (16 ounce) can whole green
  beans
1 (14½ ounce) can asparagus
  spears
1 (14 ounce) can artichoke
  hearts
1 (15 ounce) can Belgian carrots

Whisk together thoroughly the vinegar and oil. Add mayonnaise, mustard, salt and garlic powder and continue to whisk. Fold in egg and chives. Use vegetables listed or any other vegetables desired. Arrange drained vegetables separately in large Pyrex baking dish; do not mix them. Pour marinade over vegetables and refrigerate. To serve, arrange vegetables on large crystal salad platter (particularly pretty arranged in wheel fashion with artichoke hearts in the center). Decorate with sprigs of parsley. Serves 16.

Mrs. Duncan Briggs

Grease molds for congealed salads with mayonnaise.

Molded Gazpacho

10 envelopes unflavored gelatin
2 (46 ounce) cans V-8 or
    tomato juice
3 or 4 large tomatoes, peeled
    and seeded
1 white onion, quartered
2 or 3 large cucumbers,
    peeled and seeded
2 teaspoons salt

½ bunch green onions,
    chopped fine
1 teaspoon white pepper
1 teaspoon Tabasco
1 teaspoon Worcestershire sauce
¼ cup lemon juice
¾ cup olive oil
¼ cup wine vinegar
2 teaspoons celery salt
Sour cream

In a large pan soften gelatin in 1 can tomato juice. Simmer until completely dissolved. In a blender purée tomatoes, white onion and cucumbers. Add to hot mixture with rest of ingredients. This recipe fills a 3-quart mold or a bundt pan. Chill until firm. Top each slice of salad with sour cream. Serves 40-50.

Mrs. McKamy Smith

Marinated Tomatoes

1 clove garlic, minced
¼ cup sliced green onion and
    tops
1 teaspoon salt
¼ teaspoon finely ground
    pepper

¼ cup snipped parsley
½ teaspoon thyme leaves
6 fresh tomatoes, peeled
⅔ cup salad oil
¼ cup vinegar

Combine first 6 ingredients and sprinkle over tomatoes, which have been cut in half or in thick slices. Mix oil and vinegar and pour over tomatoes. Cover and chill several hours or overnight. Spoon dressing over tomatoes several times while chilling. Drain before serving. Serves 6.

Mrs. E. Ronald McAnally

Fresh Mushroom Salad

1½ cups vinegar
3 Tablespoons sugar
1½ teaspoons salt
1½ teaspoons paprika
1½ Tablespoons Worcestershire
    sauce
1½ Tablespoons salad herbs

½ cup salad oil
3 cloves garlic, pressed
¾ pound fresh mushrooms,
    sliced and sprinkled with
    lemon juice
3 heads romaine lettuce, torn
    in pieces

Blend the first 6 ingredients and cook over low heat for 8 minutes. Cool. Add salad oil and garlic. Toss with mushrooms and lettuce. Serve immediately. Serves 15.

Mrs. F. Dean Copeland, Atlanta, Georgia

Marinated Vegetable Salad

2 (16 ounce) cans French-style
  green beans
2 (17 ounce) cans early green
  peas
1 (14 ounce) can artichoke
  hearts, diced
1 (7 ounce) can pimientos,
  chopped
1 medium green pepper,
  chopped

1 medium onion, diced
1 (8 ounce) can water chestnuts,
  sliced

MARINADE:
¾ cup sugar
1 cup red wine vinegar
½ cup water
½ cup Wesson oil
1 clove garlic, minced

Combine drained vegetables. Blend all *MARINADE* ingredients and pour over the vegetables. Marinate overnight. This recipe may be prepared several days ahead. Serves 20.

Mrs. H. C. Roberts, Canton, Mississippi

Frozen Tomato Aspic

½ (10¾ ounce) can tomato
  soup
2 (16 ounce) cans tomatoes
1 large onion, quartered
1 stick cinnamon
1/8 teaspoon black pepper
2 ribs celery, quartered
2 bay leaves
½ teaspoon McCormick's
  seafood seasoning
¼ bunch parsley

2 teaspoons Worcestershire
  sauce
1/8 teaspoon ground cinnamon
½ teaspoon sugar
1 clove garlic
1 teaspoon salt
1 package unflavored gelatin,
  softened in ¼ cup cold
  water
1 cup mayonnaise

Combine all ingredients except the gelatin and mayonnaise and simmer, covered, for 20 minutes. Strain. Add the gelatin and dissolve in the hot mixture. Allow to cool. Fold in the mayonnaise, pour into individual molds and freeze. Unmold and garnish with avocado slices, if desired. For a luncheon, this salad is especially pretty frozen in individual ring molds, unmolded on a lettuce leaf, garnished with avocado slices and the center filled with Marinated Vegetable Salad. Serves 8.

Mrs. Tillman Caldwell, Canton, Mississippi

This salad is made from an old recipe which originally called for freezing the aspic with an ice cream freezer, then scooping it onto lettuce cups. It can be made that way, too.

———

Toss avocado slices in lemon juice to keep from turning brown so quickly.

Cold Pea Salad

1 (17 ounce) can English peas
2 Tablespoons chopped green
   pepper
1 teaspoon chopped pimiento
2 Tablespoons chopped celery
1 Tablespoon chopped onion

2 Tablespoons diced sharp
   Cheddar cheese
1 Tablespoon pickle relish
1 hard-cooked egg, diced
1½ Tablespoons mayonnaise

Drain peas. Combine next 6 ingredients and mix well. Add peas, egg and mayonnaise and mix gently. Chill. Serves 4-6.

Mrs. Donald A. White

Curried Stuffed Tomatoes

6 large tomatoes
Salt and pepper to taste
Dill weed (fresh, if possible)
12 large mushrooms, coarsely
   chopped
12 artichoke hearts, quartered

Oil and vinegar dressing
2 cups homemade mayonnaise
1 cup sour cream
2 teaspoons curry powder
2 teaspoons lemon juice
2 teaspoons grated onion

Pour boiling water over the tomatoes and skin them. Scoop out the seeds and juice. Season them inside and out with salt, pepper and dill. Chill. Marinate coarsely chopped mushrooms and quartered artichoke hearts in a good oil and vinegar dressing for several hours. Combine mayonnaise and sour cream and add curry powder, lemon juice and grated onion. When ready to serve, place the tomatoes on a large lettuce cup, fill with drained mushrooms and artichoke mixture and top with dressing. Sprinkle dill weed on top. Serves 6.

Mrs. Maurice Reed, Jr.

Very Special Tossed Salad

1 head iceberg lettuce
½ head each escarole and
   endive
1 cup watercress, when
   available, chopped
1 medium ripe avocado,
   chopped
1 (6 ounce) jar marinated
   artichoke hearts, chopped
   (reserve liquid)

2 tiny green onions, chopped
1 or 2 tender ribs celery with
   leaves, chopped
1 (11 ounce) can mandarin
   oranges, drained and chilled
¾ cup Wishbone Italian
   salad dressing
2 Tablespoons refrigerated
   bleu cheese dressing

Tear lettuce into bite-size pieces. Toss with next 5 ingredients. Arrange orange slices on top of salad. Place oil from artichoke hearts into a jar; add Wishbone and bleu cheese dressings. Shake well and pour over salad. Serves 16-20.

Mrs. W. F. Goodman, Jr.

Fantastic Potato Salad

12 medium white potatoes
2 Tablespoons cider vinegar
2 Tablespoons margarine,
  melted
2 Tablespoons sugar
2 teaspoons salt
1 whole bunch celery, chopped

12 hard-boiled eggs, sliced
1 cup minced parsley
2 (4 ounce) jars chopped
  pimientos
½ cup minced onion
1 (10 ounce) jar sweet pickle
  relish

Boil potatoes in skins until tender. While hot, peel, cube and toss potatoes lightly with vinegar, margarine, sugar and salt. Refrigerate until thoroughly chilled. Then add celery, eggs, parsley, pimiento, onion and pickle relish. Chill until flavors blend. Moisten with chilled MAYONNAISE-HORSERADISH SAUCE 1 hour before serving. Serves 12-15.

MAYONNAISE-HORSERADISH SAUCE

1 quart mayonnaise
  (Hellmann's preferred)

1 (5 ounce) jar prepared
  horseradish

Mix well and refrigerate. This sauce is also very good on roast beef or corned beef.

Mrs. James Kelly Wallace

Caesar Salad

1 clove garlic, crushed
½ cup olive oil
½ teaspoon salt
Pepper to taste
Juice of 1 large lemon
2 eggs, coddled 1 to 1½
  minutes

2 to 3 heads young romaine
  lettuce, torn in pieces
6 anchovy fillets, mashed
½ cup grated fresh Parmesan
  cheese
2 cups croutons

Marinate garlic in olive oil for 24 hours. In a large salad bowl, combine the salt, pepper and lemon juice. Drip in the olive oil while whipping to slightly thicken it. When the oil begins to turn cloudy, break in the coddled eggs (coddle by submerging whole egg in simmering water) and continue whipping. Drop in lettuce pieces and toss until completely coated. Add the anchovies and cheese and adjust to taste with additional salt and lemon juice if necessary. Add croutons at the last moment. Serves 8-10.

From the recipes of John B. Mason

Note: To make fresh croutons, toss 2 cups diced sourdough or French bread (which is several days old) with ¼ cup olive oil flavored with crushed garlic. Brown bread cubes in the oven, stirring several times. Drain on paper towels.

French Potato Salad

2 pounds new or boiling
   potatoes
Salt and freshly ground pepper
2 Tablespoons dry white
   vermouth
2 Tablespoons beef bouillon

2 Tablespoons wine vinegar
6 Tablespoons olive oil
2 Tablespoons minced shallots
1 teaspoon Dijon mustard
Chopped fresh parsley

Boil potatoes in their jackets until tender. Peel and slice while still hot. Place them in a shallow serving dish. Season with salt and pepper and pour vermouth and bouillon over all. Toss gently and let sit for a few minutes. Make a French dressing by combining all remaining ingredients except parsley in a screw-top glass jar. Shake well. Pour dressing over potatoes. Toss gently and sprinkle with parsley. Serves 6-8.

Mrs. William B. Wilson

Fresh Spinach Salad

¼ cup sugar
1 teaspoon salt
1 teaspoon dry mustard
1 teaspoon poppy seed
1 Tablespoon onion juice
⅓ cup cider vinegar
1 cup salad oil
¾ cup cottage cheese

2 pounds fresh spinach,
   washed and torn, heavy
   stems removed
½ pound bacon, fried crisp
2 to 3 hard-boiled eggs,
   chopped
Fresh mushrooms, sliced,
   (optional)

Mix first 8 ingredients in a jar and refrigerate overnight. (Dressing will keep up to 1 week in refrigerator.) When ready to serve, shake dressing well and toss with spinach. Add bacon, eggs and mushrooms and toss again. Serve immediately. Serves 8.

Mrs. H. K. Kent

Avocado and Bacon Salad

Juice of 2 limes
¼ cup olive oil
½ cup sour cream
¼ cup mayonnaise
Salt and coarsely ground pepper

2 cloves garlic, minced
8 strips bacon, diced
1 large head Boston lettuce,
   washed and broken into pieces
2 small avocados, cubed

Combine lime juice, olive oil, sour cream, mayonnaise, salt, pepper and garlic. Place diced bacon in a skillet and cook over low heat until crisp. Drain bacon bits. Just before serving, combine lettuce, avocado cubes and crisp bacon. Pour lime juice dressing over salad and toss gently. Serve on additional crisp greens. Serves 4-6.

Mrs. Ward Van Skiver

McInnis Salad

1 head lettuce, cored and chilled
1 cup finely chopped celery
½ cup finely chopped onion
1 green pepper, finely chopped
1 (10 ounce) package frozen
   English peas, cooked

2 cups mayonnaise, preferably
   homemade
1 (12 to 16 ounce) package
   bacon, cooked and crumbled
1 cup grated medium Cheddar
   cheese

Break lettuce into bite-size pieces. Toss with celery, onion and green pepper and place in oblong Pyrex dish. Sprinkle cooled, drained peas on top. Cover with mayonnaise, sealing edges well. Top with bacon and cheese. Seal with foil and refrigerate. Do not open for 2 days. Cut in squares to serve. Salad will keep about 1 week if kept sealed. Serves 10-12.

Mrs. W. V. Westbrook, Jr.

St. Andrew's Slaw

1 (2 pound) head cabbage
3 Tablespoons mayonnaise
   (Hellmann's or homemade)
1 teaspoon salt

3 or 4 Tablespoons sugar
4 or 5 dill pickles, chopped
2 Tablespoons prepared
   mustard

Shred cabbage. Combine remaining ingredients and mix well with cabbage. Chill overnight. Serves 6.

Mrs. Ernest Saik

Especially good as dressing for hamburgers.

German Cabbage Slaw

1 large head cabbage
1 large red onion
1 cup sugar
1 cup vinegar
1 teaspoon prepared mustard

1½ teaspoons salt
1 teaspoon celery seed
1 Tablespoon sugar
1 cup Wesson oil

Cut cabbage and onion in thin slices. Place in bowl and cover with sugar. Bring to a boil all remaining ingredients except the oil. Remove from heat, add oil and bring to boil again. Pour liquid over vegetables, mash flat with a plate, cover and refrigerate. Drain to serve. Keeps 2 weeks. Serves 12.

Mrs. Brad Dye, Jr.

EASY CABBAGE CHOPPING METHOD FOR SLAW   Wash and quarter cabbage head, removing tough center stem. Cut each quarter into smaller pieces and fill blender container half full. Fill container with water and with the top on, turn blender on and off quickly until cabbage is chopped to desired size. Drain in colander and repeat until all is chopped.

Cracked Wheat Salad

1 cup cracked wheat	Juice of 1 or 2 lemons
3 tomatoes, peeled and diced	½ cup olive oil
4 green onions, diced	Salt
½ cup chopped parsley	Pepper
½ to 1 cup chopped fresh mint	Ground allspice
½ cucumber, chopped fine	Lettuce

Wash cracked wheat well. Cover with water and let soak in the refrigerator for 1 hour. Wring water out of wheat by handfuls. Combine tomatoes, onions, parsley, mint and cucumber with wheat. Add lemon juice, olive oil and seasonings to taste. Serve in a salad bowl surrounded by bite-size pieces of lettuce. Let each person spoon a little salad mixture onto a lettuce piece and eat as finger food. Amounts given are guides and can be varied to suit individual taste. Serves 12.

Mrs. Thomas M. Elzen

Ginger Ale Salad

1 envelope plus 2 teaspoons unflavored gelatin	1 cup mandarin orange sections
2 Tablespoons cold water	1 cup canned sliced peaches or pears
½ cup boiling water	¼ cup sliced fresh strawberries
1½ cups ginger ale	¼ cup black (or green) grapes, seeded and halved or ½ cup diced canned pineapple
2 Tablespoons lemon juice	
4 Tablespoons sugar	

Soften gelatin in cold water. Add boiling water and stir until dissolved. Add ginger ale, lemon juice and sugar. Cool until mixture begins to thicken; then add fruit. Pour into a 5-cup mold or individual molds and chill. To serve, unmold and spoon STRAWBERRY SOUR CREAM DRESSING over each. Serves 6.

STRAWBERRY SOUR CREAM DRESSING

2 cups sour cream	½ cup frozen strawberries
1 teaspoon salt	

Fold the ingredients together. Makes 2½ cups dressing.

Mrs. Warren Ludlam, Jr.

POACHED PEAR SALAD

Poach, covered, 1 (16 ounce) can drained pear halves in 1 cup ruby port wine mixed with 3 Tablespoons brown sugar for 10 minutes. Chill. To serve, place 2 pear halves in each serving dish; pour wine mixture over and top each serving with a spoonful sour cream.

Nutty Golden Glow Salad

1 cup boiling water
1 (3 ounce) package lemon
   gelatin
1 cup pineapple juice
1 Tablespoon lemon juice

½ teaspoon salt
1 cup crushed pineapple
1 cup grated carrots
½ cup chopped English
   walnuts

Pour boiling water over gelatin and stir until dissolved. Add juices and salt. Allow to thicken slightly. Add pineapple, carrots and nuts and turn into 5-cup mold or individual molds. Refrigerate. Serves 6-8.

Mrs. Edward C. Nichols

Frozen Fruit Salad

1½ cups sour cream
¾ cup powdered sugar
1/8 teaspoon salt
2 Tablespoons lemon juice
½ cup sliced maraschino
   cherries

1 (20 ounce) can crushed
   pineapple, drained
¾ cup sliced seedless grapes
1 banana, diced (optional)
½ cup chopped pecans

Combine sour cream and sugar in large mixing bowl. Add salt and lemon juice, then remaining ingredients, blending evenly. Freeze in muffin tins with paper liners or 9 x 11-inch baking dish. Serves 15.

Mrs. Barry Aden

Fresh Fruit Salad

¾ cup sugar
1½ cups water
Juice of 1 lemon
1 ripe cantaloupe or other
   seasonal melon
   (about 1½ pounds)
3 navel oranges, peeled,
   sectioned
2 green apples, unpared, cored,
   diced

3 bananas, sliced
8 ounces seedless green grapes
   (about 1½ cups)
8 ounces purple or red grapes,
   halved, seeded
   (about 1½ cups)
2 red apples, unpared, cored,
   diced
¼ cup sherry wine (optional)

Dissolve sugar in water in 1-quart saucepan. Heat to boiling; reduce heat. Simmer uncovered until light syrup is formed (about 10 minutes); remove from heat. Stir in lemon juice; refrigerate covered until cold. Halve cantaloupe, remove seeds and scoop out pulp with melon ball cutter. Mix all fruits in large bowl. Pour lemon syrup over fruit and toss gently until evenly coated. Cover and refrigerate. Just before serving, stir in sherry. Serves 12.

Mrs. Richard L. Redmont, Jr.

Frozen Avocado Salad

1 (8 ounce) package cream
   cheese, softened
1 cup sour cream
¼ teaspoon salt
½ cup sugar

1 avocado, diced
1 grapefruit, sectioned
1 cup white grapes
½ cup pecans, chopped

Blend cream cheese and sour cream and add salt and sugar. Stir until smooth. Add remaining ingredients and freeze in a 9 x 5-inch pan or individual molds. Serves 8.

Mrs. Richard Warren, Jr.

Stuffed Spiced Peaches

2 (29 ounce) jars spiced peaches
   (reserve juice)
2 (3 ounce) packages orange
   gelatin

8 ounces cream cheese, softened
¼ to ½ cup chopped pecans
1 to 2 Tablespoons mayonnaise

Grease a 6-cup ring mold lightly with oil. Bring peach juice to a boil; stir in gelatin until dissolved. Cool. Mix cream cheese, pecans and mayonnaise. Remove the seed from each peach and stuff with cream cheese mixture. (Peaches tear easily, so carefully remove seeds and stuff them, squeezing slightly.) Press halves back together so that peaches appear whole. Place stuffed peaches *close* together in mold and pour gelatin over them. Refrigerate until congealed. Turn out of mold onto lettuce covered tray. Serve with mayonnaise. The ring can be cut ahead of time and will still hold its shape, making serving easier and quicker. Serves 12.

Mrs. Ed R. Mangum

24-Hour Salad

2 cups white cherries, halved
   and seeded
2 cups pineapple chunks, halved
2 cups orange sections
2 cups large marshmallow
   quarters

½ pound chopped blanched
   almonds
2 Tablespoons sugar
1 cup whipping cream, divided
Juice of 1 lemon
2 eggs, beaten lightly

Combine well drained cherries, pineapple bits and orange sections. Add marshmallows and nuts. Combine sugar, ¼ cup cream and lemon juice with eggs and cook in double boiler until smooth and thick, stirring constantly. Cool. Whip remaining cream and fold into egg mixture. Pour sauce over fruit mixture and mix lightly. Let stand 24 hours in refrigerator. Serve on lettuce leaf and garnish with whipped cream, if desired. Serves 10-12.

Mrs. Raymond S. Martin, Jr.

Apricot Melba Mold

APRICOT LAYER

½ envelope unflavored gelatin
⅓ cup orange juice
1 (17 ounce) can apricots

1 (3 ounce) package lemon
gelatin
2 Tablespoons lemon juice

Soften gelatin in orange juice. Purée apricots and apricot juice in blender; then heat to a boil. Add lemon gelatin and gelatin mixture and stir to dissolve. Add lemon juice. Pour into a 4-cup mold or into the bottom of 10 individual molds. Refrigerate to set.

CHEESE LAYER

1 (3 ounce) package cream
cheese, softened
2 Tablespoons mayonnaise

2 teaspoons milk
2 Tablespoons chopped pecans

Combine ingredients. Spread over APRICOT LAYER. Refrigerate to stiffen.

RASPBERRY LAYER

1 (10 ounce) package frozen
raspberries, thawed
2 Tablespoons lemon juice
Cold water

½ envelope unflavored gelatin,
softened in ¼ cup cold water
1 (3 ounce) package raspberry
gelatin
1 cup boiling water

Drain raspberries; combine the drained juice with lemon juice. Add cold water to make 1 cup. Dissolve gelatin mixture and raspberry gelatin in boiling water. Combine with juices. Add raspberries. Cool. Spoon over CHEESE LAYER. Chill. Unmold salad and serve with DRESSING. Serves 10.

DRESSING

¼ cup whipping cream,
whipped

1 cup mayonnaise

Fold ingredients together.

Mrs. Clyde Copeland, Jr.

The apricot and raspberry layers can be reversed for occasions, such as Christmas, when the red layer is pretty on top. For Christmas, mold in bell or star shapes.

———

To section an orange or grapefruit pare the fruit closely with a knife, cut in and out around each section close to the membrane and lift the section out.

For a pretty salad or first course scoop meat out of a cantaloupe half and fill with fresh fruits. Top with poppy seed dressing and garnish with a sprig of mint.

Tart Cherry-Pineapple Salad

Grated rind and juice of
  1 lemon
Grated rind and juice of
  1 orange
1 (16 ounce) can tart cherries
  (reserve juice)
½ cup water
1 (3 ounce) package lemon
  gelatin

1 envelope unflavored gelatin,
  softened in ¼ cup cold
  water
½ cup sugar
½ cup chopped pecans
1 (20 ounce) can crushed
  pineapple with juice

Boil the fruit juices and water and pour over the lemon gelatin and the softened unflavored gelatin. Stir well to dissolve. Cool. Add remaining ingredients. Spoon into a ring mold or individual molds. Chill to set. Serves 8-10.

Mrs. Frank Byers, St. Petersburg, Florida

Alexandria Salad

1 (3 ounce) package peach
  gelatin

1 cup orange juice
1 cup buttermilk

Dissolve gelatin in orange juice heated to boiling. Mix well, cool briefly and add buttermilk. Refrigerate. To serve, top with homemade mayonnaise or commercial mayonnaise combined with sour cream and a touch of orange juice concentrate. Serves 6.

Mrs. Chandler Clover

Apricot gelatin may be substituted for the peach. This salad is especially pretty doubled and congealed in a ring mold. Fill center and garnish outside the ring with fresh fruits in season such as strawberries, grapes and peach slices. Canned fruits such as mandarin orange sections, apricot halves and peach slices may also be used.

Frozen Waldorf Salad

½ cup pineapple juice
¼ cup lemon juice
¾ cup sugar
3 eggs
1 cup whipping cream

½ cup chopped almonds
½ cup chopped cherries
1 large apple, diced
½ cup diced celery

Mix the pineapple juice, lemon juice, sugar and eggs in double boiler and cook until thick, stirring constantly. Whip the cream and fold into cool custard mixture. Add the almonds, cherries, apple and celery. Freeze in freezer tray or individual molds. Remove from freezer 20 minutes before serving. Serves 12.

Mrs. Alexander Endy

This recipe is from the old Warwick Hotel in Philadelphia, Pennsylvania.

Bing Cherry and Grapefruit Salad

1 (16 ounce) can pitted dark
  sweet cherries (reserve juice)
2 (3 ounce) packages lemon
  gelatin, divided
1½ cups cold water, divided
½ cup port wine

1 cup unsweetened grapefruit
  juice
2 large grapefruits, peeled and
  sectioned
½ cup slivered almonds,
  toasted

Measure cherry juice and add enough water to equal 1 cup. Heat juice and stir in 1 package lemon gelatin to dissolve. Add ½ cup cold water and wine to gelatin mixture. Chill until partially set; then fold in cherries. Pour into mold or individual molds until halfway filled and refrigerate to set. Heat grapefruit juice and stir in remaining gelatin. Add remaining cup cold water. Chill until partially set; then fold in grapefruit sections and almonds. Pour over cherry layer. Chill. Serves 10.

Mrs. Ben McCarty

2 (16 ounce) cans grapefruit sections may be substituted for the fresh grapefruit and unsweetened grapefruit juice. Measure juice from grapefruit sections and add enough water to make 2 cups. Omit 1 cup of cold water from ingredients listed.

Two-Way Cranberry Salad

2 packages unflavored gelatin
½ cup cold water
1 cup pineapple juice

2 (16 ounce) cans jellied
  cranberry sauce
¼ teaspoon salt

Dissolve gelatin in cold water; then melt it over low heat. Mix together gelatin, pineapple juice, cranberry sauce and salt. Use as the gelatin base in one of the salads below.

CRANBERRY-GRAPEFRUIT SALAD

3 grapefruits, peeled and
  sectioned

½ cup blanched slivered
  almonds

Place grapefruit sections in bottom of salad mold. Allow 3 per individual salad if using individual molds. Sprinkle with almonds. Pour the above cranberry gelatin base over the grapefruit and chill to set. Serves 12.

CRANBERRY-FRUIT SALAD

1 cup chopped walnuts or
  pecans

1 cup seeded grapes, halved
1 cup pineapple tidbits

Fold these ingredients into the cranberry gelatin base and pour into a 6-cup salad mold or into individual molds. Chill to set. Serves 12.

Mrs. Clyde V. Maxwell, Jr.

Salad Dressings

Basic Homemade Mayonnaise

Juice of 1 lemon
1 teaspoon vinegar
1 teaspoon salt
¼ teaspoon paprika

Dash red pepper
2 egg yolks
2 cups salad oil
1 teaspoon boiling water

Combine lemon juice and vinegar; set aside. Mix together salt, paprika and red pepper; set aside. Beat egg yolks with 1 Tablespoon oil until slightly thick. Continue beating egg yolks constantly while adding ingredients. Add oil, a teaspoon at a time, until about ¼ cup oil has been used. Begin adding lemon juice mixture a few drops at a time, alternating with the oil, still being added by the teaspoonful, until the first cup of oil and all the lemon juice has been used. Add seasonings and continue to add remaining oil by the teaspoonful until mayonnaise is very thick. Add boiling water to set mayonnaise and beat until well blended. (If mayonnaise is to be used immediately, do not add boiling water.) Store in covered container in refrigerator. Makes 2 cups mayonnaise.

Basic Blender Mayonnaise

1 egg
1 Tablespoon vinegar
1 Tablespoon lemon juice
½ teaspoon salt

¼ teaspoon dry mustard
1/8 teaspoon paprika
Dash cayenne pepper
1 cup salad oil, divided

Place all ingredients in blender, using only ¼ cup oil at first. Blend about 15 seconds to thoroughly mix ingredients. With blender still running slowly pour in remaining oil in a thin stream until all oil has been incorporated. Makes 1 cup.

Rotisserie Salad Dressing

3 cloves garlic
1 medium onion
½ cup ketchup
½ cup chili sauce
½ cup oil
1 Tablespoon paprika
1 teaspoon pepper, or more

1 Tablespoon water
1 Tablespoon Worcestershire
  sauce
Juice of 1 lemon
1 teaspoon dry mustard
1 teaspoon salt
1 cup mayonnaise

Place ingredients in blender and mix well. Makes about 2¾ cups dressing.

Mrs. G. G. Mazzaferro

Basic French Dressing

2 Tablespoons lemon juice
2 Tablespoons wine vinegar
¾ teaspoon salt
½ to 1 teaspoon dry mustard

1 Tablespoon powdered sugar,
  or more
½ cup olive oil

Combine all ingredients in glass jar and shake well to blend. Use as a dressing over green salads or citrus salads. Makes ¾ cup dressing.

Mrs. Ralph Avery

Poppy Seed Dressing

⅔ cup sugar
1 teaspoon Colman's dry
  mustard
1 teaspoon paprika
½ teaspoon salt
⅓ cup honey

3 Tablespoons lemon juice
3 Tablespoons vinegar
2 teaspoons grated onion
1 cup salad oil
1 Tablespoon poppy seed

Mix first 4 ingredients in a bowl. Add honey, lemon juice, vinegar and onion. Stir. Pour into blender container; cover and blend on high speed 1 minute. While blender is running, slowly pour in oil through opening in cover. Stop. Pour into a container and stir in poppy seeds. Makes 1 pint dressing.

Mrs. Charlotte B. Charles

The beauty of this dressing is that it will not separate.

Crème Fraîche Dressing

3 Tablespoons fresh lemon juice
¼ cup olive oil
1 Tablespoon Dijon mustard
2 to 3 Tablespoons crème
  fraîche

1 clove garlic, minced
1 teaspoon chopped fresh
  parsley
Salt and pepper to taste

Place ingredients in a small bowl and whisk until the dressing is well blended and thick. Use as a dressing for crisp greens or lightly cooked fresh vegetables. Makes ¾ cup dressing.

Mrs. D. T. Brock

CRÈME FRAÎCHE   Combine in a screw top glass jar 1 cup whipping cream (or for fewer calories use half and half cream) and 2 Tablespoons buttermilk. Leave out of refrigerator for 12-36 hours, stirring occasionally. The cream will thicken to the consistency of commercial sour cream. Refrigerate. Cream should be made 3 days before needed and will keep 3-4 weeks in refrigerator. A touch of crème fraîche can be used for making dishes from casseroles to desserts. It has the advantage of not curdling when boiled or added to hot foods. Use also to spoon over fresh fruit or desserts instead of whipped cream.

Green Mayonnaise

½ clove garlic, minced
1 Tablespoon dill weed
1 Tablespoon chopped chives
1 egg

½ teaspoon salt
1 teaspoon dry mustard
2 Tablespoons wine vinegar
1 cup salad oil, divided

Place all ingredients except ¾ cup salad oil into blender and purée for a few seconds. Add remaining oil in a steady stream. Serve as a dressing for chilled vegetables. Makes about 2 cups mayonnaise.

Mrs. R. James Young

Cucumber Dressing

1 quart Hellmann's mayonnaise
1 large onion
1 large cucumber
1 teaspoon Accent

1 small clove garlic
Juice of 1 lemon
Dash Worcestershire sauce
Salt to taste

Blend ingredients in the blender. Refrigerate until ready to use. Keeps well. Excellent over a tossed salad or sliced tomatoes. Makes 2 quarts.

Mrs. Ken Barfield

Garlic French Dressing

½ teaspoon dry mustard
½ teaspoon sugar
½ teaspoon salt
2 Tablespoons lemon juice

2 Tablespoons wine vinegar
½ cup oil
1 clove garlic

Combine all ingredients in jar and shake well. Makes ¾ cup dressing.

Mrs. Tom Ben Garrett

Nick's Favorite Red Dressing

½ cup salad oil
¼ cup ketchup
¼ cup cider vinegar
¼ cup sugar

2 Tablespoons honey (optional)
1 teaspoon onion salt
1 teaspoon Worcestershire
sauce

Shake all ingredients in a jar and refrigerate. Serve over romaine lettuce or spinach leaves. This is also delicious over a wide variety of fresh and canned fruit combinations such as apples, bananas, cantaloupes, watermelon, white grapes, dates, raisins, pears and peaches. This is also enjoyable over salads of asparagus, artichokes and olives on lettuce. Keeps indefinitely. Makes 1 cup dressing.

Mrs. P. N. Harkins, III

Winter Salad Dressing

½ cup malt vinegar
1 cup Wesson oil
½ cup sugar
⅓ cup ketchup

1 small onion, grated
Juice of ½ lemon
½ teaspoon salt
1 teaspoon celery seed

Mix all ingredients together. Use as dressing for salad greens, orange sections and avocado slices tossed in desired proportions. Makes 1 pint.

Mrs. Ancel C. Tipton, Jr.

Tomato French Dressing

1 (10¾ ounce) can tomato soup
¾ cup vinegar
Juice of 1 lemon
1 Tablespoon sugar

1 Tablespoon salt
1 small onion, diced fine
1 clove garlic, halved
Salad oil

Combine first 7 ingredients in a quart jar and fill jar with salad oil. Shake well. Will keep indefinitely in refrigerator. Makes 1 quart dressing.

Mrs. Rowan H. Taylor

Cream Dressing for Grapefruit

3 egg yolks, beaten lightly
½ cup sugar
Juice of 1 lemon

1 Tablespoon butter
½ teaspoon salt
1 cup whipping cream

Cook egg yolks, sugar, lemon juice, butter and salt in double boiler until thick. Cool. Whip cream and fold into egg mixture. Spoon over grapefruit sections. Makes about 1½ cups dressing. Serves 12.

Mrs. Howard Nichols

Yogurt Salad Dressing

1 cup plain yogurt
½ cup mayonnaise
¼ to ½ teaspoon garlic powder
2 teaspoons minced chives

1 Tablespoon finely chopped
  parsley
1 teaspoon lemon juice

Mix all ingredients together. Prepare about 6 hours before using for flavors to blend. Delicious on green salads. Makes 1½ cups dressing.

Mrs. Reuel May, Jr.

Also good as a raw vegetable dip.

Roquefort Dressing

2 cups olive oil
1 cup vinegar
Juice of 1 lemon
2 teaspoons paprika
Dash Worcestershire sauce

A little grated onion
1/8 teaspoon cayenne pepper
1 teaspoon salt
8 ounces Roquefort cheese,
  mashed

Place oil and vinegar in a quart jar. Add all other ingredients and mix well. Refrigerate indefinitely (flavor improves with time). Shake well before serving. Makes 4 cups dressing.

Mrs. Polly H. Currie

Bleu cheese may be substituted for the Roquefort.

Fruit Salad Dressing

⅓ cup sugar
4 teaspoons cornstarch
¼ teaspoon salt
Juice of 1 lemon
Juice of 1 orange

1 cup unsweetened pineapple
  juice
2 eggs
2 (3 ounce) packages cream
  cheese, whipped

In a double boiler mix sugar, cornstarch and salt. Add lemon juice, orange juice and pineapple juice. Cook over warm water for 20 minutes, stirring constantly. Beat eggs and slowly add to cooked mixture. (It is best to add a little cooked mixture to the eggs and blend well, then return to double boiler.) Cook, stirring, 5 minutes more. Cool and blend with cream cheese. This is delicious on a fresh fruit salad made up of bananas, cantaloupe, honeydew, watermelon, grapes, cherries and apples. Stores well in refrigerator for several weeks. Makes approximately 2 cups.

Mrs. Daniel H. Draughn

Tangy Dressing

½ cup vinegar
6 Tablespoons sugar
1 teaspoon dry mustard
1 teaspoon paprika
1 Tablespoon Worcestershire
  sauce

1 teaspoon salt
¼ teaspoon pepper
1 teaspoon celery seed
1/8 teaspoon garlic powder
1 cup salad oil

Place vinegar in jar with tight lid or blender. Add all other ingredients except oil. Mix until ingredients are dissolved and then add oil and mix again. Very good served on fruit or greens. Makes 2 cups dressing.

From the recipes of John B. Mason

95

Green Goddess Salad Dressing

1 clove garlic, minced	3 Tablespoons minced chives
½ teaspoon salt	or scallions
½ teaspoon dry mustard	⅓ cup snipped parsley
1 teaspoon Worcestershire sauce	1 cup mayonnaise
2 Tablespoons anchovy paste	½ cup sour cream
3 Tablespoons tarragon vinegar	½ teaspoon pepper

Combine ingredients, blend well and refrigerate covered. Better if made day before serving. Will keep several days. May be used with raw vegetables such as cauliflower, carrots, celery, cucumbers and squash. Makes about 2½ cups dressing.

Mrs. Don Bruce

Herb Vinegars

FRESH DILL VINEGAR

2 cups sugar	3 cloves garlic
3 Tablespoons salt	4 or 5 heads and sprigs fresh
2 onions, quartered	dill
2 whole banana peppers, cut up	White vinegar

In a quart jar mix the sugar, salt, onions, peppers, garlic and fresh dill. Fill with vinegar and refrigerate for at least 1 week before using. Keep refrigerated and use as desired. To replenish, add more sugar, salt and vinegar as vinegar is used. To make into a salad dressing, combine 1 part dill vinegar with 3 parts salad oil. Use this dressing over fresh fruit or salad greens.

Howard Bishop, Gainesville, Florida

BASIL, MINT OR CHIVE VINEGAR

Fresh basil leaves	Fresh chive
Fresh mint leaves	Cider, wine or rice vinegar

Using one of the herbs listed, wash leaves, dry by patting with a towel and pack in wide mouth glass jar, vinegar bottle or cruet. Use a generous amount for best flavor. Fill with vinegar to cover herbs. Cap and store at least a week. A blend of herbs may be combined with vinegar to provide interesting flavors. Vinegars may be used alone on salads or mixed with oil to make up a dressing. Vinegars are also excellent in marinades.

Mrs. E. Leonard Posey, Jr.

Some herbs, such as chervil, chive, tarragon, sweet basil, sweet marjoram and dill leaves, freeze well packed in small plastic sandwich bags. Mixtures of herbs may be frozen together in 1 bag to be used in omelets.

Breads

Bread Making Basics

YEAST One package of dry yeast is equal to 1 package of compressed (cake) yeast. Cake yeast should be kept in a plastic bag, tightly closed and in the refrigerator. It will stay fresh for 2 weeks only. Dry yeast will keep for weeks outside the refrigerator and indefinitely inside. To proof yeast add 1 teaspoon sugar to yeast-warm water mixture in recipe. If mixture bubbles up fairly quickly, yeast is good. If nothing happens, yeast is dead. To dissolve yeast, crumble or sprinkle into warm (105°-110°F) liquid and allow to sit for a few minutes to soften. Stir with a fork until completely dissolved. One cake or package of yeast will raise as much as 8 cups of flour. To get faster action, use 1 package to every 4 cups flour.

FLOUR Unbleached, hard wheat flour makes the best yeast dough. All purpose flour may be used in any recipe unless otherwise specified. To measure flour, dip cup into flour and scrape off excess with knife. Do not pack flour. It is not necessary to sift unless recipe specifies. Because of humidity, it is sometimes necessary to add more flour than called for, but never add more than ¼ cup. Too much flour makes dough heavy. Humidity conditions may also increase rising time.

KNEADING To knead, press dough flat with heels of hands folding to center. Repeat process of pressing and folding dough in a rhythmic motion. Knead dough at least 15 minutes by the clock, unless using a mixer with a dough hook. If using dough hook, knead by hand afterwards about 5 minutes. Kneading is important because this process evenly distributes the gas bubbles, formed by the yeast, in the glutenous structure of the flour. Flat bread is usually caused by insufficient kneading, too much liquid, stale yeast or too much humidity.

RISING To facilitate final rising of bread or rolls, place, covered with a towel, in cold oven. On a lower shelf place a pan of hot water and close oven door. Dough has risen enough when a slight pressure from the fingers leaves its imprint.

BAKING Dough should be baked in a preheated oven. In cooking, bread rises during the first 15 minutes. After this it is safe to open the door. When done, loaf will shrink from sides of pan; also, if loaf sounds hollow when tapped on the bottom, it is done. If bread is not brown or done enough at end of baking time, place back in pans and cook 5 minutes longer.

FREEZING Bread should be thoroughly cooled before placing in plastic bags or foil. Breads will freeze beautifully, but all air must be eliminated from packaging to avoid formation of frost.

Sally Lunn

1 package dry yeast
¼ cup lukewarm water
1 teaspoon sugar
6 Tablespoons butter
6 Tablespoons lard or
  shortening

1 cup milk
4 cups flour
⅓ cup sugar
2 teaspoons salt
4 eggs
Melted butter

Dissolve yeast in warm water; add sugar and set aside. Warm butter, lard and milk until all is melted; then let stand until lukewarm (105°-110°F). Sift together flour, sugar, salt. Beat eggs thoroughly and combine with milk and yeast mixtures. Beat well. Add flour and beat well. Set bowl in pan of hot water to rise. Leave a wooden spoon in the batter and cover all with towel. Every 20 minutes beat dough down; then put back in pan of hot water, cover with towel and let rise again. It will rise after every beating. Do this at least 3 hours. (The wonderful texture is achieved by this beating.) After last beating put dough in well-greased bundt or other tube pan, cover with towel and let rise again (about 1½ hours). Bake at 325°F for 45-60 minutes. Baste with melted butter during the last 10 minutes of baking. Freezes beautifully wrapped in foil. Remove from freezer 1 hour before serving; heat in 350°F oven for 20-30 minutes in the foil. Serves 15.

Mrs. Lewis Prosser, Shreveport, Louisiana

This beautiful bread has a wonderful texture and makes a perfect gift at Christmas.

Brioche

½ cup lukewarm milk
1 package dry yeast
½ cup butter, melted
2 eggs

¼ cup sugar
¼ teaspoon salt
2½ cups flour, divided
Melted butter

Place milk and yeast in mixing bowl. Let stand 5 minutes. Stir well. Add butter, eggs, sugar, salt and 1 cup flour. Beat well. Add remaining flour to make a soft dough. Beat until smooth. Cover and let rise until doubled. Punch down. Let rise again. Punch down. Knead lightly to form smooth ball. (If dough is a little hard to handle, refrigerate for several hours rather than adding more flour.) Reserve a piece of dough the size of an egg. Place remainder in a large well-greased mold. Make an indentation in the top of dough. Place the egg-size piece in the indentation. Let rise until double in size. Baste top with melted butter. Sprinkle with extra sugar. Bake about 45 minutes at 375°F or until browned. Reheats well. Serves 12.

Mrs. D. T. Brock

Sourdough Variations

SOURDOUGH STARTER

2 cups milk   1 package dry yeast
3½ cups flour

Place milk in gallon jar and allow to stand in warm place for 24 hours (leave uncovered or cover with cheesecloth). Add flour and yeast and stir well. Leave uncovered for 2-5 days, or until it is sour and bubbly. Refrigerate. If starter dries out, add tepid water to keep a spongy texture.

SOURDOUGH FEEDER

1 cup flour   ⅓ cup sugar
1 cup milk

Set container of sourdough out at room temperature 2 or 3 hours before and after feeding. Mix feeder ingredients with a spatula until smooth; then stir into sourdough starter. Use these feeder amounts for every 2 cups sourdough starter. Starter may be fed as often as every other day but *must not* be kept over 7 days without feeding.

SOURDOUGH BREAD

1 package dry yeast   ½ cup shortening, melted
3 Tablespoons sugar   ½ cup sugar
1½ cups water, divided   1 cup Sourdough Starter
1 egg, beaten   6 cups flour (up to 1 cup more if
1½ teaspoons salt   needed)

Mix the yeast, sugar and ½ cup water warmed to 105°-110°F. Let mixture stand 15 minutes; then beat in remaining ingredients and the remaining 1 cup water. Knead about 10 minutes on a floured board, or until mixture does not stick to hands and is elastic. (If using a dough hook, knead only about 3-4 minutes.) Place in large greased bowl, generously greasing the top of the dough. Cover with plastic wrap and let rise until double in bulk. Punch down and let rise again. Punch down a second time and divide dough into 3 parts. Shape into oblong loaves and place on greased cookie sheets. Across top make 3 diagonal gashes. Let rise until doubled in bulk. Place in a cold oven and bake at 400°F for 15 minutes. Reduce heat to 325°F and bake 30 minutes longer. Bread will have a hard dark crust. Makes 3 loaves.

To make WHOLE WHEAT BREAD replace the flour with whole wheat flour, and use 2 packages yeast.

SOURDOUGH BISCUITS

1 cup flour   ⅓ cup shortening
3 teaspoons baking powder   1 cup Sourdough Starter
1 teaspoon salt

(Continued)

Mix together ingredients. Scoop out on floured board and knead until bread-like. Roll out or pat down on board and cut into biscuits with biscuit cutter. Bake in glass baking dish at 400°F for 12 minutes or until light brown. Makes about 24 biscuits.

Mrs. Henry H. Mounger

Homemade Bread

1 package dry yeast
½ cup warm water
½ cup Crisco
½ cup sugar

1 egg
3 teaspoons salt
8 cups flour
1½ cups water

Dissolve yeast in warm water. Cream Crisco and sugar; combine with yeast. Add egg. Mix salt and flour together. Add flour mixture and water alternately to yeast mixture until the dough is not sticky. Cover with towel, put in warm place and let rise until doubled (3-4 hours). Punch down and knead; then form dough into small loaves on floured board. Place in buttered loaf pans. Let rise again until doubled. Bake at 350°F until brown (20-30 minutes). Brush with melted butter. Makes 5 small or 3 medium loaves.

Mrs. Sam D. Knowlton, Oxford, Mississippi

Honey Whole Wheat Bread

1 package dry yeast
¼ cup lukewarm water
1¼ cups hot water
¼ cup honey
2 Tablespoons shortening

1½ teaspoons salt
2½ cups whole wheat flour, divided
2 cups sifted flour, divided

Sprinkle yeast over lukewarm water to soften. In a large bowl, combine hot water with honey, shortening and salt. Stir mixture until honey and shortening are melted. Let cool to lukewarm. Add yeast; sift in 1½ cups whole wheat flour and 1 cup sifted white flour, and beat mixture until well combined. Add 1 cup each of white flour and whole wheat flour or enough to make a moderately stiff dough. Turn dough out onto a well-floured board and knead for about 10 minutes or until very smooth and elastic. Transfer dough to a well-greased bowl, turn once, and let stand, covered, in a warm place away from drafts for about 1½ hours, or until doubled in bulk. Punch dough down, turn out onto a floured board, and form into a ball. Let dough stand covered for 10 minutes. Shape dough into a loaf and put in a well-greased loaf pan. Let dough stand, covered, until doubled in bulk (about 45 minutes). Bake loaf at 375°F for 40-45 minutes, or until golden brown and sounds hollow when tapped. Turn loaf out onto a wire rack and let it cool. Makes 1 loaf.

Mrs. James P. McKeown

No-Knead Bread

5 cups Pioneer biscuit mix
4 Tablespoons sugar
½ teaspoon salt
2 packages dry yeast

2 cups warm milk (105°-110°F)
4 eggs
¼ teaspoon cream of tartar

Sift into a large bowl the biscuit mix, sugar and salt. Soften yeast in milk. Beat eggs with cream of tartar until thoroughly mixed. Combine milk mixture with eggs and pour into dry ingredients. Stir until well mixed. This makes a heavy, sticky mixture. Set aside in a warm place covered with a damp cloth (a yeast mixture rises best at about 80°F). When doubled in bulk, stir down and fill 2 (4½ x 8½ inch) loaf pans, which have been greased, about half way. Again allow mixture to double its size before baking at 350°F about 20 minutes. Serve very hot. This bread freezes well but must be allowed to thaw completely before reheating. Makes 2 loaves.

Mrs. Rhesa Barksdale

Whole Grain Bread

2 packages dry yeast
3 cups lukewarm water, divided
1 teaspoon honey
⅓ cup oil
¼ cup molasses
1 Tablespoon salt
2 cups wheat germ

7 cups whole wheat flour,
   divided
1 egg, beaten (optional)
¼ teaspoon water (optional)
Sesame seeds, toasted
   (optional)

Dissolve yeast in 1 cup water (warmed to 105°F) to which honey has been added. Let soak 5-10 minutes. Mix oil, molasses and remaining warmed water. Stir in salt and wheat germ. Combine yeast and molasses mixtures. Mix in 3½ cups whole wheat flour; then mix in 3 more cups, blending as well as possible. Turn dough onto board and, using the remaining ½ cup flour, knead dough until it is smooth and springy (about 12 minutes). Put dough into oiled bowl, turning it in order to oil the surface. Cover with a towel and allow to rise until double in bulk (about 1½ hours). Punch dough down and let it rest for about 20 minutes. Knead dough about 5 minutes more; then divide it into 2 loaves. Place in 2 well-oiled 9 x 5 x 3-inch bread pans. If desired, brush tops with beaten egg, to which water has been added, and sprinkle with sesame seeds. Let rise until loaves are well rounded and high in pan (about 1 hour). Bake in preheated 350°F oven for 1 hour or until bread tests done. Remove from pans. Cool on rack. To serve, slice thin, and spread with butter. This is a very filling bread. Yields 2 loaves.

The Editors

To facilitate the final rising, place dough (which has been covered with towel) in cold oven with a pan of hot water on bottom shelf.

Cheese Pepper Bread

1 package dry yeast	¼ teaspoon baking soda
¼ cup hot water	1 cup sour cream
2⅓ cups flour, divided	1 egg
1 teaspoon salt	1 cup grated Cheddar cheese
2 Tablespoons sugar	½ teaspoon pepper

Grease 2 1-pound coffee cans. In large mixing bowl, dissolve yeast in hot water. Add 1⅓ cups flour. Add salt, sugar, soda, sour cream and egg. Blend ½ minute on low speed, scraping bowl constantly. Beat 2 minutes on high speed, scraping bowl occasionally. Stir in remaining flour, cheese, and pepper. Divide batter between cans. Let rise in warm place for 50 minutes. Bake at 350°F for 40 minutes (or until golden brown). Immediately remove from cans. Cool slightly before slicing. Makes 2 loaves.

Mrs. Walker W. Jones, III

Variation: Add 1 Tablespoon dehydrated minced onion to batter.

French Bread

½ cup milk	4 cups sifted unbleached flour
1 cup boiling water	2 teaspoons salt
1½ packages dry yeast	2 teaspoons sugar
¼ cup water, warmed to 85°F	Corn meal
1½ Tablespoons oil	1 egg white, beaten
1 Tablespoon sugar (optional)	1 Tablespoon cold water

Scald milk. Add boiling water. Let mixture cool to 85°F. Dissolve yeast in warm water. After yeast rests 10 minutes, add it to the milk mixture with the oil and sugar (optional). Measure into large bowl flour, salt, and sugar. Make hole in center of these ingredients and pour in yeast and milk mixture. Stir thoroughly but do not knead. Dough will be soft. Cover with damp cloth and put in warm place to rise. Allow about two hours for first rising. Break down dough. Place on lightly floured board (sometimes more flour has to be added). Form into two oblongs. Roll each oblong into a French loaf by rolling dough jelly-roll fashion. Continue rolling, pressing outward with the hands until a long thin loaf is achieved. Grease baking sheet and lightly sprinkle it with corn meal. Place loaves on sheet and cut diagonal slits across top of each loaf. Set in warm place to rise about 45 minutes. Preheat oven to 400°F. Place pie tin with hot water in bottom of oven. Bake bread 15 minutes, then reduce heat to 350°F and bake 30 minutes longer. Spray the oven intermittently with water during the last 30 minutes. Brush loaves with glazing mixture of egg white mixed with water near end of cooking time. Cool on wire rack. Makes 2 loaves.

Mrs. James P. McKeown

Seasoned Butters for French Bread

HERB BREAD

1 pound butter, melted
¾ teaspoon savory
¾ teaspoon paprika
½ teaspoon thyme

Dash red pepper
Garlic and seasoned salt to taste
2 long loaves French bread
Chopped parsley

Combine butter with seasonings. Cut bread into diamonds. Spoon seasoned butter over bread. Sprinkle with parsley. Wrap in foil and refrigerate or freeze until ready to use. Return to room temperature. Heat in foil at 350°F for 15-20 minutes. Break diamonds apart and serve or allow guests to break off pieces. Makes 2 loaves.

Mrs. Robert B. Mims

GARLIC BREAD

1 large loaf French bread
½ pound margarine
4 to 6 cloves garlic, minced

⅔ cup grated Romano cheese
Black pepper to taste

Slice bread lengthwise. Melt margarine in a small saucepan; then add garlic, cheese and pepper. Spread on both sides of bread; then put loaf back together and wrap tightly in foil. Bake in 350°F oven for 15-20 minutes, turning once so that margarine will soak through both halves. Seasons 1 loaf.

Mrs. Fred Weathersby

Bride's Biscuits

5 cups flour
5 teaspoons baking powder
1 teaspoon salt
3 Tablespoons sugar
½ teaspoon baking soda

1 cup shortening
2 cups buttermilk
1 package dry yeast
5 Tablespoons warm water

Sift dry ingredients, then cut in shortening. Add buttermilk. Dissolve yeast in warm water and add to mixture. Knead lightly. Roll out, cut with biscuit cutter and bake on greased cookie sheet at 450°F about 10-12 minutes. Dough may be stored in the refrigerator, pinching off as much as is needed each time, or may be cut and then frozen. Yields 5 dozen biscuits.

Mrs. James L. Teague

Variation: 2 cups whole wheat flour plus 3 cups white flour may be used.

A family friend gave me this recipe when I married. Included was this note: "Cut and freeze these biscuits in foil pans. Place them in a cold oven at night. Next morning, turn oven to 450°F when the bacon starts frying. Presto! Hot biscuits for breakfast!"

Everyday Biscuits

1 cup flour
¼ teaspoon salt
2 teaspoons baking powder

¼ cup Crisco
½ cup milk

Mix flour, salt and baking powder. Cut in Crisco until mixture resembles corn meal. Stir in milk. Let stand approximately one minute. Knead a few times on a floured board. Roll out and cut with biscuit cutter. Place on greased baking sheet and bake at 400°F until light brown. Baking time varies with size and thickness of biscuits. Yields approximately twelve 2-inch biscuits.

Mrs. William F. Sistrunk

Whole Wheat Biscuits

4 cups whole wheat flour
2 Tablespoons sugar
1½ teaspoons salt
½ teaspoon cream of tartar

2 teaspoons baking powder
1½ teaspoons baking soda
1 cup shortening
1½ cups milk

Mix all dry ingredients. Place shortening in the middle and pour the milk over it. With hands squeeze and mix the shortening and milk, working in the dry ingredients until a ball is formed. Roll dough about ¾ inch thick on floured board and cut in rounds. Bake on ungreased cookie sheet at 400°F until brown. May freeze before baking. Yields 20 biscuits.

Mrs. Rhesa Barksdale

This makes a heavy biscuit. It is best served for breakfast or with homemade soups.

Sweet Potato Biscuits

2 cups sifted flour
4 teaspoons baking powder
1 teaspoon salt
⅔ cup shortening

1 cup mashed, cooked sweet
  potatoes
3 Tablespoons milk, or more

Sift dry ingredients, cut in shortening and blend in sweet potatoes. Add enough milk to make a soft dough. Knead lightly. Roll on lightly floured board to about ¾ inch thick. Cut into squares or rounds with biscuit cutter. Bake on ungreased sheet at 400°F for 15-20 minutes. May be prepared ahead and stored in refrigerator covered with damp cloth or frozen until ready to bake. These are especially good for breakfast on Thanksgiving or Christmas or with the main meal. Serves 6.

Mrs. Ward T. McCraney, Jr.

Substitute 1 cup sweet potato casserole for mashed sweet potatoes for a tasty way to use leftovers.

Flaky Quick Biscuits

½ cup Crisco   ⅔ cup milk
2 cups Pioneer biscuit mix

Cut Crisco into biscuit mix. Add milk and mix well. Dough will be soft and sticky. Spoon out onto well-floured board. Sprinkle top of dough with flour. Flatten with hands to about ½ inch thick. Cut with floured biscuit cutter and place on greased baking sheet. Bake in preheated 450°F oven for 15 minutes. Yields 16 biscuits.

Mrs. Ben McCarty

Williamsburg Biscuits

½ pound sharp Cheddar cheese   ½ teaspoon salt
½ pound butter, softened   ½ teaspoon paprika
2 1/8 cups sifted flour   Powdered sugar

Cream the cheese (leave out overnight and cheese will cream like butter). Beat in butter. Add next 3 ingredients. Drop from small spoon. Bake at 450°F for 7-8 minutes. Sprinkle powdered sugar on waxed paper. Place biscuits on paper and sprinkle with sugar. Serve hot. May be prepared several days in advance. Freezes well. Yields 50 biscuits.

Mrs. J. Larry Lee

Ice Box Potato Rolls

1 package dry yeast   1 teaspoon salt
½ cup lukewarm water   1 cup mashed potatoes
1 cup milk   Flour
⅔ cup shortening   2 eggs, beaten
½ cup sugar

Dissolve yeast in lukewarm water. Scald milk and add shortening, sugar, salt and mashed potatoes. When cooled to lukewarm, add the dissolved yeast. Mix thoroughly and add just enough flour to make a thin batter. Cover and set in a warm place until double in bulk. Add eggs and stir in enough flour to make a stiff dough (dough will leave sides of bowl when stirred). Turn out on a slightly floured board and knead thoroughly until smooth and pliable. Place in a greased bowl. Cover with a cloth and place in the refrigerator. When ready to make rolls, pinch off dough, shape, place on greased baking sheet and let rise until doubled in bulk (from 1½-2 hours). Bake in a 400°F oven 15-20 minutes. Dough may be placed in greased muffin tins. Grease rolls on top and allow to rise. In baking, just as they begin to brown, brush with butter. Dough will keep about 1 week in refrigerator. Makes about 60 rolls.

Mrs. J. M. Wingate

"May-May's" Whole Wheat Rolls

½ cup sugar
½ cup Crisco
1 teaspoon salt
1 cup boiling water
2 packages dry yeast
1 teaspoon sugar
1 cup lukewarm water

1 egg, beaten
3 cups sifted flour
2 cups whole wheat flour
1 pound butter, melted
1 (13½ ounce) box graham
   cracker crumbs

Mix together and cool to lukewarm the sugar, Crisco, salt and boiling water. Dissolve yeast and sugar in lukewarm water and add to above mixture. Add egg. Add both flours and beat well. Cover tightly and put in refrigerator overnight. Roll out amount needed and cut out with small glass. Dip rolls in butter, then in cracker crumbs. Fold over pocketbook fashion and place on greased baking sheet. Let rise at room temperature for 2 hours. Preheat oven to 375 °F and bake for 15 minutes. Best when eaten immediately. May be prepared 3 days in advance. Can be frozen after cooking 10 minutes. Yields 50 large rolls.

Mrs. Sam Farrington, Jr.

Poet's Whole Grain Buns

2 Tablespoons milk
2 Tablespoons honey
2½ Tablespoons molasses
1 cup plus 2 Tablespoons water
¼ cup shortening
1 package dry yeast

1¾ cups stone ground wheat
   flour
2 to 2¼ cups flour
1½ teaspoons salt
1 egg, beaten
Bran flakes

Heat milk, honey, molasses, water and shortening, stirring to melt the shortening. Cool to 105°-110°F and add yeast. Stir to dissolve. Add both flours, salt and egg and mix on low speed of electric mixer until ingredients are well combined. Let dough rest in mixing bowl for 30 minutes (or until doubled in bulk). Remove and form into rolls or buns. Gently press bran flakes on bun or roll tops. Let rise for 30 minutes (or until doubled in size). Bake at 400°F for 15-20 minutes. Yields about 1 dozen rolls or buns.

Leslie Spencer, Poet's Restaurant

If stone ground wheat flour is unavailable, substitute whole wheat.

BLEU CHEESE BISCUIT BITES

Melt together ½ cup butter and 1 (3 ounce) package bleu cheese. Separate 2 (8 ounce) cans refrigerator biscuits and cut each biscuit into quarters. Dip each piece in butter mixture and bake at 450°F for 10-12 minutes.

Easie's Refrigerator Rolls

2 cups milk
½ cup sugar
½ cup Crisco
1 package yeast
Flour

1 teaspoon salt
1 heaping teaspoon baking
  powder
½ teaspoon baking soda
Melted butter

Heat milk, sugar and Crisco and stir to melt Crisco. Cool to 105°-110°F. Add 1 package yeast and stir to dissolve (about 5 minutes). Add enough flour to make a thin batter (about 2 cups flour). Cover and let stand in a warm place for 2 hours. Add salt, baking powder, soda and enough flour to make dough not sticky, but the right consistency to knead (about 4 cups flour). It is not necessary to knead this dough, but beat it while adding the flour. Place dough in refrigerator, covered, overnight. Roll out on floured board or wax paper. Cut rounds with biscuit cutter, dip in melted butter, fold over and place on cookie sheet. Cover and let rise 2½ hours. Bake at 400°F for 10-12 minutes. Makes about 60 rolls.

Mrs. O. B. Wooley, Jr.

Use Easie's Refrigerator Rolls dough to make CINNAMON and CARAMEL ROLLS:

CINNAMON ROLLS

1 recipe Easie's Refrigerator
  Rolls
6 Tablespoons butter, melted,
  divided

½ cup sugar
2 teaspoons ground cinnamon
½ cup raisins or currants

Divide dough into 2 parts. Refrigerate one part and roll other part into a rectangle approximately 8 x 15 inches and ¼ inch thick. Brush lavishly with 4 Tablespoons butter, then sprinkle with a mixture of the sugar and cinnamon. Scatter raisins over dough and roll up like a jelly roll along the 15-inch side, pinching edges to seal. Cut in ½-inch segments and place in greased round cake pans. Brush tops with remaining butter and allow to rise until double in bulk. Bake at 450°F until brown on top (10-15 minutes). Repeat with remaining dough or use it to make caramel rolls or refrigerator rolls. Makes 30 cinnamon rolls.

CARAMEL ROLLS

½ cup butter, melted, divided
½ to 1 cup brown sugar
⅓ cup chopped pecans

1 recipe Easie's Refrigerator
  Rolls

Cream 4 Tablespoons butter with the brown sugar. Spread over the bottom and sides of two 9-inch cake pans. Sprinkle with pecans. Divide dough into 2 parts, reserving one part in refrigerator. Roll other part into rectangle about

(Continued)

108

8 x 15 inches and ¼ inch thick. Brush with 2 Tablespoons butter; then roll up like a jelly roll. Cut into ½-inch segments and arrange over sugar-nut mixture. Brush tops with 2 Tablespoons butter. Allow to rise until double in bulk. Bake at 400°F until brown (20-25 minutes). Immediately invert on serving plate. Repeat recipe with remaining dough. Makes 30 caramel rolls.

Mrs. John E. Fontaine, III

Ingredients in either recipe may be altered to suit individual tastes.

Jennifer's Rolls

1 cup boiling water	*2 packages dry yeast*
1 cup shortening	*1 cup lukewarm water*
1 cup sugar	*½ teaspoon sugar*
1½ teaspoons salt	*6½ cups flour*
2 eggs, well beaten	

Pour water over shortening and stir until melted. Add sugar and salt and mix well. Add eggs. Place yeast in lukewarm water and add sugar to activate it. Combine the two mixtures. Sift flour into mixture, blend well and place in refrigerator. Roll out dough, cut in circles and fold like an envelope. Place on greased cookie sheet; cover and let rise for 2 hours. Bake at 350°F for 20 minutes or until brown. Dough can be kept 10 days in refrigerator. Serves 20.

Mrs. Dennis M. Ford

One-Hour Rolls

1 teaspoon salt	*1 package dry yeast*
3 Tablespoons cooking oil	*2 cups flour*
2 Tablespoons sugar	*Melted butter*
1 cup milk	

Add salt, oil and sugar to milk and heat to 120°-130°F. Pour mixture over yeast. Add flour and mix well. Scrape dough onto a heavily floured surface (dough will be sticky). Liberally sprinkle top of dough with more flour. Roll out, cut out rounds with biscuit cutter and brush with butter. Fold over and allow to rise on cookie sheet for 1 hour in warm place. Bake at 350°F for 12-15 minutes. Makes 2½ dozen rolls.

Mrs. David Ray

To make onion rolls, add to the dough ⅓ cup chopped onion, which has been sautéed in a little butter.

Shape and freeze unbaked yeast rolls on cookie sheet; then package in plastic bags and freeze. When ready to use remove, thaw, let rise and bake.

Homemade Hamburger Buns

1 cup milk
1 teaspoon salt (preferably sea
    salt)
3 Tablespoons corn oil
2 Tablespoons sugar

1 package dry yeast
1⅓ cups unbleached white flour
⅔ cup whole wheat flour
2 Tablespoons wheat germ
Melted butter

Scald milk. Add salt, oil and sugar. Cool to lukewarm and pour over yeast.
Add flours and wheat germ and mix well. Place on well-floured board and
knead in additional white flour until dough is workable. Roll to about ½ inch
thick on floured board and cut out buns approximately half the desired size.
Place on greased cookie sheet. Brush tops with melted butter and let rise about
one hour. Bake 10 minutes at 350°F. Freezes well. Yields 8-10 buns.

Mrs. Cecil A. Ford

Plain Muffins

3 cups flour
6 teaspoons baking powder
¼ teaspoon salt
½ cup sugar

2 eggs
1½ cups milk
4 Tablespoons vegetable oil

Mix dry ingredients. Add eggs and milk; beat 1 minute at low speed. Add oil.
Mix well. Fill small greased muffin tins ¾ full and bake at 400°F. This batter
freezes well. Muffins are delicious served hot for a luncheon or for breakfast.
Yields 3-4 dozen small muffins.

Mrs. William B. Fontaine

Blueberry Muffins

½ cup shortening
1 cup sugar
1¾ cups self-rising flour
⅔ cup milk
2 or 3 Tablespoons boiling
    water

3 eggs
1 teaspoon vanilla
½ teaspoon almond extract
1 (15 or 17 ounce) can
    blueberries, drained, or 1
    pint fresh blueberries

Cream shortening and sugar. Blend in flour, milk and boiling water and beat
for 2 minutes. Add eggs, vanilla and almond extract. Beat 2 more minutes.
Fold in blueberries. Spoon into greased muffin tins or tins lined with paper
muffin cups. Bake at 375°F for 20-25 minutes. Yields 24 muffins.

Mrs. W. Douglas Godfrey

---

*Peel and mash over-ripe bananas and mix in a little lemon juice. Freeze in
measured amounts. Thaw for making banana cake, bread or muffins.*

Mayonnaise Muffins

1¼ cups self-rising flour   1 cup milk
3 Tablespoons mayonnaise

Mix ingredients in order given. Spoon into greased muffin tins. Bake at 400°F for 15-20 minutes or until lightly browned. Freezes well. Yields 6-8 large muffins or 2 dozen small ones.

Mrs. Charlotte B. Charles

Six-Week Raisin Bran Muffins

1 cup boiling water
2 cups raisin bran
1 cup unprocessed wheat bran
½ cup plus 1 Tablespoon
    shortening
1½ cups sugar

2 eggs, beaten
2 cups buttermilk
2½ cups whole wheat flour
2½ teaspoons baking soda
1½ teaspoons salt
½ cup chopped pecans

Pour water over brans and shortening. Mix in other ingredients in order listed. Store in covered container in refrigerator. Bake as needed in well-greased muffin tins at 400°F for 20 minutes. Batter will keep up to 6 weeks. Makes 8 cups batter.

Mrs. Warren L. Roper

English Muffins

1 package dry yeast
¼ cup warm water
1 cup milk, scalded
3 Tablespoons butter
2 Tablespoons sugar

1 teaspoon salt
4 cups sifted flour, divided
1 egg, lightly beaten
Corn meal

Dissolve yeast in warm water. Combine milk, butter, sugar and salt. Cool milk mixture to lukewarm and stir in thoroughly 2 cups flour. Add yeast and egg, beating thoroughly. Add remaining flour or enough to make moderately soft dough. Turn out on lightly floured board and knead until smooth and satiny. Place dough in buttered bowl, butter surface slightly and cover with light towel. Let rise in warm place until double in bulk (about 1 hour). Punch down; let rest for 10 minutes. Roll out ¼ inch thick on board lightly covered with corn meal. Cut into 3-inch rounds (or smaller). Sprinkle tops with corn meal, cover with dry towel and let rise on board about 45 minutes or until double in bulk. Bake slowly on ungreased heavy griddle. For each batch of muffins have griddle hot at first and reduce heat to brown them slowly. Bake each side 7-8 minutes. Yields about 2 dozen 2½-inch muffins.

Mrs. William B. Fontaine

Oatmeal Muffins

1 cup quick-cooking rolled oats
1 cup buttermilk
½ cup brown sugar, packed
1 large egg, beaten
1 cup flour

1 teaspoon salt
1 teaspoon baking powder
½ teaspoon baking soda
½ cup melted butter, cooled

Soak oatmeal in buttermilk about 30 minutes. Add sugar, egg, flour, salt, baking powder and soda. Add melted butter. Spoon batter into greased muffin cups, filling each ⅔ full. Bake at 400°F 25-30 minutes. Yields 12 large or 18 small muffins.

Mrs. J. M. Wingate

Date Nut Muffins

2 eggs
¾ cup sugar
1 teaspoon vanilla
5 Tablespoons flour
1/8 teaspoon salt

¼ teaspoon ground cinnamon
¼ teaspoon ground allspice
1 cup chopped pecans
1 cup chopped dates

Stir (do not beat) eggs, sugar and vanilla. Mix flour, salt, cinnamon and allspice. Add pecans and dates to flour mixture. Combine the two mixtures. Using miniature muffin tins, grease tins well and fill half full. Bake at 325°F for 15 minutes. Baked muffins will keep a week or more in a tin. Makes 36 small muffins.

Mrs. Jack R. Gibson

Mississippi Spice Muffins

1 cup soft butter or margarine
2 cups sugar
2 eggs
2 cups applesauce,
   (preferably unsweetened)
3 teaspoons ground cinnamon
2 teaspoons ground allspice

1 teaspoon ground cloves
1 teaspoon salt
2 teaspoons baking soda
4 cups flour
1 cup nuts, chopped
Powdered sugar

Cream butter and sugar. Add eggs one at a time. Mix in applesauce and spices. Sift together salt, soda and flour. Add to applesauce mixture and beat well. Stir in nuts. Bake in lightly greased miniature muffin pans at 350°F for 8-10 minutes. Sprinkle with powdered sugar. Batter keeps indefinitely in refrigerator. Baked muffins freeze well (reheat before serving). Yields 84 small muffins.

Mrs. Sherwood Wise, Jr., Tallahassee, Florida

Basic Buttermilk Corn Bread

½ cup butter
1 cup self-rising corn meal
½ cup flour

1 egg, beaten
1 cup buttermilk

Melt butter in small cast iron skillet. Stir together well the corn meal, flour, egg and buttermilk and add the melted butter. Leave small amount of butter in bottom and along sides of skillet. Pour mixture into heated skillet and bake at 350°F for 25-30 minutes. Serve immediately. Freezes well after cooking. Serves 4.

Mrs. Bo Bowen

Recipe may be used for corn bread muffins or corn bread sticks.

Spoon Bread

1 cup white corn meal, sifted
1 teaspoon salt
½ teaspoon sugar
1½ cups boiling water
3 Tablespoons butter, melted

3 eggs, separated
1 cup buttermilk
½ teaspoon baking soda
¼ teaspoon baking powder

To the meal add salt and sugar; scald with boiling water. When lukewarm, add butter, well-beaten egg yolks and buttermilk with soda added to it. Mix thoroughly. Add baking powder and fold in stiffly beaten egg whites. Pour into a well-greased 1½-quart Pyrex dish and cook in a preheated 350°F oven 40-50 minutes. Test for doneness in center of bread. Serve immediately. Serves 6.

Mrs. Rabian D. Lane

Mexican Corn Bread

2 eggs
1 cup sour cream
1 cup cream-style corn
⅔ cup salad oil
1½ cups corn meal
3 teaspoons baking powder

1 Tablespoon salt
2 green Jalapeño peppers
   (seeds removed), chopped
2 Tablespoons chopped green
   pepper
1 cup grated Cheddar cheese

Mix all ingredients, except cheese, in order given. Pour half of the mixture into hot, well-greased iron skillet. Sprinkle half of the cheese over batter. Add remaining corn meal mixture and top with the rest of the cheese. Bake at 350°F for 1 hour. Bread may be sliced and buttered if so desired. Serves 8.

Mrs. H. K. Kent

Hush Puppies

1½ cups self-rising corn meal
1 Tablespoon sugar
Black pepper to taste

1 medium onion, chopped
1 egg, well beaten
Milk

Mix all ingredients except milk. Add enough milk to form balls. Drop from teaspoon into hot fat in which fish has been fried or cook along with fish. Cook until well browned and cooked throughout. Serve with hot fried catfish, bream, bass or white perch and slaw. Serves 4.

Mrs. Jerry B. Ward

Bacon Spoon Bread

¾ cup corn meal
1½ cups cold water
8 ounces Cheddar cheese,
  coarsely grated
2 cloves garlic, crushed (or ¼
  to ½ teaspoon garlic powder)
¼ cup margarine

½ teaspoon salt
1 teaspoon chopped parsley
1 cup milk
4 egg yolks, beaten
½ pound bacon, fried crisp
4 egg whites, stiffly beaten

Mix corn meal and water. Cook until the consistency of mush. Add cheese, garlic, margarine, salt and parsley. Stir to melt cheese. Add milk and egg yolks. Crumble bacon and add to corn meal mixture. Fold in egg whites. Pour into greased 2-quart soufflé dish. Bake at 325°F for 65 minutes. Serves 6.

Mrs. John S. McIntyre, Jr.

Nut Bread

2 cups flour
2 teaspoons baking powder
½ cup sugar
1 teaspoon salt

1 cup milk
1 egg, beaten
½ cup chopped pecans or
  walnuts

Sift dry ingredients together. Mix milk and egg and add to dry mixture. Mix thoroughly, but do not beat. Add nuts. Bake in greased loaf pan at 350°F about 1 hour or until straw comes out clean. Best kept for a day or two then sliced as thin as possible and served with butter or cream cheese. This bread can be made 3 or 4 days in advance. Also freezes well. Bread is good with salads or toasted with butter for breakfast. Makes 1 small loaf.

Mrs. John E. Fontaine, III

There is NO butter or shortening in this recipe, so it is excellent for low-fat diets.

Raisin Bread

2 cups white raisins
2 cups water
2 teaspoons baking soda
2 cups sugar
1 teaspoon vanilla

1 cup broken nuts
3 cups flour
½ teaspoon salt
2 eggs, beaten

Mix raisins, water and soda in saucepan. Bring to a boil. Cool overnight in refrigerator. Combine with remaining ingredients. Grease three 1-pound coffee cans and pour batter into them, filling cans slightly over half full. Bake 1 hour at 350°F. Slice immediately or cool and freeze. Makes 3 loaves.

Mrs. Leigh Watkins, III

Apricot Bread

1½ cups dried apricots, cut in
    bite sizes
½ cup butter, softened
1 cup sugar
2 eggs
¾ cup orange juice
2 cups sifted flour

3 teaspoons baking powder
¼ teaspoon baking soda
¾ teaspoon salt
1 teaspoon grated orange
    rind
1 cup chopped nuts (English
    walnuts preferred)

Soak apricots in water to cover for 30 minutes. Drain and chop. Cream butter and sugar. Beat eggs and add alternately to butter mixture with orange juice. Add dry ingredients. Add apricots, orange rind and nuts. Pour into greased 9 x 5-inch loaf pan lined with greased foil, brown or wax paper. Bake at 350°F for 1½ hours. This bread is delicious toasted, buttered and served with coffee. Freezes well. Serves 12.

Mrs. Frank H. Tucker, Jr., Meridian, Mississippi

Banana Bread

½ cup Wesson oil
1½ cups sugar
2 eggs, well beaten
¼ teaspoon salt
1½ cups sifted flour

1 teaspoon baking soda
⅓ cup buttermilk
3 very ripe bananas, mashed
1 cup walnuts, chopped

Cream oil and sugar; add eggs and salt and mix well. Add flour and soda combined with buttermilk alternately. Add bananas. Fold in nuts. Grease 2 regular size loaf pans; pour in mixture and bake approximately 45 minutes at 350°F. When bread leaves sides of pan and toothpick comes out clean, bread is done. This recipe can be doubled. Makes 2 loaves.

Mrs. John Gayden

Sour cream may be substituted for the buttermilk.

Butterhorns

1 cup soft butter or margarine
1 (12 ounce) carton cottage
  cheese
2 cups flour
Dash salt

2 cups powdered sugar
2 Tablespoons butter
2 Tablespoons milk
½ teaspoon vanilla

Cream butter and cottage cheeese until smooth. Add flour and salt. Form into a ball and refrigerate overnight. Divide dough into 3 equal parts. Roll each into a circle and cut into 12 wedges. Roll up to pointed end and place on greased cookie sheet. Bake at 350°F for 30-40 minutes. To make frosting, cream powdered sugar and butter. Add milk and vanilla. Frost rolls while warm. Makes 36 rolls.

Mrs. F. David Fowler

Italian Easter Bread

1 package dry yeast
¼ cup warm water (105°-110°F)
¾ cup butter, softened
¾ cup sugar
⅓ cup milk
½ teaspoon salt
1 Tablespoon each grated
  orange rind, crushed anise
  seed
4 eggs
1 egg yolk
About 4¾ cups flour

1 cup raisins
TOPPING:
½ cup sugar
¼ cup flour
¼ cup butter, softened
⅓ cup almond paste

1 egg white beaten with 1
  Tablespoon water
¾ to 1 cup sliced almonds
Powdered sugar

Blend yeast with warm water and allow 5 minutes for it to dissolve. Add butter, sugar, milk, salt, orange rind, anise seed, eggs and egg yolk. Add 2 cups flour and beat at medium speed of electric mixer 10 minutes. Add 1 cup flour at low speed. Add 1¾ cups flour, stirring until well blended. Cover bowl tightly with plastic wrap and let rise 1½-2 hours. Punch dough down, turn out onto floured surface and knead 10 minutes. Gently knead in raisins. Divide dough into 2 balls. Form two 9-inch flattened rounds on a greased baking sheet. Cover lightly with greased plastic wrap and allow to rise until "puffy" (40-45 minutes). Make *TOPPING* by blending ingredients with electric mixer until mixture resembles coarse crumbs. Brush top of rounds with egg white and water mixture. Place *TOPPING* over loaves; then sprinkle with almonds. Press lightly. Bake in preheated 350°F oven about 30 minutes. Serve warm dusted with powdered sugar. Makes 2 loaves.

Mrs. David Trigiani

This festive sweet bread is a family favorite on Easter morning.

Basic Pancakes

2 eggs
1 cup milk
2 Tablespoons Wesson oil
3 Tablespoons butter, melted
1¼ cups flour

3 rounded teaspoons baking
  powder
3 teaspoons sugar
¾ teaspoon salt

Beat eggs until light; add milk, oil and butter. Sift together dry ingredients and beat into liquid ingredients. Cook on a *greaseless* griddle. Heat griddle very hot; then turn to low and let cool to low temperature before cooking cakes. Serves 4-6.

Mrs. W. E. Walker, Jr.

Enriched Waffles

¾ cup flour
¼ cup whole wheat flour
2 teaspoons baking powder
¼ cup dry milk

¼ cup oil
1 cup milk
2 eggs, beaten
2 Tablespoons wheat germ

Mix all ingredients together. Bake in waffle iron. Serves 4.

Mrs. John S. McIntyre, Jr.

Batter may be used for pancakes as well as waffles.

Apricot-Almond Coffee Cake

1 cup butter, softened
2 cups sugar
2 eggs
1 cup sour cream
1 teaspoon almond extract
2 cups flour

1 teaspoon baking powder
¼ teaspoon salt
1 cup sliced almonds
1 (10 ounce) jar apricot
  preserves

Preheat oven to 350°F. Cream butter and sugar until very fluffy. Beat in eggs, one at a time, well. Fold in sour cream and almond extract. Sift together the flour, baking powder and salt and fold in also. Place about ⅓ of mixture in a greased and floured bundt pan. Sprinkle ½ the almonds and ½ the apricot preserves over batter. Spoon on rest of batter. Add the remaining preserves and top with remaining almonds. Bake at 350°F for 1 hour or until done. Cool on rack. Serves 14.

Mrs. John D. Adams

Note: May be varied by substituting vanilla for the almond extract and a mixture of ½ cup chopped pecans, 3 Tablespoons brown sugar and 2 teaspoons ground cinnamon for the almonds and apricot preserves.

117

Best Ever Buttermilk Pancakes

1¾ cups flour
2 teaspoons sugar
1 teaspoon salt
1½ teaspoons baking powder
1 teaspoon baking soda

2 eggs, well beaten
2 cups buttermilk
2 to 4 Tablespoons butter or
 margarine, melted

Sift flour before measuring; then resift with sugar, salt, baking powder and soda. Mix eggs with buttermilk. Combine the dry and liquid ingredients with a few quick strokes; then add butter or margarine. Mix ingredients well but with as few strokes as possible. Batter will be lumpy. Bake on hot griddle until browned on both sides. Yields about 20 4-inch cakes.

Mrs. John E. Ainsworth

Swedish Tea Cakes

1 package dry yeast
¼ cup warm water
2¼ cups sifted flour
2 Tablespoons sugar
1 teaspoon salt
½ cup butter, softened
¼ cup evaporated milk
1 egg
¼ cup chopped raisins

FILLING:
¼ cup butter, softened
½ cup light brown sugar
½ cup chopped pecans

ICING:
2 Tablespoons butter
1 cup sifted powdered sugar
½ teaspoon vanilla
1 to 2 Tablespoons evaporated
 milk

Soften yeast in warm water. Sift flour, sugar and salt into mixing bowl. Cut in butter until particles are fine. Add evaporated milk, egg, raisins and yeast to flour and butter mixture. Mix well. Cover. Chill at least 2 hours or overnight. Make *FILLING* when ready to roll out dough. Cream butter and brown sugar. Add pecans. Divide dough into three parts. Roll out one part on a floured surface to a 6 x 12-inch rectangle. Spread with ⅓ filling. Roll up starting with 12-inch side. Seal by pinching dough together. Make roll into crescent shape and place on cookie sheet lined with aluminum foil. Make cuts along outside edge about 1 inch apart to within ½ of center. Repeat. Let all three rolls rise in warm place (85°-90°F) until light (about 45 minutes). Bake at 350°F for 20-25 minutes. Frost with *ICING* while hot. *ICING:* Brown butter in small iron skillet. Add powdered sugar, vanilla and evaporated milk until it is of spreading consistency. Serve slightly warm and cut in small pieces. May be made 2 days in advance. Freezes well. Makes 3 crescents.

Mrs. Robert B. Mims

This recipe can be tripled if mixer has dough hook attachment. This is a great recipe for Christmas presents. Can be made, frozen and wrapped in red cellophane.

Waffles

3 eggs, separated
1 pint sour cream
1 cup flour
1/8 teaspoon salt
1 teaspoon sugar
2 teaspoons baking powder

1 teaspoon baking soda
1 Tablespoon Wesson oil
1 teaspoon ground cinnamon
½ cup chopped pecans
1 teaspoon vanilla

Mix egg yolks in bowl with sour cream. Sift together flour, salt, sugar, baking powder and soda. Blend sifted ingredients in with eggs and cream. Add oil, cinnamon, nuts, vanilla. Beat egg whites until stiff and fold in. Bake in waffle iron. Will keep in warm oven on open racks. Freeze in plastic bags. Serves 4.

Mrs. Ewing Seligman, Los Angeles, California

Mama's Coffee Cake

¾ cup sugar
¼ cup shortening
1 egg
½ cup milk
1½ cups flour
2 teaspoons baking powder
½ teaspoon salt

FILLING:
½ cup brown sugar
2 Tablespoons flour
2 teaspoons ground cinnamon
2 teaspoons butter, melted
½ cup chopped pecans

Cream thoroughly the sugar, shortening and egg. Stir in milk. Sift together the flour, baking powder and salt and stir into first mixture. Pour one half the batter into a greased and floured 9 x 5-inch loaf pan. Combine ingredients for the *FILLING* and sprinkle one half of the mixture over the batter. Pour remaining batter over all and sprinkle with remaining filling. Bake at 375°F for 45-50 minutes. Freezes. Serves 8.

Mrs. L. M. Coco, Alexandria, Louisiana

Daddy's Deal

½ cup butter
2 eggs, beaten
1 cup flour

½ teaspoon ground cinnamon
1 cup milk
Confectioners' sugar

Melt butter in heavy iron 12-inch skillet or 8 x 8-inch baking dish. Mix eggs, flour, cinnamon and milk to a rough consistency and pour mixture over butter in skillet. Bake in preheated 375° or 400°F oven for 20-25 minutes. Sprinkle confectioners' sugar on top and serve for breakfast with syrup, jelly or jam. Serves 4.

Mrs. T. Arnold Turner, Jr.

This is a delightful "baked pancake"!

Popovers

1 cup milk
1 cup sifted flour
2 Tablespoons melted butter,
    cooled

2 eggs, slightly beaten
1 teaspoon salt (optional)
1 teaspoon sugar (optional)

In food processor with steel blade or blender mix all ingredients quickly until just combined. Half fill 6 or 8 greased, warm Pyrex custard cups. Place cups on cookie sheet. Bake in preheated 425°F oven for 30 minutes or until well puffed and brown. Serve immediately with butter. Yields 6-8 popovers.

Mrs. Louis E. Ridgway, Jr.

French Breakfast Puffs

1 cup sugar, divided
1 egg
⅓ cup Crisco
1½ cups sifted flour
1½ teaspoons baking powder

½ teaspoon salt
¼ teaspoon ground nutmeg
½ cup milk
1 teaspoon ground cinnamon
Melted butter

With mixer, cream ½ cup sugar, the egg and Crisco. Sift together flour, baking powder, salt and nutmeg. Add creamed mixture alternately with milk, beating well after each addition. Fill 12 greased muffin pans ⅔ full with batter. Bake at 350°F for 20-25 minutes. When removed from oven, dip puffs, while hot, in melted butter and roll in mixture of cinnamon and remaining sugar. Freezes well. Serve hot or cold. Makes 12.

Mrs. Charles Morris

Beignets

½ cup butter or margarine
1 teaspoon sugar
¼ teaspoon salt
1 cup water
1 cup plus 2 Tablespoons sifted
    flour

1 teaspoon vanilla
4 eggs
Wesson oil for frying
Confectioners' sugar

In medium pan heat butter, sugar, salt and water to boiling. Remove pan from heat and add flour all at once; stir vigorously until ingredients are combined thoroughly and dough leaves sides of pan and forms a ball. Add vanilla, then eggs, one at a time, stirring vigorously. Dough should be smooth and glossy. In another pan, heat about 1½ inches oil to 375°F on thermometer. Drop heaping teaspoons of dough into hot oil and fry beignets, a few at a time, until golden. (Each beignet will puff up to about 2 inches in diameter when done.) Drain on paper towels. Dust beignets heavily with confectioners' sugar. Serve warm. Yields about 50 beignets.

Mrs. Chick Warner, Vicksburg, Mississippi

Easy Apple Strudel

2 (8 ounce) packages
  refrigerated crescent rolls
¼ cup butter, softened
½ cup ground walnuts
¾ cup raisins

3 cups pared and thinly sliced
  apples
½ cup sugar
2 teaspoons ground cinnamon
1 egg white, slightly beaten

Unroll crescent rolls; lay rectangles side by side, overlapping slightly. On large, lightly floured cloth, roll evenly until dough is 24 x 16 inches. Spread with butter. Two inches in from one long side, spread nuts in a strip 3 inches wide, leaving a 1-inch wide margin at each end. Top with raisins and apples. Combine sugar and cinnamon; reserve 1 Tablespoon. Sprinkle remaining sugar mixture atop fruit. Gently fold in margins and fold 2-inch border of dough over the filling. Slowly and evenly raise cloth, making the dough roll forward into a tight roll. Transfer strudel to ungreased baking sheet; form into horseshoe shape. Brush top with egg white; sprinkle with reserved sugar mixture. Bake in 350°F oven for 20 minutes. Cover with foil and bake 20-25 minutes more. Serves 10.

Mrs. Richard L. Redmont, Jr.

Almond Puff Coffee Cake

½ cup margarine
1 cup flour
2 Tablespoons water

FILLING:
½ cup margarine
1 cup water
1 teaspoon almond extract
1 cup flour

3 eggs, well beaten

FROSTING:
1½ cups confectioner's sugar
2 Tablespoons soft butter
1½ teaspoons almond extract
1½ Tablespoons warm water
1 (4½ ounce) package sliced
  almonds

Cut margarine into flour. Sprinkle water over this and mix well with fork. Form into ball and divide mixture in half. Place each half on an ungreased baking sheet. Pat each half into a 12 x 3-inch strip and place each strip about 3 inches apart on sheet. *FILLING:* Melt margarine; add water and bring to a rolling boil. Remove and quickly stir in almond extract and flour. Stir over low heat until mixture forms a ball (about 1 minute). Remove from heat once more and add eggs. Stir until mixture is smooth. Divide mixture in half and spread each half over each pastry strip. Bake 1 hour at 350°F until the top is crisp and brown. Cool. *FROSTING:* Mix ingredients except almonds until smooth and spread over top of cakes when they are cool. Sprinkle with sliced almonds. Serve warm. Serves 12.

Mrs. John H. Tatum, Cleveland, Mississippi

Easter Swirl Coffee Bread

1 package dry yeast
¼ cup warm water
½ cup soft butter or margarine
⅓ cup sugar
3 egg yolks
¾ cup milk, scalded and cooled
¼ teaspoon each salt, ground
   cardamom
3 cups flour

*CHOCOLATE STREUSEL
FILLING:*
½ cup sugar

¼ cup flour
2 Tablespoons butter
1½ teaspoons unsweetened
   cocoa
½ teaspoon ground cinnamon
¾ cup chopped pecans

POWDERED SUGAR GLAZE:
1 cup powdered sugar
4 teaspoons milk
½ teaspoon vanilla

Sprinkle yeast into warm water and let stand until dissolved. With an electric mixer cream the butter until light and beat in the sugar. Beat in egg yolks; then add yeast mixture, milk, salt and cardamom. Gradually mix in flour, beating at low speed of electric mixer. Dough will be quite soft. Turn out on a floured board and knead until smooth. Return dough to bowl and butter top lightly. Cover and allow to rise in warm place about 1½ hours or until doubled in bulk. Turn out on floured surface and knead lightly. With floured rolling pin, roll out dough 8 inches wide, 54 inches long and about ¼ inch thick. Dough can be divided and rolled in 2 lengths, each 8 inches wide and 27 inches long. *CHOCOLATE STREUSEL FILLING:* Mix ingredients except pecans until crumbly. Sprinkle filling evenly over rolled dough, covering to within 1 inch of the edges; then sprinkle with pecans. Roll up like a jelly roll from the long side, making a long rope. Pinch ends to seal. Holding one end of dough, twist it a dozen times to make a rope. The roll may be shaped into a duck or a bunny. DUCK: Cut a 3-inch length off each end of dough rope. Use one for beak and the other for feet. Shape remaining rope into a figure 8 design on a 12 x 16-inch buttered baking sheet, using ⅓ of the dough for the head and the rest for the body. Pull out tail. Shape beak and feet and pinch in place. Cover and let rise in warm place until doubled (about 45 minutes). BUNNY: Cut a 3-inch length off each end of dough rope for ears. Cut two 1½-inch pieces for feet. Shape remaining dough into a figure 8 on large buttered baking sheet using 2/5 of dough for the head and the balance for the body. Pinch ears and feet in place. Cover with towel and let rise until doubled. Bake in 325°F oven for 30-35 minutes or until browned. While still warm, spread entire surface with *POWDERED SUGAR GLAZE,* made by mixing together the sugar, milk and vanilla. Bread may be wrapped in foil and frozen, to be reheated and frosted later. Frozen bread, foil-wrapped, may be heated in 375°F oven for 40 minutes; or, if allowed to thaw, unwrap bread, place on baking sheet, heat in 350°F oven for 20 minutes and frost.

Mrs. M. S. Buckley, Newton, Mississippi

Raisins and jelly beans may be used for eyes.

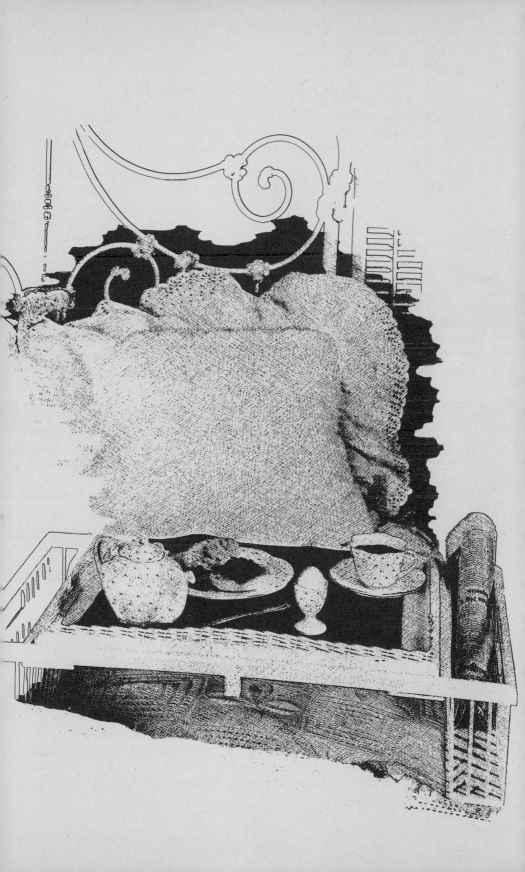

Pickles and Jellies

Preserving Basics

JAR PREPARATION   Use only standard jars and lids that are free from any chips, cracks, rust or dents. Wash jars, rims and lids in hot, soapy water. Rinse and place jars and rims in large pot. Fill with water and boil for 15 minutes, covered. Add lids and hold in hot water until ready to use.

TESTING DONENESS OF JELLY MADE WITHOUT ADDED PECTIN   *Temperature Test* - Cook the jelly to 220°F (for jams, conserves and marmalades cook to 221°F). *Spoon or Sheet Test* - Dip a cool metal spoon into boiling mixture. Raise the spoon a foot above the kettle, out of the steam, and turn spoon so that the syrup runs off the side. If the syrup forms two drops that flow together and fall off the spoon as one sheet, the jelly should be done. *Refrigerator Test* - Pour a small amount of boiling jelly on a cold plate and place it in the freezing compartment of the refrigerator. If the mixture gels, the jelly should be done.

SEALING JARS   Fill jars with hot jelly or fruit mixture to within 1/8 inch of top. Wipe the rim and threads clean with a damp cloth to prevent improper sealing. A two-piece metal cap (flat metal lid and metal screw band) is the most common lid used for sealing. Metal screw bands may be reused. Place the hot lid on the jar with the sealing compound next to the glass. Screw the metal band down tightly. After jar has cooled, check for seal.

WATER BATH METHOD FOR SEALING PICKLES AND RELISHES   Heat processing is recommended for all pickle products. Pack pickle products into glass jars according to the recipe being used. Adjust lids and immerse the jars into actively boiling water in a canner or deep kettle, making sure jars do not touch each other. Water must cover jar tops by an inch or two. Cover the container with a close-fitting lid and bring water back to a boil as quickly as possible. Start to count processing time when the water returns to a boil and boil gently for time specified in recipe. Remove jars and set upright to cool on a wire rack.

GUARDING AGAINST SPOILAGE   A jar is properly sealed if the lid is slightly concave in the center or has "popped down" after the contents have cooled. Store in dark, dry, cool place.

When making jellies or jams without adding artificial pectin, use ¼ under-ripe fruit and ¾ ripe fruit in order to provide the necessary natural pectin.

For heating pickling liquids, use utensils of enamelware, stainless steel, aluminum or glass. Copper, brass, galvanized or iron utensils may react with acids or salts and cause undesirable color changes in the pickles or form undesirable compounds.

Basic Bread and Butter Pickles

4 quarts sliced medium
   cucumbers
6 medium white onions, sliced
3 cloves garlic
⅓ cup salt

5 cups sugar
3 cups cider vinegar
1½ teaspoons turmeric
1½ teaspoons celery seed
2 teaspoons mustard seed

Do not peel cucumbers; slice thin. Add onions, whole garlic cloves and salt. Cover with cracked ice; mix thoroughly. Let stand for 3 hours. Drain well. Combine remaining ingredients and bring to a boil. Pour over cucumbers. Heat just to a boil. Seal in hot, sterilized jars. Yield: 8 pints.

Mrs. Julian Henderson

Grandmother's Tomato Relish

30 large tomatoes
10 large onions
5 large green peppers
1 teaspoon ground cinnamon
1 teaspoon ground allspice

1 teaspoon ground cloves
3 Tablespoons salt
1½ cups sugar
2 cups cider vinegar

Peel tomatoes. Chop tomatoes, onions and peppers. Combine with rest of in-gredients and cook on medium to low heat for several hours until relish turns a deep red color and is very thick. Spoon into sterile jars and seal. This is ex-cellent on hamburger patties, leftover roast and black-eyed peas. It can be made with canned tomatoes, about 7 (28 ounce) cans of a good brand, frozen chopped onions and green peppers. Yield: 6-8 half pints.

Mrs. G. Richard Greenlee

Pickled Squash

1 gallon yellow squash, sliced
   paper thin
8 small white onions, chopped
   thin
1 green pepper, chopped
1 sweet red pepper, chopped
½ cup ice cream salt

5 cups sugar
½ teaspoon turmeric
½ teaspoon ground cloves
2 Tablespoons mustard seed
2 Tablespoons celery seed
5 cups vinegar

Layer squash, onions and peppers in large pot. Cover with ice cream salt and fill with ice and water. Cover and set aside for 3 hours. Combine remaining in-gredients and bring to a boil. Drain ice and water from squash and place pot on stove. Pour hot vinegar mixture over squash. Bring back to a boil. Stir to coat squash well. Spoon immediately into hot jars. Seal. Yield: 8 pints.

Mrs. McWillie Robinson

Zucchini may be substituted for the squash in this recipe.

Green Tomato Relish

6 green peppers, chopped
1 hot pepper, chopped
12 green tomatoes, chopped
6 onions, chopped
½ cup salt

3 cups sugar
1 quart vinegar
1 Tablespoon turmeric
¼ box whole mixed pickling
  spice

Soak peppers, tomatoes, onions and salt overnight in water to cover. Drain and wash off. In a pot place sugar, vinegar, turmeric and spices tied in cheesecloth. Bring to a boil. Add the drained vegetables. Return to a boil. Spoon into jars and seal. Yield: 6 pints.

Mrs. Suzy McKay, Pickens, Mississippi

Red Pepper Relish

24 sweet red peppers, ground
  (reserve juice)
7 medium onions, chopped fine
  (reserve juice)

3 cups white vinegar
3 cups sugar
2 Tablespoons salt
2 Tablespoons mustard seed

Drain some, but not all, of juice from peppers. Combine peppers, onions with juice and all other ingredients in a pot. Bring to boil and simmer 30 minutes, stirring occasionally. Seal at once in jars. Process in boiling water bath for 20 minutes. Excellent with meat or vegetables. Especially good on cream cheese as an appetizer served with crackers. Yield: 2 quarts.

Mrs. George M. Wilkinson

Tarragon Pickles

8 pounds whole cucumbers
Salt
Water
⅓ gallon vinegar (5⅓ cups)
2 Tablespoons alum

4 pounds sugar
2 Tablespoons whole mixed
  pickling spice
1 (12 ounce) bottle tarragon
  vinegar

Wash cucumbers and place in salt water (2 cups salt per gallon water) for 10 days, removing scum as it accumulates on the top. Pour off salt water. Wash cucumbers and place in cold water for 3 days. Drain cucumbers. Mix vinegar and alum. Add cucumbers and let stand in mixture for 3 days. Slice pickles thin. In wide-mouth gallon jar alternate layers of pickles and sugar until all are used. Add pickling spice. Pour tarragon vinegar over all. Stir mixture occasionally for several hours until sugar is dissolved. Pack in jars and cover. *Sealing is unnecessary.* Yield: 1 gallon.

Mrs. Slater Gordon, Florence, Mississippi

Emma's Cabbage Relish

4 pounds hard white cabbage, chopped fine
12 medium onions, chopped fine
8 medium green peppers, chopped fine
2 quarts white vinegar

2½ Tablespoons salt
3 Tablespoons celery seed
4 Tablespoons turmeric
3 Tablespoons dry mustard
4 cups sugar
1 cup flour
1 cup Wesson oil

Combine all ingredients except flour and oil and bring to a boil. Immediately add the flour which has been dissolved in a small amount of water. Stir in well. Remove from heat and add the oil. Mix. Fill jars and seal. Yield: about 6 pints.

Mrs. Hobart Hector, Jr.

Pickled Pole Beans

30 to 40 fresh, young Kentucky Wonder pole beans
Red pepper
Cloves garlic

Fresh heads dill weed
Cider vinegar
Water
Salt

Sterilize pint jars and tops and vertical pack beans. To each pint add ½ teaspoon red pepper, 1 or 2 cloves garlic, and 1 head fresh dill. For each pint bring to a boil a solution of ½ cup cider vinegar, ½ cup water and 1 Table-spoon salt. Fill jars of beans with boiling solution and seal at once, preferably in boiling water bath for 5 minutes. Do not open for at least 3 weeks. Serve as an hors d'oeuvre or condiment. Serves 10.

Mrs. James H. Creekmore

Pear Relish

12 pounds hard pears (about 40) peeled, cored and quartered
2 pounds onions, peeled and quartered
4 green peppers, seeded and quartered

5 cups white vinegar
4 cups sugar
2½ Tablespoons salt
2 Tablespoons whole mixed pickling spice
2 Tablespoons turmeric

Run pears, onions and peppers through food grinder. Drain off all liquid. Combine vinegar, sugar, salt, pickling spice and turmeric. Boil 10 minutes. Add pears, onions and peppers. Boil 15 minutes. Spoon into hot jars and seal quickly. This is very good with meats or vegetables. Yield: 8-9 pints.

Mrs. Dick B. Mason, III

Hot Dill Pickles

4 pounds cucumbers (4 to 5 inches long)
8 Tablespoons dill seed
4 teaspoons caraway seed
2 teaspoons minced garlic
1 teaspoon crushed red pepper

2 quarts water
2 cups cider vinegar
½ cup pickling salt, coarse or kosher
¼ teaspoon alum

Thoroughly wash and dry cucumbers. Pack 4 into each of four 1-quart sterilized preserving jars. Into each jar place 2 Tablespoons dill seed, 1 teaspoon caraway seed, ½ teaspoon garlic and ¼ teaspoon crushed pepper. In a large saucepan bring water, vinegar, salt and alum to boiling point. Pour over cucumbers to cover, leaving ¼ inch head space. Seal with lids. Process in water bath for 15 minutes. Let stand at least 8 weeks before serving. Yield: 4 quarts.

Mrs. Richard L. Redmont, Jr.

Pear Chutney

1 quart cider vinegar
½ pound light brown sugar
1½ pounds white sugar
30 to 35 firm, unripe pears, peeled, cored, sliced
7 onions, coarsely chopped
7 cloves garlic, sliced
1 pound seedless golden raisins
1 pound currants
2½ Tablespoons salt
1 teaspoon cayenne red pepper
2 teaspoons paprika
2 (2½ ounce) cans mustard seed

1 cup orange marmalade
Grated rind of ½ orange
2 lemons, sliced thin
2 Tablespoons curry powder
3 Tablespoons crystallized ginger, coarsely chopped
1 teaspoon each ground cinnamon, ground cloves, ground allspice, ground nutmeg
½ pound dried apples, halved
½ pound dried apricots, halved
1 cup sherry wine (optional)

Simmer vinegar and sugar 15 minutes. Add all ingredients except apples and apricots. Cook slowly 1 hour. Add apples and apricots. Cook 30 minutes longer or until thick. Remove from heat. Add sherry, if desired. Place in sterilized jars and seal. Yield: 25 half pints.

Mrs. Robert Ratelle

In pickling, do not use iodized table salt; it may darken pickles.

Hollow pickles usually result from poorly developed cucumbers, holding cucumbers too long before pickling, too rapid fermentation or too strong or too weak a brine solution.

Jerusalem Artichoke Pickle

8 quarts small Jerusalem
  artichokes
1 gallon distilled vinegar
1 (1.12 ounce) can dry mustard
1 cup salt

1 Tablespoon whole mixed
  pickling spice in cheesecloth
  bag
4 pounds sugar
12 small onions, sliced

Scrub artichokes with a stiff brush until clean. If artichokes are large, cut into pieces. Let vinegar, mustard, salt, spices and sugar come to a boil; then allow to get cold (this mixture may be prepared ahead). Layer artichokes and onions in sterilized jars until full; then cover with cold vinegar mixture and seal. Store jars upside down. *Do not open for 5 weeks.* Yield: 24 pints.

Mrs. Clyde X. Copeland, Sr.

Spiced Pears

7 pounds cooking pears
2 cups vinegar
4 cups sugar
½ cup water

2 sticks cinnamon, broken
1 Tablespoon whole cloves
1 lemon, sliced and seeded

Peel and core pears and cut in half. Immediately place in cold water to which a little lemon juice has been added to prevent turning dark. Combine all other ingredients and bring to a boil. Boil 5 minutes, then add drained pears. Reduce heat and simmer until pears are tender and can be pierced with a straw. Place pears in jars. Continue boiling syrup 10 minutes and pour over pears, including some spices in each jar. Seal. Red or green food coloring may be added to jars if pears are to be used for Christmas. Yield: about 6 pints.

Mrs. James L. Enochs, Orange Beach, Alabama

Pear Mincemeat

7 pounds cooking pears
1 pound raisins
1 Tablespoon ground cinnamon
1 Tablespoon ground nutmeg
1 Tablespoon ground cloves

1 Tablespoon salt
2 cups vinegar
2 lemons, grated (juice and
  rind)
3 pounds sugar

Grind together the pears and raisins. Add all remaining ingredients. Cook until thick and seal in jars while hot. Allow to age for several weeks. Yield: at least 8 pints.

Mrs. Don T. Caffery, Franklin, Louisiana

To make PEAR MINCEMEAT PIE add ½ cup broken nuts, 1 Tablespoon rum or rum flavoring and 1 apple, peeled and finely diced, to 3 cups mincemeat. Pour into unbaked 9-inch pie shell, cover with a lattice of pastry and bake.

129

Pickled Okra

4½ pounds okra, small or
   medium
8 cups cider vinegar
1 cup water
½ cup salt

10 cloves garlic, peeled
10 hot red peppers
10 teaspoons dill seed
10 teaspoons mustard seed

Wash okra and brush lightly with a piece of nylon net or brush to remove "fuzz". Trim okra stems without cutting too close. Sterilize 10 pint jars and keep hot until ready to use. Combine vinegar, water and salt and bring to a boil. Into each jar pack okra in 2 vertical layers. The first layer should be packed with the stems down and the next layer with the stems up. Also add to each jar 1 clove garlic, 1 hot red pepper, 1 teaspoon dill seed and 1 teaspoon mustard seed. Pour hot vinegar mixture over okra and seal. To insure a good seal, process 5 minutes in boiling water bath. Let stand several weeks before opening. If very small okra is used, then half pint jars should be used instead. Very small pickled okra is delicious in a martini. Yield: 10 pints.

Mrs. Louis J. Lyell

Cranberry Surprise

2 (1 pound) bags cranberries
2 pounds plus 2 cups sugar
1 cup white wine vinegar
1 teaspoon ground cinnamon

½ teaspoon ground cloves
¾ (14½ ounce) box raisins
Juice of 1 lemon
3 large oranges (navel preferred)

Wash and stem berries. Cover with sugar and all other ingredients except oranges. Stir and allow to stand while preparing oranges. Peel thin skin from oranges and chop skin very fine. Add to berries. Cut oranges in half and remove as much meat and juice as possible (fruit spoon helps). Add to mixture. Cook and stir over high heat, bringing to a boil for about 5 minutes (berries will pop open). Turn heat down, continue to stir until mixture turns very dark and most berries are cooked down (about 35 minutes). Cool. Serve hot or cold as a relish. Store in refrigerator. To use as a molded salad, soften 2 packages unflavored gelatin in ½ cup cold water. Add to mixture a few minutes before removing from heat. Yield: 2 quarts.

Mrs. William Menge, New Orleans, Louisiana

Variation: An easy HEAVENLY CRANBERRY SAUCE can be made by washing and draining well 2 pounds cranberries. Place in shallow baking dish and cover with 2 cups coarsely chopped walnuts, 3 cups sugar, juice and grated rind of 2 lemons and 2 cups orange marmalade. Cover tightly and bake for 45 minutes at 350°F. Makes 2 quarts.

Mrs. Louis H. Shornick

Mango Chutney

6 mangoes
1 pound dates
2 pounds brown sugar
¼ pound crystallized or
   preserved ginger, chopped

1 pound seedless raisins
¾ Tablespoon salt
1 clove garlic, minced
Cayenne red pepper
1 quart cider vinegar

Peel and slice mangoes. Pit dates and dice. Place all ingredients in large heavy pot. Simmer until thick. Stir when necessary to prevent sticking. Pour into sterilized 8-ounce jars and seal. Serve with curry and rice. Yield: 6 pints.

Mrs. W. Calvin Wells, Jr.

Mixed Fruit Chutney

2 Tablespoons whole mixed
   pickling spice
1 pound apples, pared and diced
½ pound pitted prunes, cut up
1 cup cider vinegar

1 (8 ounce) package apricots,
   cut up
1½ cups dark brown sugar
1½ teaspoons salt
1 large clove garlic, minced

Tie pickling spices in double thickness of cheesecloth. Combine all ingredients in stainless or enameled 5 or 6-quart kettle. Bring to a boil. Mixture will be thick. Reduce heat and simmer 1 hour, covered, stirring frequently until soft. If mixture becomes too thick add several Tablespoons of water. Discard spices. Spoon into hot, sterilized jars. Seal. Yield: 6 half pints.

Mrs. Reuel May, Jr.

Jellies

Pyracantha Jelly

3 pounds pyracantha berries,
   or more
4 Tablespoons lemon juice

5 Tablespoons vinegar
1 (1¾ ounce) box Sure-Jell
7 cups sugar

Pick pyracantha berries when deep red. Wash, remove stems and place in a large pot. Add 1 cup of water for each pound. Boil for 25 minutes or until berries pop open. Drain in dampened, double-thickness cheesecloth bag. (The clearest jelly comes from dripped juice without pressing the bag, but yield of juice can be increased by pressing bag when the dripping stops.) Measure 3 cups of juice. Mix the juices and vinegar with the Sure-Jell. Bring to a hard boil, stirring occasionally. Add the sugar all at once. Bring to a hard rolling boil for 1 minute, stirring constantly. Remove from heat and skim off foam. Pour into jars, leaving ½ inch head space. Seal or cover with 1/8 inch hot paraffin. Cool and store. Yield: 7 half pints.

Mrs. James Wheeler

Peeled Fig Preserves

6 cups sugar   1 lemon, sliced
4 pounds peeled figs

Layer sugar, figs and lemon slices in large pot and cook covered on very low heat until sugar dissolves (about 1 hour). Uncover and cook about 45 minutes longer, until figs are transparent. Lift out figs with a slotted spoon and cook the syrup about 15 minutes longer, until thicker. Put figs back into pot and let sit overnight. The following morning, heat figs to a boil and seal in jars. Yield: 7 half pints.

Mrs. Charles Craft

Unpeeled Fig Preserves

2 pounds figs, unpeeled   1 cup water
3 cups sugar   8 thin lemon slices

Rinse figs well in cool water. Soak for 15-20 minutes. Make a syrup by boiling the sugar and water together. When syrup is clear and slightly thick (about 10 or 15 minutes), add figs and sliced lemon. Bring back to a boil and boil for 1 minute. Lower heat and simmer for 30 minutes. Seal in jars. This recipe is easily doubled. Yield: 3 half pints.

Mrs. Warren Roper

Wild Plum Jelly

Wild plums (about 6 pounds,   Water
   using a mixture of ¾ ripe   Sugar
   and ¼ unripened plums)

Wash and remove stems from plums. Place in an enamel, stainless steel or brass container. Do not use aluminum. Add water to almost cover the plums. Bring to a boil and allow to boil until plums burst open. Strain juice through several layers of cheesecloth. For every 6 cups of juice use 4 cups of sugar. Place sugar and juice in kettle. Bring to a boil, stirring until sugar dissolves. Do not stir any longer. Five or ten minutes after juice comes to a boil, begin testing to see if jelly is ready. The best test is with a sterling silver fork. The jelly will sheet immediately and completely between all tines. When the jelly is ready, remove from heat and let sit for a minute. Skim off foam. Pour into hot, sterilized jars and seal with lids or with 2 layers of paraffin. Extra juice can be frozen for use at another time. Yield: about 8 half pints.

Mrs. James P. McKeown

Plum jelly using domestic plums can be made by this same recipe. For 6 cups of juice use 3-3½ cups of sugar.

Strawberry Preserves

1 quart strawberries   4 cups sugar
2 teaspoons vinegar

Wash and stem strawberries. Add vinegar and cook 3 minutes. Add sugar and bring to a full rolling boil. Cook 10 minutes. Skim. Place in a shallow pan or dish overnight. When ready to jar, place jars, lids and rings in boiling water. Fill drained, hot jars with preserves and seal immediately with hot lids. Yield: 2 pints.

Mrs. G. B. Shaw

Fig Jam

3¼ pounds fully ripened figs   ½ cup water
½ cup lemon juice   1 (1¾ ounce) box Sure-Jell
1 teaspoon grated lemon rind   3¼ pounds (or 7½ cups) sugar

Trim stems, grind figs and place in large saucepan. Stir in lemon juice, grated lemon rind and water. Add Sure-Jell. Mix well. Place figs over high heat until a hard boil is reached. Immediately add all sugar. Let come to a quick rolling boil that will not stir down. Boil hard for one minute, stirring constantly. Remove from heat and skim with metal spoon. Stir and skim for 5 minutes. Ladle into jelly glasses leaving ½ inch space at top. Cover with hot melted paraffin or seal with tops. Cool. Yield: 12 half pints.

Mrs. R. B. Layton

Variation: Add a little preserved ginger or chopped nuts.

Scuppernong or Muscadine Jelly

4 quarts scuppernong or   2⅔ cups sugar
   muscadine grapes

Wash grapes, mash and place in preserving pot with enough water to cover. Simmer for 20 minutes. Press out juice through a colander; then strain through cheesecloth. For one recipe of jelly use 4 cups of grape juice. Reserve the remaining juice in the refrigerator for a week or freeze for future use. Pour grape juice into preserving pot and boil for 5 minutes. While juice is boiling, warm the sugar in a 200°F oven. Pour sugar into juice and cook over medium heat until it reaches 220°F on candy thermometer (about 25 minutes). Skim off foam. Add a few drops of yellow food coloring if using scuppernongs to give it a richer color. Pour into jars and seal. Yield: 4 half pints.

Mrs. Clyde Copeland, Jr.

———

Cranberries may be frozen in the plastic bags in which they are bought.

Blackberry Jam

2 quarts fresh blackberries
(¼ of which are unripe)

6 cups sugar

Wash berries and cook in saucepan over moderate heat until juice begins to flow and berries are soft. Run through a food mill to obtain juice and pulp. Measure out 4 cups of juice and pulp mixture and place in preserving pot. Bring to a boil. Add sugar and cook over moderate heat until candy thermometer reaches about 221 °F (about 30 minutes). Pour into jars and seal. Extra juice and pulp may be kept in refrigerator for 2 weeks or frozen for making another batch of jam later. Yield: 6 half pints.

Mrs. Steven Lucas, Washington, D. C.

Aimée's Mint Jelly

1½ cups packed fresh mint,
    washed
3¼ cups water
Green food coloring

½ teaspoon lemon juice
1 (1¾ ounce) box Sure-Jell
4 cups sugar

Crush mint leaves and stems. Add water. Bring to a boil. Remove from heat, cover and let stand ten minutes. Strain and measure 3 cups of mint infusion. Add food coloring and lemon juice. Add Sure-Jell, dissolve and bring to a rapid boil. Add sugar. Cook fast, stirring occasionally until it comes to a rapid boil that cannot be stirred down; then cook one minute more. Pour into sterilized jelly glasses and seal. Very nice to serve with lamb. Yield: 6 half pints.

Mrs. John H. Walsh

Golden Marmalade

6 ounces dried apricots, halved
1¼ cups water, divided
1 (8 ounce) can pineapple
    tidbits or sliced pineapple,
    cut into bits, with juice
1 large or 2 medium oranges,
    cut in pieces, seeds removed

1 small lemon, cut in pieces,
    seeds removed
2½ cups sugar
2 pounds peaches, peeled and
    chopped
2 sticks cinnamon

In preserving kettle set aside apricots, 1 cup water and pineapple bits with juice. Blend in blender ¼ cup water, oranges and lemon. Add to fruit in kettle along with the sugar, peaches and cinnamon. Heat to boiling, then lower heat and simmer gently for 1½ hours, or until thickened. Stir occasionally during cooking. Seal in sterilized jars. Yield: 5 half pints.

Mrs. Buford Yerger, Sr.

Easy Hot Pepper Jelly

6 green peppers
12 hot peppers
2 cups water
5½ cups sugar

1 cup white vinegar
⅓ cup lemon juice
1 (6 ounce) bottle Certo

Cut stems and chop peppers, leaving in seeds. Cover with water and simmer until tender. Mash through strainer to obtain more juice, then strain juice through cheesecloth in order to have clear jelly. Add sugar and vinegar to juice. Rapidly bring to a boil and add lemon juice and Certo. Boil hard for 1 minute. Remove from heat and skim off foam. Pour into sterile jars and seal. Delicious served with cheese and crackers or spread on cream cheese. Yield: 8 half pints.

Mrs. G. Richard Greenlee

Ginger Pear Honey

10 pounds cooking pears, peeled
   and quartered
1 lemon
Grated rind and juice of 2
   lemons

4 ounces ginger root, grated, or
   2 Tablespoons powdered
   ginger
7½ pounds sugar

Grind pears and lemon with a meat grinder. Add grated rind and juice of other 2 lemons. Place all ingredients in large canning kettle. Start on high heat and bring to a boil. Turn to medium low and cook until amber and as thick as desired (approximately 1½ hours). Place in jars and seal. Good with hot breads or can be used as an ice cream topping. Recipe may be cut in half. Yield: 15 pints.

Mrs. Hugh McInnis, Jr.

Spicy Peach Marmalade

1 (1¾ ounce) box Sure-Jell
3 pounds ripe peaches, peeled
   and chopped fine or put
   through a meat grinder
   (about 4 cups)

Juice of 1 lemon
5½ cups sugar
¼ teaspoon each ground
   cinnamon, ground cloves,
   ground nutmeg

Mix Sure-Jell, fruit and lemon juice and place in large pot over high heat. Bring to a boil, stirring constantly. Add sugar all at one time and bring back to a rolling boil. Boil hard for 1 minute, stirring constantly. Remove from heat; skim off foam with a metal spoon. Add spices. Pour into jars and seal. Yield: 7 half pints.

Mrs. William F. Goodman, Jr.

Rosy Peach Conserve

18 peaches, peeled, pitted
5 medium oranges, quartered,
   seeded
Sugar

1 cup maraschino cherries,
   chopped
½ cup chopped nuts

Run peaches and oranges through food chopper, using coarse blade. Measure fruits and add 1½ times as much sugar as fruit. Cook until 2 drops of syrup hang side by side from spoon. Add cherries and nuts. Seal in hot sterilized jars. Yield: about 12 half pints.

Miss Ellen Robinson

Horseradish Jelly

3¼ cups sugar
½ cup prepared horseradish

½ cup cider vinegar
½ cup liquid pectin

In large pan heat and stir sugar, horseradish and vinegar until sugar dissolves. Bring to boil; then stir in pectin all at once. Bring to full rolling boil while stirring. Take off heat and skim foam off top. Pour at once into hot sterilized jelly jars. Seal with paraffin. Excellent with roast beef or chicken. Yield: 3 half pints.

Mrs. Ancel C. Tipton, Jr.

Crab Apple Jelly

5 pounds whole crab apples
5 cups water
2 (4 ounce) blocks paraffin

1 (1¾ ounce) package
   powdered fruit pectin
8 cups sugar

Wash apples and remove blossom ends. Leave crab apples whole. Do not peel or core. Add water to apples; cover and simmer for 15 minutes. Crush with masher and simmer 5 minutes longer. Place in jelly bag and allow to drip overnight for clearest jelly. (A man's cotton handkerchief clipped with clothes pins to a strainer or colander makes a very handy jelly bag.) If in a hurry, juice may be squeezed out. There should be about 7 cups of juice. If there is a slight shortage of juice, add water. Sterilize jars and lids; drain. Melt paraffin in heavy glass jar in boiling water. Mix fruit pectin with juice in a 6-8-quart saucepan over high heat. Bring to a hard boil, stirring occasionally. Add sugar at once. Bring to a hard rolling boil that cannot be stirred down, stirring constantly. Boil 1 minute, remove from heat and skim off foam with a metal spoon. Pour into jelly glasses, leaving ½ inch space at top, and cover with melted paraffin. Jelly will keep in refrigerator for 2 months without paraffin but sealed with lid. Allow jelly to sit for 24 hours before moving to store. Crab apples make a tart jelly. Yield: 12-13 half pints.

Mrs. Reynolds Cheney

For softer jellies, use ¼ cup more juice. For stiffer jellies, use ¼ cup less juice.

Eggs, Cheese and Grains

Basic Poached Egg

Water
1 Tablespoon white vinegar

1 teaspoon salt
1 egg, at room temperature

In a shallow pan or skillet pour enough water to cover egg. Add vinegar and salt and bring to a boil. Break 1 egg into a saucer or cup. With the tip of a slotted spoon or spatula swirl the water and carefully slip the egg into the center of the whirlpool. Reduce heat to low and let egg steep in hot water for about 3 minutes. Remove egg from water with a spatula or slotted spoon. Note: As many as 4 eggs may be poached at one time in an 8-inch skillet.

SERVING VARIATIONS FOR POACHED EGGS

The term, poached egg, brings to mind the several specialty dishes which are built around the basic poached egg and which have been made famous by restaurants throughout the world.

EGGS BENEDICT denotes either a round of Holland rusk or an English muffin covered with a slice of broiled ham and then topped with two poached eggs. All of this is then capped with hollandaise sauce.

EGGS HUSSARDE is described in Brennan's own souvenir cookbook as "the most complex of the Brennan egg dishes, primarily because it has several elements which must be prepared separately." The marchand de vin sauce must be prepared ahead. One should then grill the ham, tomato slices and toast before preparing the hollandaise sauce. The eggs should then be poached. The ham is placed immediately on top of the toast and is covered with the marchand de vin sauce. Two poached eggs are placed on top of this mound before the hollandaise sauce is added. The dish is garnished with a grilled tomato on the side.

EGGS SARDOU is a creamed spinach dish topped with artichoke bottoms, covered with 2 poached eggs per artichoke bottom and then capped with hollandaise sauce.

EGGS PORTUGUESE is a dish containing chopped vegetables in pastry shells and covered with 2 poached eggs before the hollandaise sauce is ladled over the entire serving.

EGGS ST. CHARLES is a fried trout dish, the trout being topped with 2 poached eggs and capped with hollandaise.

EGGS A LA NOUVELLE ORLEANS is the Cadillac of the poached egg dishes. It consists of lump crab meat covered with 2 poached eggs and then coated with a brandy cream sauce.

Basic Omelet

3 eggs
1½ teaspoons water
Salt and pepper

3 teaspoons butter
Fillings (optional)

Break eggs into a bowl. Add water, salt and pepper and beat well. Place butter in a heavy, cold skillet or omelet pan and melt it over medium heat until frothing. Just as it settles and begins to clear, pour the eggs directly into the middle of the pan and turn the heat up slightly. Lift the edges of the omelet with a narrow spatula to let the uncooked egg run under the cooked portion. Shake the pan back and forth over the flame while lifting. When the omelet is soft, creamy and slightly set, lay the warm precooked FILLING or herbs across the center of the omelet. Grasp the pan handle from underneath with the left hand and with the right hand flip one third of the omelet over the center. Tilt the omelet pan up and roll the omelet out onto a warmed plate. This process takes only 15 seconds. Making an omelet only takes a minute, so do not double recipe; just make two. Serves 1 or 2.

SUGGESTED FILLINGS

Crumbled bacon
Strips of thinly sliced ham
Fried minced onions, scallions,
    green peppers
Chopped fresh herbs (chives,
    parsley, tarragon)

Freshly grated Gruyère,
    Parmesan, Romano, Swiss
    or Cheddar cheese
Minced lobster, crab or shrimp
Creamed or sautéed
    mushrooms

Mrs. Rhesa Barksdale

The chief difference between an omelet and scrambled eggs is that an omelet has class.

Clam Omelet Filling

2 Tablespoons butter, divided
1 Tablespoon flour
½ cup milk
1 Tablespoon chopped shallots

2 Tablespoons canned minced
    clams
¼ teaspoon tarragon

Make small amount of white sauce with 1 Tablespoon butter, flour and milk. In small skillet sauté shallots, clams and tarragon in 1 Tablespoon butter. When onions are barely brown, add to white sauce. Set aside while making omelet. Place filling on one side of eggs and fold other side over the filling. Cover and let cook until omelet is puffed up. Serve immediately. Filling may be made in larger quantities for more omelets. Will fill 1 omelet.

Miss Charlotte Skelton

Polly's Easy Cheese Omelet

To serve 4:
1 Tablespoon margarine, melted
3 eggs, well beaten
Salt and pepper to taste
½ cup grated sharp cheese
1 cup milk

To serve 2 to 3:
1 Tablespoon margarine, melted
2 eggs, well beaten
Salt and pepper to taste
⅓ cup grated sharp cheese
½ cup milk

Have water in bottom of double boiler hot, but not boiling hard. Mix ingredients well and place in top of double boiler. Cover and leave for exactly 20 minutes without lifting lid. Serve immediately.

Mrs. Rivers Y. Lurate

Willie's Omelet Fillings

RUSSIAN OMELET FILLING

1 pound lump crab meat
2 Tablespoons olive oil
1 teaspoon Worcestershire sauce
1 Tablespoon soy sauce
1 teaspoon rosemary
½ teaspoon chives

1 teaspoon Parmesan cheese
1 (2 ounce) can sliced
  mushrooms
½ cup sherry or red wine
Salt and pepper to taste
1 (2 ounce) jar black caviar

Pick shells from crab meat. Mix all ingredients except caviar and marinate overnight. Sauté briefly in skillet to warm. Use to fill inside of an omelet, reserving a little to sprinkle on top. Top with a sprinkling of caviar. Will fill 4 omelets.

SWISS OMELET FILLING

1 (2 ounce) can sliced
  mushrooms
½ cup sherry wine
Salt and pepper
3 Tablespoons olive oil
2 bay leaves, crumbled
1 bunch green onions, finely
  chopped

½ cup finely chopped parsley
½ teaspoon Worcestershire
  sauce
1 teaspoon soy sauce
1 (2 ounce) can pimientos, diced
½ teaspoon dry mustard
Dash Accent
½ teaspoon Italian seasoning

Marinate mushrooms overnight in wine. Salt and pepper them to taste. Heat olive oil; add bay leaves first and cook briefly. Add onions and other ingredients. Cook for 10 minutes, stirring constantly. Add mushrooms and sherry. Reduce heat and cook until dry. Use to fill an omelet, reserving some to spoon on top. Will fill 2 omelets.

Willie Braxton, Little Rock, Arkansas

Note: For a special omelet use 1 part Swiss Omelet Filling and 2 parts Russian Omelet Filling inside basic omelet. Garnish with anchovies on top.

Basic Hard-Cooked Eggs

Place the number of eggs desired, 2 Tablespoons water per egg and a pinch salt in a pan with a tight-fitting cover. Place covered pan on heating unit and turn heat to high until steam appears. Turn off heat but leave pan on unit for 25 minutes. Plunge eggs into ice water to cool. Peel immediately. Yolks will not darken by this method.

Pickled Eggs

2½ to 3 dozen small eggs,
    hard-boiled
1 (16 ounce) bottle Wishbone
    Italian dressing
¾ cup vinegar

Garlic salt to taste
Juice from 1 (16 ounce) can
    beets
Red food coloring, as needed

Place eggs in large-mouth glass gallon jar. Combine dressing, vinegar, garlic salt, beet juice and red food coloring to make up marinade. Pour over eggs. Let eggs marinate in refrigerator for about a week. Eggs should take on a purplish-red color. Stir occasionally. Color will penetrate completely through egg white.

Mrs. Harry Weir

Shrimp Curried Eggs

STUFFED EGGS:
8 hard-boiled eggs, halved
⅓ cup mayonnaise
½ teaspoon salt
⅓ teaspoon curry powder
½ teaspoon paprika
¼ teaspoon dry mustard

SAUCE:
2 Tablespoons margarine
2 Tablespoons flour

1 (10½ ounce) can cream of
    shrimp soup
½ soup can milk
½ cup shredded sharp cheese
1 cup small, cooked shrimp

TOPPING:
1 cup fresh bread crumbs
1 Tablespoon butter or
    margarine

STUFFED EGGS: Push egg yolks through a sieve or mash and mix with remaining ingredients. Fill egg whites with mixture and arrange egg halves in rectangular baking dish. SAUCE: Melt margarine and add flour gradually, making a paste. Slowly add soup and milk and cook until thick. Add cheese and stir until melted. Add shrimp. Pour sauce over eggs in baking dish. TOPPING: Sauté bread crumbs in butter. Sprinkle over top of casserole. Bake in 350°F oven until thoroughly heated (about 25 minutes). This is a delicious brunch or luncheon entrée. Serve it with a spinach salad. Serves 6.

Mrs. Bob Carroll

Cheese Nest Eggs

1 (2 pound) box Velveeta
   cheese, grated
12 to 16 eggs
1 to 2 teaspoons whipping
   cream per egg used

1 teaspoon ground mustard
   per egg used
Salt
Red pepper

Butter a 3-quart casserole. Line with cheese, making a nest to hold each egg. Break eggs into nests. In a bowl mix whipping cream and mustard. Spoon mixture on top of each egg yolk until coated. Sprinkle with salt and red pepper. Cook at 325°F for 20 minutes. Watch carefully. Shortly before done, sprinkle a tiny bit of salt on each egg. Dish may be assembled and refrigerated the day before, but let it come to room temperature before cooking. Serves 12-16.

Mrs. Edward J. Peters

Stuffed Egg and Mushroom Casserole

12 hard-boiled eggs
3 (4 ounce) jars button
   mushrooms, drained, divided
2 Tablespoons butter, melted
Salt to taste
Dash white and red pepper

1 Tablespoon Worcestershire
   sauce
¼ teaspoon Tabasco
½ pound bacon, fried, divided
¾ pound sharp cheese, grated,
   divided

Slice eggs lengthwise; remove and mash yolks. Mince 1 jar mushrooms and warm in butter. Add to yolks. Season mixture with salt and peppers, Worcestershire sauce and Tabasco. Mix well and stuff back into whites. Press two halves together. Arrange in lightly greased casserole dish. Sprinkle remaining 2 jars mushrooms over eggs. Crumble bacon; sprinkle half of bacon and half of cheese over eggs. Reserve remainder for SAUCE.

SAUCE

4 Tablespoons butter
¼ cup flour
2 cups milk
Salt to taste
White and red pepper

1 Tablespoon Worcestershire
   sauce
¼ teaspoon Tabasco
¼ cup white wine
2 Tablespoons chopped parsley

Melt butter; add flour and blend in milk. Cook until thick; remove from heat. Season with salt and peppers to taste, Worcestershire sauce and Tabasco. Add wine and blend well. Pour sauce over eggs and top with remaining bacon and cheese. Refrigerate at this point, if desired. Bring to room temperature and bake 25 or 30 minutes at 350°F until bubbly. Garnish with parsley; serve warm. May be prepared 1 day in advance. Serve for brunch with cheese grits soufflé, hot or fresh fruit and a favorite spinach casserole. Serves 8-10.

Mrs. John Ainsworth

Robin's Cheese Strudel

1 pound Monterey Jack cheese
4 ounces green chilies, chopped
1 quart cottage cheese (large
   curd)

½ cup flour
1 teaspoon baking powder
½ cup butter, melted
10 eggs, well beaten

Grate cheese. Add chilies and cottage cheese. Sift flour and baking powder. Add to mixture. Add other ingredients and mix well. Pour into well-greased 3-quart oblong baking dish. Bake 15 minutes at 400°F and then 30 minutes at 350°F. Serves 8.

Mrs. T. Arnold Turner, Jr.

Curried Eggs

4 Tablespoons butter
4 Tablespoons flour
2 cups milk
2 teaspoons curry powder

6 Tablespoons cream
Salt and white pepper
12 hard-boiled eggs, sliced
Pimiento strips

To make cream sauce, melt butter in top of double boiler. Add flour and cook, stirring with wooden spoon, for about 2 minutes. Remove from heat and add milk slowly, stirring. Return to heat and stir constantly until sauce thickens. Mix curry powder and cream, and add to thickened sauce. Add salt and pepper to taste. Place sliced eggs in buttered casserole and top with pimiento strips. Pour cream sauce over all, lifting eggs gently so sauce reaches bottom of casserole. Bake at 400°F for 20 minutes. Should be served immediately over rice with some or all of the usual curry accompaniments: chutney, shredded coconut, chopped peanuts, raisins. This is a delicious brunch dish and is very good served with a broiled tomato, French bread and a fresh fruit compote. Serves 6-8.

Mrs. Louis J. Lyell

Sausage-Egg Soufflé

1 pound mild bulk sausage
6 slices bread, toasted
6 eggs
2 cups milk

½ teaspoon dry mustard
Salt and pepper to taste
1 cup grated Cheddar cheese

Brown the sausage; drain. Cut each slice of toast into 4 pieces. Beat together the eggs, milk and seasonings. In a casserole layer half the toast, half the sausage and sprinkle on half the cheese. Pour half the custard over the layers. Repeat layers once more. Cover and bake in a 325°F oven for 45 minutes to 1 hour (or until soufflé has puffed up). Let sit for 5 minutes before serving. Casserole is best made 24 hours ahead and refrigerated until ready to bake. Serves 4.

Mrs. James L. Brown

Variation: Substitute Swiss cheese for the Cheddar; use rye bread instead of white.

Grains

Basic Rice Cooking Methods

BASIC BOILED RICE

4 quarts water   1⅓ cups raw rice
1 Tablespoon salt

In a heavy saucepan bring water and salt to a rolling boil. Sprinkle in rice, stir and reduce heat. Cook over moderate heat for about 18 minutes. Drain rice in colander and rinse under running cold water. Put the colander over a pan of boiling water making sure water level does not touch bottom of colander. Cover rice with a lid and steam for 15-20 minutes. Serves 4.

BASIC BOILED RICE, COVERED

1 cup raw rice   1 teaspoon salt
1½ cups water

Combine ingredients in saucepan and bring to a boil. Cover. Reduce heat to low and cook for 23 minutes without removing lid. Remove pan from heat and let stand for 5 minutes. Fluff with a fork. Serves 4.

BASIC WILD RICE

1 cup wild rice   1 teaspoon salt
6 cups water

Wash rice several times. Drain. In heavy saucepan bring water, salt and rice to a boil, covered. Uncover and boil for 50 minutes. Drain. To fluff rice further, steam in a colander. Serves 4.

Oriental Rice

1½ cups raw rice
2 Tablespoons butter or
   margarine
1 bunch green onions and tops,
   chopped
1 (5 ounce) bottle soy sauce

1 (8 ounce) can water
   chestnuts, sliced
1 (2 ounce) can mushrooms,
   stems and pieces or sliced
½ cup slivered almonds

Cook rice in 2¼ cups unsalted water according to cooking instructions for Basic Boiled Rice, Covered (see Index). Melt butter in skillet and sauté onions until tender (about 5 minutes). Add cooked rice, soy sauce, water chestnuts and mushrooms. Bake covered for 40 minutes in 325°F oven. Sprinkle almonds on top for last 10 minutes of cooking. Uncover, and fluff with a fork. Serves 6.

Mrs. Clyde Copeland, Jr.

Aunt Robin's Oyster-Sausage-Rice Casserole

3 cups raw brown rice
2 pounds hot bulk sausage
2 cups chopped onion

2 cups chopped celery
2 pints oysters, well-drained
2 cups minced parsley, divided

Cook brown rice according to package directions. Crumble sausage and cook in skillet. Drain grease into another skillet and cook onion and celery in this until tender. Drain off grease. Mix vegetables, sausage, oysters, rice and 1 cup parsley. Place in casserole with 1 cup parsley on top. Bake in 350°F oven for 30 minutes. Serves 8-10.

Mrs. Bill E. McCrillis

Aunt Louise's Red Rice

3 Tablespoons butter
1 medium onion, chopped
1 large green pepper, chopped
1 (8 ounce) can tomato sauce
½ cup water

1 cup Uncle Ben's Converted Rice,
  washed
1 teaspoon salt
1 teaspoon pepper
Pinch sugar

Melt butter in double boiler, adding onion and green pepper. Cook until transparent and tender (about 15 minutes). Add tomato sauce, water, rice, salt, pepper and sugar. Cook 1½ hours or less, turning occasionally with a fork. This is a very good side dish for meats with no gravy. Serves 6.

Mrs. William L. Watson, III

Wild Rice with Snow Peas

2 (6 ounce) boxes Uncle Ben's
  Long-Grain and Wild Rice
½ cup chopped onion
⅓ cup chopped celery
¼ cup chopped parsley
¼ cup chopped green pepper
2 Tablespoons vegetable oil

½ pound fresh mushrooms,
  sliced
2 Tablespoons butter
1 (8 ounce) can water
  chestnuts, sliced
1 (7 ounce) package frozen
  Chinese pea pods, thawed
½ cup slivered almonds, toasted

Cook rice according to package directions. Sauté the onion, celery, parsley and green pepper in the oil until tender. Sauté the fresh mushrooms in the butter for 5 minutes. Combine the cooked rice, vegetables, mushrooms, water chestnuts and pea pods and toss gently. Spoon into a buttered 2-quart casserole. Dish may be prepared ahead of time to this point. When ready to serve, heat covered in a 350°F oven for 15-20 minutes. Sprinkle with almonds for last 5 minutes of cooking. Serves 8.

Mrs. Robert L. Abney

Western Rice

1 cup Uncle Ben's Converted
  Rice
2 Tablespoons oil
½ cup margarine
2 bunches spring onions, chopped
1 large green pepper, chopped
1 teaspoon Italian seasoning
2 (4 ounce) cans sliced or
  button mushrooms

2 (3 ounce) jars pimientos, cut
  into thin strips
1 Tablespoon soy sauce
1 Tablespoon Worcestershire
  sauce
2 teaspoons salt
¼ teaspoon pepper
1 teaspoon Accent
1 cup chopped parsley

Cook rice according to package directions. Place in colander to steam. In oil and margarine sauté onions first; then add green pepper and cook until tender. Add rest of ingredients except parsley and rice to sautéed vegetables. When ready to serve, add parsley and rice, toss and serve immediately. Casserole may be put together several days ahead, refrigerated and heated at serving time. Freezes well. Serves 8.

Willie Braxton, Little Rock, Arkansas

Wild Rice and Cheese Casserole

1 (6 ounce) box wild rice
½ cup margarine or butter
2 Tablespoons flour
1 cup milk

1 (3 ounce) package cream
  cheese
1 teaspoon salt
1 cup button mushrooms

Cook wild rice according to directions on box (about 25 minutes). Pour into colander and drain well. Melt margarine in top of double boiler; add flour and stir well until it forms a thick paste. Begin to add milk very slowly. Stir constantly. Add cream cheese and stir until melted and sauce is smooth. Add salt. Butter a 1½-quart casserole. Alternate layers of rice, mushrooms and cream sauce. Repeat until dish is filled. Be sure to put generous amount of sauce on top. Bake at 325°F for 20-30 minutes or until mixture is hot throughout and is golden brown on top. Serves 12.

Mrs. Steven H. Brasfield

Substitute 1 (6 ounce) box Uncle Ben's Long-Grain and Wild Rice (cooked by package directions) for the wild rice. Use 3 (3 ounce) packages of cream cheese instead of one.

Mrs. Willard Boggan, Jr.

———

Leftover cooked rice will freeze. To reheat, steam, covered, in a colander until thoroughly heated. Fluff occasionally with a fork.

For a quick curried rice add 1 teaspoon curry powder to ingredients in Basic Boiled Rice, Covered.

Aunt Clemy's Rice

6 Tablespoons butter
1 cup Uncle Ben's Converted
  Rice
1 medium onion, chopped

1 green pepper, chopped
1 (10½ ounce) can cream of
  mushroom soup
1 (10½ ounce) can consommé

Melt butter. Add rice and sauté until golden brown. Place onion and green pepper in a 1½-quart casserole dish. Add the cream of mushroom soup to the rice and stir well. Then add consommé and blend. Pour this mixture into casserole and mix with onion and green pepper. Bake uncovered at 325°F for 1½ hours, stirring once after 45 minutes. Good with beef or barbecued chicken. May be prepared in advance on day of serving. Serves 6.

Mrs. Roger P. Friou

Rice Pilaf

2 cups raw long-grain rice
⅓ cup butter
4 cups chicken broth
¾ cup chopped or coarsely
  ground carrots

¾ cup chopped celery
¾ cup chopped parsley
½ cup chopped green onion
1 cup slivered almonds

Stir rice in melted butter until a little brown. Have casserole very hot and broth boiling; add the rice. Cook, covered, approximately 20 minutes in 350°F oven. Add vegetables and almonds to rice and toss lightly. Place back into oven for 15 or 20 minutes. Serves 12.

Mrs. Marie Allen, Raymond, Mississippi

Garden Rice

1 bunch green onions with
  tops, chopped
1 small green pepper, chopped
1½ pounds zucchini or yellow
  squash (or combination),
  sliced
¾ cup butter or margarine,
  divided
1 (12 ounce) can Mexicorn,
  drained

1 teaspoon lemon-pepper
  seasoning
½ teaspoon coriander
¾ teaspoon leaf oregano
1 teaspoon salt
1 teaspoon dried parsley or
  chopped fresh parsley
1½ cups raw rice

Sauté onions, green pepper and squash in 4 Tablespoons butter until tender. Add corn, seasonings and parsley. Set aside. Cook rice. Place drained rice in large bowl. Pour ½ cup melted butter or margarine over rice and toss lightly. Add vegetables, tossing again. Place in a buttered casserole. Cover. Heat in 350°F oven for 15-20 minutes. Serves 10-12.

Mrs. Charlotte B. Charles

Sausage-Almond Rice Casserole

1 pound bulk sausage
½ cup chopped onion
½ cup chopped celery
1½ cups raw rice

2 (14 ounce) cans chicken
broth
½ cup slivered almonds, toasted
1 Tablespoon soy sauce

Cook sausage, onion and celery until done. Drain and pour into 3-quart covered casserole. Add rice, chicken broth, almonds and soy sauce. When ready to serve, bake in 375°F oven for 45 minutes to 1 hour. May be prepared ahead, refrigerated and baked when ready to use. Serves 6.

Mrs. Betty Nell St. Clair

Green Rice

1 clove garlic, crushed
2 ribs celery, minced
1 medium onion, minced
1 bunch green onions and tops,
   chopped
½ green pepper, minced
½ cup butter
1 cup grated sharp cheese

1 (4 ounce) can sliced
   mushrooms, drained
2 cups cooked rice
1 chicken bouillon cube,
   dissolved in 2 Tablespoons
   hot water
Salt and red pepper to taste

Cook vegetables in butter until limp. Add cheese and mushrooms. Then add rice, chicken bouillon and seasonings. Place in buttered casserole and heat in 350°F oven for 10-15 minutes. Slivered almonds, diced pimiento and slivered water chestnuts may also be added. Serves 6.

Mrs. Rabian Lane

Brazilian Rice

1 (10 ounce) package frozen
   chopped spinach
1 cup raw rice, cooked without
   salt
¼ cup butter or margarine,
   melted
4 eggs, beaten
1 pound cheese, grated

1 cup milk
1 Tablespoon chopped onion
1 Tablespoon Worcestershire
   sauce
2 teaspoons salt
½ teaspoon each marjoram,
   thyme, rosemary

Cook spinach without seasoning and drain well. Combine with remaining ingredients and bake in a 2-quart baking dish at 350°F for 30 minutes. Cut into squares and serve. May be prepared one day in advance. Serves 6-8.

Mrs. Sherman L. Muths, Jr., Gulfport, Mississippi

Parsleyed Rice with Mushrooms

1 green pepper, chopped
1 onion, chopped
3 Tablespoons butter
1½ cups raw rice, cooked
1 (3 ounce) can sliced
 mushrooms, drained

1 cup chopped parsley
2 cups milk
2 cups grated sharp cheese
2 eggs, well beaten
1½ teaspoons salt
Dash pepper

Sauté green pepper and onion in butter. Mix with the rice, mushrooms and parsley. Add milk, cheese, eggs, salt and pepper. Blend together and bake in preheated 325°F oven for 1 hour. Cut into squares and serve. Serves 8.

Mrs. David L. Ross

Hominy Casserole

2 (29 ounce) cans yellow
 hominy, drained
½ cup butter, divided
2 (4 ounce) cans chopped
 green chilies

1 cup sour cream
Salt and pepper to taste
½ cup half and half cream
1 cup grated Monterey Jack
 cheese

Cook hominy briefly in 2 Tablespoons butter. In buttered casserole alternate layers of hominy and green chilies, dotting each layer with remaining butter and sour cream and seasoning with salt and pepper. Pour cream over all and sprinkle with cheese. Bake at 350°F for 25-30 minutes. May be prepared 1 or 2 days ahead. Serve with steak in place of potatoes or rice. Serves 8.

Mrs. Ben McCarty

Baked Grits and Corn Meal

1 cup quick grits, cooked
 according to directions on
 box
⅓ to ½ cup corn meal
⅓ cup margarine

½ teaspoon salt
1⅓ cups milk
3 eggs, beaten
Pinch baking powder (optional)

Stir into the cooked grits while they are still warm the corn meal, margarine, salt and milk. Allow to cool a little; then add eggs. Add baking powder. Pour into greased 2-quart casserole and bake about 1 hour and 20 minutes in preheated 350°F oven until brown and firm. Serve immediately with pat of butter or gravy from meat. Can be cooked ahead and reheated. Doubling this recipe in a larger dish requires more baking time. Good served with broiled or fried chicken, ham, roast, steak, doves, or as brunch dish with eggs and sausage. Serves 7-8.

Mrs. Henry Barksdale

Monterey Rice

1 cup raw rice
1½ pints sour cream
2 (4 ounce) cans chopped
    green chilies, drained

1½ teaspoons salt
½ teaspoon white pepper
12 ounces Monterey Jack
    cheese, thinly sliced

Cook rice. Mix with sour cream, chilies, salt and pepper. In a deep casserole dish, place a layer of rice mixture and top with cheese slices. Repeat layers, ending with a layer of rice mixture. Bake in preheated oven at 350°F for 30-40 minutes. Serves 6.

Mrs. John Mosal, Jr.

Cheese

Cheese Grits Soufflé

2 teaspoons salt
7 cups water
2 cups uncooked grits
1 (6 ounce) roll Kraft nippy cheese
1 (6 ounce) roll Kraft garlic cheese

1 cup butter, melted
4 eggs, well beaten
½ cup milk
Salt and pepper to taste
Yellow food coloring (optional)

Add salt to boiling water and cook grits covered, on low heat, until done (about 25 minutes). Stir in cheese cut into small pieces, butter, eggs, milk, salt and pepper. Spoon into a 3-quart casserole and bake at 350°F for 1 hour. For even fluffier soufflé, separate eggs. Add beaten yolks to grits mixture and fold in stiffly beaten egg whites last. Serves 12.

Mrs. Louis E. Ridgway, Jr.

Gourmet Fettuccine

¼ cup olive oil
4 Tablespoons butter
1 Tablespoon flour
1 cup chicken broth
1 clove garlic, pressed
2 teaspoons lemon juice
1 teaspoon paprika
½ teaspoon salt

¼ teaspoon pepper
¾ cup Prosciutto (or thinly sliced
    ham), in julienne strips
1 (14 ounce) can artichoke
    hearts, sliced
½ cup grated fresh Parmesan
    cheese
6 ounces fettuccine noodles

Cook olive oil, butter, and flour for 3 minutes. Add other ingredients (except noodles). Keep warm. When ready to serve, toss in saucepan with noodles, which have been cooked and drained. Sauce may be prepared ahead. Serve with Veal Marsala, pork chops, steak or Italian dishes. Serves 4-6.

Mrs. W. R. Newman, III

Basic Quiche Pastry

2 cups flour
½ teaspoon salt
Pinch sugar

½ cup butter, chilled
3 Tablespoons shortening, chilled
4 to 5 Tablespoons cold water

Place flour, salt, sugar, butter and shortening into a mixing bowl. Mix together rapidly with fingers. Add cold water 1 Tablespoon at a time and work dough into a large ball. Dough should not be sticky. Chill dough for several hours (dough can be refrigerated for several days). Roll dough out into a circle 1/8 inch thick and 3 inches larger than flan ring. Trim the excess dough and mold the sides of the pastry shell as if making a pie. Prick the bottom of the pastry shell; then fill with buttered brown paper or foil. Fill with dried beans (beans will hold pastry against the mold while cooking). Precook the pastry shell at 400°F for 8-10 minutes. Remove paper and beans. Cool. Pastry shell is ready to be filled. *Do not unmold the flan ring until after the filling has been cooked in the pastry.* Makes one 11-inch shell or two 7-inch shells.

Artichoke Quiche

1 (9 inch) pie shell or Basic
    Quiche Pastry, partially
    cooked
1 bunch green onions and tops,
    minced
2 (6½ ounce) jars marinated
    artichoke hearts, cut in
    thirds (reserve oil)
3 eggs

1½ cups whipping cream
Pinch ground nutmeg
1/8 teaspoon white pepper
1 teaspoon salt
Dash red pepper
½ cup grated Swiss or Cheddar
    cheese
Butter

Prepare pastry shell. Sauté onions in the oil reserved from the artichokes until limp and shiny. Beat the eggs, cream and seasonings in a mixing bowl to blend. Stir in onions and artichoke pieces and check seasonings to taste. Pour into quiche shell. Spread the cheese on top and distribute dots of butter over it. Bake in upper third of preheated 375°F oven for 25-30 minutes, or until puffed and browned. Quiche can be frozen and reheated for 12 minutes but will not puff again. Serves 8.

Mrs. Henry H. Mounger

This makes a beautiful brunch or luncheon dish with Canadian bacon, sautéed cherry tomatoes, fresh fruit and assorted homemade breads.

———

Allow ¼ pound cheese for each 1 cup shredded cheese.

Hard cheese can be frozen. Wrap airtight in small packages or grate and store in convenient serving amounts in freezer.

John Bennett's Quiche Lorraine

2 (9½ inch) pie shells or
  Basic Quiche Pastry,
  partially cooked
¾ pound bacon, finely diced
4 Tablespoons butter,
  preferably unsalted
2 large onions, finely diced
  (about 10 ounces)
3 cloves garlic, finely diced
1¼ cups half and half cream

6 eggs plus 2 egg yolks, well
  beaten
1 cup whipping cream
¾ pound Swiss cheese, grated
3 Tablespoons finely chopped
  fresh parsley
½ teaspoon ground nutmeg
1½ teaspoons salt
1 teaspoon freshly ground
  pepper

Prepare pastry shells. Sauté bacon until crisp; drain and set aside. Melt butter in remaining bacon fat; add onion and garlic, cooking until lightly browned. Drain and cool. Mix with half and half, beaten eggs and yolks and whipping cream. Fold in bacon, grated cheese and parsley. Add seasonings. Pour mixture into partially baked pie shells and bake at 350°F for 30 minutes or until a knife inserted in custard comes out clean. Serves 14-16.

William N. Warren

Crayfish Quiche

1 (10 inch) pie shell or Basic
  Quiche Pastry, partially
  cooked
1 pound shelled crayfish tails
4 Tablespoons minced shallots
3 Tablespoons butter
Salt
Dash ground nutmeg
White pepper
5 Tablespoons dry white wine
½ to ¾ pound mushrooms, sliced

3 or 4 eggs
1½ cups whipping cream
½ Tablespoon tomato purée
  (preferably fresh)
¼ teaspoon salt
Pinch pepper
¼ cup grated Swiss cheese
¼ cup grated Gruyère cheese
½ cup grated fresh Parmesan
  cheese, or less

Prepare pastry shell. Sauté the crayfish and shallots in butter for 2-3 minutes or until tender. Add salt, nutmeg and pepper. Add the wine and cook another minute. Allow to cool. Sauté mushrooms in a small amount of butter and set aside. Beat the eggs in a bowl with cream, tomato purée, salt and pepper. Gradually blend in crayfish and taste for seasoning. Add the sautéed mushrooms to the mixture. Pour the mixture into thè pastry shell and sprinkle the cheeses over it. Bake in the upper third of the oven for 30 minutes at 375°F or until quiche has puffed. Unmold and slip onto rack. Serves 6 as a main course. Serves 8 as a first course.

Mrs. James Keeton

Hamburger Quiche

1 (9 inch) pie shell or Basic
  Quiche Pastry, partially
  cooked
1 pound hamburger meat
⅓ cup minced onion

1 cup shredded sharp Cheddar
  cheese
3 eggs
1 cup whipping cream
1½ teaspoons salt
1/8 teaspoon white pepper

Prepare pastry shell. Preheat oven to 425°F. Brown hamburger meat in skillet, then drain off excess fat. Mix meat and onion. Reserve a small amount and place remaining meat mixture in pastry shell. Sprinkle cheese over meat. Beat eggs, cream and seasonings and pour over meat and cheese. Bake 15 minutes. Reduce oven temperature to 300°F and bake 30 minutes longer. Sprinkle remaining meat on top and bake 5 minutes more. Let pie stand 10 minutes before serving. This quiche is good for family supper with a salad accompaniment. Will freeze. Serves 4-6.

Mrs. Robert H. Thompson, Jr.

Primia Servia

2 (24 ounce) cartons creamed
  cottage cheese
2 pounds sharp Cheddar
  cheese, grated
6 eggs, beaten
6 Tablespoons flour

½ cup butter, melted
Salt to taste
1 (10 ounce) package frozen
  chopped spinach, cooked
  and drained

Mix all ingredients and bake at 350°F for 1 hour. Serve hot. May be prepared 1 day in advance. Serves 12.

Mrs. John Mosal, Jr.

Wild Rice Quiche

1 (10 inch) pie shell or Basic
  Quiche Pastry, partially
  cooked
1 egg, lightly beaten with
  1 Tablespoon water
1 (6 ounce) package long-grain
  and wild rice
2 cloves garlic, minced

2 Tablespoons oil
1 (16 ounce) can Progresso
  Italian-style tomatoes with
  basil
1 (8 ounce) package cream
  cheese, softened
1 teaspoon each salt, pepper
4 eggs, beaten

Glaze pie shell with egg and water mixture and place in 400°F oven for 3 minutes. Cook rice according to package directions. Brown garlic in oil. Add tomatoes, drained and cut up, then cooked rice. Cut up cream cheese into bits and add, stirring until melted. Add salt and pepper. Add beaten eggs and stir in well. Pour into pie shell and bake in 375°F oven for 25 minutes. Will freeze. This quiche is good served with poultry or wild game. Serves 8.

Mrs. Hunter Gates

Crab Quiche

1 (9 inch) pie shell or Basic
   Quiche Pastry, unbaked
4 ounces Swiss cheese, shredded
1 (7½ ounce) can white crab
   meat, drained (or ½ pound
   fresh)
2 green onions with tops, minced

3 eggs, beaten
1 cup half and half cream
½ teaspoon salt
½ teaspoon grated lemon rind
¼ teaspoon dry mustard
Pinch mace
¼ cup slivered almonds

Prepare pastry shell. Sprinkle cheese evenly over bottom of pastry shell. Top with crab meat and sprinkle with green onions. Combine remaining ingredients except almonds and pour over crab meat. Sprinkle almonds over top. Bake in a 350°F oven until custard sets (about 40 minutes). Let stand after removing from oven about 15 minutes before cutting. Serves 6 generously.

Mrs. Bob Carroll

Rosa's Macaroni Pie

1½ cups uncooked macaroni
4 Tablespoons margarine, melted
1 pound sharp Cheddar cheese,
   grated

2 eggs
1 cup milk
Salt and pepper to taste (at least
   1½ teaspoons salt)

Cook macaroni until done. While still hot, add the margarine and all but ½ cup cheese. Mix well. Beat the eggs and add to macaroni mixture. Add milk and seasonings. Return to stove and cook, stirring, over medium heat for 3 minutes. Pour into greased 1½-quart casserole and sprinkle with remaining cheese. Bake in 350°F oven until cheese has melted (about 20 minutes). Serves 6.

Mrs. R. Baxter Brown

Mystery Casserole

1 (5 ounce) package Ronco
   medium egg noodles
1½ teaspoons salt
½ cup butter or margarine
1 cup chopped pecans
¾ cup chopped parsley (or 3
   Tablespoons dried)

3 cloves garlic, chopped (or 1
   teaspoon garlic powder)
6 soda crackers, crushed
Salt and pepper
Grated Parmesan cheese
1 cup half and half cream

Cook noodles in salted water until done. Drain and rinse with hot water. Melt the butter in a saucepan and sauté the pecans, parsley, garlic and cracker crumbs for about 5 minutes. In a buttered 1½-quart casserole place a layer of ⅓ of the noodles and top with ⅓ the pecan mixture. Salt and pepper the layer; then sprinkle liberally with Parmesan cheese. Repeat 2 more times. Pour cream over assembled casserole and run knife around sides to insure saturation. Bake covered 45 minutes to 1 hour in 350°F oven. Serves 6.

Mrs. John Bookhart

Game

Basic Handling of Game

ALL GAME   Clean as quickly as possible after killing. Rinse thoroughly until water runs clear; then cook or freeze. Freeze small game in water to prevent freezer burn. Wrap large cuts of meat in plastic wrap, then in freezer paper, sealing all seams and making the package as airtight as possible. Do not keep game frozen more than a year. Most game must be cooked slowly to make it more juicy and tender.

DOVES   After cleaning, soak overnight in salted water in refrigerator. Cook 1½-2 hours at a low temperature. Wrap each bird in a piece of bacon while cooking to add flavor and fat. 3-4 birds are needed per serving.

DUCK   Soak in pan of cold water with 2 teaspoons baking soda and 2 teaspoons salt added for 20 minutes to help purify and remove wild taste. To prevent dryness, baste with cooking juices or liquid while cooking and roast breast-side-down. Stuff with pieces of either celery, apple or onion (or a combination) while roasting to remove excessive wild flavor. One duck serves 2.

QUAIL   As for dove, soak in salted water overnight. Quail are best smothered, roasted or fried. Allow 2 quail per serving.

SQUIRREL   Quarter the squirrel and fry or combine with vegetables in a stew. Allow ½ squirrel per person.

VENISON   Marinate in wine or wine vinegar or soak in vinegar water (1 part vinegar to 3 parts water) overnight or for several hours to remove excessive wild taste. Prepare as one would any meat. One pound venison serves 2.

Sauce for Wild Game

1 pint cider vinegar	5 ounces Louisiana hot sauce
Juice of 3 lemons	1 ounce soy sauce
1 ounce black pepper	2 Tablespoons salt
10 ounces Worcestershire sauce	2 Tablespoons sugar

Combine all ingredients and refrigerate. This is a good marinade for any wild game or meat. Keeps indefinitely. Makes 1 quart.

Mrs. A. M. White

Tart or sweet and sour fruit is the best garnish or accompaniment for game. Use such jellies as currant, gooseberry, sour plum or apple.

Mississippi Pan-Broiled Quail

Quail
Salt and pepper

4 Tablespoons butter for each
quail

Clean and dry quail thoroughly. Sprinkle each with salt and pepper on both sides. Melt butter in large iron skillet. Place quail in skillet (breasts down) and cook over medium heat until brown. Turn over and brown other sides. Turn breasts down again, cover and cook until done. Pour brown butter on crisp toast and top with quail. Serve 1 or 2 quail per person.

Mrs. William B. Fontaine

Doves in Orange Sauce

12 doves, cleaned and rinsed
4 Tablespoons butter

1½ teaspoons salt
2 cups orange juice

Brown doves in butter in heavy skillet. Add salt and orange juice. Cover tightly. Bake at 325°F about 1½ hours. Serves 6-8.

Mrs. James L. Moore

Delicious Baked Dove

18 doves
2 Tablespoons butter
2 Tablespoons cooking oil
Salt and pepper
1/8 teaspoon garlic salt
Juice and grated rind of
½ lemon

2 teaspoons liquid smoke
1 Tablespoon Worcestershire
sauce
4 strips bacon
¼ cup sherry wine
¼ cup water

Brown doves in a mixture of butter and oil; salt and pepper liberally while browning. Remove doves to a baking dish. Sprinkle with garlic salt, lemon juice and rind, liquid smoke, Worcestershire sauce and more salt and pepper. Cover the doves with bacon. Deglaze the skillet in which the doves were browned with the sherry and water. Pour over doves. Cover and bake in a 325°F oven for 1½ hours. Serves 6.

Mrs. William S. Cook

GRILLED QUAIL

Cook quail over a low charcoal fire for 30 minutes. Baste frequently with a mixture of the juice of 3 lemons, ½ cup butter and ½ teaspoon salt.

Smothered Dove

12 doves
6 Tablespoons butter
3 Tablespoons flour

2 cups chicken broth
½ cup sherry wine
Salt and pepper to taste

Brown doves in heavy skillet or Dutch oven in melted butter. Remove doves to baking dish, breast down. Add flour to skillet and stir well. Slowly add chicken broth, sherry, salt and pepper; blend well and pour over doves. Cover baking dish and bake at 350°F at least 1 hour. Serve over cooked rice. Serves 4.

Mrs. Frank M. Duke

Smothered Quail

Salt and pepper
6 to 8 cleaned quail
Flour

½ cup butter
Milk

Salt and pepper quail all over and roll in flour. Melt butter in very large skillet with a lid and brown quail over medium heat. Remove quail from skillet and add 3 Tablespoons (or more) flour and salt and pepper to taste. Brown flour lightly and slowly stir in enough milk to make a white gravy. Add more salt and pepper if needed. Return quail to skillet and roll in the gravy; cover skillet. Simmer on low heat for 45 minutes, basting every 15 minutes. Serve the gravy on rice and biscuits. Serves 3-4.

Thomas E. Ward

This is the old Southern way to fix quail. It is simple but very good.

Quail in Wine

Salt and pepper
Flour
6 to 8 quail
6 Tablespoons butter
2 cups sliced fresh mushrooms

1 cup Madeira wine
1 cup consommé
1 rib celery, quartered
1 thin slice lemon per bird
Chopped parsley

Lightly salt, pepper and flour each bird; then brown until golden in melted butter. (If butter burns in this process, discard and replace with 2-3 more Tablespoons.) Remove birds to baking dish. Sauté mushrooms in remaining butter; add wine and consommé and bring to boil. Pour over birds. Add celery and lemon slices; sprinkle with parsley. Cover and bake at 350°F for 1 hour or until tender. When done, remove celery and lemon slices from sauce. Serve with wild rice topped with sauce. Serves 4.

Mrs. James L. Teague

Mom's Dove Pie

12 whole doves or breasts
1 Tablespoon salt
1 small onion, quartered
1 rib celery, sliced
1 bay leaf
3 to 4 peppercorns
Pie pastry for double-crust pie

4 Tablespoons butter, sliced,
  plus enough to dot pastry
1 pint oysters
Salt and pepper to taste
2 Tablespoons flour
¼ cup minced parsley
Paprika

Cover doves with water. Add salt, onion, celery, bay leaf and peppercorns and bring to a boil. Cover and simmer until doves are tender (45-50 minutes). Cool in broth. Line a greased deep 1½-quart casserole with pastry and dot with butter. Drain doves. Strain and reserve broth. Drain oysters and stuff each dove with 3-4 oysters. Place in pastry-lined baking dish with any remaining oysters. Sprinkle generously with salt and pepper. Blend 2 cups reserved dove broth with flour. Pour over doves. Add parsley and 4 Tablespoons sliced butter and cover with top pastry. Dot with butter and sprinkle with paprika. Bake at 350°F for 45 minutes. Serves 4.

Mrs. James L. Enochs, Jr.

Bean City Ducks

2 mallard ducks
½ cup vegetable oil
Salt and pepper
½ cup butter
1 large apple, peeled and
  chopped
1 large turnip, peeled and
  chopped
1 onion, chopped

2 ribs celery, chopped
1 medium potato, peeled and
  chopped
1 green pepper, chopped
2 large carrots, peeled and
  chopped
1 orange, sliced
4 strips bacon

Place each duck on a large piece of aluminum foil. Rub ducks with oil, salt and pepper. Stuff each with 4 Tablespoons butter and a mixture of apple and vegetables. Place remaining vegetables and orange slices around each duck and cross 2 strips bacon over each. Wrap tightly in foil so that no juices can escape. Bake at 300°F for 1½ hours. Serve hot. Serve vegetables used for stuffing over bed of long grain and wild rice. Serves 4.

James H. Creekmore

———

A delicious duck sauce can be made by adding 1 cup fig-orange marmalade to the pan drippings from baked duck.

159

Duck 'n Orange Sauce

4 wild ducks
Celery
Onion
Apple slices

Salt and pepper
Bacon
Worcestershire sauce

Wash and dry the ducks. Stuff each duck with equal amounts of celery, onion and apple. Salt and pepper all over and place bacon strips over the top of each. Place in baking pan. Add about ½ inch of water to the bottom of the pan and sprinkle with enough Worcestershire sauce to slightly color the water. Cook ducks at 300° or 325°F for about 2 hours, basting every 30 to 45 minutes. When done, remove stuffing from duck and discard. Reserve bacon and place around duck for serving. Serve with ORANGE SAUCE. Serves 8.

ORANGE SAUCE

⅔ cup brown sugar
⅔ cup white sugar
2 Tablespoons flour

2 cups orange juice
Dash salt
A little grated orange peel

Combine ingredients and simmer until thickened. Spoon over duck slices.

Mrs. Edward J. Peters

Wild Duck Skewers

1 Tablespoon curry powder
1 Tablespoon chili powder
1 teaspoon freshly ground
   black pepper
⅔ cup soy sauce
⅓ cup lime juice

2 Tablespoons honey
⅔ cup olive oil, divided
1 cup chopped onion
3 cloves garlic, chopped or minced
4 mallard ducks

Place curry powder, chili powder, black pepper, soy sauce, lime juice, honey and ⅓ cup olive oil in a jar; shake vigorously to blend. Sauté onion and garlic in remaining olive oil; add to jar. Remove each duck breast half as intact as possible from bone and skin. Cut each half into 2 strips. Combine with marinade and refrigerate for 3 hours. Thread each strip on bamboo skewers which have been soaked 1 hour in water. Grill over hot coals with grill top down. (If using gas grill, preheat to high.) Cook 3-4 minutes on each side. Do not overcook, as this is best served rare to medium rare. Heat remaining marinade and serve in gravy boat. Serves 6-8.

Mrs. Joseph L. Speed

Note: By cutting each breast half into 3 strips and cutting cooking time to 2-3 minutes per side, recipe will make 24 skewers and can be used as an appetizer. Remaining duck carcass may be used in gumbo or duck pie.

Ducks Burgundy

2 wild ducks
4 Tablespoons butter
4 Tablespoons flour
2 cups chicken broth
1 cup Burgundy wine
4 Tablespoons chopped onion

2 small bay leaves
½ teaspoon salt
Dash pepper
1 (6 ounce) can sliced
  mushrooms

Simmer ducks, covered, in small amount of salted water for 30 minutes and drain. Brown ducks in butter, then remove. Blend flour into butter. Add broth, Burgundy, onion, bay leaves, salt and pepper. Cook and stir until thick and bubbly. Add mushrooms and ducks. Cover and cook over low heat 2 hours or until tender. May be served over wild rice. Freezes well after cooking. Serves 4-6.

Mrs. William L. Crim

Gus's Wild Ducks with Turnips

4 wild ducks
Salt and pepper
½ cup butter
6 medium turnips
1 (16 ounce) jar small white
  onions or 6 small white
  onions

Sugar
1½ cups white wine
Juice of 1 lemon
1 quart beef stock
6 ounces fresh mushrooms
Butter

Season ducks inside and out with salt and pepper. Using 2 skillets with 4 Tablespoons butter in each, brown the ducks on all sides and set aside. Peel turnips and quarter. Roll the turnips and the onions in sugar. Brown in skillet in the butter in which the ducks were browned for about 15-20 minutes. Add more butter if needed. Set vegetables aside. Divide the wine between the 2 skillets and deglaze the pans, adding the lemon juice to each. Boil the liquid down in each skillet until it is reduced by half. In separate pan boil down the beef stock and reduce it to 2 cups. Add the beef stock to the wine. Remove ducks to roasting pan breast side up and pour gravy over them. Cover pan with foil and cook ducks in a preheated 300°F oven for 1 hour. For last 30 minutes of cooking add the onions to the pan. For the last 20 minutes of cooking add the turnips. Last 10 minutes remove the foil, baste ducks, turn oven up to 400°F and brown ducks. Do not overcook. Stop when the juices run out clear when pricked. Sauté fresh mushrooms in additional butter and add to ducks when cooking is completed. Remove ducks from pan; cool. Bone out both sides of breasts. While cutting up the ducks, boil down the juices to thicken. Serve duck breasts with the gravy and garnish with onions, turnips and mushrooms. Ducks may be cooked a day ahead and breast halves warmed in gravy to serve. Serves 8.

Gus Primos

Joanna's Duck Pie

3 wild ducks, well cleaned
1 large onion, chopped
3 to 4 ribs celery, sliced
Salt and pepper
Sliced water chestnuts (optional)
Canned early green peas
 (optional)

Parsley (optional)
Chopped green onions
 (optional)
2 Tablespoons flour or
 1 Tablespoon cornstarch
Pie pastry for 1-crust pie

Cover ducks with water; add onion, celery, salt and pepper. Bring to a boil, cover and simmer until tender. When ducks are cool enough to handle, remove all meat and place in a shallow baking dish. Add some of the onion and celery from the broth. Also add optional ingredients in any amount and combination desired. Strain broth and skim off grease. To about 2 cups strained broth, add flour or cornstarch and shake in a jar until smooth. Pour over but do not cover duck meat. Cover top of casserole with pie pastry. Bake at 325°F until crust is nicely browned. Older ducks are perfect for this recipe. Serves 6.

Mrs. Joseph L. Speed

Barbecued Duck Breasts

1 (10½ ounce) can onion soup
½ cup ketchup
¼ cup margarine
4 drops Tabasco
¼ teaspoon salt
2 cloves garlic, finely chopped

¼ teaspoon freshly ground
 pepper
1 medium green pepper,
 finely chopped (optional)
4 wild ducks
8 slices bacon

Combine in saucepan first 8 ingredients. Bring to boil and simmer about 10 minutes, stirring often. Remove from heat and allow to cool while preparing ducks. Remove each breast half from duck as intact as possible, removing skin if preferred. Wrap each breast side with a slice of bacon and secure with toothpick. Cover breasts with sauce and marinate 3 hours in refrigerator. Grill over hot coals 3-4 minutes on each side for rare to medium. (Duck is juicy and best when pink.) Reheat remaining marinade for gravy. Marinating time may be adjusted to suit each individual's taste. Using the freshest of ducks or properly frozen ones is most important. Remaining duck carcass may be used for gumbo or duck pie. Serves 4-8.

Mrs. Joseph L. Speed

Warm a glass of currant jelly with about ½ as much port wine. Serve hot with any kind of game.

Breasts of Wild Duck

2 wild ducks
10 Tablespoons butter, divided
2 Tablespoons oil
1 onion, roughly chopped
2 carrots, roughly chopped
1 rib celery, roughly chopped
2 leeks or green onions, roughly
chopped
2 cloves garlic
1 teaspoon coarse salt
3 peppercorns

Bouquet garni (¼ teaspoon
thyme leaves, 2 whole cloves,
5 sprigs parsley, ½ bay leaf)
½ cup dry white wine
3½ to 4 cups homemade
chicken stock
4 Tablespoons flour
3 Tablespoons imported
Madeira wine
Salt and pepper

Skin and debone the breasts of the ducks. Remove the membrane from the fillet of the breasts. Set aside. Chop the bones that remain and brown them in a large pan in 2 Tablespoons of butter and the oil. Add the vegetables to the pan along with the salt, peppercorns and bouquet garni. Brown the vegetables; then add the white wine and enough chicken stock to cover the bones. Simmer for at least 2 hours. Strain and degrease the stock. Make a brown roux of the flour and 4 Tablespoons of butter. Off the heat, add the hot stock to the hot roux. Cook over low temperature for 1 hour or more, reducing the sauce until it is just thick enough to coat a spoon. When ready to serve, add Madeira and taste for salt and pepper. This sauce may be cooked a day or two ahead and freezes well. When ready to serve, dip the duck breasts in 4 Tablespoons melted butter. Salt and pepper them and place in a single layer, not touching, in a baking pan. Cover with buttered parchment. Cook in a preheated 400°F oven for about 15 minutes. Do not overcook; the breasts should be rare. Cooked this way the breasts will always be juicy and tender. Serve immediately with the duck sauce. Serves 4.

Mrs. Clarence H. Webb, Jr.

Venison Cutlets

Venison (any cut)
1 egg
½ cup milk
1 (4 ounce) package soda
crackers, crushed

½ cup flour
Oil
1 lemon
Salt and pepper

Cut venison into slices about ¼ inch thick and hamburger patty size. Remove *all* fat from meat. Pound thoroughly with a tenderizing hammer. Mix egg and milk in bowl and dip venison slices into mixture. Remove and roll in cracker and flour mixture. Fry in hot cooking oil until golden brown, turning once. Remove and place on paper towel to drain. Squeeze lemon juice on venison immediately after removing from skillet; salt and pepper to taste and serve.

Heber Simmons, Jr.

Barbecued Venison Steaks

Venison hindquarter
Lawry's unseasoned tenderizer
  (optional)
Pepper (optional)
MULE JAIL BARBECUE
  SAUCE:
1 pound butter or margarine
2 cups water

1 (5 ounce) bottle
  Worcestershire sauce
Juice of 6 lemons (reserve rinds
  of 3)
2 onions, quartered
2 teaspoons salt
½ teaspoon pepper

Slice hindquarter across the grain into steaks ½ inch thick. Trim all fat and gristle. Tenderize and lightly pepper each side at this point, if desired. Make MULE JAIL BARBECUE SAUCE by melting butter in saucepan. Add remaining ingredients, including lemon rinds, and bring to a boil. Turn off heat immediately. Cook steaks over charcoal grill, with hickory chips added, basting with sauce. Steaks should be cooked medium to medium well in order to be juicy and tender. Cooked well done, they will be tough. Sauce is also good spread on toasted bread.

Mrs. Lewis L. Culley, Jr.

Venison Stroganoff

2 pounds venison steak
1 teaspoon salt
5 Tablespoons flour, divided
4 Tablespoons butter, divided
2 cups sliced mushrooms
1 cup chopped onion

3 cloves garlic, minced
2 Tablespoons tomato paste
2 cups beef stock
2 cups sour cream
3 Tablespoons cooking sherry

Cut venison into ¼-inch strips; salt and dust with 2 Tablespoons flour. In heated heavy skillet add 2 Tablespoons butter and place steak strips in skillet, browning quickly on all sides. Add mushrooms, onion and garlic. Cook 3-4 minutes until onion is barely tender. Remove meat and add remaining butter to pan drippings. Blend in remaining flour, tomato paste and beef stock. Stir mixture constantly until it thickens. Return meat to skillet. Stir in sour cream and sherry and heat briefly. Serve with rice or noodles, if desired. Serves 4.

Billy Joe Cross, Clinton, Mississippi

Squirrel, a delicate meat, is one of the most nutritious meats because of the squirrel's straight diet of pine nuts.

Smoked Venison

Venison (any cut)
Dry wine
½ cup cooking oil
¼ cup lemon juice

1 teaspoon black pepper
Sour cream
Hot pepper jelly

Marinate venison in wine for at least 24 hours. Prepare a light fire in covered grill. Place meat on spit and cook, basting with sauce made with oil, lemon juice and black pepper. When the meat gets warm, add wet hickory chips to the fire (and more briquets as necessary to keep an even heat). Smoke venison for 3 hours with continued basting. Remove meat from spit and baste with wine. Wrap in foil and allow meat to cool to room temperature. Reheat, when ready to serve, in foil for 20 minutes at 250°F. To serve, place a dab of sour cream and a teaspoon of hot pepper jelly on each piece of meat.

Jack McIntyre, Sr., Utica, Mississippi

Excellent Rabbit

1 rabbit, cut in pieces
1 medium onion, sliced
4 whole cloves
4 peppercorns
1 bay leaf
½ teaspoon mace

1 cup dry red wine
1 cup water
Salt and pepper
Flour
½ cup butter or margarine

Place rabbit in glass or plastic container. Combine next 7 ingredients and pour over rabbit. Let marinate in refrigerator for 2-12 hours, turning several times. The longer it stands, the better the flavor. Remove rabbit from marinade and pat dry. Season with salt and pepper and sprinkle with flour. Brown on all sides in butter in heavy skillet. Strain marinade and add to rabbit. Cover and simmer rabbit about 45 minutes until tender. Good served with rice or hot grits. Serves 4.

Mrs. James L. Enochs, Orange Beach, Alabama

EASY VENISON CHILI

Sauté 1 cup each minced green pepper and minced green onion in a little oil. Add 2 pounds ground venison and sear until brown. Add 1 (8 ounce) can tomato sauce, 2 cups water and all packets in 1 package 2-Alarm chili mix. Cook about 1 hour over low heat. Serve on buns.

———

Venison which is overcooked or started with not enough heat will be tough.

Pheasant with Scotch Whiskey

4 Tablespoons butter
Salt and pepper to taste
1 pheasant, cleaned and
    quartered (or an equal
    amount of any game
    bird except duck)

½ cup consommé or 3 chicken
    bouillon cubes
½ cup Scotch whiskey (or any
    wine or whiskey preferred)

Melt butter in heavy frying pan on low heat (an electric skillet may be used). Salt and pepper pheasant quarters and add to skillet. Turn heat up to 260°F and sauté, uncovered, turning frequently until golden brown on all sides. While pheasant is browning, line a small roasting pan (or any oven-proof pan with lid of an appropriate size) with aluminum foil. Transfer the sautéed bird to the roaster. Add enough water to cover the meat about halfway. Add the consommé or bouillon cubes. Add whiskey at this point, or pour it over the birds about 30 minutes before the end of the cooking period if a stronger taste is desired. Seal tightly with foil and a lid. Place in a 350°F oven for about 3 hours. The liquid from the pan is a wonderful addition to gravy. Serve pheasant with tongs or large serving spoon as the meat is very moist and tender and easily falls off the bone. Serve with wild rice. Serves 3-4.

Mrs. John F. Anderson, Jr.

Squirrel Mulligan

6 large squirrels, cut up
1 pound butter or margarine
3 teaspoons salt
6 medium potatoes, peeled and
    chopped
6 medium onions, chopped
1 cup chopped celery

1 quart peeled tomatoes,
    chopped
1 (17 ounce) can cream-style
    corn
1 teaspoon red pepper
3 Tablespoons sugar
1 cup bread crumbs

Cook squirrels slowly in large pot with just enough water to cover the squirrels. Add butter and salt and cook until tender. Cool. Remove meat from bones and return to stock. Add potatoes, onions and celery. Cook slowly until vegetables are tender. Add tomatoes, corn, pepper and sugar. Bring to a boil. Simmer on low heat until mushy. Thicken with bread crumbs. Serve with green salad and garlic bread. Serves 8.

Billy Joe Cross, Clinton, Mississippi

FRIED QUAIL, DOVE OR SQUIRREL

Sprinkle quail, dove or squirrel pieces liberally with seasoned salt. Soak overnight in a mixture of 1 egg beaten with ½ cup milk. Drain, dip in pancake flour and fry in deep fat (375°F) for about 10 minutes.

Poultry

My Mother's Chicken Spaghetti

(The Dish Mother Used to Make)
Craig Claiborne

Recently, we were interviewed on a radio program, and when the subject veered around to childhood foods, we described in some detail the dish that had given us most pleasure in early youth and adolescence and still gives us comfort as we approach senility. It was a family creation known as chicken spaghetti. It consisted of spaghetti or spaghettini and sometimes vermicelli baked in a casserole, layered with a tomato and cream sauce, a meat sauce, boneless chicken and two kinds of grated cheese. It was almost always served when large numbers were invited for special occasions. Subsequent to the program we received numerous requests for the recipe and discovered with some astonishment that we had somehow never had occasion to use it in a story. The recipe follows.

1 (3½ pound) chicken with
　giblets
Chicken broth
Salt
3 cups canned tomatoes,
　preferably Italian peeled
7 Tablespoons butter, divided
3 Tablespoons flour
½ cup whipping cream
1/8 teaspoon grated nutmeg
Freshly ground pepper to taste
½ pound fresh mushrooms or
　canned button mushrooms,
　drained
2 cups finely chopped onion

1½ cups finely chopped celery
1½ cups chopped green pepper
1 Tablespoon or more finely
　minced garlic
¼ pound ground beef
¼ pound ground pork
1 bay leaf
½ teaspoon hot red pepper
　flakes (optional)
1 pound spaghetti or
　spaghettini
½ pound Cheddar cheese,
　grated (about 2 to 2½ cups)
Grated Parmesan cheese

One of the stipulations in the original recipe for this dish is that all the ingredients be combined at least 4 hours before baking. Place the chicken with neck, gizzard, heart and liver in a kettle; add chicken broth to cover and salt to taste. Bring to the boil and simmer until the chicken is tender without being dry, 35-45 minutes. Cool. Remove the chicken and take the meat from the bones. Shred the meat, cover and set aside. Return the skin and bones to the kettle and cook the stock down 30 minutes or longer. There should be 4-6 cups of broth. Strain and reserve the broth. Place tomatoes in a saucepan and cook down to half the original volume, stirring. There should be 1½ cups. Melt 3 Tablespoons butter in a saucepan and add the flour, stirring to blend with a wire whisk. When smooth, add 1 cup of the reserved hot broth and the cream, stirring rapidly with the whisk. When thickened and smooth, add the nutmeg, salt and pepper. Continue cooking, stirring occasionally, about 10 minutes. Set aside. If fresh mushrooms are not available, as they frequently weren't when this recipe was prepared some 50 years ago, use drained canned button mushrooms. If the mushrooms are very small or button mushrooms, leave them whole. Otherwise, cut them in half or quarter them. Heat 1 Tablespoon butter in a small skillet and add the mushrooms. Cook, shaking the skillet occasionally and stirring the mushrooms until they are golden brown. Set aside. Heat 3 Tablespoons butter in a deep skillet and add the onions. Cook, stirring, until wilted. Add the celery and green pepper and cook, stirring, about 5 minutes. Do not overcook. The vegetables should remain crisp-tender. Add the garlic, beef and pork and cook, stirring and chopping down with the edge of a large metal spoon to break up the meat. Cook just until the meat loses its red color. Add the bay leaf and red pepper flakes. Add the tomatoes and the white sauce made with the chicken broth. Add the mushrooms. Cook the spaghetti or spaghettini in boiling salted water until it is just tender. Do not overcook. It will cook again when blended with the chicken and meat sauce. Drain the spaghetti and run under cold running water. Spoon enough of the meat sauce over the bottom of a 5 or 6-quart casserole to cover it lightly. Add about ⅓ of the spaghetti. Add about ⅓ of the shredded chicken, a layer of meat sauce, a layer of grated Cheddar cheese and another layer of spaghetti. Continue making layers, ending with a layer of spaghetti topped with a thin layer of meat sauce and cheese. Pour in up to 2 cups of the reserved chicken broth or enough to almost but not quite cover the top layer of spaghetti. *Cover and let the spaghetti stand for 4 hours or longer.* If the liquid is absorbed as the dish stands, add a little more chicken broth. When this dish is baked and served, the sauce will be just a bit soupy rather than thick and clinging. When ready to bake, preheat the oven to 350°F. Place the spaghetti casserole on top of the stove and bring it just to the boil. Cover and place it in the oven. Bake 15 minutes and uncover. Bake 15 minutes longer or until the casserole is hot and bubbling throughout and starting to brown on top. Serve immediately with grated Parmesan cheese on the side. Yields 12 or more servings.

*From CRAIG CLAIBORNE'S FAVORITES
FROM THE NEW YORK TIMES, VOL. II*

Craig Claiborne, author of seven cookbooks, restaurant critic and food editor of the NEW YORK TIMES for about twenty years, was born in Sunflower, Mississippi, and grew up in nearby Indianola. He now resides in Springs on Long Island, New York.

RICH CHICKEN BROTH Made by combining the bony parts of the chicken such as backs, necks and wings with water to cover a depth of about 1 inch above the pieces, adding salt to taste and simmering to the desired richness of flavor. Vegetables such as chopped celery, carrots, leeks, an onion stuck with cloves, peppercorns and parsley sprigs may also be added with the water, and although they will improve the flavor of the broth, they are not essential.

To Bake a Turkey

1 (11 to 12 pound) turkey
(Swift's Butterball
recommended)

Wesson oil
Salt and pepper

Preheat oven to 325°F. Remove giblets from turkey; set aside for gravy. Wash and dry turkey well and rub inside and out with Wesson oil, salt and pepper. Make dressing and spoon dressing into neck cavity. Bring skin of neck over back and fasten with poultry pin. Spoon dressing into body cavity. *Do not pack.* Bake any leftover dressing in covered casserole. With long piece of twine, lace cavity closed, bootlace fashion; tie with knot. Fasten wings of turkey to body with poultry pins. With twine, tie ends of legs together. Brush turkey generously all over with Wesson oil. Roast turkey on rack in roasting pan breast side up, allowing 25 minutes per pound for a 12-pound turkey. When turkey begins to brown, cover loosely with a square of foil. Turkey is done when meat thermometer registers 185°-190°F, leg joint moves freely when twisted and fleshy part of drumstick feels soft. When fork is inserted in meatiest part of the breast closest to the bone, the juices should run clear. Remove from oven and let stand 20-30 minutes before slicing.

Mrs. Townsend Stallworth

Southern Corn Bread Dressing

5 cups crumbled corn bread
4 cups toasted bread pieces
1½ cups chicken stock
1½ cups chopped onion
1⅓ cups chopped celery
1 green pepper, chopped
10 Tablespoons margarine,
    divided
⅓ cup chopped parsley
½ teaspoon sage

½ teaspoon thyme
Salt and pepper to taste
2 eggs, beaten
2 hard-boiled eggs, chopped
1 (1 pint) jar raw oysters,
    simmered until edges curl
    (optional)
Turkey giblets, cooked and
    chopped (optional)

Soak corn bread and bread pieces in chicken stock. Cook onion, celery and green pepper in 2 Tablespoons margarine until tender. Mix together the breads, cooked vegetables, remaining margarine, melted, and rest of ingredients, using the oysters or giblets, if desired. Use dressing to stuff turkey. Or shape into patties, place in greased casserole and bake uncovered at 400°F for about an hour or until as done as desired. Serves 12.

The Editors

To clarify chicken stock, combine 3 quarts stock with 2 egg whites and shells. Cook for 10 minutes, remove from heat and let stand for 10 minutes, allowing egg particles to sink to bottom. Strain through several layers of cheesecloth.

Oyster Dressing for Turkey

10 to 12 slices white bread
4 to 6 dozen oysters (reserve
    liquid)
4 large onions
1 whole bunch celery
1 small green pepper
4 or 5 sprigs parsley
1 clove garlic
2 green onions

6 to 8 Tablespoons butter
1 Tablespoon Crisco
½ pound ground beef
½ teaspoon curry powder
¼ teaspoon thyme
1 bay leaf, broken
Salt and pepper to taste
Dash cayenne pepper

Place bread in oven at 300 °F to dry out and toast to a golden brown. Remove and cool. Scald oysters in their own liquid. Grind or cut fine the onions, celery, green pepper, parsley, garlic and green onions. Sauté in combined butter and Crisco. Add ground beef. Cook on low heat for approximately 1 hour. Grind or chop oysters. Strain oyster liquid over crumbled bread. Add bread and oysters to cooked vegetables. Add curry powder, thyme, bay leaf, salt, pepper and cayenne pepper. If dressing is not moist enough, add a little milk. Stuff turkey with dressing. Bake any leftover dressing in baking dish for about 1 hour at 400 °F. Also excellent stuffed in celery. Makes enough dressing for a 10-12 pound turkey.

Mrs. Earl P. Bartlett, Sr., Metairie, Louisiana

Smoked Turkey

Juice of 1 lemon
1 teaspoon red pepper
1 teaspoon black pepper
2 teaspoons prepared mustard
1 or 2 cloves garlic, pressed
½ teaspoon sugar

½ teaspoon salt
2 teaspoons flour
White wine vinegar
1 cup margarine, melted
1 (12 to 16 pound) turkey

In a one-cup measuring cup combine first 8 ingredients. Fill to the 1 cup mark with wine vinegar. Mix well by shaking in a jar. Add marinade to the melted margarine and cook until thickened. Place turkey on charcoal grill, adding several hickory chips that have been soaked in water to the fire. Cook turkey for 1 hour; then begin basting frequently with the marinade, being sure to saturate the cavity. Cook over medium fire until a meat thermometer registers *almost* done (between 4½-5½ hours for this size turkey). Take off fire and let sit at least 15 minutes before serving. The turkey can be marinated overnight, but cover it with a foil tent for the first hour of cooking so that it will not get too brown.

Mrs. Joseph L. Speed

Add leftover stuffing to soups to enhance their flavor and thicken them.

Grandmother's Turkey Hash on Waffles

4 Tablespoons butter
½ cup flour
1 quart turkey or chicken stock
½ Tablespoon salt
¼ teaspoon pepper
½ teaspoon paprika

8 cups diced cooked turkey
¼ cup chopped pimiento
¼ pound mushrooms, fresh or
   canned
1½ Tablespoons chopped
   parsley

In a double boiler melt butter and slowly add flour to make a thick paste. Add turkey stock, stirring constantly to prevent lumping, and cook until smooth. Season with salt, pepper and paprika. Add remaining ingredients. (If fresh mushrooms are used, prepare by sautéing until brown in additional melted butter.) Heat thoroughly over boiling water and keep hot until ready to serve. Serve hash over waffles or patty shells. May be prepared in advance. Serves 15.

Mrs. F. Coleman Lowery, Jr.

This is Grandmother's recipe which has been used for 65 years at special family gatherings. It is a good use for leftover turkey.

Glazed Cornish Hens

1 cup wild rice
6 to 8 cups boiling water
2½ teaspoons salt, divided
1 cup raw rice
1 medium onion, chopped
2 (4 ounce) cans sliced
   mushrooms, drained or
   ½ pound fresh, sliced

1¾ cups butter, melted, divided
½ cup slivered almonds
8 Cornish hens
¼ teaspoon pepper
½ cup bourbon
1 chicken bouillon cube
   (optional)
8 Tablespoons currant jelly

Wash wild rice thoroughly. Pour into boiling water with 1 teaspoon salt added and cover. Cook 15 minutes. Add white rice. Cook 30 minutes longer. Sauté onion and mushrooms 5 minutes in ¼ cup butter. Stir in almonds, then the cooked and drained rice. Stir until mixed. Stuff cavity of hens with rice mixture and lace with string or skewers. Tie legs together and make triangle out of wings behind neck. Place hens on shallow baking sheet, breast side up. Mix remaining salt and pepper with ½ cup butter and pour over hens. Place in 425°F oven. Roast for 20 minutes, basting 3 times with bourbon mixed with remaining cup of butter. Reduce heat to 350°F; roast for 30 minutes more, basting every 15 minutes with bourbon and butter mixture. Turn breast side down. Roast for 15 minutes more. If drippings evaporate, add bouillon cube dissolved in 1 cup boiling water. Baste regularly so that fowl will be juicy. Pour melted jelly over hens the last half hour of cooking to glaze. Serves 8.

Mrs. Richard Redmont, Sr.

---

1 (3½ pound) chicken will give 3 cups diced cooked chicken.

Smoked Rock Cornish Hens

Hickory chips (plus apple and cherry chips, if available)

7 Cornish hens (or as many as grill will accommodate)

1 Tablespoon soy sauce per hen

3 Tablespoons white wine vinegar per hen

½ cup vegetable or corn oil

1 Tablespoon lemon juice

5 to 7 dashes Tabasco

Mix equal parts of hickory, apple and cherry chips for smoke. Soak in water for *at least* 48 hours for maximum smoke. If apple and cherry chips are unavailable, use all hickory. Thaw, unstuff, wash and truss hens well. Sprinkle liberally (in proportions listed) with soy sauce and wine vinegar. Marinate 3-4 hours, basting and turning frequently. Start fire and when coals are red add handful of wet chips. When fire is ready and smoke is ample, pour marinade from hens into a bowl (add a little more wine vinegar and soy sauce if necessary) and add oil, lemon juice and Tabasco. Place hens on rack in smoker. Baste with sauce every 15 or 30 minutes until done. Add more wet chips as required to maintain smoke. Total cooking time is approximately 3-3½ hours, depending on cooker and smoke. The smoked hens may be cooled, securely wrapped and frozen for later use. Thaw hens and place in slow oven (250°-275°F) for about 30 minutes. This allows the "smoke" to repenetrate the hens. Great with a wild rice dish, green vegetables and fruit salad. Serves 7.

Reuel May, Jr.

Cornish Game Hens with Grapes

2 Cornish hens

Salt and pepper

2 slices bacon

½ cup Cognac

½ cup whipping cream

1 Tablespoon butter

2 scallions, minced

1 cup white seedless grapes, parboiled in water for 3 minutes

½ cup port wine

Cayenne pepper

Lemon juice

Sprinkle hens with salt and pepper; cover each breast with half a slice of bacon and roast at 350°F for 50 minutes to 1 hour, basting occasionally. Remove; cut in half and keep warm. To juices in pan add Cognac and reduce by half. Then add cream and cook until creamy. In a saucepan melt the butter and sauté the scallions for 2 minutes. Add grapes and port and flame. Stir until flames die. Strain cream sauce into the pan with grapes and season to taste with salt, cayenne and lemon juice. Serve each half bird on a triangle of bread previously sautéed in butter. Serves 2-4.

Mrs. William B. Wilson

Boning a Chicken Breast

Use whole or half breasts from a 2½-3 pound fryer. Slip fingers between skin and flesh and pull off skin. Cut against the ridge of the breast bone to loosen flesh from bone. Disjoint the wing where it joins the carcass and continue down along the rib cage, cutting flesh from the bone until the meat from one side of the breast separates from the bone in one piece. Remove wing. Cut and pull out the white tendon that runs about two thirds of the way down the underside of the meat. Flatten the breasts lightly with the side of a heavy knife. The breasts are now ready for cooking. If not used immediately, wrap in wax paper and refrigerate.

Sherried Swiss Chicken Breasts with Brown Rice

4 whole chicken breasts, split
   and boned
8 slices Swiss cheese
2 Tablespoons Cognac
2 teaspoons fines herbes
2 teaspoons ground coriander
1 teaspoon crushed thyme

½ teaspoon salt
¼ teaspoon pepper
2 Tablespoons margarine
1 cup beef broth
½ cup sherry wine
Fresh mushrooms, sliced
   (optional)

Flatten breasts with a tenderizer; then wrap each piece of chicken around a slice of cheese, encasing it completely. Secure with a toothpick. Dry with paper towel. Place in bowl and coat with Cognac. Cover and let stand 5 minutes. Toss again in Cognac; cover and let stand another 5 minutes. Drain and rub with a mixture of the fines herbes, coriander, thyme, salt and pepper. Melt margarine in heated skillet; brown chicken quickly. Place chicken in casserole dish, pour beef broth and sherry over and bake, covered, at 375 °F for about 1 hour (or until done). To serve, remove toothpicks and serve with BROWN RICE. Spoon gravy over rice. Sprinkle sautéed sliced mushrooms over chicken breasts, if desired. Serves 8.

BROWN RICE

2¼ cups beef broth
1 cup raw Riceland brown rice
¼ cup sherry wine
2 Tablespoons dried parsley

1 Tablespoon margarine
½ teaspoon fines herbes,
   crushed
1 teaspoon salt

Bring broth to a boil. Add remaining ingredients. Cover, turn heat down to simmer and cook 45 minutes to 1 hour.

Mrs. Thomas M. Howe

———

A stewing chicken is done when its meat is tender if pierced with a fork; roasters, fryers and broilers are done when the meat is pricked deeply with a fork and the juices run clear yellow with no trace of rosy color.

Orange Chicken

2 cups diced celery
1⅓ cups water
7 cups crumbled day old whole
   wheat bread

1 teaspoon salt
6 Tablespoons chopped onion
1 cup margarine
8 half chicken breasts, boned

Simmer celery in water 20 minutes. Drain, reserving ⅔ cup liquid. In a large bowl combine bread crumbs, celery, celery liquid and salt. Cook onion in margarine until tender. Add to bread mixture. In a baking pan make 8 mounds of dressing. Place an uncooked chicken breast over each mound. Pour ORANGE WINE SAUCE over chicken and mounds of stuffing. Bake at 350°F for 1½ hours. Serves 8.

ORANGE WINE SAUCE

⅔ cup sugar
3 Tablespoons flour
2 eggs, beaten

3 cups orange juice
½ cup white wine

Mix sugar and flour in double boiler; add eggs, orange juice and wine. Cook, stirring constantly, until thickened.

Mrs. W. Henry Holman, Jr.

Chicken Kiev

4 large whole chicken breasts,
   split, skinned, boned
½ cup butter, softened
1 clove garlic, crushed
2 Tablespoons chopped parsley

1 teaspoon thyme or marjoram
Flour
2 eggs, beaten
1 cup fine bread crumbs
Salt

Pound breasts thin between plastic bags, keeping the smooth side of breast down. Mix next 4 ingredients. Shape into 8 elongated oval pieces and freeze. Wrap chicken completely around butter and dip each chicken piece into flour. Next dip into eggs and finally coat with bread crumbs. Fry in hot oil (375°F) for 10-12 minutes or bake at 350°F for 45 minutes. Drain on paper towels. Salt after cooking. Chicken will keep in a 200°F oven if placed, uncovered, on a metal tray. Serves 8.

Mrs. Joe Ross, Jr.

Variation: Serve with CRAB MEAT SAUCE to ladle over each portion. Marinate 2 cups white crab meat in ¼ cup dry vermouth. Sauté 1 cup sliced mushrooms in 4 Tablespoons butter until tender. Stir in 4 Tablespoons flour and cook several minutes; then add 2 cups sour cream and 2 cups milk and cook, stirring until thickened. Fold in 1 Tablespoon chopped chives and the crab meat. Makes 6 cups sauce.

---

6 half chicken breasts equal 2⅔ cups diced cooked chicken.

Chicken Veronique

2 large whole chicken breasts,
   split and boned
Salt and pepper
½ cup butter, divided
1 teaspoon olive oil
4 cups chicken broth, divided

⅓ cup flour
1 cup dry vermouth
Dash cayenne pepper
1 cup green seedless grapes,
   chilled

Season chicken breasts with salt and pepper. Melt 2 Tablespoons butter in a heavy skillet and add olive oil to prevent burning. Over moderate heat sauté chicken breasts until golden brown on both sides. Add 1 cup chicken broth and simmer until tender, about 15 minutes. Make a white wine sauce by melting remaining butter in heavy saucepan and stirring in flour. Gradually add remaining 3 cups hot chicken broth. Stir until partially reduced. Add vermouth; season with salt and cayenne pepper. Continue cooking until thick and reduced, stirring frequently. Place chicken breasts on serving dish. Add grapes and pour sauce over all. Serve at once. Serves 4.

Mrs. Maurice Reed, Jr.

Chicken Breast Mediterranean

3 whole chicken breasts, halved
   and deboned
1½ teaspoons monosodium
   glutamate, divided
½ teaspoon salt
¼ teaspoon paprika
½ cup butter
1 medium eggplant, peeled and
   cut in ½-inch slices

½ cup chopped onion
1 clove garlic, chopped
1 green pepper, cut in strips
2 zucchini, cut in ½-inch slices
3 tomatoes, peeled and diced
¼ teaspoon Tabasco
¼ teaspoon thyme
¼ teaspoon oregano
2 Tablespoons chopped parsley

Sprinkle chicken with 1 teaspoon monosodium glutamate, salt and paprika. Heat butter in skillet and brown chicken. Remove chicken from skillet. Sauté eggplant in skillet and place in buttered casserole. Add onion, garlic and green pepper to skillet and cook until tender. Add zucchini and tomatoes and cook until tomatoes are cooked down and part of liquid evaporated. Add remaining monosodium glutamate, Tabasco and herbs to mixture. Arrange chicken over eggplant and spoon tomato mixture over chicken. Bake uncovered in 350°F oven for 45 minutes or until chicken is done. Baste several times. Serves 6.

Mrs. William Atkins, Shreveport, Louisiana

CHICKEN BREASTS BRAZILIA

Wrap boneless chicken breasts around hearts of palm stalks and attach with a toothpick. Place each seam-side-down in a buttered pan and cover with melted butter. Season with salt and pepper. Bake at 400°F for 25 minutes. To serve, top with hollandaise sauce and chopped chives.

Chicken Florentine Joseph

10 ounces fresh spinach
7 Tablespoons butter, divided
Lemon juice
Salt and pepper to taste
20 fresh mushrooms, sliced
1 cup dry sherry wine
4 half chicken breasts
Flour
1 egg, beaten with 1 Tablespoon
    water
⅔ cup fine bread crumbs
⅔ cup grated Parmesan cheese
Oil
Chopped pimiento

Cook spinach in salted water. Drain, chop and season with 1 Tablespoon butter, lemon juice and salt to taste. Sauté mushrooms in sherry for about 10 minutes. Add remaining butter and salt to taste. Set aside. Debone chicken and flatten with meat tenderizer. Salt and pepper; then dust with flour and dip in egg. Coat chicken with mixture of bread crumbs and Parmesan cheese. Fry in oil until tender. To serve, place spinach on plate. Top with chicken and pour mushroom sauté on top. Garnish with chopped pimiento. Canned or frozen spinach or canned mushrooms may be substituted. Recipe can be easily increased for as many as desired. This is good with Rice Pilaf (see Index), green salad and hot rolls. Serves 4.

Joseph A. Mitchell

Chicken Breasts Supreme

¼ cup flour
2½ teaspoons salt
1 teaspoon paprika
6 whole chicken breasts, halved
    and skinned
¼ cup butter
⅓ cup water
4 teaspoons cornstarch
3 cups half and half cream,
    divided
½ cup cooking sherry
2 teaspoons grated lemon rind
2 Tablespoons lemon juice
1 cup grated Swiss cheese
½ cup chopped parsley

Combine flour, salt and paprika on wax paper and coat chicken breasts. In large skillet melt butter and lightly brown chicken. Add water and simmer covered for 30 minutes or until chicken is almost tender. Arrange breasts in 9 x 13-inch baking dish. Mix cornstarch and ¼ cup cream and stir into drippings in skillet. Stir over low heat, gradually adding remaining cream, until thickened. Add sherry, lemon rind and juice. Pour sauce over chicken and bake covered at 350°F for 35 minutes. Uncover, sprinkle grated cheese and parsley over top and continue to bake until cheese bubbles. May be frozen after sauce is added if boneless chicken breasts are used. Serve hot with rice and green vegetables. Serves 12.

Mrs. Robert B. Mims

Creamed chicken or turkey dishes will freeze, except those containing hard-cooked eggs.

Helen Mary's Chicken

8 half chicken breasts
Salt and pepper
1 (10½ ounce) can cream of
  mushroom soup
1 (10½ ounce) can cream of
  celery soup
½ cup butter or margarine,
  melted
1 teaspoon horseradish
1 Tablespoon Worcestershire
  sauce

½ cup lemon juice
1 large onion, sliced
1½ fresh tomatoes, sliced
1 (15 ounce) can whole
  potatoes, drained
1 (4 ounce) can sliced
  mushrooms, drained
1 (14 ounce) can artichoke
  hearts, drained
Chopped fresh parsley

Sprinkle chicken breasts with salt and pepper and brown them in a 375°F oven in a 9 x 13-inch Pyrex dish. Mix thoroughly the mushroom and celery soups, butter, horseradish, Worcestershire sauce, lemon juice and additional salt and pepper to make a sauce. To chicken add the onion, tomatoes, potatoes, mushrooms and artichokes. Sprinkle parsley on top. Pour sauce over this and cook 2 hours at 300°F. Delicious served over noodles. Serves 8.

Mrs. Thomas M. Elzen

Bernàrd's Poulet au Curry

2 broilers (or 10 half breasts)
Salt and pepper
Flour
6 Tablespoons butter, divided
3 apples, finely diced
3 medium onions, diced
2 ribs celery, diced
2 Tablespoons curry powder
Dash ground ginger
4 cups beef bouillon

1 cup plus 1 Tablespoon dry
  white wine
½ cup chopped pimiento
⅓ cup raisins, simmered in
  water for 5 minutes
5 ounces chutney, diced
1 cup whipping cream
Salt and white pepper
Banana slices
Fresh flaked coconut

Split broilers and remove spinal columns. Salt, pepper and dust each half with flour. Sauté chicken in 4 Tablespoons butter until golden brown. In a large skillet or pot sauté apples, onions and celery in 2 Tablespoons butter until yellow and wilted. Add curry and ginger and cook for 5 minutes. Add bouillon and white wine. Place chicken in bouillon sauce and simmer for 1 hour. Remove chicken and finish sauce by adding pimiento, drained raisins, chutney, cream, salt and pepper. Serve the chicken in the sauce over buttered white rice. Garnish with banana slices and coconut. Serves 8.

Bernard Sarme, Bernard's Restaurant

Chicken Island Supreme

1 broiler-fryer chicken, cut
   in parts
3 Tablespoons fresh grated
   ginger root
1 lemon, sliced
1 teaspoon salt

1 teaspoon Accent
½ teaspoon ground mace
¼ teaspoon curry powder
¼ teaspoon black pepper
¼ cup Mazola corn oil
¼ cup water

Place chicken in shallow baking pan in single layer, skin side up. Sprinkle over all ginger root, lemon, salt, Accent, mace, curry powder and pepper. Pour over corn oil and water. Bake in 350°F oven, covered, ½ hour. Remove cover and add more water, if necessary. Continue baking until chicken is well browned, about ½ hour, or until fork can be inserted with ease. Serve with rice. Serves 4.

Mrs. Margaret L. Gutierrez, Biloxi, Mississippi

This recipe was the Mississippi state winner and was entered in the 1977 National Chicken Cooking Contest held in Jackson in July of that year.

Coronation Chicken

8 half chicken breasts
¾ pint mayonnaise (1½ cups)
1 (7½ ounce) jar apricot purée
   (baby food)
1 Tablespoon olive oil
2 ounces onion (1 small), finely
   chopped
1 dessert spoonful curry powder
   (about 1 Tablespoon)
1 good teaspoon tomato purée

1 glass red wine (about ¾ cup)
¾ wine glassful water
   (about ½ cup)
1 bay leaf
A little salt, pepper, sugar
A slice or two of lemon
A squeeze of lemon juice
3 Tablespoons whipping cream,
   lightly whipped

Cook chicken breasts in seasoned water until done. Drain, cool and cut meat into bite-size pieces. Mix mayonnaise and apricot purée and set aside. Heat oil and sauté onion 3-4 minutes. Add curry powder and cook 2 minutes more. Add tomato purée, wine, water and bay leaf. Bring to a boil and add salt, pepper, sugar, lemon and lemon juice. Simmer uncovered 5-10 minutes. Strain and cool; then add slowly to the mayonnaise mixture. Add cream. Serve cold over the chicken bits. Good for a cold buffet. Serves 8-10.

Mrs. Tom B. Scott, Jr.

This recipe was given me by Lady Elsie Newton of Leek, Staffs (United Kingdom). The recipe was, in fact, written by hand by Lady Elsie. Lady Elsie's husband, Sir Hubert Newton, Hon. MA (Keele), is Chairman of the Britannia Building Society, Newton House, Leek, Staffs. The terminology of the ingredients is Lady Newton's and I have left it just as she wrote it.

Oven-Barbecued Chicken

1 chicken, cut up, or desired
   pieces
1 teaspoon salt

½ teaspoon paprika
½ cup butter

Rinse chicken and pat dry. Mix salt and paprika in bag and shake chicken until coated. Pieces may also be seasoned individually with these ingredients. Melt butter in baking dish at 350°F. Place chicken in dish, skin side down. Bake 45 minutes. Turn chicken and cover with BARBECUE SAUCE. Bake another 30 minutes until tender. Spoon sauce over pieces when serving. May be prepared ahead and warmed for serving. Serves 4.

BARBECUE SAUCE

¼ cup butter
1 large onion, chopped
¼ cup vinegar
1 cup water
1 teaspoon dry mustard
½ cup Worcestershire sauce

1½ cups chili sauce
½ cup lemon juice
2 teaspoons chili powder
2 teaspoons salt
¼ cup brown sugar

Melt butter and sauté onion. Add all other ingredients and simmer 30 minutes.

Mrs. McDonald Jones

Barbecue Sauce for Chicken

For 100 chicken halves:
1 gallon cider vinegar
½ gallon cooking oil
1 (2 ounce) bottle Tabasco
1 (4 ounce) box black pepper
1 (1 7/8 ounce) box crushed
   red pepper
1 (¾ ounce) jar onion powder
1 (2 ounce) bottle liquid garlic
2 pounds salt
100 chicken halves

For 8 to 10 chicken halves:
2 cups cider vinegar
1 cup cooking oil
1 teaspoon Tabasco
½ teaspoon black pepper
1 teaspoon crushed red pepper
1 Tablespoon onion powder
¼ teaspoon liquid garlic
4 Tablespoons salt
8 to 10 chicken halves

Combine all ingredients except chicken halves in saucepan. Simmer. Sprinkle chicken halves lightly with additional salt. Place chicken on grill. Baste after first turning. Turn and baste chickens frequently until done. Basting sauce may be prepared ahead and refrigerated, tightly covered, for up to 1 month.

Mississippi Department of Agriculture and Commerce

This barbecue sauce was developed to be used by the MDAC Cooking Team in promotion of Mississippi agricultural products.

---

1 Tablespoon vinegar or lemon juice in 1 cup milk equals 1 cup buttermilk.

Buttermilk Chicken

4 to 6 half chicken breasts,
  skinned
1½ cups buttermilk, divided
¾ cup flour
½ teaspoon salt

¼ teaspoon pepper
¼ cup margarine
1 (10½ ounce) can cream of
  mushroom soup

Preheat oven to 425°F. Dip chicken into ½ cup buttermilk. Then roll chicken in mixture of flour, salt and pepper. Melt margarine in a 9 x 13-inch pan. Place chicken in pan, breast side down. Bake 30 minutes, uncovered. Turn chicken and bake for 15 minutes more. Turn chicken again and pour mixture of 1 cup buttermilk and mushroom soup over chicken, baking 15 minutes more. Remove chicken to platter and garnish with parsley. Serve with pan gravy. Serves 4-6.

Mrs. J. L. Alford, Jr.

Clyde's Barbecued Chicken

Salt and pepper
4 broilers, halved

BARBECUE SAUCE:
1 pound margarine
1 cup lemon juice

2 Tablespoons Worcestershire
  sauce
2 teaspoons salt
½ teaspoon black pepper
6 drops Tabasco
½ cup sherry wine

Salt and pepper chicken. Combine all *BARBECUE SAUCE* ingredients in saucepan and heat slowly, stirring occasionally, until margarine is melted. Paint chicken with sauce. Grill over low charcoal fire to which 2 or 3 hickory chips, presoaked in water, have been added. Cook until tender (about 1½ hours or until meat leaves bone on drumstick). Turn and baste often. Serves 8.

Clyde X. Copeland, Sr.

Diet Herb Chicken Bake

1 fryer, quartered
1 teaspoon salt
½ teaspoon black pepper
1 Tablespoon garlic salt
2 Tablespoons Worcestershire
  sauce
2 Tablespoons soy sauce

1 Tablespoon lemon juice
1 teaspoon rosemary
1 Tablespoon Italian herb
  seasoning
1½ teaspoons thyme
2 chicken bouillon cubes,
  dissolved in ½ cup hot water

Sprinkle chicken with salt, pepper and garlic salt. Place in shallow pan or casserole and sprinkle with remaining ingredients. Bake uncovered 30 minutes in 325°F oven, turning once after 15 minutes. Baste occasionally. Turn skin side up, cover and bake 30 minutes more or until tender. Serves 4.

Mrs. Lois Anderson

Country Captain

1 (3 pound) hen, or larger
2 medium onions, diced
1 large green pepper, diced
1 clove garlic, minced
2 Tablespoons butter
2 (16 ounce) cans stewed
 tomatoes

1 teaspoon salt
½ teaspoon pepper
1 teaspoon powdered thyme
1 teaspoon curry powder
4 ounces slivered blanched
 almonds, toasted
½ cup raisins or currants

Stew hen in seasoned water; remove meat from bone and cut into bite-size pieces. Sauté onions, green pepper and garlic in butter. Add tomatoes and cook 10 minutes. Add salt, pepper, thyme and curry powder. Cook five minutes longer. Pour sauce over chicken and bake 45 minutes at 325°F. When ready to serve, add almonds and raisins. May be prepared ahead. Freezes well. Serve with brown or wild rice. Serves 12.

Mrs. Brad Dye, Jr.

This is an old Georgia recipe given by Daisy Bonner to President Roosevelt at Warm Springs, Georgia. It was President Roosevelt's favorite, so Daisy Bonner went to Washington to show the chef how to make it. The recipe came to me from my mother, who received it from Mrs. Melville Dye, Roosevelt's secretary when he was at Warm Springs, Georgia, December 21, 1939.

Oven-Fried Chicken

2 cups sour cream
¼ cup lemon juice
4 teaspoons Worcestershire
 sauce
4 teaspoons celery salt
2 teaspoons paprika

1 teaspoon garlic salt
1 teaspoon salt
½ teaspoon pepper
8 half chicken breasts
2 cups cracker crumbs
½ cup margarine, melted

Combine all ingredients except chicken, crumbs and margarine. Roll breasts in mixture and refrigerate overnight. Before cooking, roll chicken in crumbs and place in shallow pan. Pour half of margarine over chicken and bake uncovered in a 350°F oven for 45 minutes or 1 hour. Baste occasionally. Pour rest of margarine over and bake 15 minutes longer. If chicken begins to brown too quickly, cover loosely with foil. Serves 6.

Mrs. G. Leighton Lewis

This recipe may be varied by using 1 cup Italian seasoned crumbs mixed with 1 cup grated Parmesan cheese and ¼ cup chopped parsley for coating the chicken.

Mrs. Tom Kizer, Senatobia, Mississippi

———

As a substitute for sour cream blend together until smooth 1 cup cottage cheese, ¼ cup buttermilk and ½ teaspoon lemon juice. Makes 1 cup.

Teriyaki Chicken

¾ cup chopped onion
2 cloves garlic, minced
1 pinch ground ginger
2½ Tablespoons sugar

½ cup soy sauce
1 cup water
1 fryer chicken, cut in pieces

Mix first 6 ingredients. Cover chicken with mixture. Marinate for 12-14 hours. Cook on grill for approximately 45 minutes. Serves 4.

Mrs. W. Timothy Jones

Florence's Open-Faced Sandwich

8 whole chicken breasts,
　deboned
Carrots
Celery

Onion
Salt and pepper
16 slices dark rye bread
16 slices Swiss cheese

Cook chicken breasts in water to cover seasoned with carrots, celery, onion, salt and pepper. Remove skin and cool. To assemble sandwich, spread each slice of bread with AVOCADO BUTTER, top with a slice of cheese and a half chicken breast. Pour THOUSAND ISLAND DRESSING over all. Pass extra dressing to be added to sandwich as desired. Serves 16.

AVOCADO BUTTER

3 large ripe avocados
2 Tablespoons fresh lime juice,
　or more

2 cups butter, softened
¼ teaspoon ground ginger
Finely chopped almonds

Purée avocados in blender with lime juice, butter and ginger. Form into several balls and roll in almonds. Chill. Any butter not used on sandwich freezes well and is good as a spread on crackers or as a butter seasoning for a charcoaled steak. Makes 3 cups butter.

THOUSAND ISLAND DRESSING

2 cups mayonnaise
1 green pepper, finely chopped
8 ribs celery, finely chopped
1 large onion, finely chopped
1 cup sour cream

1 teaspoon Worcestershire sauce
1 cup chili sauce
1½ Tablespoons salt
Pepper to taste
4 hard-boiled eggs, chopped

Combine ingredients and chill. Dressing will keep in refrigerator for a week or 10 days. Makes 5 cups dressing.

Mrs. Dick B. Mason, III

In freezing egg yolks beat in 1 teaspoon sugar or ½ teaspoon salt to every 6 yolks to prevent coagulation.

Sweet and Sour Chicken

6 half chicken breasts
½ cup flour
⅓ cup salad oil
1 teaspoon salt
¼ teaspoon pepper
1 (13½ ounce) can pineapple chunks (reserve juice)
1 cup sugar

2 Tablespoons cornstarch
¾ cup cider vinegar
1 Tablespoon soy sauce
¼ teaspoon ground ginger
1 chicken bouillon cube
1 green pepper, cut in ½-inch strips

Coat chicken with flour and brown in oil in skillet. Remove to roasting pan and sprinkle with salt and pepper. Preheat oven to 350°F. Drain pineapple, pouring juice into a 2-cup measure. Add water to make 1¼ cups. In saucepan combine sugar, cornstarch, pineapple juice, vinegar, soy sauce, ginger and bouillon cube. Bring to boil, stirring constantly. Boil 2 minutes; then pour over chicken. Bake uncovered for 30 minutes. Baste occasionally. Add pineapple and green pepper. Bake 30 minutes longer, or until chicken is tender. Place chicken on serving platter, on rice bed if desired, and pour pan juices and pieces of pineapple and green pepper over chicken. Serve immediately. Serves 4-6.

Mrs. Anson Bob Chunn

Skillet Coq au Vin

½ cup flour
1½ teaspoons salt, divided
¼ teaspoon pepper
1 (3 to 3½ pound) fryer, cut up
6 slices bacon
6 small onions
8 ounces fresh mushrooms, sliced
½ teaspoon thyme leaves

1 bay leaf
2 large sprigs parsley
4 carrots, halved
1 teaspoon instant chicken broth or 2 chicken bouillon cubes
1 cup hot water
1 cup Burgundy wine
1 clove garlic, crushed

Mix flour, 1 teaspoon salt and pepper and coat chicken with mixture. Fry bacon in large skillet until crisp; remove and brown chicken in bacon fat over medium heat. Remove chicken; cook onions and mushrooms until tender, about 5 minutes. Drain fat. Tie thyme leaves, bay leaf and parsley in cheesecloth. Crumble bacon. Stir bacon, herbs in cheesecloth and remaining ingredients into skillet. Add reserved chicken and vegetables and cover. Simmer until done, 1 hour or longer. Remove cheesecloth. Spoon off fat. Serve in individual bowls. Garnish with a sprig of parsley if desired. Serves 4-6.

Mrs. Richard L. Redmont, Jr.

Skillet Coq au Vin is borrowed from French country cooking. The chicken is simmered in wine and bouillon and accompanied by many good things. To serve, spoon into large shallow bowls. Dunk hot French bread or crusty hard rolls into the gravy.

Chicken Livers Français

2 (4 ounce) cans sliced
  mushrooms
¼ cup butter
¾ pound chicken livers
1 small clove garlic, crushed
4 Tablespoons flour, divided
1 teaspoon salt
¼ teaspoon pepper

1 cup milk
2 (10 ounce) packages frozen
  broccoli spears, thawed and
  drained
1 Tablespoon lemon juice
1 cup sour cream
2 Tablespoons grated Parmesan
  cheese

Drain mushrooms, reserving half the liquid. Set aside. In a large skillet melt butter; add chicken livers and garlic. Sauté livers until brown and tender. Stir in 3 Tablespoons flour, mushrooms (with reserved liquid), salt and pepper. Add milk; heat, stirring constantly, until mixture thickens. Arrange broccoli in 2-quart buttered baking dish. Sprinkle with lemon juice. Top with liver mixture. Combine sour cream and remaining flour. Spread over liver mixture. Top with Parmesan cheese. Bake in preheated 350°F oven 30-35 minutes. Serves 6.

Mrs. Alexander Endy

Dutch Chicken Pie

1 large or 2 small chickens
Salt
Pepper
2 onions, quartered
3 ribs celery, quartered
2 carrots, chopped
1 cup half and half cream

4 Tablespoons butter, divided
2 cups flour
2 teaspoons baking powder
1 teaspoon salt
1 egg, beaten
1 cup milk

Simmer chicken in water to cover with salt, pepper, onions, celery and carrots until tender. Remove chicken from bones and cut in large chunks. Place in a 2-inch deep oblong baking dish. Reduce stock to 2 cups. Add cream and 2 Tablespoons butter. Correct seasonings. Pour over chicken in baking dish. Sift together flour, baking powder and salt. Work in 2 Tablespoons butter with pastry mixer or finger tips. Add egg and milk. Drop by spoonfuls over chicken and gravy. Bake in a 400°F oven until batter is puffed up and brown. Cut in squares to serve. Serves 8.

From the recipes of Mrs. Harold Dever

To slice cooked chicken breasts, chill them well. Carefully remove meat from bone and lay each piece flat on cutting board. With sharp knife slice breast lengthwise parallel to board. Three thin slices can be obtained from each half breast.

Chicken and Shrimp Supreme

6 to 8 half chicken breasts
1 cup finely chopped onion
1 cup finely chopped celery
¼ cup chopped parsley
2 Tablespoons margarine
3 cups shredded bread (½ pumpernickel and ½ white)
2 cups mayonnaise

2 teaspoons Worcestershire sauce
2 Tablespoons prepared mustard
6 teaspoons capers
½ cup sherry wine
½ teaspoon curry powder
1 cup water
2 pounds peeled, cooked shrimp

Boil chicken in seasoned water. Remove skin and bones and cut meat into medium-size chunks. Sauté onion, celery and parsley in margarine. Shred bread in blender, if desired. Set aside. Mix the next 6 ingredients together well. To the sauce add the chicken pieces, vegetables, bread and remaining ingredients. Bake uncovered in a 3-quart casserole at 350°F for 30-45 minutes. This can be prepared 1-2 days ahead. Serves 8-10.

Mrs. Albert H. Green

Chicken Tetrazzini

1 (8 ounce) package spaghetti, broken in 2-inch pieces
1¾ cups grated Cheddar cheese, divided
4 Tablespoons Parmesan cheese, divided
2 cups diced cooked chicken or turkey
1 (2 ounce) can diced pimientos

¼ green pepper, cut in thin slivers
½ small onion, minced
1 (10½ ounce) can cream of mushroom soup
½ cup chicken broth
¼ cup dry vermouth
Salt and pepper to taste

Cook and drain the spaghetti. Combine 1¼ cups Cheddar cheese, 2 Tablespoons Parmesan cheese and all remaining ingredients. Toss with the spaghetti. Place in greased casserole and sprinkle with reserved cheeses. Cook, covered, for 45 minutes at 350°F. Serves 6-8.

Mrs. Christoph Keller, Little Rock, Arkansas

SOUTHERN FRIED CHICKEN

Cut 1 fryer into pieces and salt and pepper each piece liberally. Combine ¾ cup flour, 1 teaspoon salt and ¼ teaspoon pepper in a plastic bag. Shake each chicken piece in bag one at a time to coat well with flour. Fry in deep fat covered for the first 5 minutes, then uncovered until golden brown (about 15 minutes total cooking time). Turn pieces occasionally.

Poulet d'Artichoke

2 (14 ounce) cans artichoke
   hearts
2⅔ cups diced cooked chicken
   breasts
2 (10½ ounce) cans cream of
   chicken soup
1 cup mayonnaise

1 teaspoon lemon juice
½ teaspoon curry powder
1¼ cups grated sharp Cheddar
   cheese
1¼ cups bread cubes
2 Tablespoons butter, melted

Drain artichoke hearts and arrange in 8 greased ramekins or a 9 x 13-inch casserole. Spread chicken on top (⅓ cup per ramekin). Combine the soup, mayonnaise, lemon juice and curry powder and pour over chicken. Sprinkle with cheese. Toss bread cubes with butter and place on top. Bake at 350°F for 25 minutes. Can be prepared in advance. Serve with rice for a dinner, or in the ramekins for a luncheon dish. Serves 8.

Mrs. James P. McGaughy, Jr.

Paella Terrisita

1 chicken, cut into pieces
Paprika
3 Tablespoons olive oil
3 Tablespoons butter
2 cloves garlic, peeled
2 onions, chopped
1 green pepper, chopped
1 sweet red pepper, chopped
1 (5¾ ounce) can ripe olives,
   sliced
½ pound mushrooms, sliced

1 cup cubed ham
Juice of 1 lemon
1 teaspoon thyme
1 teaspoon oregano
Salt and pepper to taste
2 cups dry white wine
2 uncooked lobster tails
1½ pounds raw shrimp, peeled
1 cup raw rice
2 cups chicken broth (see Note)
Parsley

Dry pieces of chicken, sprinkle with paprika and brown on one side in oil and butter in a *very* large skillet or paella pan. Turn and brown on other side. Place garlic in oil in skillet and sauté. Discard garlic. Add onions and peppers and simmer until clear. Add olives, mushrooms, ham and lemon juice, stirring well. Crush spices in palm of hand and sprinkle over ingredients. Add salt and pepper. Pour wine over chicken. Cut lobster tails into chunks, about 4 or 5 pieces per tail. Place lobster and shrimp in pan around edge. Make a hollow in center of pan and pour rice into it. Pour chicken broth over rice slowly. Stir only to moisten rice. Cover and simmer 15-20 minutes or just until rice is done. Serves 6.

Mrs. John E. Ainsworth

Note: Cook chicken back, trimmings and giblets in approximately 3 cups of water before browning chicken. This will make the broth to add at the end.

Minnie Porter's Chicken and Dumplings

4 Tablespoons lard or shortening
1½ cups sifted flour
1 teaspoon salt
¼ teaspoon baking soda
Pinch sugar
½ cup buttermilk
1 egg, beaten
1 fryer, cut in pieces
2 cups water

2 cups chicken stock,
   preferably unsalted
2 Tablespoons butter
1½ teaspoons salt (if stock is
   salted, use less)
½ teaspoon freshly ground
   black pepper
¾ to 1 cup milk

To make dumplings cut lard into the flour, salt, soda and sugar; make a well in the flour mixture and add buttermilk and egg. Mix as for biscuits. Roll into a ball and place in freezer while chicken is cooking. Place chicken pieces into a 3 or 4-quart saucepan with the water, stock, butter, salt and pepper. Simmer (do not boil) for 30-40 minutes or until tender. Remove chicken pieces. Skin and debone. Roll out dumplings as for pie crust, using ample flour on board and rolling pin, as the dough is sticky. Cut pastry into 1-inch squares. Bring stock to a boil. Drop dumplings into stock slowly enough to keep stock boiling, stirring constantly to avoid sticking. Place chicken on top when all the dumplings are in, and pour the milk over all. Bring stock back to a boil, place top on saucepan and turn heat down to a fast simmer. Do not remove lid or dumplings will be tough. After 20 minutes remove top. Add more milk if too dry. Salt and pepper to taste and serve at once. Dish may be reheated by pouring a little hot milk in bottom of a casserole, adding the chicken and dumplings, covering with foil and placing in a 350°F oven until warmed. Serves 6.

Mrs. Herbert A. Kroeze, Jr.

Chicken Jambalaya

1 cup chopped onion
1 cup chopped green pepper
2 cloves garlic, minced
2 Tablespoons salad oil
1 cup diced cooked ham
12 small pork sausage links,
   sliced

1 cup diced cooked chicken
2 (16 ounce) cans tomatoes
1 cup raw rice
1½ cups chicken broth
½ teaspoon thyme
1 teaspoon salt
1 Tablespoon chopped parsley

Sauté onion, green pepper and garlic in hot oil in skillet, stirring frequently until tender. Stir in meats and cook for 5 minutes. Add all remaining ingredients and place in greased casserole dish. Cover dish and bake at 350°F for 1 hour. Serves 8.

Bobby Ginn, Chef, LeFleur's Restaurant
This dish was served to banquet parties at the Heidelberg Hotel.

Hot Chicken Salad

2 cups croutons, toasted
2 cups diced cooked chicken
1½ cups chopped celery
1½ cups grated sharp cheese
¼ cup slivered almonds, toasted

2 Tablespoons minced onion
¾ cup mayonnaise
½ teaspoon salt
1 Tablespoon lemon juice

Combine half of the croutons with all the remaining ingredients. Turn into baking dish and cover with remaining croutons. Bake at 350°F for 35 minutes. May be prepared ahead, but if so, do not put in croutons until baking time. This is good for a luncheon or light dinner with a congealed or fruit salad and rolls. Serves 6.

Mrs. Ward T. McCraney, Jr.

Mexican Noodles

1 (5 to 6 pound) hen
About 4 quarts water
½ large onion, quartered
4 sprigs parsley with stems
4 bay leaves, divided
Tops and leaves of 3 ribs celery
3 Tablespoons salt
3 Tablespoons chicken fat or
   butter
2 cups diced celery
2 cups diced onion
1 cup diced green pepper
1 cup minced parsley
1 clove garlic, minced

1 teaspoon chili powder
1 teaspoon garlic salt
1 (10¾ ounce) can tomato soup
2 teaspoons Worcestershire
   sauce
5 cups broth from chicken
1 cup chopped pimiento
1 (8 ounce) can mushrooms,
   stems and pieces, with liquid
1 (6 ounce) can pitted black
   olives, drained
1 (12 ounce) package broad egg
   noodles

Boil hen, breast side down, in large pot with water, onion, parsley, 2 bay leaves, celery and salt until tender (about 2½ hours). Remove hen, strain broth and reserve. When cool, remove meat from bones and cut into large pieces. Discard skin and bones. Melt butter or chicken fat in large pot. Sauté in the fat the celery, onion, green pepper, parsley and garlic until soft. Add remaining 2 bay leaves, chili powder, garlic salt, tomato soup, Worcestershire sauce and chicken broth. Simmer on low about 20 minutes. Add pimiento, mushrooms with liquid, black olives and about ⅔ of the chicken meat. Cook noodles in salted water. Drain. Combine hot noodles gently with hot sauce using wooden or plastic spoons. Pour into 2 (2 quart) shallow casseroles. Place the remaining chicken pieces on top. Heat, covered, in 350°F oven for about 20 minutes or longer if noodles have been chilled. This recipe is better if made the day before serving. If the noodles absorb too much of the sauce, more broth may be added before heating in oven. Freezes well. Serves 20.

Mrs. Sherwood Wise

Almond Chicken with Rice

6 half chicken breasts
Salt
Pepper
Paprika
½ cup slivered almonds
½ cup margarine
½ cup chopped onion

1 (3 ounce) can sliced
    mushrooms
Juice of 1 lemon
¼ cup cooking sherry
1 cup raw rice, cooked
Parsley

Skin and debone chicken; cut meat into large pieces. Place in baking dish and sprinkle with salt, pepper and paprika. Brown almonds in margarine. Remove almonds and in same skillet sauté onion and drained mushrooms. Add lemon juice, sherry and almonds, stirring well. Spoon mixture over chicken pieces. Cover with foil and bake 1 hour and 15 minutes at 350°F. Spoon rice on serving platter and place chicken on top. Garnish with parsley. Serves 6.

Mrs. Richard C. Turner, III

Green Chicken Enchiladas

1 (16 ounce) bag fresh spinach,
    stems removed
2½ cups chicken broth
1 clove garlic, minced
2 (10½ ounce) cans cream of
    mushroom soup
2 (4 ounce) cans chopped green
    chilies
1 Tablespoon flour
1 large onion, chopped, divided

2 teaspoons salt, divided
1 pound fresh mushrooms,
    sliced, divided
2 pounds small-curd cottage
    cheese
1 cup chopped ripe olives
4 cups chopped cooked chicken
24 flour tortillas, thawed
8 ounces sharp cheese, grated
2 (8 ounce) cartons sour cream

Place spinach in blender with chicken broth and blend until puréed. Pour spinach mixture into large pan and add garlic, mushroom soup, chilies, flour, ½ the onion, 1 teaspoon salt, and ½ the mushrooms. Bring to a boil and turn off. In a separate bowl, combine cottage cheese, olives, chicken, and the remaining salt, onion and mushrooms. Add 1 cup of the spinach sauce to this mixture and stir until combined. Place a heaping Tablespoon of the chicken mixture in the center of each tortilla and roll up. Place side by side in 2 greased 9 x 13-inch Pyrex dishes. Divide spinach sauce and pour half over each casserole. Bake at 350°F for 20 minutes or until bubbly. Remove from oven and sprinkle with cheese. Place under broiler until cheese melts. Remove from oven and cover each casserole with 1 carton sour cream. Return to oven for 3-5 minutes. Serve immediately. This may be prepared ahead and frozen. Defrost before cooking and adding the cheese and sour cream. Serves 12-16.

Mrs. J. Tim Mitch

Swiss Enchiladas

1 onion, chopped
Cooking oil
1 clove garlic, minced
2 cups tomato purée
2 (4 ounce) cans chopped
    green chilies
2 cups chopped cooked chicken

Salt
12 tortillas
6 chicken bouillon cubes
3 cups half and half cream
½ pound Monterey
    Jack cheese, grated

Sauté onion in 2 Tablespoons oil until soft. Add garlic, tomato purée, green chilies and chicken. Season with salt to taste and simmer 10 minutes. Fry tortillas in 1 inch hot oil. Do not let them become crisp, as they are to be rolled. Dissolve bouillon cubes in hot cream. Dip each tortilla in cream, cover generously with chicken filling and roll up. Arrange rolls in baking dish and pour remaining cream mixture over them. Top with cheese. Bake at 350°F for 30 minutes. Freezes well. Serves 6.

Mrs. Edwin S. Graham, III

Chicken Chow Mein

12 to 14 large half chicken
    breasts, boned and skinned
Oil
1 whole bunch celery
2 bunches green onions
1 pound fresh mushrooms,
    sliced, or 2 (8 ounce) cans
    sliced mushrooms, drained
1 (20 ounce) bag frozen
    Oriental-style vegetables or
    2 (10 ounce) packages frozen
    broccoli spears, thawed
2 Tablespoons La Choy brown
    gravy sauce
1 cup soy sauce

1 (13¾ ounce) can chicken broth
1 cup water
2 (10½ ounce) cans cream of
    chicken soup
2 (16 ounce) cans bean sprouts,
    drained
1 (8 ounce) can water chestnuts,
    drained and sliced
1 (8 ounce) can bamboo shoots,
    drained
1 (4 ounce) jar diced pimientos,
    drained
1 Tablespoon cornstarch,
    or more
Chow mein noodles

Cut chicken breasts into bite-size chunks. Sauté chicken pieces in hot oil; remove from pan. Cut celery and green onions diagonally ½ inch thick. Add celery, green onions, mushrooms and Oriental vegetables or broccoli spears, which have been cut into 1½-inch pieces, to pan. Add gravy sauce, soy sauce, chicken broth and water. Cover and steam until vegetables are barely crisp. Do not overcook. Add chicken and next 5 ingredients. Thicken with cornstarch mixed with broth from vegetables. Serve over chow mein noodles. Freezes well. Thaw before reheating so vegetables will be crisp. Serves 12-14.

Mrs. W. V. Westbrook, Jr.

Chicken Verde

2 (3½ pound) fryers or 1 fryer
   and 5 chicken breasts
3 ribs celery with leaves
1 onion, sliced
1 Tablespoon salt
1 teaspoon poultry seasoning
2 teaspoons lemon-pepper
   seasoning, divided
1 green pepper, chopped
1 cup chopped celery
1 bunch green onions and tops,
   chopped
½ cup butter or solidified
   chicken fat from stock
¾ cup flour

3 cups chicken broth
1½ cups evaporated milk
¼ pound sharp cheese, grated
¼ cup grated Parmesan cheese
1 teaspoon Worcestershire sauce
½ teaspoon salt
1/8 teaspoon black pepper
1/8 teaspoon red pepper
3 Tablespoons sherry wine
1 (6 ounce) can sliced
   mushrooms
1 (2 ounce) can pimiento,
   chopped
1 (8 ounce) package green
   noodles

Quarter chickens, place in large pot and cover with water. Add celery, onion, salt, poultry seasoning and 1 teaspoon lemon-pepper seasoning and cook until tender. Let chicken stand 30 minutes in stock. Remove chicken, cool, skin, bone and cut into bite-size pieces. Strain stock, cool and refrigerate overnight. Sauté chopped vegetables in butter or fat. Add flour and stir; then blend in warmed chicken broth and evaporated milk, stirring constantly until thickened. Remove from heat. Add cheeses, then remaining lemon-pepper seasoning, other seasonings and wine, stirring to mix well. Fold in mushrooms, pimiento and chicken. Cook green noodles according to package directions, using remaining chicken broth for liquid. Drain noodles and fold into chicken sauce. Place in well-greased 3-quart casserole. Heat at 350°F for about 30 minutes. Serves 12-15.

Mrs. Charlotte B. Charles

Chicken Salad Turnovers

1 cup diced cooked chicken
1 cup chopped celery
½ cup sliced pecans
3 Tablespoons lemon juice
¼ teaspoon salt
Pepper to taste

¼ cup grated cheese
¼ cup mayonnaise
1 (10 ounce) package frozen
   puff patty shells, thawed
1 cup hollandaise sauce (see
   Index)

Mix first 8 ingredients gently. Roll out patty shells about ¼ inch thick. Place 2-3 Tablespoons chicken mixture in center of each shell and fold over turnover-style, sealing edges by pressing with a fork. Place on cookie sheet and bake at 425°F for 15 minutes or until golden brown. Serve turnovers topped with hollandaise sauce. Filling can be made a day in advance. Serves 6.

Mrs. G. G. Mazzaferro

Crispy Chicken Casserole

2 cups diced cooked chicken
1 (10½ ounce) can cream of
   mushroom soup
¾ cup mayonnaise
1 cup diced celery
1 cup cooked rice (cooked in
   chicken broth)

1 Tablespoon lemon juice
1 teaspoon grated onion
1 (3½ ounce) can sliced
   mushrooms, drained
½ cup sliced almonds, toasted
1 cup corn flakes, crumbled
3 Tablespoons butter, diced

Mix first 9 ingredients together in a greased 2-quart casserole. Sprinkle corn flakes and butter on top. Bake 30 minutes at 350°F. Serves 6.

Mrs. W. Henry Holman, Jr.

Chicken Croquettes

1 (5 or 6 pound) hen or 2 large
   fryers
Salt and pepper to taste
Grated onion to taste
1 (4 ounce) can mushrooms,
   stems and pieces, chopped
   (reserve liquid)

2 Tablespoons butter
½ cup flour
2 cups milk
Cracker crumbs
1 egg, beaten with 1 Tablespoon
   water
Cooking oil

Cook chicken in seasoned water until very tender. Remove from bones, chop fine and season with salt, pepper and grated onion. Add chopped mushrooms. Make a thick white sauce by cooking melted butter and flour together for several minutes. Add milk and stir until very thick. Mix sauce with chicken mixture and correct seasonings. Place in shallow dish, cover and refrigerate for at least 2 hours (or overnight). Shape croquettes into cones, cylinders or round balls. Roll in cracker crumbs, then in egg, then back in cracker crumbs. At this point croquettes can be refrigerated or frozen. Fry in deep fat until golden brown. Croquettes are best served at once, but may be kept warm for a short time in the oven. Serve with MUSHROOM SAUCE. Serves 8-10.

MUSHROOM SAUCE

2 Tablespoons butter
¼ cup flour
1 cup milk
Salt to taste
Onion juice to taste
1 teaspoon vinegar

Worcestershire sauce to taste
1 (4 ounce) can sliced
   mushrooms, (reserve liquid)
   or fresh, sautéed in a little
   butter

Combine melted butter and flour and cook several minutes. Add milk and stir until thickened. Stir in seasonings and mushrooms. Thin sauce with mushroom liquid, if desired.

Mrs. William H. Hight, Louisville, Mississippi

Roast Duckling Bigarade

4 (4½ to 5 pound) Long
  Island ducklings
Onions, chopped
Apples, chopped

1 teaspoon Maggi's seasoning
1 teaspoon garlic salt
1 teaspoon Accent
Dash Tabasco

Stuff duck cavitites with onions and apples. Place ducks in roasting pan and sprinkle with remaining seasonings. Roast in a preheated 400°F oven 25-30 minutes. Remove from oven and cool. Split ducks with a cleaver down center of the breast bone and separate. Remove back bone, splitting the ducks in half. Remove legs. The breast meat may then be deboned, if desired. Return duck meat to the roasting pan and heat in a 350°F oven 15-20 minutes to get rid of surface fat. Remove from oven and drain well. Arrange duck breasts in a deep casserole dish and pour BIGARADE SAUCE over them. Bake at 350°F 35-45 minutes longer. This dish can be very attractively served by leaving 1 duck whole and placing it in the center of serving platter. Arrange duck pieces around it and garnish with parsley. Serves 8.

BIGARADE SAUCE

½ cup butter
1 medium onion, chopped
½ cup flour
3 cups beef stock or consommé
½ cup tomato purée
1 cup dry red wine
Bouquet garni (½ teaspoon
  thyme, 6 sprigs parsley tied
  in cheesecloth)
1 bay leaf

1 cup Dundee butter orange
  marmalade
1 (6 ounce) can orange juice
  concentrate, thawed
½ cup brandy
Juice of 1 lemon
3 or 4 large navel
  oranges
½ cup Grand Marnier or
  Cointreau

Melt butter and sauté onion until transparent. Add flour; stir and cook until light brown. Add next 5 ingredients and bring to a boil, stirring. Simmer 25-30 minutes. Remove bouquet garni; strain sauce through a sieve. Add remaining ingredients except oranges and liqueur. Bring to a boil; then simmer 20-30 minutes. Coarsely grate the orange rinds and blanch in water to cover for 10 minutes. Drain well and add to the sauce. Section the oranges and add liqueur and orange sections to sauce.

Mrs. A. Arthur Halle, Jr., Memphis, Tennessee

TOAST RINGS FOR CREAMED DISHES

Cut unsliced bread in ¾-inch slices. Cut one slice with a large round cookie cutter. Cut a second slice with a medium-size cutter and remove center with a smaller cutter, making a doughnut. Brush large round with melted butter or margarine. Top with doughnut and brush with melted butter or margarine. Toast in 375°F oven for 10-12 minutes.

Meats

Individual Beef Wellingtons

Salt and pepper
6 (5 ounce) fillets of beef
Vegetable oil
1 cup chopped fresh
   mushrooms
1 cup beef consommé

¼ cup red wine
1 (2¾ ounce) tin pâté
   de foie gras
2 (10 ounce) packages frozen
   puff patty shells, thawed
1 egg, well beaten

Salt and pepper fillets and brush both sides with a thin coating of vegetable oil; sear in a medium hot skillet for a few minutes on each side. Remove from skillet, cool and chill in refrigerator about 15 minutes. Meanwhile cook the mushrooms in consommé and wine until tender. When done, mix drained mushrooms with pâté and add enough of the consommé and wine to make of spreading consistency. Spread mushroom-pâté mixture over top of fillets and chill for 30 minutes. Preheat oven to 400°F. Separate the patty shells so that there are 2 for each fillet. Press the pastry with fingers until flat. Place each fillet on a round and bring up sides. Top with the matching pastry round, pinching the dough until each fillet is completely covered with pastry. Bake fillets 12 minutes for rare, 16 minutes for medium or 20 minutes for well done. After baking them for 5 minutes, brush with egg to make them shiny and pretty. Serve hot with MARCHAND DE VIN SAUCE. Serves 6.

MARCHAND DE VIN SAUCE

3 Tablespoons butter
2 Tablespoons chopped
   scallions or onion
3 Tablespoons flour
1 cup beef consommé

1 Tablespoon tomato paste
⅓ cup red wine
Salt and pepper
2 Tablespoons butter
2 Tablespoons chopped parsley

Melt butter and add scallions. Cook until scallions are clear; then add the flour. Cook over medium heat, stirring constantly. When the roux is brown, add the boiling consommé, stirring until sauce thickens. Turn down heat to simmer; add tomato paste and wine. Cook over low heat for 20 minutes or until thick, stirring occasionally. Season with salt and pepper to taste. Take off heat and swirl in butter and parsley. Serve in sauceboat with Beef Wellington. Makes 1½ cups sauce.

Mrs. James B. Furrh, Jr.

When buying foie gras the label is important. Only "foie gras pur" of goose or duck has the right to the title. The mousses, purées, blocs de foie gras, blocs de foie d'oie, foies gras entiers, massifs and terrines legally do not have to be more than 50% pure.

Basic Beef or Brown Stock

2 pounds beef shin, cut into
   cubes
1 pound marrow bones, cracked
2 onions, quartered
1 carrot, quartered
4 quarts water, divided

2 ribs celery, quartered
1½ teaspoons salt
Pinch thyme
Pinch marjoram
Bouquet garni (4 sprigs parsley,
   1 bay leaf)

In a flat baking pan spread beef shin, marrow bones (if marrow bones are unavailable, brown the meat and shin bones in 2 Tablespoons shortening), onions and carrot. Brown the meat, bones and vegetables well on all sides in a preheated 450°F oven; then transfer them to a kettle. Deglaze the pan with 2 cups water over high heat, stirring in the brown bits clinging to the bottom and sides, and add the liquid to the kettle with 3½ quarts cold water and remaining ingredients. Bring the water to a boil, reduce the heat to low, and skim the froth as it rises to the surface. Simmer the stock, adding more boiling water if necessary to barely cover the ingredients, for 5-6 hours, or until it is reduced to about 2 quarts. Do not cover stock completely while it is cooking. Strain the stock through a fine sieve into a bowl and let it cool. Chill and remove fat. The stock freezes well. Makes 2 quarts stock.

Emergency Beef Stock

2 (10½ ounce) cans beef
   bouillon
3 Tablespoons finely minced
   onion
3 Tablespoons finely minced
   carrot

1 Tablespoon chopped celery
½ cup red or dry white wine
2 sprigs parsley
½ bay leaf
1/8 teaspoon thyme

Canned beef bouillon may be substituted in some recipes. However, since it tends to be sweet, it can be enriched by combining all ingredients listed. Simmer 30 minutes and strain through a fine sieve. Makes 3 cups stock.

Shish Kabob Marinade

1½ cups salad oil
¾ cup soy sauce
¼ cup Worcestershire sauce
2 teaspoons dry mustard
2¼ teaspoons salt

1 teaspoon pepper
½ cup wine vinegar
½ teaspoon chopped parsley
2 cloves garlic, minced
½ cup lemon juice

Mix all ingredients together. Place sauce in glass bowl and add cubed meat. (Up to 3 large sirloin or round steaks, cubed, can be marinated in sauce for several hours for use in making shish kabobs.) Yields 3½ cups marinade.

Mrs. Gene A. Stumpff

Bearnaise Sauce

¼ cup wine vinegar
¼ cup dry white wine or dry
   white vermouth
1 Tablespoon minced green
   onion
1½ teaspoons dried tarragon

1/8 teaspoon pepper
Pinch salt
3 egg yolks
3 Tablespoons boiling water
1 cup butter, sliced in thin
   pieces

Boil first 6 ingredients over medium heat until liquid has been reduced to 2 Tablespoons. Cool. Place egg yolks and water in top of double boiler. Have water barely boiling and shallow enough so that it does not touch the bottom of the upper saucepan. Stir egg mixture constantly with a wire whisk until it begins to thicken. Remove boiler from heat. Add butter a slice at a time, beating until dissolved. Remove top of double boiler from hot water. Blend in wine and vinegar mixture. Makes 1½ cups sauce.

Mrs. Ben McCarty

Sweet and Hot Mustard

1 cup sugar
1 cup vinegar
½ teaspoon salt

2 (2 ounce) cans Colman's
   dry mustard
3 eggs

Blend ingredients in blender. Cook in top of double boiler, stirring until thick. Cool and store in refrigerator. Yields about 20 ounces or enough to fill 3 large baby food jars.

Mrs. Robert Ratelle

This mustard is good on any sandwich or in any recipe calling for prepared mustard. For a lighter sauce, substitute tarragon vinegar and use only 1 (1.12 ounce) can dry mustard.

Henry Bain Sauce

1 (12 ounce) bottle Major
   Grey's chutney
½ bottle pickled walnuts
2 (14 ounce) bottles tomato
   ketchup
1 (10 ounce) bottle A-1 sauce

2 (12 ounce) bottles chili
   sauce
1 (5 ounce) bottle
   Worcestershire sauce
½ (2 ounce) bottle Tabasco or
   to taste

Place chutney and pickled walnuts in blender; set on low speed so they are chopped but not completely smooth. Mix with remaining ingredients, bottle and refrigerate. Use with any meat. Makes 4 pints sauce.

William N. Warren

This sauce is a standard in Louisville and was invented years ago by a chef, Henry Bain, at the Pendennis Club. Bottled, it makes special Christmas gifts.

Marinated Brisket

Make a paste of 1½ Tablespoons salt, 1½ Tablespoons paprika, 1 teaspoon garlic powder and a little water. Smear on both sides of a 2 or 3 pound brisket that has not been trimmed of fat. Wrap in foil and bake for 1 hour at 425°F; turn heat down to 375°F and bake 2 more hours. Serves 6.

Mrs. Ralph D. Farr

Marinated Beef Short Ribs

2 quarts cider vinegar or red
   wine
2 quarts water
½ cup brown sugar
2 Tablespoons dry mustard
6 whole cloves
2 sticks cinnamon

3 Tablespoons pickling spice
1 Tablespoon ground ginger
2 Tablespoons salt
1 Tablespoon pepper
4 or 5 pounds lean beef short
   ribs

Combine first 10 ingredients and simmer 30-40 minutes. Allow to cool. Pour marinade over short ribs which have been seasoned with additional salt and pepper and marinate 24 hours in refrigerator. Cook about 4-5 hours on Cajun Cooker or on covered grill. Do not place meat directly over fire. Serves 4-6.

Joseph Daschbach

Steak Butters

WINE BUTTER

1 Tablespoon minced green
   onion
1 cup dry red wine

½ cup butter, softened
2 teaspoons chopped parsley
Salt and pepper to taste

Cook onion and wine in a small saucepan until the liquid is reduced to ¼ cup. Remove from heat and cool. With beater, cream butter and parsley. Gradually beat in the wine mixture. Season to taste with salt and pepper. Makes ¾ cup butter.

HERB BUTTER

½ cup butter, softened
1 Tablespoon lemon juice
½ teaspoon salt
1/8 teaspoon pepper

2 Tablespoons chopped parsley
1 Tablespoon chopped chives
½ teaspoon tarragon leaves

Cream butter. Beat in the rest of the ingredients until smooth. Makes ½ cup butter.

The Editors

Lobster-Stuffed Tenderloin

1 (3 to 4 pound) beef tenderloin
3 long lobster tails or
   2 (8 ounce) boxes frozen
1 Tablespoon margarine, melted
1½ teaspoons lemon juice

6 slices bacon
½ cup sliced green onion
½ cup margarine
½ cup dry white wine
1/8 teaspoon garlic salt

Butterfly roast; boil lobster tails and remove from shells. Place lobster inside beef. Combine margarine and lemon juice. Drizzle over lobster. Tie roast together. Place partially cooked bacon over roast. Preheat oven to 500°F. Place roast in oven for 5 minutes. Reduce heat to 350°F. Cook to desired doneness, allowing 10 minutes per pound for rare, 15 minutes for medium. Cook green onion in margarine; add wine and garlic salt and serve over meat. Serves 6-8.

Mrs. Dan Hodges, Jr.

Steak à la Moutarde

1 thick fillet steak
Salt and pepper
2 Tablespoons butter

1 Tablespoon Cognac
2 Tablespoons whipping cream
1 teaspoon prepared mustard

Season steak with salt and pepper and sear on both sides in hot butter in frying pan. Remove and keep hot. Rinse pan with Cognac; add cream. Stir well and reduce liquid by half. Just before serving add mustard. Stir well and pour over steak. Serves 1.

From the recipes of John B. Mason

Roast Tenderloin

1 (3½ to 5 pound) beef
   tenderloin
Kitchen Bouquet
Garlic powder
Salt and cracked black pepper

½ cup water
½ cup red wine
Minced parsley (optional)
Sliced mushrooms (optional)

Using hands, coat roast well with Kitchen Bouquet. Season with garlic powder, salt and pepper. Allow to stand until roast is at room temperature. Preheat oven to 450°F. Cook 20 minutes. Remove roast from pan; cover meat lightly with foil. To pan juices add water, wine, parsley and mushrooms, if desired. Simmer and serve as sauce. Tenderloin will be brown and crusty on outside, pink and juicy on inside. If more doneness is desired, return to oven, but watch carefully because every minute counts at this temperature. Serves 8.

Mrs. Harrison Russell

This can only be prepared shortly before dinner is served. But don't worry. It turns out perfectly!

Beef Shish Kabobs

½ cup Burgundy wine
1 teaspoon Worcestershire sauce
½ teaspoon monosodium
  glutamate
1 clove garlic, crushed
½ cup salad oil
½ teaspoon salt
2 Tablespoons ketchup
1 teaspoon sugar
1 Tablespoon vinegar

½ teaspoon marjoram
½ teaspoon rosemary
2 pounds trimmed sirloin steak,
  cut into 1½-inch cubes
1 (8 ounce) can large button
  mushrooms, drained
Onion wedges
Green pepper, cut into 1-inch
  squares
Cherry tomatoes (optional)

Mix first 11 ingredients for the marinade. Place marinade, sirloin cubes and mushrooms in covered container and refrigerate for 1-2 days. After this time the contents may be divided and frozen in separate containers, if desired. When ready to cook, thaw meat. Blanch onion wedges and green pepper squares in boiling water. Alternate on skewers with mushrooms and meat. Cherry tomatoes may be added, if desired. Cook over medium coals. Yields 4-5 kabobs.

Reuel May, Jr.

Braised Sirloin Tips over Almond Rice

1½ pounds mushrooms, sliced
¼ cup butter or margarine,
  melted, divided
1 Tablespoon salad oil
1 (3 pound) sirloin steak, cut
  into 1-inch cubes
¾ cup beef bouillon
¾ cup red wine
2 Tablespoons soy sauce

2 cloves garlic, minced
½ onion, grated
2 Tablespoons cornstarch
⅓ cup beef bouillon
½ (10½ ounce) can cream of
  mushroom soup
Salt to taste
Cooked rice
Slivered almonds, toasted

Sauté mushrooms in 2 Tablespoons butter until lightly browned; spoon into a 3-quart casserole. Add remaining butter and salad oil to skillet; add meat and brown on all sides. Spoon over mushrooms. Combine ¾ cup bouillon, wine, soy sauce, garlic and onion; add to skillet, scraping bottom to salvage all particles. Blend cornstarch with ⅓ cup bouillon; stir into wine mixture. Cook, stirring constantly, until smooth and thickened. Spoon over meat, stirring gently to mix. Cover and bake at 275 °F for 1 hour. Add mushroom soup, stirring until smooth. Add salt to taste. Bake 10-15 minutes longer. Serve over cooked rice into which toasted almonds have been tossed. Serves 8.

Mrs. Richard L. Redmont, Jr.

Permit meat to stand at room temperature for an hour or two before roasting.

Marinated Eye of the Round

1 (5 pound) eye of the round
  roast
¼ cup salad oil
2 Tablespoons lemon-pepper
  seasoning
½ cup wine vinegar
½ cup lemon juice
½ cup soy sauce
½ cup Worcestershire sauce

Marinate roast in mixture of next 6 ingredients for 1-3 days, turning at least once a day. Cook uncovered with marinade in a Dutch oven at 250°F for 3 hours. Refrigerate overnight. Slice thin and serve with heated marinade. Garnish with parsley and cherry tomatoes. This is delicious for a buffet supper. Freezes well. Serves 10-15.

Mrs. J. Edward Ruff, II

London Broil

1 (2 pound) flank steak
1 Tablespoon salad oil
2 teaspoons chopped parsley
1 clove garlic, crushed
1 teaspoon salt
1 teaspoon lemon juice
1/8 teaspoon pepper

Trim excess fat from steak and wipe with damp paper towels. Combine remaining ingredients. Brush half of mixture over 1 side of steak; let stand 45 minutes. Place steak, oil side up, on lightly greased broiler pan; broil 4 inches from heat for 5 minutes. Turn steak; brush with remaining mixture and broil 4-5 minutes longer. Remove steak to board or platter and slice thinly on the diagonal across the grain. This steak will be rare—the only way London Broil should be served! Serves 4.

Mrs. George P. Hewes, III

Barbecued Brisket

1 (5 or 6 pound) beef brisket
  (flat cut), trimmed
3 ounces liquid smoke
Celery salt
Garlic salt
Onion salt
Worcestershire sauce
Salt and pepper
6 ounces barbecue sauce
2 Tablespoons flour
½ cup water

Place brisket in oblong baking dish; sprinkle with liquid smoke and salts. Cover and refrigerate overnight. When ready to bake, sprinkle with Worcestershire sauce, salt and pepper. Place foil loosely over meat. Cook at 275°F for 5 hours. Uncover and pour barbecue sauce over meat. Cook without foil for another hour. Remove to platter and let cool before slicing. Remove fat from sauce remaining in dish. Add flour and water to sauce and stir. Cook until sauce thickens. Serve sauce hot with meat. Serve with rice or potatoes and tossed green salad. Serves 10.

Mrs. William R. Wright

Goza's Pepper Roast and Gravy

5 to 6 pounds boneless beef rib
   eye (or eye of round or top
   round)
½ cup coarsely cracked pepper
½ teaspoon cardamom seed
1 Tablespoon tomato paste
1 teaspoon paprika

½ teaspoon garlic powder
1 cup soy sauce
¾ cup vinegar
1½ cups water, divided
1½ Tablespoons flour
   (optional)

Rub roast with pepper and cardamom to cover. Press in with heel of hand. Place in shallow baking pan. Mix together tomato paste, paprika and garlic powder. Gradually add soy sauce and vinegar. Pour over roast and marinate overnight in refrigerator. Let stand at room temperature 1 hour. Remove roast from marinade and wrap in foil. Reserve marinade for gravy. Cook in shallow pan at 300°F for 2 hours. Open foil and ladle off drippings. Brown uncovered at 350°F. While meat is browning, strain and defat pan drippings. To 1 cup drippings add 1 cup water and bring to a boil. Add ½ cup reserved marinade. Thicken with flour mixed with remaining water, if desired. Slice roast thinly and diagonally and serve with gravy. Serves 12.

Mrs. Thomas G. Abernethy, Jr.

Tangy Pot Roast

1 (4 pound) boned, rolled beef
   arm, blade or bottom round
   pot roast
3 Tablespoons flour
2 teaspoons salt
¼ teaspoon freshly ground
   black pepper
3 Tablespoons bacon drippings
   or oil
1 cup beef broth

1 cup whole berry cranberry
   sauce
½ cup freshly grated
   horseradish or 1 (4 ounce)
   jar horseradish, drained
1 stick cinnamon, halved
4 whole cloves
16 small white onions
1 bunch carrots, cut in 3-inch
   lengths

Dredge meat in the flour mixed with the salt and pepper. Rub the mixture into all surfaces. Heat the drippings or oil in a heavy Dutch oven or casserole and brown the meat well on all sides over high heat. Pour off drippings into a skillet and reserve. Mix together the broth, cranberry sauce, horseradish, cinnamon and cloves and add to the meat. Bring the mixture to a boil, cover tightly and simmer gently about 2 hours or until the meat is barely tender. Meanwhile, brown the onions in the reserved drippings in the skillet. Add the carrots and cook 2 minutes longer. Add drained vegetables to the meat broth. Cover and cook about 25 minutes longer or until the vegetables and meat are tender. Note: The quantity of horseradish is correct. It loses its pungency as it cooks. Serves 8.

Mrs. Richard L. Redmont, Jr.

Cold Marinated Beef

2 cups water
Few drops lemon juice
Dash salt
1 large onion, sliced in rings
15 large mushrooms, sliced
1½ pounds cold cooked roast
   beef, thinly sliced

½ cup red wine vinegar
2 teaspoons Dijon mustard
1 teaspoon salt
¼ teaspoon crushed marjoram
¼ teaspoon pepper
1 cup salad oil
2 Tablespoons chopped parsley

Bring to a boil the water, lemon juice and salt. Drop in the onion rings; remove immediately and drain. Place onions and mushrooms on top of meat slices. Mix together the remaining ingredients, except the parsley, and pour over the meat. Refrigerate until time to serve; then sprinkle with parsley. Serves 6-8.

Mrs. Walker L. Watters

Steak Diane à la Richard

2 rib eye steaks, well trimmed
1 Tablespoon butter
Salt and pepper to taste
2 Tablespoons Cognac
1 Tablespoon dry sherry wine
2 Tablespoons butter

Juice of ½ lemon
½ teaspoon hot English mustard
2 teaspoons chopped parsley
2 teaspoons Worcestershire
   sauce
1 Tablespoon chopped chives

Sauté steaks in butter over medium high heat to desired doneness, adding salt and pepper as they cook. Reduce heat and add Cognac and sherry. Flame. When flame dies, remove steaks and keep warm in oven. Add remaining ingredients to pan juices. Heat to bubbling and pour over steaks. Serve immediately. Serves 2.

Mrs. W. R. Newman, III

Barbecued Beef Cubes

5 pounds beef, cut in 2-inch
   cubes
Oil
1 medium onion, chopped
4 Tablespoons butter
3 Tablespoons vinegar
4 Tablespoons brown sugar
4 Tablespoons lemon juice

1 (14 ounce) bottle ketchup
3 Tablespoons Worcestershire
   sauce
2 teaspoons prepared mustard
1 cup water
1 cup chopped celery
Salt and pepper to taste

Brown beef cubes in small amount of oil in heavy skillet. Drain and set aside. Brown onion in butter. Add remaining ingredients, mix well and simmer until slightly thickened, about 30 minutes. Pour sauce over beef cubes either in Dutch oven or casserole. Cover and cook in 300°F oven until beef cubes are tender, about 2 hours. Good served over noodles. Serves 12.

Mrs. W. H. Hight, Louisville, Mississippi

Mediterranean Oven Stew

2½ Tablespoons butter
¼ cup chopped celery
¼ cup chopped green pepper
  (optional)
1 clove garlic, minced (optional)
½ cup chopped onion
2 pounds cubed lean beef
2½ Tablespoons flour
1½ teaspoons salt

¼ teaspoon pepper
½ teaspoon sugar
1 (16 ounce) can whole
  tomatoes, cut up
1 (4 ounce) can sliced
  mushrooms, drained
2 beef bouillon cubes, dissolved
  in 2 cups hot water
½ cup dry red wine

Melt butter in skillet. Add celery, green pepper, garlic and onion. Sauté until softened and browned. Dust meat with flour, salt and pepper. Add meat to skillet and brown on all sides. Stir in remaining ingredients. Place in a large buttered casserole and cover. Refrigerate for 24 hours. To serve, bake at 350°F for 2 hours. The sauce is also good over biscuits or toast. Serves 8-10.

Mrs. James C. Jenkins, Jr.

Boeuf à la Bourguignonne

½ pound bacon, diced
4 pounds beef (chuck or
  round), cut in 2-inch cubes
Flour
2 cloves garlic, minced
3 carrots, sliced
3 cups sliced onion
¼ cup Cognac or brandy
½ teaspoon salt
¼ teaspoon freshly ground
  pepper

1 bay leaf
½ teaspoon thyme, crumbled
3½ cups Burgundy wine,
  divided
1 pound fresh mushrooms,
  sliced
2 Tablespoons butter or
  margarine
24 small white onions, peeled
¼ cup chopped parsley

Cook bacon until crisp and brown; remove from grease. Roll beef cubes lightly in flour. Brown in bacon fat. Transfer to Dutch oven or large oven-proof casserole. Sauté garlic, carrots and onion in bacon fat until soft and lightly browned. Warm Cognac and ignite; pour over beef. When flame dies, add garlic, carrots, sliced onion, salt, pepper, bay leaf, thyme and 3 cups Burgundy. Cover and cook 2-2½ hours or until meat is tender. While meat is cooking, sauté mushrooms in butter or margarine. Remove. In same skillet sauté onions until brown (more fat may be added if needed). Add ½ cup wine to skillet. Cover and simmer 15 minutes. When meat is done, skim any excess fat. Sauce may be thickened by blending 1 Tablespoon flour and 1 Tablespoon butter or margarine and stirring into hot wine liquid bit by bit. Add bacon, mushrooms and onions. Cook 5 minutes. Sprinkle with parsley. Serves 6-8.

Mrs. John B. Mason

Slow and Easy Chuck Roast

3 to 4 pounds lean boneless
   chuck roast
Cavender's Greek seasoning
Lemon-pepper seasoning

1 package onion-mushroom
   dry soup mix
½ cup water

Cut away as much fat as possible from roast. Sprinkle roast with next 3 ingredients and place in crock-pot. Add water and cook on low for 8-10 hours. Thicken gravy with flour or cornstarch, if desired. Any lean roast is good cooked this way. Serves 6.

Mrs. W. V. Westbrook, Jr.

Beef Chicona

5 pounds stew meat
Olive oil
3 cups chopped onion
2 Tablespoons paprika
1½ teaspoons garlic powder
2 Tablespoons onion powder
2 Tablespoons ground cumin
2 Tablespoons monosodium
   glutamate

1 (16 ounce) can whole
   tomatoes
1 (6 ounce) can tomato paste
4 beef bouillon cubes
2¼ cups water
3 Jalapeño peppers, chopped
2½ cups chopped green pepper
Salt to taste
Flour tortillas

Brown stew meat in olive oil. Add all other ingredients except tortillas and simmer 2 hours or more. Serve on flour tortillas which have been heated in oven. Leftover sauce mixed with browned ground beef makes delicious sloppy joes. Serves 10.

Mrs. Alex A. Alston, Jr.

Chinese Pepper Steak

¼ cup vegetable oil
1 clove garlic, crushed
1½ to 2 pounds sirloin steak,
   cut in small thin pieces
1 teaspoon ground ginger
Salt to taste
½ teaspoon pepper
½ cup beef bouillon
3 large green peppers, sliced

2 large onions, sliced
4 green onions, chopped
¼ cup soy sauce
½ teaspoon sugar
¼ cup cold water
1 Tablespoon cornstarch
1 (8 ounce) can water
   chestnuts, sliced
Cooked rice

Heat pan; add oil and garlic. When garlic browns, remove. Add beef and fry a few minutes. Season with ginger, salt and pepper. Add bouillon and continue to cook, adding green peppers and onions. Add soy sauce, sugar, water and cornstarch mixed together. Cook until mixture thickens, stirring slowly. Fold in water chestnuts. Serve over cooked rice. Serves 4.

Mrs. Ken P. Toler

Tomato Beef

1½ to 2 pounds flank steak
3 Tablespoons soy sauce
2 Tablespoons dry sherry wine
1 clove garlic, minced
½ teaspoon ground ginger
1/8 teaspoon black pepper
2 Tablespoons oil
1 medium green pepper, sliced

1 medium onion, sliced
½ cup sliced celery
1 beef bouillon cube
¾ cup boiling water
2 Tablespoons cornstarch
2 Tablespoons cold water
4 ripe medium tomatoes

Slice beef thinly on the diagonal. Place snugly in small bowl. Combine soy sauce, sherry, garlic, ginger and pepper; pour over meat. Cover and refrigerate 8-10 hours. In a large skillet, heat oil. Add green pepper, onion and celery; sauté 2 minutes. Dissolve bouillon cube in boiling water. Add to skillet along with beef and marinade. Bring to boiling point. Reduce heat and simmer covered for 8-10 minutes. Blend cornstarch with cold water. Stir into mixture in skillet. Stir until thickened. Cut tomatoes into wedges; add to skillet and stir gently. Simmer just until tomatoes are hot. Serve hot over rice with scallions or green onions. Serves 6-8.

Mrs. J. T. Noblin

Chunky Chili

2 Tablespoons vegetable oil
3 pounds boneless chuck, cut in
    1-inch cubes
2 cloves garlic, chopped
4 Tablespoons chili powder
2 teaspoons ground cumin
3 Tablespoons flour
1 Tablespoon leaf oregano
2 (13¾ ounce) cans beef broth

1 teaspoon salt
½ teaspoon pepper
1 (15½ ounce) can Trappey's
    Jalapeño pinto beans,
    drained
4 cups cooked rice
1 cup sour cream
2 limes, cut in wedges

Heat oil in a heavy 4-quart pan over medium heat. Add beef, stirring frequently with a wooden spoon, until meat changes color but does not burn. Lower heat and stir in garlic. Combine chili powder, cumin and flour. Sprinkle meat with chili mixture, stirring until meat is evenly coated. Crumble oregano over meat. Add broth and stir until liquid is well blended. Add salt and pepper. Bring to a boil, stirring occasionally. Reduce heat and simmer 2 hours. Cool thoroughly. Cover and refrigerate overnight. Reheat chili slowly. Add beans. Place cooked rice in individual serving bowls. Spoon chili mixture over rice. Add 1 Tablespoon sour cream to each serving. Garnish with lime wedges to squeeze over each portion. Serves 8-10.

Mrs. O. J. Lange, Florence, Mississippi

Grillades

8 pounds beef round steak
1 cup oil or bacon grease, divided
1 cup flour
3 cups chopped onion
1 bunch green onions, chopped
5 ribs celery and tops, chopped
3 cups chopped green pepper
2 (8 ounce) cans tomato sauce
2 teaspoons thyme
2 cups Burgundy wine

1 to 2 cups water
1½ Tablespoons salt
1 teaspoon cracked pepper
1½ teaspoons instant minced garlic
1 bunch parsley, chopped
2 teaspoons Tabasco
4 Tablespoons Worcestershire sauce
6 to 8 bay leaves

Cut meat into strips and brown in a little oil or bacon grease in heavy skillet or Dutch oven. Set aside. Add rest of oil or grease to pan and stir in flour. Continue stirring until a rich brown roux has been made. Add onions, celery and green pepper and stir until tender. Add tomato sauce and thyme, stirring until sauce has lost its bright red color. Add wine and water necessary to make enough gravy to cover meat. Return meat to gravy and bring to a boil. Add all seasonings. Reduce heat and simmer 2 hours, or until done. Adjust seasonings. Serve over grits or rice. May be prepared 1-2 days ahead. Freezes well. Serves 24.

Mrs. George W. Newton

Calf Liver à l'Orange

6 slices calf liver (about 1½ to 2 pounds)
½ cup flour
½ teaspoon salt
¼ teaspoon pepper
¼ teaspoon dry mustard
Dash cayenne pepper
5 Tablespoons butter or margarine, divided

1 medium onion, finely chopped
1 clove garlic, crushed
⅓ cup beef stock
¼ cup red wine
1½ teaspoons chopped parsley
1½ teaspoons thyme
1 navel orange, unpeeled
Sugar

Remove membrane from liver slices and dredge liver in flour seasoned with salt, pepper, dry mustard and cayenne. In large skillet, melt 3 Tablespoons butter and sauté liver slices quickly on both sides. Transfer liver to heated platter and keep warm. To skillet add 1 Tablespoon butter, onion and garlic. Cook until onion is golden. Add beef stock, red wine, parsley and thyme. Cook sauce for 1 minute and pour over liver. Cut orange into thin slices, brown on both sides in 1 Tablespoon butter and sprinkle with sugar. Garnish platter with orange slices. Serve with fluffy white rice. Serves 6.

Mrs. Reuel May, Jr.

Virginia Ham with Dressing Patties

1 (12 to 14 pound) Virginia ham	Vinegar
3 cups sherry wine	Brown sugar
3 bay leaves	Prepared mustard
2 Tablespoons whole cloves	Bread crumbs

Soak ham in water to cover several hours or overnight, depending on how strong the salt and flavor is. Place ham in large pan; mix sherry, bay leaves and cloves and pour over ham. Cover and bake at 275°F for 20-25 minutes per pound, turning periodically. Cool overnight in mixture. Skin. Make a paste of remaining ingredients (approximately 1 part vinegar, 2 parts sugar, 1 part mustard and 3 parts bread crumbs) and spread over ham. Dot with additional cloves. Bake uncovered at 400°F for about 30 minutes to brown. Slice thinly and serve with DRESSING PATTIES. Serves 25.

DRESSING PATTIES

1½ cups hand-crumbled white bread	¼ teaspoon cayenne pepper
	2 eggs, beaten
3 cups hand-crumbled corn bread	1 teaspoon sugar
	⅓ cup cider vinegar
1 teaspoon dry mustard	2 Tablespoons ham fat, melted
½ teaspoon black pepper	1 teaspoon salt
2 Tablespoons celery seed	½ cup milk
1 medium onion, chopped	3 Tablespoons ham liquid

Grease cookie sheet or miniature muffin tins. Mix together all ingredients. Taste for seasoning, adding more pepper or vinegar as desired. Heat baking pans. If using muffin tins, fill about half full, using about 1 Tablespoon of mixture for each muffin. If making patties, use same amount on cookie sheet. Bake in a preheated 400°F oven for 30 minutes. Serve hot preferably, but can use cold. Can store patties in refrigerator or freezer. Patties are hot and are intended more as a taste enhancer with the ham than as a dressing. Great for a cocktail buffet. Yields about 4 dozen patties.

Mrs. Sydney A. Smith

Jezebel Sauce

1 (5 ounce) jar horseradish	1 (18 ounce) jar apple jelly
1 (1.12 ounce) can dry mustard	2 Tablespoons coarsely ground
1 (18 ounce) jar pineapple preserves	pepper, or less

Mix the horseradish and dry mustard well. Combine with remaining ingredients. Will keep in refrigerator for years. Especially good on sliced ham. Makes 4 cups sauce.

Miss Lynda Wright

Jean Enochs's Glazed Ham Loaf

2 pounds ground smoked ham
2 pounds ground lean pork
1½ cups cracker crumbs (not
    packaged cracker meal)
⅓ cup chopped onion
4 eggs, well beaten
2 cups milk
2 Tablespoons chopped parsley

GLAZE:
1 cup brown sugar (packed)
½ cup cider vinegar
1½ Tablespoons dry mustard

SAUCE:
½ cup mayonnaise
½ cup sour cream
¼ cup prepared mustard
1 Tablespoon minced olives
2 Tablespoons horseradish
Salt
Lemon juice

Mix well the first 7 ingredients and shape in loaf pan. Bake at 350°F for 30 minutes. Pour off fat. While this is baking, prepare GLAZE by mixing glaze ingredients and boiling 1 minute. Pour over ham loaf and bake 1 hour longer. Serve ham loaf cold with SAUCE prepared by mixing well the sauce ingredients. Serves 10.

Mrs. Ben Lampton

Italian Cheese and Ham Pie

1 (16 ounce) carton cottage
    cheese
1 (15 or 16 ounce) carton
    ricotta cheese
2 cups diced cooked ham
    (¾ pound)
⅔ cup grated Parmesan cheese
3 eggs
2 teaspoons Italian seasoning
½ teaspoon salt
¼ teaspoon pepper
2 packages pie crust mix or pie
    crust sticks for 4 crusts
1 egg yolk, beaten

In a medium bowl mix well the first 8 ingredients. Preheat oven to 375°F. In a large bowl prepare pie crust as package directs, making up both packages at once. Shape ⅔ of the pastry into a large ball and shape the remaining ⅓ into a smaller ball. On a lightly floured surface, roll the large ball into a 16-inch circle. Fold circle into fourths and carefully lift into a 10-inch springform pan. Lightly press into bottom and sides of pan. Trim edges even with rim of pan and brush pastry with egg yolk. Spoon cheese mixture into pan and fold edges of pastry over filling; then brush edges with egg yolk. Roll remaining pastry into a 10-inch circle and place over filling in pan, pressing lightly around edges to seal. Brush top with egg yolk. Bake pie 1 hour or until a knife inserted in the center comes out clean. Cool pie in refrigerator. Serve chilled. Serves 8-10.

Mrs. Robert H. Thompson, Jr.

This pie looks especially nice if leftover dough is rolled out and cut into attractive shapes with a cookie cutter and then placed on top crust of pie before brushing top with egg yolk. It is great for picnics since it is served cold and can be transported easily in the springform pan in a cooler.

Cherry Sauce for Ham

1 (10 ounce) bottle maraschino
   cherries (reserve juice)
Slivered almonds
⅓ cup wine vinegar
2 teaspoons pickling spice, tied
   in cheesecloth

1 cup brown sugar
2 Tablespoons cornstarch
2 Tablespoons butter
1 to 2 teaspoons juice from
   prepared horseradish (optional)
Red food coloring

Measure cherry juice and add water to make 1½ cups. Stuff each cherry with 3 almond slivers. Combine cherry juice and all ingredients except cherries in saucepan and cook, stirring, until thick. Remove from heat, remove pickling spice and add cherries. Serve at room temperature. Makes 2 cups.

Mrs. Elaine Ford Eaton, Taylorsville, Mississippi

Ham and Mushroom à la King

1 pound fresh mushrooms, sliced
½ cup butter or margarine,
   divided
¼ cup flour
2 cups milk
¼ cup port wine

1½ cups shredded Cheddar
   cheese, divided
1/8 teaspoon cayenne red pepper
8 ounces sliced cooked ham,
   divided
Toast points

Cook mushrooms in ¼ cup butter or margarine in large skillet until tender. Set aside. Melt remaining butter in 2-quart saucepan over low heat; stir in flour. Cook over low heat, stirring until mixture is smooth and bubbly. Remove from heat; stir in milk. Heat to boiling, stirring constantly. Boil and stir 1 minute; reduce heat. Stir in wine, 1 cup cheese and red pepper. Heat oven to 350°F. Chop half the ham slices. Stir chopped ham and mushrooms into sauce. Cover bottom and sides of 1-quart baking dish with remaining ham slices. Pour sauce over ham; sprinkle with remaining cheese. Bake at 350°F until hot and bubbly (20-25 minutes). Serve over toast points. Serves 8.

Mrs. Richard L. Redmont, Jr.

Pork Loin Roast with Apple Glaze

1 pork loin roast with
   backbone loosened
1 Tablespoon flour
1 teaspoon dry mustard
1 teaspoon salt

¼ teaspoon pepper
2 cups sweetened applesauce
¼ cup brown sugar
¼ teaspoon ground cinnamon
¼ teaspoon ground cloves

Rub roast with mixture of flour, mustard, salt and pepper. Roast 35 or 40 minutes to the pound at 350°F. About an hour before roast is done, spread with apple glaze made by combining remaining ingredients. Return to oven until meat is done. Serves 6-8.

Mrs. Richard L. Redmont, Jr.

Chow Mein

½ pound diced pork
½ pound diced beef or chicken
2 Tablespoons oil
3 medium onions, chopped
1 whole bunch celery, diced
6 Tablespoons soy sauce
½ cup water or 1 (10½ ounce)
    can beef broth

2 to 3 Tablespoons cornstarch
1 (8 ounce) can water
    chestnuts, sliced
1 (16 ounce) can bean sprouts,
    drained
Salt to taste

Sauté meat in oil until it browns. Remove meat from skillet. Sauté onions until tender. Add celery. Cover with small amount of water and cook until tender. Add browned meat and simmer 1½-2 hours. Add soy sauce, broth and cornstarch, mixed with a little water to make a paste. Add water chestnuts and bean sprouts. Season with salt. Serve over rice or chow mein noodles. Serves 6-8.

Mrs. Lee R. Reid

Roast Loin of Pork

6 pounds loin of pork, trimmed
3 teaspoons salt
1 teaspoon thyme
1 teaspoon pepper
½ teaspoon ground nutmeg
2 onions, peeled and sliced
2 carrots, peeled and sliced
2 cloves garlic, crushed

Parsley
Celery leaves
4 whole cloves
3 bay leaves
1¼ cups dry white wine, divided
1¼ cups beef consommé,
    divided
½ cup water

Season roast by rubbing with a mixture of the salt, thyme, pepper and nutmeg. Place roast in roasting pan and place vegetables, herbs and spices around it. Combine ½ cup wine and ½ cup consommé and pour over roast. (Add more wine and consommé later if needed. Do not let roast dry out.) Place uncovered in preheated 475°F oven and roast 20 minutes. Reduce heat to 350°F and roast covered about 35 minutes per pound or until meat registers well done on meat thermometer. Remove roast and vegetables from pan. Strain pan juices and mix with remaining consommé, remaining wine and water. Return to pan and boil down rapidly, scraping bottom of pan. Cook until slightly thick. Serve as a gravy for the roast. Serves 12.

Mrs. Frank R. Briggs

———

Cook a pork loin roast in foil until well done. Remove foil and baste with a mixture of 4 Tablespoons Cointreau and ¾ cup Marsala wine while cooking in 400°F oven to achieve a ruby red glaze.

Pork Chop Gravy

3 Tablespoons ketchup
2 Tablespoons white vinegar
1 Tablespoon lemon juice
2 Tablespoons Worcestershire
   sauce
4 Tablespoons water

1 teaspoon paprika
2 Tablespoons butter
3 Tablespoons brown sugar
1 teaspoon salt
1 teaspoon prepared mustard
½ teaspoon pepper

Mix all ingredients in saucepan over low heat until butter is melted. Serve over broiled chops or any type pork roast. Serves 4.

Mrs. James Dent May

Maple Barbecued Spareribs

1½ cups maple syrup
2 Tablespoons chili sauce
2 Tablespoons cider vinegar
1½ Tablespoons chopped onion
1 teaspoon salt

1 Tablespoon Worcestershire
   sauce
½ teaspoon dry mustard
1/8 teaspoon pepper
3 pounds spareribs, cut in pieces

Preheat oven to 350°F. Combine maple syrup with all ingredients except meat. Brush sauce on both sides of ribs. Place ribs in single layer on rack in roasting pan. Roast 1½ hours. Brush frequently with sauce, turning occasionally to glaze. Serves 3-4.

From the recipes of Mrs. John R. Countiss, III

Barbecued Ribs

6 pounds country-style pork ribs
3 cloves garlic, minced, sautéed
   in 2 Tablespoons margarine
1½ cups water
¾ cup chili sauce
1 cup ketchup
¼ cup brown sugar
2 Tablespoons Worcestershire
   sauce

2 Tablespoons soy sauce
2 Tablespoons prepared mustard
2 teaspoons chili powder
1 Tablespoon celery seed
¼ teaspoon liquid smoke
½ teaspoon salt
Tabasco to taste
1 large onion, sliced
1 lemon, thinly sliced

Place ribs in shallow roasting pan. Cover and bake 45 minutes at 450°F. Meanwhile, combine remaining ingredients except onion and lemon and heat to boiling. Remove ribs and drain off all fat. Arrange in pan, placing a slice of onion and a slice of lemon on each piece. Pour sauce over the ribs and continue baking uncovered at 350°F for about 1½ hours. Baste ribs with sauce about every 15 minutes. Serves 6.

Mrs. John Crawford

Hot Tamales

5 pounds pork roast (loin end)
5 pounds chuck roast
Salt to taste
3 cloves garlic
Peppercorns
2 to 3 bay leaves
2 (4 ounce) cans green chilies
1 (9 ounce) jar salad olives
5 large onions, chopped
3 Tablespoons oil
2 pounds dried corn shucks
16 cups prepared masa or
    homemade using Masa
    Harina

5⅓ cups lard or shortening
4 Tablespoons baking powder
11 cups meat liquid
2 (15 ounce) cans tomato
    sauce
4 (6 ounce) cans tomato paste
5 teaspoons Mole or chili
    powder to taste if Mole is
    not available
1 (1 pound) box dark brown
    sugar
Ground cinnamon to taste
¾ (15 ounce) box raisins

In a large kettle cover meat with water. Add salt, garlic, peppercorns and bay leaves. Cook on low setting until meat is fork tender. While meat is cooking chop green chilies (reserve juice) and olives (reserve juice). Cook onions until tender in oil; set aside until next day. Cook olives and green chilies in their own juice until tender; refrigerate until next day. When meat is ready, strain and save liquid. Pull meat apart by hand. Refrigerate meat and liquid until next day. When ready to roll tamales remove meat, liquid, onions and olive mixture from refrigerator. Remove any fat that formed on meat liquid. Heat the liquid for use in making the dough. Clean and separate corn shucks; soak in *hot* water to cover to soften. In a large bowl beat the masa, lard or shortening, baking powder and some of the meat liquid, adding a little at a time. Mix well until the dough is glossy or soft enough to spread easily. Remove ⅓ of dough mixture and set aside for sweet tamales. To the remaining meat liquid, add the shredded meat, olives, onions, peppers, tomato sauce and tomato paste. If the mixture is not covered with liquid, add water. Add Mole or chili powder to taste. Simmer mixture on low for about 1 hour, or long enough for the flavors to blend. When the meat mixture is ready, *strain* the mixture, saving the liquid for the sauce. Spread 3 Tablespoons masa on a corn shuck. Add 2 Tablespoons meat mixture. Roll up and fold over one end. Place on steaming rack. (If dough has become hard to spread, add a little water and mix until it can be spread easily.) After all the meat tamales are rolled, take the remaining masa dough and add the dark brown sugar, cinnamon and raisins. Take mixture and spread on remaining corn shucks. Roll up as before. Place the sweet tamales on top of the meat-filled tamales and steam in the oven or in an electric cooker for 2 hours at 325°F or until the dough is completely cooked. (To test for doneness, unwrap one tamale; if dough is firm and does not stick to husk it is ready.) With remaining liquid make sauce to serve over tamales. Divide liquid in half to make one hot and one regular sauce. For hot sauce add more chili

(Continued)

powder or Tabasco to taste. Add a little cornstarch or flour to thicken. Any remaining meat may be used for taco filling. Freezes well. Makes about 9 dozen meat tamales and 5 dozen sweet tamales.

Mrs. Ernest Thomas, II

Sweet and Sour Pork

Cooking oil
1 egg
¼ cup flour
1 teaspoon salt
Dash pepper
3 Tablespoons milk
1 pound lean pork, cut in
   1-inch cubes
1 cup pineapple chunks
⅓ cup vinegar

1 large green pepper, cut in
   pieces
½ cup brown sugar
1 chicken bouillon cube,
   dissolved in 1 cup boiling
   water
2 teaspoons soy sauce
2 Tablespoons cornstarch
1 tomato, cut in 6 pieces

Heat oil to 350°F. Mix egg, flour, salt, pepper and milk to make a thin batter. Dip pork in batter and fry in deep oil until golden brown. Combine pineapple, vinegar, green pepper, brown sugar, ¾ cup chicken bouillon and soy sauce. Bring to a boil. Mix cornstarch and remaining ¼ cup bouillon and stir into sauce. Cook until thickened. Fold in tomato and pork. Cook about 2 minutes more. Serve immediately with hot cooked rice. Serves 6.

Mrs. Arnold Hederman, Jr.

Noisettes de Pork aux Pruneaux
(Pork Tenderloin with Prunes)

24 large dried pitted prunes
1 cup dry white wine
6 pork tenderloin medallions,
   1½ inches thick
Salt and freshly ground pepper

Flour
3 Tablespoons butter
½ cup chicken broth
½ cup whipping cream
2 teaspoons red currant jelly

Soak prunes at room temperature in white wine for 12 hours. Simmer for 10 minutes in the same liquid. Drain, reserving liquid. Sprinkle pork with salt, pepper and flour. Sauté tenderloins in butter until brown on both sides; remove to a side dish. Pour out almost all fat from the pan and add the prune-flavored wine. Boil briskly until almost cooked away. Add chicken broth and bring to a boil; add tenderloins, cover and simmer gently for 30-40 minutes, until tender. Remove meat. Add cream to pan and bring to a boil, scraping up all the brown tidbits. Cook, stirring, until slightly thickened. Add jelly and stir to dissolve. Add prunes, heat through and taste for seasoning. Arrange tenderloins on serving dish with prunes around them and spoon sauce over. Serves 3-6.

Mrs. William B. Wilson

Pork Chops Danish-Style

6 center-cut pork chops
¼ cup butter
1 large onion, chopped

1 large apple, chopped
½ cup dry white or port wine

Brown pork chops in butter. Remove to baking dish. Brown onion and apple in butter and pork drippings in same skillet. Spread over pork chops. Add wine and bake at 350°F until done, about 30 minutes. Serve immediately. Serves 4.

Mrs. J. S. Owen, Jr.

Recipe is from a farm-home demonstration in Copenhagen.

Marinated Pork Roast

½ cup soy sauce
½ cup dry sherry wine
2 cloves garlic, minced
1 Tablespoon dry mustard

1 teaspoon ground ginger
1 teaspoon thyme
1 (4 to 5 pound) pork loin
   roast, boned, rolled and tied

Combine first 6 ingredients. Place roast in large clear plastic bag. Pour in marinade and close bag tightly. Marinate 2-3 hours at room temperature or overnight in refrigerator. Remove meat from marinade. Place on rack in shallow roasting pan. Roast uncovered at 325°F for 3 hours or until meat thermometer registers 175°F. Baste occasionally with marinade during last hour of roasting time. Serves 8-10.

Mrs. Trenton H. Shelton

Sour Cream Pork Chops

4 pork chops
2 Tablespoons oil
1 cup beef bouillon
1 (8 ounce) can sliced mushrooms
2 teaspoons prepared mustard

2 Tablespoons chopped parsley
1 teaspoon paprika
Salt and pepper to taste
1 onion, sliced into rings
1 cup sour cream

Brown pork chops in oil in skillet. While they brown, mix all remaining ingredients, except the onion rings and sour cream, in a bowl. Separate onion rings and place on pork chops. Pour above mixture over chops and simmer for 1¼ hours. Add the sour cream and cook for another 15 minutes. Especially good served over rice. Serves 4.

Mrs. A. Y. Brown, Jr., Memphis, Tennessee

To season pork chops for cooking on a charcoal grill, sprinkle with lemon-pepper seasoning, meat tenderizer, soy sauce, a dash of ground cloves and a little butter.

Mint Sauce for Lamb

Mix together 8 Tablespoons chopped mint, 8 teaspoons sugar, salt and pepper to taste. Stir in 8 Tablespoons vinegar gradually until sugar is dissolved. Serve as a sauce to spoon over lamb. Makes ¾ cup.

Mrs. Fred J. Lotterhos, Jr.

Braised Shoulder of Lamb

1 (5 pound) shoulder of lamb
Garlic cloves, slivered
5 Tablespoons olive oil
6 tomatoes, peeled, halved and
*   seeded*

12 small onions
2 teaspoons salt
¾ teaspoon each thyme, pepper
Chopped fresh parsley
Lemon juice

Bone and roll lamb and stud with garlic. In Dutch oven brown meat well on all sides in olive oil. Add vegetables and seasonings. Cover the pot and simmer the meat slowly 1½ hours. Transfer the lamb to a heated platter; arrange the vegetables around it. Bring sauce to a boil; reduce it over high heat for 4-5 minutes. Pour over lamb and vegetables. Sprinkle lavishly with chopped parsley and lemon juice. Serves 6-8.

From the recipes of John B. Mason

Lamb Brochettes (Souvlakia)

1 leg of lamb (approximately
*   3 pounds boned weight)*
½ cup lemon juice
2 teaspoons oregano

1 Tablespoon olive oil
2 teaspoons salt
Pepper
1 onion, sliced thin

A good butcher will age his lamb at least 5 days after he receives it so that it will be tender. Try to get aged lamb. Bone and cut lamb into 1½-2-inch pieces. Whisk remaining ingredients together; then add lamb pieces and turn to coat them well. Marinate 4 hours in plastic bag or covered bowl outside the refrigerator or overnight in the refrigerator. Stir occasionally. Drain off marinade and discard or keep for another purpose. Push the meat onto skewers, crowding the pieces close together. Preheat broiler for 15 minutes. Place broiler pan at top position so that the meat will be only about 1 inch from the heat source. Baste meat with additional olive oil. Arrange brochettes on broiler pan, allowing at least ½ inch between each one for circulation. Broil 4-5 minutes, then turn brochettes to the other side. Broil 4-5 minutes more; then serve on a bed of rice and spoon over any juices that collect in the pan. Brochettes may be barbecued outside on a very hot grill close to the coals. Cut into smaller pieces and serve as a hot hors d'oeuvre on small bamboo skewers. Serves 6.

Mrs. Joe Ross, Jr.

Roast Leg of Lamb Barbecue-Style

1 leg of lamb
¼ cup shortening
¼ cup butter or margarine
¼ cup flour
¼ cup vinegar
1 clove garlic
2 cups water

1 Tablespoon Worcestershire
* sauce*
1 Tablespoon salt
1 teaspoon sugar
¼ teaspoon cayenne pepper
2 lemon slices

Have butcher remove gland from leg of lamb. With a very sharp knife remove as much skin and fat as possible; then score the lamb. Melt shortening and butter in saucepan and stir in flour. Add remaining ingredients and cook for several minutes, stirring. Keep basting sauce warm on top of stove. Place lamb in a preheated 500°F oven for 15 minutes; lower heat to 425°F for 15 more minutes per pound. As soon as roast is well seared begin basting. Baste every 15 minutes with basting sauce. When roast is done, a delicious gravy may be made by adding a little water to the pan. Add a little flour if a thicker gravy is preferred.

Mrs. Edward C. Nichols

Saltimbocca

4 thin veal cutlets
Salt
Pepper
Powdered sage
2 thin slices prosciutto (or
* cooked ham)*
2 thin slices Provolone cheese
* (or other mild cheese)*
Corn oil

6 or 8 fresh mushrooms, sliced
* (or 2 ounces canned sliced*
* mushrooms, drained)*
4 teaspoons chopped parsley
1/8 to ¼ teaspoon garlic powder
* (or 1 clove garlic, crushed)*
3 Tablespoons butter or
* margarine, divided*
2 cups Rhine wine

Season 2 cutlets with salt, pepper and sage. On top of each cutlet, layer a slice of ham, cheese and the other cutlet. Press edges of veal together firmly to hold filling and secure with wooden toothpicks. In skillet heat oil and brown sides of veal well. Remove veal and keep warm. In small pan sauté mushrooms, parsley and garlic in 1 Tablespoon butter. To skillet in which veal was browned, add wine; heat, and scrape remaining browned bits into wine. Add mushrooms and parsley to wine. Return veal to skillet and ladle sauce over meat. Add remaining butter and cook slowly over low heat until tender. Remove toothpicks before serving. This dish is easily multiplied to serve any number of people. Serves 2.

Mrs. Reuel May, Jr.

Veal Marsala

8 veal medallions, sliced in
  thin strips
¼ cup oil or melted margarine
  (or combination)
1 (4 ounce) can sliced
  mushrooms, drained, or
  fresh, sliced

¼ cup chopped onion
2 green peppers, sliced in thin
  strips
½ teaspoon celery salt
¼ teaspoon black pepper
½ teaspoon Italian seasoning
½ cup Marsala wine

Sauté veal in oil. Add vegetables and seasonings. Cook over low heat until tender. Add wine and simmer 3-4 minutes. Serves 4.

Mrs. W. R. Newman, III

Gypsy Schnitzel

6 veal scallops
Salt and pepper
1 egg, lightly beaten
1 cup bread crumbs
2 Tablespoons oil
2 Tablespoons butter
2½ medium onions, chopped
2 green peppers, thinly sliced

2 sweet red peppers, thinly
  sliced
1 cup hot water
1 beef bouillon cube
6 ounces fresh mushrooms,
  sliced
¼ cup whipping cream
1 Tablespoon flour

Pound meat very thin. Salt and pepper. Dip veal into egg, then in bread crumbs. Heat oil and butter together over medium heat. Sauté veal until golden (about 15 minutes). Remove to another pan and keep warm. Add onions to skillet used for cooking veal. Sauté until limp but not brown. Add green and red peppers, water, bouillon cube and mushrooms. Cook until *just* tender. Combine cream and flour; then stir into vegetable mixture. Heat until just thickened. Pour over warm veal and serve hot. Serves 6.

Mrs. James J. Hudgins

BREADED STEAK CUTLETS

Cut 1½ pounds round steak into serving pieces, removing all fat. Cube with a tenderizing hammer and sprinkle with salt and pepper. Dip each piece into 1 egg beaten with 1 teaspoon water. Dip into cracker crumbs and coat well. Fry in hot grease until brown on both sides. Drain. Pour off grease and add 1 (8 ounce) can tomato sauce to pan and deglaze pan. Serve tomato sauce with cutlets.

Before cooking on a charcoal grill, marinate as many as 8 hamburger patties for several hours in a mixture of 1 Tablespoon each dry mustard, Worcestershire sauce, ½ cup melted butter or margarine and the juice of 2 lemons.

Italian Red Sauce

5 pounds pork or beef neck
  bones
1½ cups olive oil
3 pounds or 5 large onions,
  chopped
1 small whole bunch celery with
  leaves, chopped
1 whole garlic bulb, minced
2 (28 ounce) cans tomatoes

1 (12 ounce) can tomato paste
20 (8 ounce) cans tomato
  sauce
2 (8 ounce) cans water
3 Tablespoons oregano leaves
4 Tablespoons basil
5 Tablespoons parsley flakes
1 (4 ounce) bottle Kitchen
  Bouquet

In large pot brown neck bones in olive oil. Add onions, celery and garlic. Mash tomatoes with hands and add to the bones. Add remaining ingredients and simmer 5-6 hours. Remove bones. Serve over spaghetti or use as a sauce in any Italian dish such as pizza or lasagne. May be prepared ahead. Freezes well. Yields 12 pints.

Mrs. James R. Galyean, III

Kibbie

2 cups cracked wheat
1 small onion, grated
2 pounds very lean ground
  round beef

½ teaspoon pepper
1 Tablespoon salt
1 Tablespoon ground allspice
1 teaspoon sweet basil

Wash and drain wheat; refrigerate for 30 minutes. Grate onion into meat and add spices. Remove wheat from refrigerator and cover with ice water or ice. Squeeze the water out of the wheat and add by handfuls to the meat. When well mixed, sprinkle with a little ice water to soften and lightly knead. Taste for seasonings. Kibbie may be eaten raw, fried or BAKED WITH FILLING. To fry, shape into patties and deep fry in corn oil. Serves 12.

BAKED KIBBIE WITH FILLING

4 Tablespoons butter
1 pound ground chuck
1 medium onion, chopped
1 teaspoon salt
½ teaspoon ground allspice

½ teaspoon pepper
⅓ cup pine nuts
1 recipe Kibbie
½ cup Mazola oil

To make filling, melt butter and sauté the meat, onion and spices about 15 minutes. Add pine nuts. Grease a 9 x 11-inch pan. Spread a layer of Kibbie ¼ inch thick. Spread filling over Kibbie; then top with remaining Kibbie. Cut into diamond shapes and cover with oil. Bake at 350°F for approximately 1 hour. Serve hot or cold. Can be made ahead, frozen and baked later. Serves 16.

Mrs. Ernest E. Saik

Lynda's Meat Sauce

2 pounds ground chuck
1 onion, chopped
2 cloves garlic, minced
1 (15 ounce) jar Ragu spaghetti
    sauce with mushrooms
1 (15 ounce) jar Ragu
    spaghetti sauce with meat
2 (10½ ounce) cans Franco-
    American beef gravy

2 (5¾ ounce) cans Dawn
    Fresh mushroom steak sauce
2 (2 ounce) cans sliced
    mushrooms and liquid
3 (6 ounce) cans tomato paste
1 (8 ounce) can tomato sauce
2 Tablespoons sugar
1 Tablespoon chili powder
¼ teaspoon oregano
Bay leaf

Brown meat. Drain off fat and set aside. Sauté onion and garlic in small amount of fat. Add meat and all other ingredients and simmer 30 minutes, covered. Taste to adjust seasonings as desired. Serve over spaghetti or use as lasagne sauce. May be prepared 2 days in advance. Freezes well. Makes enough for 1 (2 pound) package spaghetti.

Mrs. Roger P. Friou

Lasagne

1¼ pounds ground chuck
¼ cup olive oil
1 large onion, chopped
3 cloves garlic, minced
1 (28 ounce) can tomatoes
1 (8 ounce) can tomato sauce
1 teaspoon salt
1 teaspoon oregano
¼ teaspoon chili powder

Pinch black pepper
Dash Worcestershire sauce
2 cups water
½ pound lasagne noodles
2 (1 pint) cartons cottage
    cheese
2 (6 ounce) packages sliced
    Mozzarella cheese
1 cup grated Romano cheese

In Dutch oven brown meat in olive oil with onion and garlic. Add tomatoes, tomato sauce, seasonings and water. Simmer slowly, about 1½ or 2 hours, until sauce is thick. Cook noodles in boiling water with salt and a Tablespoon of oil until tender. Drain well. In a 9 x 13-inch baking dish, place a thin layer of meat sauce (just enough to cover the bottom). Over this place a layer of ½ the noodles. Spread with 1 carton cottage cheese. Cover with 1 package Mozzarella. Add a layer of meat sauce and repeat layers of noodles, cottage cheese and Mozzarella. Top with remaining meat sauce. Sprinkle with grated Romano cheese. Bake at 375°F about 45 minutes until cheese is well melted. Remove from oven and let stand at least 10 minutes before cutting into squares. This recipe may be prepared the day before baking and serving. Freezes well before baking. Serves 8.

Mrs. John Crawford

Cannelloni

TOMATO SAUCE:
4 Tablespoons olive oil
1 cup finely chopped onion
4 cups canned tomatoes, coarsely chopped (reserve liquid)
6 Tablespoons tomato paste
2 teaspoons dried basil
2 teaspoons sugar
1 teaspoon salt
Black pepper

MEAT FILLING:
2 Tablespoons olive oil
¼ cup finely chopped onion
1 teaspoon minced garlic
1 (10 ounce) package frozen chopped spinach, thawed, squeezed dry
1 Tablespoon butter
1 pound ground round beef

5 Tablespoons grated Parmesan cheese
2 Tablespoons whipping cream
2 eggs, lightly beaten
½ teaspoon oregano
Salt and pepper

BESCIAMELLA:
4 Tablespoons butter
4 Tablespoons flour
1 cup milk
1 cup whipping cream
1 teaspoon salt
1/8 teaspoon white pepper

1 (1 pound) box lasagne noodles
4 Tablespoons grated Parmesan cheese
2 Tablespoons butter, cut in pieces

TOMATO SAUCE: Heat oil in a 2 or 3-quart saucepan until a light haze forms over it. Add onion and cook until soft. Add tomatoes with liquid and other remaining ingredients. Reduce heat to very low and simmer for 40 minutes with pan partially covered. Stir occasionally. Blend tomato mixture in blender and taste for seasoning. Correct if necessary. May be made up to a week before serving and stored in refrigerator. Makes 3 cups. MEAT FILL-ING: Heat oil in a skillet. Add onion and garlic. Cook over moderate heat, stirring frequently, for 7-8 minutes until soft. Stir in spinach and cook 3-4 minutes, stirring constantly. When all the moisture has cooked away, transfer to large mixing bowl. Melt butter in same skillet and lightly brown meat, stir-ring. Add meat to spinach mixture. Add cheese, cream, eggs and oregano. Mix and season with salt and pepper. BESCIAMELLA: In a heavy 2 or 3-quart saucepan melt butter over moderate heat. Remove from heat and stir in flour. Add milk and cream all at once, stirring constantly with whisk. When the sauce comes to a boil and is smooth, reduce heat. Simmer, still stirring, for 2-3 minutes or until sauce is thick enough to coat the whisk wires heavily. Remove from heat and season with salt and white pepper. To assemble cannelloni, cook lasagne until done. Cut each whole lasagne noodle into 3 equal sections. Pour a light film of the tomato sauce into 2 (10 x 14 inch) shallow baking dishes. Place a Tablespoon of the meat filling on the bottom third of each of the pasta rectangles and roll them up. Lay the cannelloni side by side, seam-side-down, in 1 layer on the tomato sauce. Pour besciamella over cannelloni and spoon the

(Continued)

rest of the tomato sauce on top. Sprinkle the Parmesan cheese over the assembled cannelloni and dot with butter. Cannelloni may be assembled to this point the day before serving, then refrigerated until time to heat and serve. It may be wrapped and frozen. When ready to cook, bake cannelloni in 375 °F oven uncovered for 20 minutes or until cheese is melted and sauce bubbling. For a complete meal serve with a crisp tossed salad, a loaf of Italian bread and fresh fruit. Serves 8-9.

Mrs. James L. Teague

Variation: Use tufoli or manicotti, cut in half after cooking, for pasta.

Mama's Meatloaf

¾ cup cornflakes, crushed crackers or torn bread	1/8 teaspoon pepper
½ cup milk	¼ teaspoon celery seed
1 (10½ ounce) can cream of mushroom soup	1 Tablespoon dried parsley
1 soup can milk	½ teaspoon Worcestershire sauce
1 pound ground beef	½ onion, finely chopped
1 teaspoon salt	1 egg, well beaten
	1½ Tablespoons ketchup
	1½ Tablespoons barbecue sauce

Soak cornflakes in ½ cup of milk until soft. Heat mushroom soup and soup can of milk for sauce. Mix cornflakes and all other ingredients together in a 2-quart casserole dish and shape into loaf. Pour ½ of the sauce over loaf. Bake at 350°F. After 15 minutes of cooking, pour remaining sauce over loaf and continue baking for 25 more minutes. Serves 6.

Mrs. J. Lawrence Hollis

Reuben Pie

1 egg, beaten	1 (8 ounce) can sauerkraut, drained and snipped
⅓ cup evaporated milk	12 ounces corned beef, chopped (1½ cups thinly sliced)
¾ cup rye bread crumbs	
¼ cup chopped onion	
¼ teaspoon salt	
Dash pepper	Pie pastry for 1 deep-dish pie crust
½ teaspoon prepared mustard	
½ pound ground chuck, browned	6 ounces Swiss cheese, grated

In mixing bowl combine first 7 ingredients. Add chuck, sauerkraut and corned beef. Mix well. Place ½ of meat mixture into pastry shell and sprinkle with ½ of cheese. Cover with remaining meat mixture. Top with cheese and bake at 400°F for 25-30 minutes. Serves 6.

Mrs. John M. Roach

Aunt Lou's Baked Spaghetti

2 large onions, chopped
2 green peppers, chopped
¾ cup chopped celery
1 bunch parsley, chopped
2 cloves garlic, chopped fine
3 Tablespoons oil
3 (28 ounce) cans tomatoes, cut
   up, and juice
1 (8 ounce) can tomato sauce
1 (6 ounce) can tomato paste
2 bay leaves

2 teaspoons salt
1 Tablespoon ground allspice
1 Tablespoon ground cinnamon
Red and black pepper to taste
3 pounds ground beef
1 (4 ounce) can mushrooms,
   stems and pieces
1 cup sherry wine
1½ pounds spaghetti, cooked
Grated Parmesan cheese
Grated Cheddar cheese

Cook onions, green peppers, celery, parsley and garlic in oil until tender. Drain. Add tomatoes and juice, tomato sauce and paste, bay leaves and spices and simmer for 1 hour. Brown ground beef, drain and add to sauce. Add mushrooms and sherry and simmer 30 minutes. Mix spaghetti sauce and cooked spaghetti. Place in greased casseroles and bake at 350°F for 20 minutes, or a little longer. Serve with Parmesan and Cheddar cheeses. This recipe divides by thirds easily for making a smaller quantity. Sauce freezes well. Serves 16-18.

Mrs. V. Q. Ricks, Canton, Mississippi

Zucchini-Beef Casserole

1 pound ground beef chuck
1 (8 ounce) can tomato sauce
1 teaspoon salt
¼ teaspoon Tabasco
½ teaspoon sugar
1 teaspoon Worcestershire sauce
2 green onions, finely chopped
1 pound zucchini

½ Tablespoon butter or
   margarine
½ (8 ounce) package cream
   cheese, softened
½ pint sour cream
1/8 teaspoon paprika
½ cup seasoned bread crumbs
   or grated Parmesan cheese

Allow heavy skillet to become very hot over high heat and brown beef, stirring constantly. Lower heat to medium, add tomato sauce, salt, Tabasco, sugar and Worcestershire sauce and cook about 5 minutes until well blended. Add green onions. Remove from heat. Slice zucchini in ½-inch rounds. In buttered 10 x 6-inch casserole, place a layer of meat mixture and a layer of zucchini, repeating process. In large bowl blend cream cheese and sour cream. Spread over top of casserole and sprinkle with paprika. Cover with bread crumbs or Parmesan cheese. Bake in preheated 350°F oven for 35 minutes. Serve hot. If prepared in the morning, add bread crumbs just before baking. Serves 6-8.

Mrs. Reynolds Cheney

Stuffed Cabbage Rolls

1 large head cabbage
1 pound ground chuck
1 cup raw rice
1½ teaspoons salt
1/8 teaspoon pepper
1 Tablespoon chili powder
1 (28 ounce) can tomatoes,
 drained and chopped
 (reserve juice)

1 medium onion, grated or
 chopped fine
2 raw chicken wings (last two
 end joints only)
2 Tablespoons ketchup
½ cup brown sugar
Juice of 2 lemons
1 bay leaf, crumbled
1 (8 ounce) can tomato sauce

Soak cabbage in hot water until pliable. Carefully peel off leaves and place in boiling water for 5 minutes to soften. Mix well the meat, rice, salt, pepper, chili powder, tomatoes and onion. Place 1 Tablespoon of meat mixture (or less) on each cabbage leaf (cut the large leaves in half). Wrap and secure with a toothpick. Place chicken wing tips on bottom of Dutch oven and arrange cabbage rolls atop wings and over bottom of pan. Make a second layer if necessary. Sprinkle each layer liberally with additional salt. Add enough water to the ketchup and reserved tomato juice to make 2 cups liquid. Pour over cabbage rolls. Sprinkle brown sugar, lemon juice and bay leaf over rolls. Pour tomato sauce over all. Cover dish tightly and bake in 350°F oven for 1 hour and 15 minutes. Serves 8.

Mrs. Julian Henderson

Noodles Marmaduke

¼ cup sliced onion
2 Tablespoons butter
1 pound ground beef
3 Tablespoons sherry wine
1 (10½ ounce) can beef
 consommé
1 (6 ounce) can mushrooms,
 stems and pieces, and juice

3 Tablespoons lemon juice
1 teaspoon salt
¼ teaspoon pepper
Dash garlic salt
¼ pound medium noodles
1 cup sour cream
Chopped parsley

Sauté onion in butter. Add meat and brown. Stir in sherry, consommé, mushrooms and juice, lemon juice, salt, pepper and garlic salt. Simmer uncovered for 15 minutes. Stir in uncooked noodles and cook for 10 minutes or until noodles are tender. Stir in sour cream. Top with parsley to serve. Serves 6.

Mrs. Ralph B. Boozman

A favorite dish for Wednesdays at St. Andrew's Episcopal Cathedral luncheons, this recipe is easily doubled, tripled or quadrupled. If prepared in advance, it may be stored in Pyrex casseroles and heated at 325°F until hot. It may also be frozen, thawed and reheated.

Meat Balls and Spaghetti

SAUCE:

2 cloves garlic, minced
1 large onion, chopped
3 Tablespoons olive oil
1 (6 ounce) can tomato paste
1 (8 ounce) can tomato sauce
1 (16 ounce) can tomatoes
1 (4 ounce) can sliced
   mushrooms with liquid
2 teaspoons sugar
2 cups water
¼ cup chopped parsley
¼ teaspoon each rosemary,
   basil, thyme, oregano
   leaves, pepper
1 bay leaf

1 teaspoon salt

MEAT BALLS:

1½ pounds ground chuck
2 Tablespoons chopped onion
2 Tablespoons chopped celery
   leaves
½ cup dry bread crumbs
¼ cup milk
1 egg
½ teaspoon each salt, pepper
1 clove garlic, minced
¼ cup grated fresh Parmesan
   cheese

Cooked spaghetti

SAUCE: In large saucepan cook garlic and onion in oil until golden brown. Add remaining ingredients. Cover and simmer gently for 2 hours or longer. MEAT BALLS: Combine all ingredients. Shape into balls and brown in hot skillet. Drain off fat. Add meat balls to sauce and simmer 30 minutes longer. Serve over spaghetti. Serves 6-8.

Mrs. Julian Henderson

Chalupas

1 (16 ounce) can refried beans
1 (10 ounce) can Rotel
   tomatoes, puréed in blender
1 (8 ounce) package frozen
   corn tortillas
¼ cup oil
Salt and pepper

1 pound ground chuck
½ teaspoon ground cumin seed
1 large onion, chopped
1 head lettuce, shredded
2 large tomatoes, diced
1 cup grated Cheddar cheese

In separate pans heat the beans and the Rotel tomatoes. Fry the tortillas in oil for 1 minute on each side or until lightly browned. Drain on a paper towel and salt. Discard oil and brown ground chuck. Add cumin and salt and pepper to taste. Stir. Spread hot beans on each tortilla. Sprinkle over beans a layer of meat, onion, lettuce and diced tomatoes. Spoon over each the hot Rotel tomatoes and top each with cheese. Two chalupas make a meal. Serves 12.

Mrs. Hobart Hector, Jr.

Variation: Top each chalupa with AVOCADO DRESSING made by combining 1 large avocado (puréed or mashed), 1 Tablespoon lemon juice, 2 Tablespoons mayonnaise, 2 Tablespoons sour cream and salt and seasoned salt to taste.

Seafood

Chilled Smoked Fish with Horseradish Sauce

Whole redfish
Garlic salt
Lemon-pepper seasoning
Juice of 3 lemons
½ cup butter, melted

2 Tablespoons Worcestershire
  sauce
Dash Tabasco
1 teaspoon chopped parsley

Sprinkle fish with garlic salt and lemon-pepper seasoning. Combine next 5 ingredients to make basting sauce. Place aluminum foil over tail and head of fish and smoke on covered grill over low fire (to which wet hickory chips have been added) for about 1 hour. Baste every 15 minutes. Do not overcook. Fish should flake easily. Cool, refrigerate and serve with HORSERADISH SAUCE. The fish makes an excellent buffet dish. For an appetizer, serve a piece of smoked fish on a Melba round with a dab of sauce on top. Yields about 1 serving per pound.

HORSERADISH SAUCE

2 cups sour cream
1 Tablespoon horseradish
2 teaspoons lemon juice
¼ teaspoon lemon-pepper
  seasoning

Salt to taste
1 Tablespoon chopped chives or
  1 teaspoon dill seed or fresh
  dill
Paprika

Mix together all ingredients and spoon into bowl. Sprinkle with paprika. Makes 2 cups sauce.

Alvin E. Brent, Jr.

Basic Fish Stock

2 pounds skinned fresh or
  frozen fish (halibut, whiting
  or flounder), heads, bones,
  trimmings, shellfish
1 onion, thinly sliced
6 parsley stems
1 teaspoon lemon juice

¼ bay leaf
Pinch thyme leaves
¼ teaspoon salt
1 cup dry white wine
¼ cup fresh mushroom stems
  (optional)

Place ingredients in large non-aluminum pot with water to cover. Bring to a simmer and cook uncovered for 30 minutes. Strain. Fish stock may be refrigerated or frozen. Boil before using. Makes 2 cups stock.

Emergency Fish Stock

1½ cups bottled clam juice
1 cup water
1 cup dry white wine
1 onion, thinly sliced

6 parsley stems
¼ cup fresh mushroom stems
  (optional)

Place ingredients in saucepan and simmer uncovered 30 minutes. Strain. If too salty, dilute with water. Makes 2 cups stock.

Sauce for Cold Fish

2 egg yolks
1/8 teaspoon salt
¾ cup olive oil
Juice of ½ lemon
1/8 teaspoon lemon-pepper
  seasoning

½ cup whipping cream,
  whipped
1 Tablespoon capers
1 Tablespoon minced parsley
Few drops onion juice

Beat egg yolks; add salt and oil, beating well. Add lemon juice, a few drops at a time, then lemon-pepper. Fold in cream and add remaining ingredients. Serve as sauce for boiled shrimp or chilled salmon. Serves 6.

Mrs. J. S. Owen, Jr.

Baked Trout with Shrimp

5 pounds raw shrimp, unpeeled
5 pounds trout or pompano
  fillets (preferably fresh)
1½ teaspoons salt
½ teaspoon pepper
⅔ cup butter, melted, divided
½ (6 ounce) can pitted black
  olives, halved
5 (10½ ounce) cans cream of
  shrimp soup
6 drops Tabasco

1/8 teaspoon cayenne pepper
2 Tablespoons Worcestershire
  sauce
3 Tablespoons lemon juice
1 teaspoon powdered thyme
2 Tablespoons chopped parsley
1 teaspoon Jane's Krazy Mixed-
  Up Salt seasoning
⅓ cup sherry wine
½ cup sliced almonds
1 cup grated Parmesan cheese

Boil shrimp in seasoned water. Drain, cool, peel and devein. Wash fish fillets and dry well on paper towels. Sprinkle with salt and pepper. Grease bottoms of 3 (7½ x 11¾ inch) casseroles with ⅓ cup butter. Lay fillets skin side down in casseroles. Distribute shrimp equally over fish; then sprinkle with olives. Cover all with a sauce made by combining next 9 ingredients. Correct seasoning. Top sauce with almonds and drizzle remaining butter over all. Sprinkle Parmesan cheese over tops of casseroles. Bake at 350°F for 25 minutes or until bubbly and lightly browned. Serves 20.

Mrs. Vernon T. Johnston

Charlie's Turban of Sole

1 cup raw rice or 1 (6 ounce)
  box long-grain and wild rice
3 pounds fillet of sole (flounder
  or trout may be substituted)
Salt

Butter
A few whole cooked shrimp
Paprika
Fresh parsley

Cook rice. Flatten fillets slightly with a moistened wooden mallet. Season with salt. Butter a 6-cup ring mold generously. Lay fillets in mold, overlapping them and with tail ends over inner edges of mold. Line mold completely with fillets. Fill with rice, pressing down gently with spoon. Bring tail ends over rice to cover top side. Cover with aluminum foil. Set mold in larger pan and pour in boiling water to a depth of 1 inch. Poach in 400°F oven for 15 minutes. To serve turban, remove from oven and leave for a few minutes to set. Drain off accumulated liquids by turning upside down on a plate but *do not unmold*. Unmold on serving platter. Fill center with ROUFFIGNAC SAUCE. Garnish top with a few whole cooked shrimp and sprinkle with paprika. Surround the turban with parsley and serve. Serves 8.

ROUFFIGNAC SAUCE

1 cup butter
¾ cup finely chopped fresh
  mushrooms
½ cup finely chopped shallots
½ cup finely chopped onion
1 cup finely chopped cooked
  shrimp
1 Tablespoon finely chopped
  garlic

4 Tablespoons flour
1 teaspoon salt
½ teaspoon pepper
2 dashes red pepper
1 (16 ounce) jar oysters
  with liquid
1 cup red wine
1 teaspoon arrowroot

Lightly sauté in butter the mushrooms, shallots, onion, shrimp and garlic. When onion is a golden brown, add flour, salt and peppers. Brown well, about 10 minutes. Blend in oyster liquid and wine and simmer 10 minutes. Remove some of the liquid to a separate bowl and blend in arrowroot. Add little by little to the sauce until sauce is consistency of thick gravy. Gently stir in oysters and simmer 10-15 minutes. Makes about 4 cups sauce.

Charles E. White, Memphis, Tennessee

A magnificent main course!

TARTAR SAUCE

Combine 1 cup mayonnaise (preferably homemade) with ½ medium onion (chopped), 2 large pimiento-stuffed olives (chopped), 1 medium sweet gherkin (chopped), 1 Tablespoon chopped parsley and 1 Tablespoon capers. A touch of Sweet and Hot Mustard (see Index) is a good addition.

Broiled Speckled Trout

1 small onion, chopped
½ cup butter, melted
½ cup sauterne wine
½ cup water
½ teaspoon garlic powder

3 lemons, sliced
Salt and pepper
2 or 3 pounds fresh speckled
   trout fillets
Paprika

In saucepan sauté onion in butter; add wine, water and garlic powder. Remove seeds, partially squeeze lemon slices into saucepan and add slices to mixture. Bring mixture to a boil. Salt and pepper fillets and place in baking dish skin side down. Pour sauce over fillets. Broil 6-8 inches from heat at 450°F until fish turns white and flakes apart throughout. Cooking time will be about 15-20 minutes. Do not overcook. To serve, sprinkle paprika over fish and top with lemon slices. Serves 4.

Thomas E. Ward

Paupiettes de Poisson Dugléré
(Rolled Fish Fillets in Creamy Tomato Sauce)

4 large ripe tomatoes
8 Tablespoons butter, divided
Pinch salt
Pinch sugar
¼ cup each chopped shallots
   and chopped onion or
   ½ cup chopped onion
2 pounds fish fillets (fresh sole,
   speckled trout or red
   snapper)

⅔ cup dry white wine
½ cup white wine fish stock
½ cup whipping cream
White pepper
1 Tablespoon beurre manié
   (½ Tablespoon flour rubbed
   into ½ Tablespoon butter)
3 Tablespoons minced parsley

Peel, seed and chop tomatoes. Melt 2 Tablespoons butter in a pan; add tomatoes, salt and sugar. Cook, stirring occasionally, until reduced to a thick purée. Butter baking dish generously using about 4 Tablespoons butter. Sprinkle shallots and onions over the bottom and spread half the tomato purée over that. Cut fish fillets into 6 serving pieces. Roll fish in tight cylinders, secure with toothpick and place upright side by side in the pan. Spread the remaining tomato purée on top. Pour in wine and fish stock. Cover with buttered wax paper. Poach fillets at 350°F for 10-15 minutes or until they flake easily. Remove fillets, cover loosely and keep warm. Strain the juices into a pan, reduce them to a cup, whisk in the whipping cream, pepper and *beurre manié* and simmer, stirring, for about 5 minutes or until sauce is thickened and smooth. Correct seasoning. Remove from heat and swirl in remaining 2 Tablespoons butter. Remove toothpicks from fillets and place on serving plate. Add any accumulated juices to the sauce and pour it over the fish. Decorate with parsley. Serve with rice or boiled potatoes. Serves 6.

Mrs. William B. Wilson

Stuffed Flounder Fillets

6 flounder or sole fillets
⅔ cup finely chopped celery
1 medium onion, finely chopped
2 Tablespoons butter
1 pound shrimp, cooked and
chopped

½ cup crab meat
½ cup seasoned bread crumbs
1 Tablespoon chopped parsley
1 egg, slightly beaten
Bread crumbs, buttered
Grated Parmesan cheese

Wash fillets and drain well on paper towels. Sauté celery and onion in butter. Add shrimp, crab meat, bread crumbs, parsley and egg. Mix. Spread on fish fillets. Roll up and place in lightly greased baking dish. Pour WHITE WINE SAUCE over fillets. Top with bread crumbs, Parmesan cheese and additional chopped parsley. Refrigerate overnight at this point, if desired. Bake at 350°F for 30 minutes. Serves 6.

WHITE WINE SAUCE

2 Tablespoons butter
2 Tablespoons flour
2 cups milk
¼ teaspoon salt

White pepper
1 (2 ounce) can sliced
mushrooms, drained
¼ cup dry white wine

Melt butter in saucepan. Stir in flour until smooth. Add milk. Cook, stirring, until thick. Remove from heat; add salt, white pepper, mushrooms and wine. Makes 2½ cups sauce.

Mrs. J. T. Noblin

Flounder Florentine

2 (10 ounce) packages frozen
chopped spinach
4 Tablespoons chopped onion
2 teaspoons salt
½ teaspoon pepper
4 Tablespoons salad oil
2 Tablespoons butter

1½ Tablespoons flour
1 cup milk
4 Tablespoons dry vermouth
1 pound flounder fillets, cut in
serving pieces
1 cup grated Cheddar cheese

Cook and drain spinach. Place in greased shallow casserole. Sprinkle with onion, seasonings and oil. In saucepan melt butter. Stir in flour until smooth. Blend in milk and stir until thickened. Season with additional salt. Add vermouth. If using frozen fish, thaw and squeeze out water between paper towels. Place fillets over spinach. Pour white sauce over all. Sprinkle with cheese. Bake at 350°F for 45 minutes. Serves 4-6.

Mrs. E. E. Laird, Jr.

Allow ⅓ pound fish fillets per serving; allow ½ pound per serving if fish is whole.

Baked Fish Fillets in Sauce

1 pound fresh or frozen fish
   fillets
1 Tablespoon butter

¼ cup sour cream
¼ cup mayonnaise
Juice of ½ lemon

Place fish fillets in buttered baking dish and bake 10 minutes in 350°F oven. Mix sour cream, mayonnaise and lemon juice; spread over fish. Bake 10-15 minutes longer. Serves 2-3.

Mrs. Donald A. White

Red Snapper Court Bouillon

4 pounds red snapper or red
   fish fillets, cut in serving
   pieces
1 pint oysters, drained
2 pounds peeled, raw shrimp

1 (4 ounce) can sliced
   mushrooms, drained
¼ cup sherry wine
1 lemon, thinly sliced
2 Tablespoons chopped parsley

Place fillets in large rectangular casserole dish. Sprinkle oysters, shrimp and mushrooms over fish. Cover with CREOLE SAUCE. Sprinkle with wine, then lemon slices and parsley. Bake 20-25 minutes at 350°F. Serve over rice. Serves 12-15.

CREOLE SAUCE

¼ cup flour
¼ cup bacon drippings
2 cups chopped onion
½ cup chopped green onion
1 cup chopped green pepper
2 cloves garlic, minced
1 cup chopped celery and leaves
1 teaspoon thyme
2 bay leaves

3 teaspoons salt
½ teaspoon pepper
1 (16 ounce) can tomatoes
1 (6 ounce) can tomato paste
1 (8 ounce) can tomato sauce
1 teaspoon Tabasco
½ cup chopped parsley
1 Tablespoon lemon juice
½ cup sherry wine

In a large skillet or Dutch oven make a dark brown roux using the flour and bacon drippings. Add onions, green pepper, garlic, celery, thyme, bay leaves, salt and pepper. Sauté over medium heat until onions are soft. Add tomatoes, tomato paste and sauce. Cover and simmer over low heat about 2 hours, stirring occasionally. Add remaining ingredients. Stir, cover and remove from heat. Let stand several hours before pouring over fish. Makes about 6 cups sauce.

Mrs. Fred Weathersby

PAN-FRIED TROUT Melt ½ cup butter in an iron skillet over medium heat. Roll whole trout or fillets in a mixture of half corn meal and half flour and lay fish in melted butter. Turn frequently and watch carefully to keep butter from burning. Take out when golden brown.

Fish Marguery

2 to 3 pounds fish fillets
(preferably speckled
trout or bass)
Salt
1 Tablespoon oil
¾ cup water
½ cup plus 3 Tablespoons
butter, divided
4 Tablespoons flour

½ cup half and half cream
½ cup milk
3 egg yolks
2 Tablespoons lemon juice
Red pepper
2 pounds peeled, boiled shrimp
1 (4 ounce) can sliced
mushrooms, drained
Paprika

Cut fish into serving portions and salt lightly. Place in shallow baking dish. Add oil and water. Cover with foil and bake at 450°F until just done, about 15-45 minutes (depending on thickness of fillets). Do not overcook. Drain; place on serving tray and keep warm. Melt 3 Tablespoons butter and stir in flour. Add ¼ teaspoon salt, cream and milk. Stir until thick and smooth. Remove from heat. Mix egg yolks and lemon juice slightly in blender. Heat remaining butter to almost boiling. Slowly add butter to egg mixture with blender on high speed. Blend until thick. Add to cream sauce. Season with additional salt and red pepper. Keep in double boiler over hot water until ready to serve. If mixture separates, add more cream and stir. Just before serving, add shrimp and mushrooms. Pour sauce over hot fish. Sprinkle with paprika. Serve immediately. Green grapes and crab meat may be substituted for shrimp and mushrooms. Serves 6-8.

Mrs. William F. Sistrunk

Shrimp and Feta Cheese

4 ripe medium tomatoes
2½ pounds unpeeled, raw
medium shrimp
6 Tablespoons olive oil
¼ cup finely chopped onion
½ cup dry white wine
½ teaspoon oregano

3 Tablespoons finely chopped
parsley, divided
1 teaspoon salt
Freshly ground pepper
4 ounces feta cheese, cut in
¼ inch cubes

Skin tomatoes; squeeze out juice and seeds. Shell shrimp, leaving tails on, if desired. In skillet heat oil. Add onion and cook 5 minutes. Stir in tomatoes, wine, oregano, 2 Tablespoons parsley, salt and pepper. Cook until mixture forms a light purée, stirring constantly. Add shrimp and cook 5 minutes more or until shrimp are pink. Stir in cheese. Taste for seasoning and correct if necessary. Sprinkle with remaining parsley. Serve as first course in individual ramekins or use as a luncheon entrée. Serve with crusty French bread for "sopping up" juices, which are delicious. Serves 6.

Mrs. James Savage, Jr.

Instant Rémoulade Sauce

½ Tablespoon Creole mustard,
  or more
2 Tablespoons grated onion
1 pint mayonnaise
¼ cup horseradish, or more

½ ounce frozen chopped chives
¼ teaspoon salt
1 Tablespoon lemon juice
¼ teaspoon pepper

Mix all ingredients. Serve over cold boiled shrimp for a shrimp rémoulade main course. Can be used as a dip for boiled shrimp. Sauce is best after 24 hours. Makes 2¼ cups sauce.

Mrs. Polly H. Currie

Shrimp Cocktail Sauce

Combine 1 (12 ounce) bottle Heinz chili sauce, 1 Tablespoon creamed horseradish, 1 Tablespoon Worcestershire sauce, 1 teaspoon lemon juice and freshly ground pepper. Heat thoroughly and serve with boiled shrimp. Season with more horseradish, if desired. Cocktail sauce can be prepared without heating, if preferred. Makes 1 cup sauce.

Mrs. H. Vaughan Watkins, Jr.

Basic Fried Breaded Shrimp

¼ cup flour
Salt and pepper
1 egg
2 Tablespoons vodka

¾ cup fine bread crumbs
40 large raw shrimp, shelled
  but with tails intact
Oil for frying

Mix flour with a little salt and pepper and place in a bowl. In a second bowl beat well the egg and vodka. In a third bowl place the bread crumbs mixed with salt and pepper. Toss the shrimp, one at a time, in the flour; dip into egg mixture; toss in the bread crumbs to coat. Drop into hot grease (360°F) and deep fry quickly until golden brown. Do not overcook. Shrimp may be breaded several hours ahead and refrigerated until time to fry. Serve with a tartar and a cocktail sauce. Serves 3-4.

The Editors

BOILED GULF SHRIMP

Bring to a boil 1 gallon water seasoned with 1 (3 ounce) box Zatarain's crab boil, ½ cup salt, 2 lemons (sliced), 6 peppercorns, 2 bay leaves and 1 teaspoon Zatarain's concentrated instant crab and shrimp boil (optional). Drop in 5 pounds raw shrimp in the shell. When water returns to a boil, cook jumbo or large shrimp 12-13 minutes and medium shrimp 7-8 minutes. Remove from heat and add 1 quart ice water. Let sit for 10 minutes. Drain.

Pink Cocktail Sauce

1 cup mayonnaise
1 cup chili sauce
1 teaspoon anchovy paste

10 drops Tabasco
2 Tablespoons tarragon vinegar

Mix ingredients and chill. Serve as dip for boiled shrimp, crab fingers or other seafoods. Makes about 2 cups sauce.

Mrs. Sherwood Wise

Grilled Shrimp

2 pounds unpeeled large or
  jumbo shrimp
1 cup salad oil
1 cup lemon juice
2 teaspoons Italian salad
  dressing mix

2 teaspoons seasoned salt
1 teaspoon seasoned pepper
1 teaspoon Worcestershire sauce
4 Tablespoons brown sugar
2 Tablespoons soy sauce
½ cup chopped green onion

Wash shrimp and drain on paper towels. Mix oil, lemon juice, salad dressing mix, salt, pepper and Worcestershire sauce. Place shrimp in bowl and cover with marinade. Marinate in refrigerator 2-4 hours or overnight, stirring occasionally. Lift shrimp from marinade with slotted spoon and push onto skewers. Place on charcoal grill about 6 inches from hot coals. Grill about 10 minutes, turning once and brushing with marinade. Pour remaining marinade into pan. Stir in brown sugar, soy sauce and onion. Heat to boiling. Serve as dip for shrimp. Serves 8.

Mrs. Richard L. Redmont, Jr.

Shrimp Curry

2 cups chopped unpeeled apple
1½ cups finely chopped onion
¾ cup butter
4 Tablespoons curry powder
1 teaspoon salt
Dash cayenne pepper
2 carrots, finely chopped
2 cups tomato juice

1 bay leaf
1 (8½ ounce) bottle chutney
½ (3½ ounce) can grated
  coconut
5 pounds shrimp, cooked,
  peeled, deveined
Cooked rice
Curry condiments

Cover and cook the first 7 ingredients until soft. Gradually add the next 4 ingredients. Reduce heat and simmer for ½ hour, stirring frequently. Let cool, remove bay leaf, and run through blender. When ready to serve, add shrimp and reheat. Serve over hot rice with some or all of the following condiments: chopped hard-boiled egg, chopped peanuts, raisins and chopped bacon. Curry sauce can be frozen. Serves 10.

Mrs. James Y. Palmer

Baked Stuffed Shrimp

24 jumbo shrimp
1 medium onion, minced
1 green pepper, chopped
6 Tablespoons butter, divided
1 cup fresh crab meat or
    1 (7½ ounce) can
1 teaspoon dry mustard
1 teaspoon Worcestershire sauce

½ teaspoon salt
2 Tablespoons mayonnaise
2 Tablespoons flour
1 cup milk
1 Tablespoon sherry wine, or
    more
Grated Parmesan cheese
Paprika

Clean and remove heads and shells from shrimp, leaving tails. Split shrimp and open flat. Sauté onion and pepper in 4 Tablespoons butter until soft but not brown. Add the crab meat, dry mustard, Worcestershire sauce, salt and mayonnaise. Set aside. Make white sauce using remaining 2 Tablespoons butter, flour and milk. Add to crab meat mixture along with the sherry. Mix well, stuff the butterflied shrimp with the crab meat and dot with extra butter. Sprinkle lightly with Parmesan cheese and paprika. Arrange in shallow baking pan and bake at 350°F for 25-30 minutes. Serves 4-6.

Mrs. Douglas Swayze

Black Iron Pot Shrimp Stew

1 cup flour
1 cup salad oil (or half olive oil)
3 large yellow onions, chopped
1 bunch green onions and tops,
    chopped, divided
2 green peppers, chopped
½ cup Worcestershire sauce
Dash Tabasco
1 (8 ounce) can tomato sauce
1 (10½ ounce) can cream of
    mushroom soup
1 (10 ounce) can Rotel tomatoes

Salt and pepper
Dash oregano
Dash thyme
2 (8 ounce) cans sliced
    mushrooms, drained
4 ribs celery, chopped
½ pound smoked sausage,
    sliced and parboiled
6 bay leaves
¾ cup cooking sauterne
5 pounds raw shrimp, shelled
½ cup minced fresh parsley

Make a rich brown roux by stirring flour and oil in iron pot or skillet about 45 minutes to 1 hour. Do not let burn. Add to roux the onions and green peppers, reserving some green onion. Sauté for 45 minutes. Add remaining ingredients except shrimp and parsley. Simmer about 1 hour. Add shrimp and cook 30 minutes. Keep heat constant and stir frequently. Before serving add parsley and reserved green onion. Serve over buttered and fried French bread slices or fluffy rice. Can be prepared a day ahead. Serves 8-10.

Mrs. D. T. Brock

Note: To have basic roux on hand, brown dry flour in 350°F oven for 1½-3 hours. Shake or stir often. Store in covered jar in refrigerator. It is ready to use; add oil according to recipe proportions.

Sautéed Shrimp

2 green onions, chopped
½ cup butter
Garlic salt
4 Tablespoons sherry wine
Juice of 1 lemon

2 pounds peeled, raw shrimp
1 pound fresh mushrooms,
  sliced
Grated Parmesan cheese

In skillet sauté onions in butter. Season with garlic salt. Add sherry, lemon juice, shrimp and mushrooms. Sprinkle with Parmesan cheese. Simmer until shrimp are done. This is good served in a small bowl with the juices or over curried rice. Freezes well after cooking. Serves 4.

Mrs. Lyle Bates, Jr.

Curried Shrimp in Zucchini Shells

2 pounds zucchini
1 Tablespoon minced onion
3 Tablespoons butter
2 (8 ounce) cans shrimp or
  1 pound peeled, cooked
  medium shrimp

1 teaspoon curry powder
½ teaspoon salt
¼ cup evaporated milk or half
  and half cream
2 Tablespoons flour
½ cup dry bread crumbs

Parboil, then split zucchini lengthwise. Scoop out center and reserve pulp. Sauté onion in butter and add to pulp. Add shrimp and remaining ingredients. Stuff mixture into zucchini shells. Bake at 350°F for 30 minutes. Serves 8.

Mrs. Richard Redmont, Sr.

Creamed Shrimp with Brown Rice

4 Tablespoons butter or
  margarine
3 Tablespoons flour
2 cups half and half cream or
  milk
4 Tablespoons ketchup
4 teaspoons Worcestershire
  sauce

1 teaspoon dry mustard
2 Tablespoons lemon juice
Salt, pepper and red pepper
  to taste
Seasoned salt to taste
⅓ cup dry sherry wine
1 pound shelled, cooked shrimp
1 cup raw brown rice, cooked

Melt butter in saucepan. Stir in flour until smooth and add cream. Stir until thickened. Season cream sauce with the next 7 ingredients. Fold in shrimp. Serve over brown rice. Serves 4.

Mrs. Julian Lee Owen

For best results freeze any kind of seafood in water. Store in freezer for 3 months.

Shrimp Broiled with Tarragon

1 pound peeled, raw jumbo
  shrimp
2 Tablespoons minced tarragon
  or 1 Tablespoon dried
Salt

Freshly ground white pepper
2 Tablespoons butter
¼ cup Cognac
1 cup whipping cream

Place shrimp in shallow ovenproof dish and sprinkle with tarragon, salt and pepper. Dot with butter and broil 10-15 minutes or until done. Remove shrimp and keep warm. Deglaze pan with Cognac; add cream and reduce by ⅓ or until slightly thickened. Arrange shrimp on plates or in ramekins, pour sauce over and serve with French bread or toast. Serves 4.

Mrs. William B. Wilson

Shrimp-Stuffed Artichokes

6 fresh artichokes
1 lemon, sliced
1 package Good Seasons Old
  Fashion French salad
  dressing mix, made up
  according to package
  directions, or 8 ounces
  favorite French dressing
6 cups peeled, cooked shrimp
1 cup chopped celery

1 cup mayonnaise
⅓ cup ketchup
½ teaspoon Worcestershire
  sauce
1/8 teaspoon salt
¼ teaspoon seasoned salt
Dash onion powder
Dash white pepper
Juice of ½ lemon

Remove artichoke stems and trim tips of leaves. Make several cuts in bottom of stem. Boil until tender in salted water to which sliced lemon has been added, about 40 minutes. Drain, remove choke with a spoon and cool. Pour French dressing into artichoke centers and around leaves. Marinate overnight. Combine shrimp and celery. Blend remaining ingredients and fold into shrimp. Two hours before serving, drain off excess French dressing and spoon shrimp into center of artichokes. Chill until ready to serve. This recipe makes a delicious luncheon entrée accompanied by individual cheese soufflés. It can also be used as a salad. Serves 6.

Mrs. Clyde Copeland, Jr.

Milanese Scampi Romano

On each hot plate place a serving of cooked spaghetti, 8 cooked medium shrimp, 1 cup Italian Red Sauce (see Index) and top with grated fresh Romano and Swiss cheeses. Place under broiler or in microwave oven to melt cheeses.

Ronald Cook

Shrimp Stroganoff

¼ cup minced onion
5 Tablespoons butter, divided
1½ pounds shelled, raw shrimp
½ pound fresh mushrooms,
   quartered
1 Tablespoon flour

1½ cups sour cream, at room
   temperature
1¼ teaspoons salt
Pepper to taste
Cooked yellow rice
Artichoke hearts, quartered

In a large skillet sauté onion in ¼ cup melted butter until softened. Add shrimp and sauté for 3-5 minutes or until pink and just cooked. Transfer mixture to a heated dish and keep warm. In the same skillet sauté mushrooms in remaining butter over moderately high heat until browned. Sprinkle mushrooms with flour and cook mixture, stirring, for 2 minutes. Reduce heat to moderately low and stir in the shrimp mixture, sour cream, salt and pepper. Cook mixture, stirring, for 2-3 minutes or until shrimp are thoroughly heated. Do not let mixture boil. Serve immediately over saffron rice tossed with quartered artichoke hearts. Serves 4.

Mrs. John B. Mason

Shrimp Newburg with Green Rice Ring

3 Tablespoons butter
2 Tablespoons flour
2 cups milk
1 teaspoon paprika
½ teaspoon dry mustard
¼ teaspoon salt
¼ teaspoon pepper

Pinch red pepper
5 Tablespoons Madeira wine,
   divided
1 cup whipping cream
2 egg yolks, lightly beaten
2 pounds peeled, cooked shrimp

Melt butter in top of double boiler. Stir in flour and cook several minutes. Gradually add milk and stir until smooth and thick. Add seasonings and 4 Tablespoons wine. Beat together cream and egg yolks. Gradually add cream to wine sauce. Cook over boiling water for 15 minutes. Add shrimp and remaining Tablespoon wine. Pour shrimp newburg into center and around GREEN RICE RING and garnish with parsley. Serves 10.

GREEN RICE RING

2 cups cooked rice
2 Tablespoons chopped green
   onion

1 cup chopped parsley
½ cup butter, melted
3 eggs, separated

Combine the rice, green onion, parsley, butter and slightly beaten egg yolks. Fold in stiffly beaten egg whites. Pour mixture into buttered 1½-quart ring mold and bake in a 350°F oven 25 minutes. Unmold on a hot platter.

Willie Braxton, Little Rock, Arkansas

Shrimp Manale

½ cup butter
2 Tablespoons Worcestershire
  sauce
Freshly ground black pepper

8 to 10 unpeeled, fresh jumbo
  shrimp
Lemon juice (optional)

Melt butter in saucepan. Add Worcestershire sauce and *plenty* of pepper.
Allow sauce to cool. Rinse shrimp lightly but do not dry. Place in baking dish.
Pour sauce over shrimp, sprinkle with lemon juice, if desired, and place in
400°F oven 20 minutes. Turn shrimp. Broil 3 minutes. Serve hot in a bowl with
the juices, accompanied by French bread to "sop up" the sauce. Serves 2.

Mrs. Gibbs J. Fowler

Deluxe Shrimp Soufflé

8 slices slightly dry bread,
  trimmed, buttered and cubed
2 cups cooked or canned shrimp
1 (3 ounce) can broiled sliced
  mushrooms, drained
½ pound sharp cheese, grated

3 eggs
½ teaspoon salt
½ teaspoon dry mustard
Dash pepper
Dash paprika
2 cups milk

Place half the bread cubes in a greased 7 x 11-inch baking dish. Add shrimp,
mushrooms and half the cheese. Top with remaining bread and cheese. Beat
together eggs and seasonings; add milk and pour over all. Bake at 325°F for
45-50 minutes. This is best made and refrigerated overnight before cooking.
Serves 8.

Mrs. Robert E. Taylor, Jr.

Shrimp and Mushrooms

1 cup flour
1 cup butter
1 cup chopped green onion and
  tops
2 pounds raw shrimp, shelled
  and deveined
2 (10½ ounce) cans beef
  bouillon

6 (8 ounce) cans mushrooms,
  stems and pieces or sliced
  (reserve liquid)
1 cup chopped parsley
Juice and grated rind of
  6 lemons
Salt and pepper

Brown flour in butter; add onion and sauté until tender. Add shrimp, bouillon
and mushroom liquid. Cook until thick. Stir in mushrooms, parsley, lemon
juice and rind, salt and pepper to taste. Add more lemon juice, if desired.
Serve in patty shells for a main course or in chafing dish as an hors d'oeuvre
with Melba toast rounds. Serves 15 as a main course.

Mrs. Thad J. Ryan, Jr., Monroe, Louisiana

Shrimp and Wild Rice Bake

2½ pounds shrimp
3 (10½ ounce) cans cream of
   mushroom soup
¾ cup water
1 (6 ounce) box Uncle Ben's
   Long-Grain and Wild Rice

1 large green pepper, chopped
1 (2 ounce) jar diced pimientos
2 cups finely chopped onion
1 cup finely chopped celery
1 pound Cheddar cheese,
   shredded

Boil, peel and devein shrimp. Dilute soup with water. Cook rice according to package directions. Combine all ingredients. Pour into a 3-quart casserole or rectangular Pyrex dish. Bake uncovered at 350°F for 45 minutes to 1 hour. Serve at once. Serves 8.

Mrs. Robert J. Johnson, Jr.

Cantonese Shrimp and Snow Peas

1½ pounds frozen peeled, raw
   shrimp
1½ teaspoons chicken stock
   base
1 cup boiling water
¼ cup thinly sliced green onion
1 clove garlic, crushed
1 teaspoon salad oil

½ teaspoon salt
1 teaspoon ground ginger, or
   less
Dash pepper
1 (6 ounce) package frozen
   Chinese pea pods, thawed
1½ Tablespoons cornstarch
1 Tablespoon soy sauce

Thaw shrimp. Dissolve chicken stock base in boiling water. In a skillet cook onion, garlic and shrimp in oil for 3 minutes, stirring frequently. If necessary add a little of the chicken broth to prevent sticking. Stir in salt, ginger, pepper, pea pods and chicken broth. Cover and simmer 5-7 minutes longer or until peas are tender but still slightly crisp. Dissolve cornstarch in a little water. Add cornstarch mixture to shrimp and cook until thick and clear, stirring constantly. Season with soy sauce. Serves 6.

Mrs. W. T. Mitchell, Jr., New Orleans, Louisiana

Beer Batter for Seafood

1½ cups flour, divided
½ cup corn meal
1 (12 ounce) can beer

1 Tablespoon salt
1 Tablespoon paprika

In one bowl combine ½ cup flour and corn meal. In second bowl combine remaining flour, beer, salt and paprika. Dip oysters, shrimp or any fish into dry mixture first and then into beer mixture. Fry in hot grease.

Mrs. Steven H. Brasfield

Crayfish Étouffée

1 Tablespoon flour
1 Tablespoon crayfish fat or
  margarine
1 cup chopped celery
½ cup chopped green pepper
4 Tablespoons chopped green
  onion tops
2 cups chopped onion
3 to 4 cloves garlic, finely chopped
½ cup oil
2 bay leaves

1 Tablespoon prepared mustard
Tabasco to taste
Cayenne pepper to taste
1½ teaspoons salt
½ cup tomato sauce (optional)
3 pounds peeled crayfish tails,
  or more
2 Tablespoons lemon juice
2 Tablespoons chopped parsley
Cooked rice

Make a roux of the flour and crayfish fat. Sauté vegetables in oil until tender, about 15 minutes. Add bay leaves and seasonings and blend well. Add vegetables to roux and stir for a few minutes. Thin with tomato sauce if needed. Cook on low heat for 30 minutes, stirring occasionally. Add crayfish tails. Simmer 5 additional minutes, or until crayfish tails are tender. Remove bay leaves. Correct seasonings. Add lemon juice and parsley just before serving. Serve over rice. Best made 1 day ahead. Freezes well. Serves 12.

Mrs. James P. Evans, Jr.

Shrimp may be substituted for the crayfish.

Coquilles St. Jacques

1½ pounds fresh scallops
Juice of 1½ to 2 limes or
  lemons
½ cup dry vermouth
Salt and pepper
½ pound fresh mushrooms,
  sliced

¼ cup minced green onion
3 Tablespoons butter
2 Tablespoons cornstarch
1 cup whipping cream, scalded
1 egg yolk, beaten
6 Tablespoons grated Parmesan
  cheese

If using large scallops, cut in 1-inch cubes. Dry and marinate in a mixture of the lime juice, vermouth, salt and pepper for an hour. Simmer scallops in liquid for about 5 minutes. Drain and reserve liquid. Sauté mushrooms and onion in butter for a few minutes. Set aside. Blend reserved liquid with cornstarch and add cream. Stir over low heat. When sauce thickens, stir in egg yolk. Butter 6 scallop shells or individual ramekins. Place scallops and mushrooms in shells. Cover with sauce. Sprinkle cheese on top and broil until hot and brown. Serves 6.

Mrs. Yandell Wideman

This is great for a ladies' luncheon or as a first course for dinner.

Bones's Frog Legs

10 pairs frog legs
1 (13 ounce) can evaporated
    milk
2 eggs, beaten

Salt and pepper
Self-rising flour
Cooking oil

Split pairs of legs to make single legs. Soak legs in mixture of milk, egg, salt and pepper for at least 30 minutes. Dip in flour seasoned with salt and pepper. Fry in medium-hot oil in deep-fat fryer or large pot until golden brown. Serves 4-6.

John Cossar

Escargot

3 scallions or green onions
1 cup white wine, divided
1 (4½ ounce) can large
    snails
Snail shells

½ cup butter, softened
2 Tablespoons finely chopped
    parsley
2 teaspoons garlic salt
Bread crumbs

Finely chop onions, using some of green tops. Sauté in ¾ cup wine for about 5 minutes. Rinse snails and cut large ones in half if necessary to make 24. Place 1 teaspoon sautéed onions in snail shell. Add snail. Combine butter, parsley and garlic salt, then "seal" the shell with butter mixture. Place shells in escargot pan. Add 1 Tablespoon wine to each pan and sprinkle shells lightly with bread crumbs. Bake in preheated 400°F oven for 10 minutes. Serve immediately with fresh French bread (to soak up the butter). May be prepared several hours in advance, adding wine and bread crumbs just before heating. Cover lightly with plastic wrap; place in refrigerator. Serves 4 as appetizer.

Mrs. John E. Ainsworth

Hot Tuna on Toast

2 tomatoes
1 green pepper, chopped
2 hard-boiled eggs, chopped
2 (6½ ounce) cans tuna fish
½ teaspoon salt

1 teaspoon lemon juice
Dash cayenne pepper
Worcestershire sauce
1000 Island Dressing (see Index)
Parsley

Peel and chop tomatoes; place in top of double boiler. Add green pepper and eggs to tomatoes. Drain tuna and add with remaining seasonings to tomato mixture. Toss lightly and steam, covered, for 20 minutes. Serve on toast topped with 1000 Island Dressing. Garnish with parsley. Serves 6.

Mrs. Sherwood Wise

Good for a luncheon or for cocktail or afternoon parties on small Melba rounds.

Tuna-Noodle Florentine

1 (10 ounce) package egg
noodles, cooked

2 (10 ounce) packages frozen
chopped spinach, cooked
and drained

2 (6½ ounce) cans tuna,
drained

2 (2 ounce) jars diced
pimientos, drained

2 (10½ ounce) cans cream of
mushroom soup

1 teaspoon minced onion

2 cups grated sharp cheese

Combine noodles, spinach and remaining ingredients, reserving some cheese to sprinkle on top. Cook in covered casserole in 350°F oven until cheese bubbles. May be prepared a day ahead. Freezes well. Serves 6-8.

Mrs. Ed R. Mangum

Oysters Bienville

36 select raw oysters
(about 1 quart)

1 large bunch green onions or
2 yellow onions, finely
chopped

½ cup butter

8 Tablespoons flour

1 pint fish stock, clam juice or
chicken stock

1½ pounds boiled shrimp,
finely chopped

1 (2 ounce) can mushrooms,
drained, finely chopped

3 egg yolks

6 Tablespoons white wine or
vermouth

½ cup half and half cream

Salt, white pepper and cayenne
pepper to taste

Tabasco

Oyster shells

¼ cup bread crumbs

¼ cup grated Parmesan cheese

1/8 teaspoon paprika

Rock salt

Place oysters in a baking pan in a 375°F oven and bake about 10 minutes or until they curl around the edges. Remove pan and set aside. Reserve liquid. Cook onions in butter, stirring until golden and soft. Do not brown. Add the flour. Stir over low heat until mixture is smooth. Slowly add the fish stock which has been scalded but not boiled. Add shrimp and mushrooms. Simmer until the sauce is smooth and begins to thicken. Set aside and allow to cool. Beat the egg yolks well with the wine and cream. Slowly pour the warm sauce into the egg mixture, beating constantly to keep mixture from curdling. Add reserved liquid from prebaked oysters to sauce and cook over low heat, stirring constantly for 10 minutes until well thickened. Season with salt, peppers and Tabasco. Place oysters in oyster shells. Spoon thick sauce over each oyster and sprinkle with a mixture of bread crumbs, cheese and paprika to form a thick cover. Place shells in 400°F oven until tops begin to turn golden brown. Serve shells on a bed of rock salt with French bread and a good tossed salad. Serves 6.

Mrs. Henry H. Mounger

Mississippi Fried Oysters

Raw oysters
2 eggs, beaten
2 cups corn meal
1 teaspoon sugar

2 teaspoons salt
1 teaspoon pepper
2 Tablespoons flour

Drain oysters and soak in eggs. Mix corn meal, sugar, salt, pepper and flour. Dip oysters in corn meal mixture and fry in deep fat until golden brown. Drain on paper towels.

Mrs. William S. Hamilton

Oysters and Artichoke Bottoms

3 fresh artichokes
3 dozen oysters
½ cup butter
5 Tablespoons flour
½ cup chopped shallots or
    green onion
½ cup chopped parsley

3 cloves garlic, crushed
1 teaspoon monosodium
    glutamate
Juice and grated rind of
    ½ lemon
Dash cayenne pepper
Salt and pepper to taste

Cook artichokes in boiling, salted water until tender, about 40 minutes. Remove leaves and choke. (Scrape leaves and reserve pulp for another use.) Slice each artichoke bottom in half. Place one slice in each of 6 ramekins. Drain oysters; chop coarsely and drain again, reserving all oyster liquid. Melt butter. Add flour and stir over *low* heat to make a golden brown roux. Add shallots, parsley, garlic and monosodium glutamate. Sauté vegetables in roux until wilted. Add lemon juice and rind, cayenne pepper, salt and pepper. Slowly add enough reserved oyster liquid to make a rather thick sauce. Cook sauce over low heat 20 minutes. Add oysters and cook 3-4 minutes or until oysters curl at edges. Pour oyster sauce over artichoke bottoms. Bake at 350°F until thoroughly heated. Serves 6.

Mrs. Mary S. Brister

Mother's Baked Oysters

Place raw oysters in oyster shells on a cookie sheet lined with foil. Cover oysters *heavily* with black pepper. Place on low oven rack and broil 10-15 minutes or until shriveled. Remove from oven and place a strip of bacon cut to fit on top of each oyster. Return to oven and cook at 350°F until bacon is done. Remove from oven. Combine 4 Tablespoons melted butter and the juice of 1 lemon and spoon a little over each oyster. Serve at once.

Mrs. Edward J. Peters

Oyster Spaghetti

2 bunches shallots or green
    onions and tops, chopped
1 large onion, chopped
1 large green pepper, chopped
2 cloves garlic, minced
1 bunch parsley, chopped
3 ribs celery, chopped
Cooking oil
¼ teaspoon thyme
3 bay leaves
2 (8 ounce) cans tomato sauce
2 teaspoons salt

½ teaspoon pepper
2 (4 ounce) cans button or
    sliced mushrooms or
    8 ounces fresh mushrooms,
    sliced and sautéed in butter
4 dozen raw oysters or
    4 (12 ounce) jars oysters
    (reserve liquid)
12 ounces vermicelli
10 ounces sharp Cheddar
    cheese, grated, divided
Grated fresh Parmesan cheese

Cook onions, green pepper, garlic, parsley and celery in a small amount of cooking oil until tender. Add thyme, bay leaves, tomato sauce, salt and pepper and simmer, partially covered, for 30 minutes. Add mushrooms. If oysters are large, cut in half. Add oysters and oyster liquid and cook for 15 minutes. Taste and correct seasonings. Cook vermicelli in boiling, salted water until tender. Drain and rinse in hot water. Combine in large mixing bowl the vermicelli, oyster sauce and Cheddar cheese, reserving about 2 ounces cheese for top. Mix thoroughly. Pour into 9 x 13-inch baking dish. Sprinkle top with reserved cheese. Bake covered for 30 minutes at 350°F. Let sit for 10 minutes before serving. Serve freshly grated Parmesan cheese as an accompaniment. Serves 16.

Mrs. John F. Potter

Baked Oysters in Shells

½ cup butter, divided
½ cup minced green onion
½ cup finely chopped celery
4 dozen or 1 pint medium
    oysters, drained and finely
    chopped
4 hard-boiled eggs, finely
    chopped

½ cup finely chopped parsley
8 crackers, crumbled, divided
1 teaspoon salt
Dash red pepper
1 Tablespoon Worcestershire
    sauce
2 or 3 dashes Louisiana hot
    sauce

In 10-inch iron skillet melt ¼ cup butter; add onion and celery and cook until tender. Add oysters and juice that accumulated while chopping. Add eggs, parsley and half the cracker crumbs. Add seasonings. Cook until oysters curl. If the mixture seems too runny to spoon into shells, cook a little longer. If too stiff, add a little liquid. Spoon mixture into 10 small clam or oyster shells; sprinkle with remaining cracker crumbs and melted butter. Bake in 450°F oven for about 10 minutes. This recipe may also be served in a casserole. Serves 10.

Mrs. Jay A. Travis, Jr., McComb, Mississippi

Oven Fried Oysters

½ cup butter, melted
Dash Worcestershire sauce
Dash Tabasco

Salt and pepper to taste
1 pint oysters, drained
1 cup bread crumbs

Mix butter and seasonings. Dip oysters in mixture; then roll in crumbs. Place close together in 10 x 7-inch pan. Pour any remaining butter sauce over oysters. Refrigerate 3-4 hours or overnight. *Refrigeration is important.* Bake in preheated 350°-400°F oven for 15-20 minutes or until crumbs are golden brown and oysters begin to juice. Serves 4.

Mrs. Charles Morris

Oysters Mosca

1 large onion, chopped
½ cup butter
3 cloves garlic, minced
2 Tablespoons chopped fresh
  parsley
½ teaspoon thyme
¾ teaspoon oregano
1/8 teaspoon red pepper

Salt and pepper to taste
4 dozen oysters, drained
  (reserve liquid)
1 cup bread crumbs
2 slices bacon, fried and
  crumbled
10 almonds, crushed
Grated Parmesan cheese

Sauté onion in butter until clear. Add garlic, parsley, seasonings and oysters. Cook until oysters curl at the edges; then add reserved oyster liquid. Fold in bread crumbs, bacon and almonds. Spoon into casserole or individual ramekins. Sprinkle with cheese. Bake at 350°F for 15-20 minutes. Serves 4.

Mrs. Albert Simmons

Oyster Ramekins

1 quart oysters
¾ cup butter, divided
2 cups chopped onion
2 small cloves garlic, minced
1½ bay leaves, broken
1/8 teaspoon thyme

1½ teaspoons salt
Pepper
Tabasco to taste
1½ cups cracker crumbs,
  divided

Drain and chop oysters, reserving liquid. Melt ½ cup butter in heavy skillet; add onion, garlic and bay leaves. Sauté until onions are light brown. Add oysters and seasonings. Moisten 1 cup crumbs with reserved oyster liquid. Add to oyster mixture and cook 20-30 minutes or until oysters have stopped drawing water. Add 3 Tablespoons butter and cook until melted. Place in buttered casserole or individual ramekins and cover with remaining crumbs. Dot with remaining butter. To serve, place in 350°F oven until thoroughly heated. May be prepared 1 day ahead. May also be served from a chafing dish. Serves 6-8.

Mrs. Edward C. Nichols

Crab Mornay

2 bunches green onions, minced
¾ cup minced parsley
6 Tablespoons butter, divided
¼ cup flour
1½ cups chicken stock
½ cup whipping cream
Salt and pepper
1 teaspoon lemon juice

1 cup grated Swiss or Gruyère
   cheese, or more
1 pound fresh lump crab meat
   or 3 (7½ ounce) cans lump
   or king crab
1 (2 ounce) jar pimientos,
   chopped
3 Tablespoons sherry wine
Tabasco to taste

Sauté onions and parsley in 2 Tablespoons butter. Set aside. Melt remaining butter in a saucepan and stir in flour. Remove from heat and add hot chicken stock and cream. Return to heat and stir until thickened. Season with salt, pepper and lemon juice. Stir in cheese until melted. Fold vegetables and crab meat into sauce. Add remaining ingredients. Keep warm or reheat over hot water. Serve in tart shells for a main course or in a chafing dish with BREAD CRISPS for a party. Serves 6.

BREAD CRISPS

With an electric knife trim crusts from day old bread slices. Cut each slice lengthwise into 3 pieces. Place on cookie sheet and brush each side with melted butter. Toast in 250°-300°F oven until very crisp and slightly brown. Crisps keep well in a tin box.

Mrs. Chick Warner, Vicksburg, Mississippi

Stuffed Eggplant à la Galatoire's

2 large eggplants
Olive oil
6 Tablespoons butter
1 cup chopped green onion
Chopped parsley

Salt and pepper to taste
1 pound lump crab meat
Bread crumbs
Grated Parmesan cheese

Cut eggplants in half lengthwise; rub the cut surface with olive oil and place cut-side-down in roasting pan. Bake 30 minutes at 350°F. Scrape pulp from skin, leaving a shell with skin intact. Melt butter in heavy skillet and sauté in it the onion and a generous amount of parsley. Season mixture with salt and pepper and allow to simmer a few minutes. Add eggplant pulp and cook a few more minutes. Add crab meat and mix well. Stuff eggplant shells with mixture and sprinkle with bread crumbs and Parmesan cheese. Bake in 350°F oven for 30 minutes. Serves 4.

Mrs. Maurice Reed, Jr.

A very attractive dish!

Creamed Crab Meat with Artichoke Hearts

½ cup butter
½ cup flour
¼ cup grated onion
½ cup chopped green onion
2 Tablespoons chopped parsley
2 cups whipping cream
¾ cup dry white wine
2½ teaspoons salt

½ teaspoon white pepper
¼ teaspoon cayenne pepper
2 Tablespoons lemon juice
2 pounds fresh crab meat
1 (14 ounce) can artichoke
  hearts, drained, quartered
½ pound fresh mushrooms,
  thickly sliced

In a 2-quart saucepan melt butter and stir in flour. Cook 5 minutes over medium heat, stirring often. Add onions. Cook 2-3 minutes without browning. Stir in parsley. Gradually add cream and heat well. Add wine, salt, white pepper and cayenne pepper. Blend well. Bring to a simmer, stirring occasionally. Remove from heat. When sauce has cooled to lukewarm, stir in lemon juice. In a 3-quart casserole, alternate layers of crab meat, artichoke hearts and mushrooms, spreading sauce between layers. Bake uncovered at 350°F 30-45 minutes. May be prepared in advance. Freezes well. Serves 8.

Mrs. Thomas Yates, III

Stuffed Lobster Thermidor

6 (1 pound) frozen lobster tails
10 Tablespoons butter, melted
1 cup sliced fresh mushrooms
4 Tablespoons flour
1 teaspoon dry mustard
2 dashes ground nutmeg
2 dashes cayenne pepper
1 teaspoon salt

1 cup milk
1 cup half and half cream
2 egg yolks, slightly beaten
1 teaspoon lemon juice
2 Tablespoons sherry wine
½ cup fine bread crumbs
2 Tablespoons grated Parmesan
  cheese

Preheat oven to 450°F. Place the lobster tails in large pot of boiling water and cover. Cook until tender, about 20 minutes; drain. Cut each tail in half lengthwise and dice lobster meat. Set aside empty lobster tails. Pour ¼ cup butter in saucepan; add mushrooms and sauté until slightly browned. Blend in flour and mix in seasonings. Add milk and cream gradually to mixture, stirring constantly until thick. Add small amount of hot mixture to egg yolks, stirring constantly; then return egg yolk mixture to cream sauce, again stirring constantly and cooking until thickened. Stir in lemon juice, sherry and lobster meat; spoon into lobster shells. Combine bread crumbs, Parmesan cheese and remaining butter; sprinkle over stuffed lobster tails. Place on cookie sheet and bake at 400°F for 15 minutes. Serves 6.

Bobby Ginn, Chef, LeFleur's Restaurant

Norma's Crab Meat

1 pound lump crab meat
2 slices bread, trimmed and
   crumbled
1 cup mayonnaise
1 Tablespoon dry mustard
1 Tablespoon Worcestershire
   sauce

1 Tablespoon lemon juice
Dash Tabasco, or more
Cracker crumbs
Butter
Lemon wedges
Chopped fresh parsley

Combine first 7 ingredients and fill greased seafood shells. Top with cracker crumbs and dot with butter. Heat in a 350°F oven 30 minutes. Serve each with a lemon wedge and sprinkle with parsley. Serves 4.

Mrs. John Fontaine, Sr.

Mrs. Bradley's Crab Meat in Wine Sauce

4 Tablespoons butter
4 Tablespoons flour
2 cups half and half cream
2 egg yolks, well beaten
½ teaspoon salt
1 teaspoon Worcestershire sauce
¼ cup Rhine wine

1 pound lump crab meat, flaked
   and drained
½ pound fresh mushrooms,
   sliced and sautéed in butter,
   or 1 (3 ounce) can sliced
   mushrooms, drained
3 Tablespoons chopped parsley
Buttered bread crumbs

Melt butter; stir in flour. Add cream and stir until thickened. Remove from heat and add egg yolks, salt and Worcestershire sauce. Fold in wine, crab meat, mushrooms and parsley. Pour into greased 1½-quart baking dish. Bake at 350°F for 15 minutes. Cover with bread crumbs and bake for 15 minutes more. Serves 4.

Mrs. Donald A. White

Barbecued Rock Lobster Tails

Frozen rock lobster tails (2 per
   person)
½ cup butter, melted
1 clove garlic, minced

½ teaspoon salt
½ teaspoon pepper
¼ cup lemon juice

Using kitchen shears, snip off thin shell on the underside of the lobster tail; then starting at the tail end, split the lobster shell up the back about ¾ of the length. Combine remaining ingredients for a basting sauce; refrigerate sauce and lobster tails until time to cook. Prepare bed of coals in charcoal grill and cook lobster tails, shell side down, 3 inches above coals, for 8 minutes, brushing with sauce. Turn lobster tails; brush with sauce and cook 6 minutes on the other side. Keep turning and brushing with sauce until lobster tails are done. Sauce is sufficient to baste 12 tails.

Robert Swittenberg

Deviled Crab with Shrimp and Eggplant

1 small eggplant
Salt
2 Tablespoons chopped shallots
and tops
1 clove garlic, minced
2 Tablespoons chopped flat
parsley
1 Tablespoon chopped celery
leaves
1 Tablespoon chopped fresh
basil or 1 teaspoon dried
1 teaspoon chopped fresh
marjoram or ⅓ teaspoon
dried

10 peeled, raw shrimp
4 Tablespoons butter
2 teaspoons olive oil
Zest of ¼ lemon
1 teaspoon Worcestershire sauce
1 teaspoon dry mustard
12 single soda crackers, crushed
½ cup whipping cream
1 egg, beaten
1 pound lump crab meat
Freshly ground black pepper to
taste
½ cup grated fresh Parmesan
cheese, divided

Peel eggplant and slice; sprinkle with salt and let stand 30 minutes. Squeeze out dark juice and drain. Drop into a large quantity of boiling water. Cook a few minutes; drain and drop into more boiling water and cook until tender. Drain, mash and set aside. Sauté the shallots, garlic, parsley, celery, herbs and raw shrimp in butter and olive oil until shrimp turn pink. Stir in lemon zest, Worcestershire sauce, dry mustard, crackers, cream and egg. Mix well. Add crab meat and eggplant. Salt and pepper mixture to taste. Mix in ¼ cup cheese. Place in medium-size casserole or in individual shells. Sprinkle with remaining cheese. Cover loosely. Bake at 350°F for 30 minutes. Remove cover; cook 10 minutes more. Serve hot with fresh lemon slices if desired. Serves 5-6.

Mrs. Herbert A. Kroeze, Jr.

Lump Crab Meat and Shrimp

½ cup butter
1 Tablespoon flour
1 cup whipping cream
¼ cup sherry wine
2 Tablespoons Worcestershire
sauce
Salt and red pepper to taste
Chopped celery to taste

Chopped parsley to taste
1 cup mayonnaise
1 pound lump crab meat
½ pound shrimp, shelled and
cooked
Potato chips, crushed
Grated Cheddar cheese

Make a rich cream sauce by melting butter and adding flour. Stir until smooth. Add whipping cream gradually. Add next 5 ingredients and cook slowly until thickened. When mixture has cooled, add mayonnaise. Add crab meat and shrimp to sauce. Spoon into individual buttered shells or a buttered casserole dish. Sprinkle potato chips and cheese on top. Bake about 25 minutes in 325°F oven. Freezes well. Serves 6-8.

Mrs. Rabian D. Lane

Vegetables

Freezing Fresh Vegetables

SELECTION AND PREPARATION OF VEGETABLES FOR FREEZING Choose only the very best vegetables for freezing, those that were harvested at their peak. If not using vegetables from the home garden, buy fresh produce early in the day from a truck farmer, farmers' market or roadside stand. Everything should be in readiness for a freezing project so that there are no delays between harvesting the produce and storing it. Ideally vegetables should be stored in the freezer within 2 or 3 hours after picking. If vegetables cannot go directly from garden to freezer, they must spend the interim in the refrigerator or be held on ice to prevent overripening. Wash vegetables. Sort according to size, as blanching time varies according to size. Imperfect, immature or overripe vegetables should be discarded and any bruised parts of larger ones cut away.

BLANCHING PROCESS Almost all vegetables should be blanched before freezing to preserve flavor, vitamins, color and tenderness. Blanching in boiling water preserves nutritional value of vegetables, destroys almost all bacteria that may be present, permits longer freezer storage and helps ensure cleanliness of the food. 1 to 1½ pounds of prepared vegetables can be blanched at a time. Using a vegetable blancher with a perforated blanching basket and its own lid or a kettle with a 2-gallon capacity, bring to a boil over high heat at least 1 gallon water. Lower the vegetables into boiling water in the basket, a deep-frying basket, colander or cheesecloth bag. If the water is boiling hard and the correct amount of vegetables is added, the boil will stop only for a few seconds. Cover blancher tightly and keep heat high. Start timing at once and remove the vegetables from the water immediately at the end of the blanching time. Vegetables should not be overcooked. The water in the blancher can be used several times, adding fresh water to make up for any loss. Lower drained blanched vegetables, still in their container, into another container holding ice water. Let them cool thoroughly in the water, allowing about the same length of time for cooling as for blanching. Remove from water and drain well. Vegetables must be cooled to their centers before packaging or excess ice crystals will form among them when frozen. As soon as vegetables are cooled and well drained, pack for freezing.

BLANCHING TIMES

Asparagus - 2 to 4 minutes (depending on size)
Lima Beans - 2 to 4 minutes (depending on size)

Green Beans - 3 minutes (whole); 2 minutes (cut); 1 minute (French-style)
Cabbage - 1½ minutes

(Continued)

Carrots - 5 minutes (small whole);
  2 minutes (sliced)
Corn-on-the-cob - 6 to 10 minutes
  (depending on size)
Greens and spinach - 2 minutes
Okra - 2 minutes (cut into rounds
  after blanching)

Peas, English - 1½ minutes
Peas, black-eyed, crowder, lady -
  2 minutes
Squash and zucchini, sliced -
  3 minutes
Tomatoes, peeled and quartered -
  cook 10 to 20 minutes; cool

Basic Hollandaise Sauce

7/8 cup butter, divided
3 egg yolks
1 Tablespoon cold water

1 Tablespoon lemon juice
Pinch salt
White pepper to taste

Melt ¾ cup butter and set aside. Beat egg yolks until thick. Place yolks in top of double boiler and add water, lemon juice and salt. Beat well; place over barely simmering water. Add 1 Tablespoon cold butter and stir with wire whisk until thick enough to see bottom of pan between strokes, about 2 minutes. Remove pan from hot water and immediately beat in 1 Tablespoon cold butter. Pour melted butter *very slowly* into mixture, beating it in constantly. Add white pepper to taste and additional salt and lemon juice, if desired. If sauce curdles beat in 1 Tablespoon cold water; or mix together 1 teaspoon lemon juice and 1 Tablespoon sauce and beat in the rest of the sauce slowly. Will keep several days in refrigerator. Freezes well. To use, thaw and let sauce reach room temperature. Makes approximately 1 cup.

Blender Hollandaise Sauce

3 egg yolks
1 to 2 Tablespoons lemon juice
¼ teaspoon salt

Dash cayenne pepper
½ cup butter, melted

Blend first 4 ingredients in blender on high speed. Slowly add melted butter. Sauce will keep at room temperature for an hour before serving. Yields about 1 cup sauce.

Mrs. Taylor Holland

Mock Hollandaise Sauce

1 (3 ounce) package cream
  cheese, softened
2 egg yolks

2 Tablespoons lemon juice
Dash salt
¼ cup butter, melted

Blend ingredients. Refrigerate if desired. Heat over hot water before serving. Yields about 1 cup sauce.

Mrs. James Y. Palmer

Perfect White Sauce

Use ingredient amounts specified in recipe. Scald liquid ingredient. Melt butter or margarine in a heavy-bottomed saucepan. (Do not use aluminum pan as it may discolor sauce.) Stir the flour into the melted butter until mixture is smooth. Cook over low heat for several minutes, stirring, to eliminate any raw flour taste. Remove pan from heat and add hot liquid all at one time, beating constantly with a wire whisk. Return sauce to medium heat and cook until thickened, stirring. Add seasonings. If sauce is not used immediately, float a thin film of milk, stock or melted butter on top to prevent a skin from forming; set aside uncovered. May also keep hot over simmering water, refrigerate or freeze.

Scalloped Pineapple

4 cups fresh bread crumbs
1 (20 ounce) can pineapple
   chunks, drained

3 eggs, beaten
2 cups sugar
1 cup butter, melted

Toss together bread crumbs and pineapple chunks and place in a greased 2-quart baking dish. Combine remaining ingredients and pour over pineapple. Bake at 350°F for 30 minutes. Casserole can be made up and refrigerated overnight before baking. Reheats well. Good with ham. Serves 8.

Mrs. Samuel H. White, Jr.

Red Candied Apples

1½ cups sugar
1 cup water
½ cup cinnamon gems (red hots)
½ teaspoon red food coloring
6 to 8 cooking apples

2 (3 ounce) packages cream
   cheese, softened
Mayonnaise
Milk
Chopped pecans

Mix sugar and water in medium-size boiler. Add cinnamon candies and coloring and simmer until candies are dissolved. Peel and core apples. Add apples to simmering mixture. Turn frequently. Cook until apples are just tender. Cool. Refrigerate. Combine cream cheese with a little mayonnaise and milk. Add a few chopped pecans. Stuff apples with cheese mixture. Apples can be cut into rings before cooking and served as rings with cheese stuffing in the center. Goes well with game. May be made several days ahead. Serves 6-8.

Mrs. Jack R. Gibson

BROILED PEARS   Sprinkle peeled fresh pear halves with a small amount of sugar and ground cinnamon. Dot with butter or margarine. Broil in 450°F oven for 5 minutes or until butter is melted. Serve immediately.

Fruit Stacks

Make as many fruit stacks as desired, beginning with a pineapple slice, topping that with a peach half, an apricot half and a seeded whole prune. Stir together ½ cup melted butter, ¼ cup dark brown sugar and 2 Tablespoons dark rum. Spoon over fruit stacks and bake in 350°F oven for 10 minutes. Baste with extra sauce and serve as an accompaniment to poultry or game. Sauce is sufficient for at least 8 fruit stacks.

Mrs. Clyde Copeland, Jr.

Country French Applesauce

2 pounds tart apples
½ cup water
½ to ⅔ cup sugar
1 teaspoon lemon juice
¼ teaspoon ground cinnamon
1/8 teaspoon ground nutmeg

½ cup sour cream
1 Tablespoon flour
Ground blanched almonds
Crushed almond macaroons
Butter

Cut unpeeled apples into quarters and remove cores. (Red-skinned apples make the most attractive sauce.) Place apples in saucepan; add water and cook the fruit, covered, for about 20 minutes or until soft. Force fruit through a sieve or food mill and discard skins. Add sugar, lemon juice, cinnamon, nutmeg and sour cream mixed with flour. Place in buttered baking dish and sprinkle with almonds and macaroon crumbs. Dot with butter and bake at 400°F for 15 minutes. Serve warm. Yields approximately 3 cups applesauce.

Mrs. James L. Alford, Jr.

Festive Curried Fruit

1 (29 ounce) can pear halves
1 (29 ounce) can Freestone
  peach halves
1 (17 ounce) can Royal Anne
  light sweet cherries, pitted
1 (20 ounce) can pineapple
  chunks
1 (11 ounce) can mandarin
  orange sections

1 (17 ounce) can apricots
  (preferably peeled)
½ cup white raisins
¾ cup sugar
¼ teaspoon salt
3 Tablespoons butter
3 Tablespoons flour
½ to 1 teaspoon curry powder
½ cup white wine

Drain all fruit, reserving juice. Measure ¾ cup fruit juice and set aside. Soak raisins in hot water to cover for 10 minutes. Drain. Mix fruit juice with sugar, salt, butter and flour. Heat but do not boil. Stir until thick. Fold sauce into drained fruit and raisins. Add curry powder and wine. Let stand 3 hours. Cook 30 minutes at 350°F. May be refrigerated and reheated next day. Improves with age. Serves 8-10.

The Editors

Baked Stuffed Oranges

6 large navel oranges
4 cups crushed pineapple
  with juice
Juice of 1 lemon

½ cup sugar or to taste
¼ cup sherry wine
½ cup walnuts, finely
  chopped

Cut oranges in half and scoop out pulp. Place pulp in 3-quart saucepan with pineapple and add lemon juice and sugar. Cook over low heat, stirring occasionally, until mixture becomes the consistency of a thin marmalade. As mixture cooks, scallop edges of orange shells, if desired, using small scissors. Stir sherry into pineapple mixture and refill shells. Sprinkle with walnuts. Bake at 350°F for 20 minutes. Do not refrigerate. Serve at room temperature. Can be held at room temperature overnight. Serves 12.

Mrs. Reuel May, Jr.

Artichokes Willie

3 (14 ounce) cans
  artichoke hearts, drained
1 cup butter, melted
2 (4 ounce) cans sliced
  mushrooms, drained
½ cup lemon juice

1 (2 ounce) jar diced
  pimientos
½ teaspoon Italian seasoning
Salt and pepper to taste
½ cup slivered almonds
Paprika

Combine all ingredients except almonds and paprika in a casserole. Top with slivered almonds and sprinkle with paprika. Warm at 350°F until hot throughout. Serve immediately. Serves 8.

Willie Braxton, Little Rock, Arkansas

Mrs. Morse's Asparagus Casserole

1 cup crushed Ritz crackers
2 (14½ ounce) cans cut green
  asparagus, drained
1 cup grated sharp cheese

¾ cup butter, diced
1 cup blanched almonds,
  toasted and finely ground
1 cup milk

Line a casserole with a few cracker crumbs. Alternate layers of asparagus, cheese, cracker crumbs, butter and almonds. Pour the milk in one side of the dish. Prepare the night before or at least 2 hours in advance. Bake at 350°F for 1 hour. Serves 6.

Mrs. George F. Woodliff

Simmer 4 pineapple slices in a mixture of ¼ cup vinegar, 2 Tablespoons each brown sugar and brandy and 1 cinnamon stick for 10 minutes. Chill. Cut into chunks, if desired, and serve as a fruit accompaniment with ham, pork or chicken.

Asparagus Soufflé

4 eggs
1 (15½ ounce) can asparagus
    spears, drained
1 cup shredded Cheddar cheese

1 cup mayonnaise
1 (10½ ounce) can cream of
    mushroom soup

Beat eggs in blender. Add remaining ingredients and blend. Pour into lightly greased 1½-quart soufflé dish. Place soufflé dish in a second pan and add 2 inches of water. Bake at 350°F for 55-60 minutes or until knife inserted in center comes out clean. Serves 6.

Mrs. Robert Allen Smith

Avocado Zapata

½ pound ground lean meat
½ cup chopped onion
⅓ cup raisins
¼ cup chopped walnuts or
    pecans
1 clove garlic, chopped
½ teaspoon ground cinnamon
½ teaspoon sugar

1 Tablespoon chopped green
    chilies
¼ teaspoon ground cumin
¼ cup chopped tomatoes and
    juice
½ teaspoon salt
3 large avocados (or 4 small)

Sauté meat until brown. Add onion and cook until soft. Add remaining ingredients except avocados and simmer 10 minutes. Set aside. Peel and cut avocados in half. Fill each cavity with meat mixture. Place avocados filled side down in greased baking dish or individual ramekins. Pour ZAPATA SAUCE over and bake until warm at 375°F (about 15 minutes). Serves 6-8.

ZAPATA SAUCE

½ cup chopped onion
¼ cup chopped green pepper
2 Tablespoons chopped green
    chilies
1 Tablespoon oil

1 Tablespoon tomato paste
1 (16 ounce) can tomatoes,
    diced (or 2 cups chopped
    fresh)
¼ teaspoon salt

Sauté onion, green pepper and chilies in oil until soft. Add additional ingredients and simmer 5 minutes. Makes 2½ cups sauce.

Mrs. G. G. Mazzaferro

Variation: Stuffed avocados may be briefly deep-fried, then topped with warmed sauce to serve.

FRIED ASPARAGUS Wash fresh asparagus and cut off white ends. Cut diagonally into 1-inch pieces. Drop into hot peanut oil and fry 3-4 minutes. Salt lightly and serve.

Norma Watkins's Green Bean Casserole

1 Tablespoon butter, divided
2 teaspoons flour
1 teaspoon salt
¼ teaspoon pepper
1 teaspoon sugar
1 teaspoon grated onion

1 pint sour cream
½ pound Swiss cheese, grated
2 (16 ounce) cans Jack and the
    Beanstalk whole green beans,
    drained
Cracker crumbs

Melt 2 teaspoons butter and stir in flour, salt, pepper, sugar and onion. Add sour cream. Stir until thickened. Stir in cheese until melted. Grease a 1½-quart casserole. Place beans in first and top with cheese sauce. Cover with cracker crumbs and sprinkle with remaining butter. Bake in 400°F oven for 20 minutes. Serves 8.

Mrs. W. Thad McLaurin

Green Beans Supreme

3 (16 ounce) cans French-style
    green beans, drained
1 (10½ ounce) can beef
    consommé
1 (4 ounce) can sliced
    mushrooms and liquid

½ cup butter, sliced
2 teaspoons Maggi's seasoning
1 teaspoon salt
½ teaspoon seasoned salt
1 teaspoon soy sauce

Combine all ingredients in casserole. Bake at 325°F for 45 minutes. May be prepared 2 days ahead, then cooked when needed. Serves 10-12.

Mrs. Sherwood Wise

Favorite Red Beans and Rice

1 pound dried red beans
1 meaty ham bone
1¾ quarts water (or enough to
    cover ham bone)
3 cups chopped Bermuda onion
1 bunch green onions, chopped
1 cup parsley, chopped
2 large cloves garlic, crushed
1 Tablespoon salt
Dash red pepper

1 teaspoon black pepper
½ teaspoon sugar
Dash Tabasco
¼ teaspoon oregano
¼ teaspoon thyme leaves
1 Tablespoon Worcestershire
    sauce
½ (8 ounce) can tomato sauce
Seasoned salt to taste
Cooked rice

Soak beans overnight in water to cover. Drain. Cook beans and ham bone in water slowly for 3 hours. Add all ingredients except seasoned salt. Cook slowly for 1½ hours. Cool. Reheat and simmer for 1 hour. Add seasoned salt to taste. For thicker red beans, remove a few beans from the pot. Mash beans and return to pot. This recipe may be prepared a day in advance and is better served the second day. Serve over cooked rice. Serves 8.

Mrs. E. B. Robinson, Jr.

Old Fashioned Baked Beans with Spices

1 (31 ounce) can pork and
   beans
1 teaspoon dry mustard
1/8 teaspoon pepper
2 teaspoons salt
¼ cup brown sugar or
   2 Tablespoons brown sugar
   and 2 Tablespoons molasses
1 green pepper, chopped

1 large onion, peeled and thinly
   sliced
1 Tablespoon sweet pickle juice
   or vinegar
1/8 teaspoon each ground
   cinnamon, ground cloves
¼ cup ketchup or chili sauce
½ lemon, quartered
3 slices bacon

Combine all ingredients except bacon, including lemon quarters which are squeezed, then added to mixture. Pour beans into a casserole dish; lay slices of bacon on top and bake covered at 300°F for at least 2 hours. Serves 6.

Mrs. Clyde Copeland, Jr.

Tangy Green Beans

2 (15½ ounce) cans whole
   string beans

Bacon strips, cut in half

Wrap 6 or 7 string beans in half piece of bacon. Secure with pick. Repeat with remaining string beans. Broil until bacon is done. Pour hot VINAIGRETTE SAUCE over beans and serve. Serves 8.

VINAIGRETTE SAUCE

3 Tablespoons butter
2 Tablespoons vinegar
1 Tablespoon tarragon vinegar
1 teaspoon salt

1 teaspoon paprika
1 Tablespoon chopped parsley
1 teaspoon grated onion

Combine all ingredients and bring to a boil. Makes ½ cup sauce.

Mrs. Charles E. Carmichael

Chinese Pickled Beets

1 cup sugar
2 Tablespoons cornstarch
1 cup vinegar
24 whole cloves
3 Tablespoons ketchup
3 Tablespoons Crisco oil

Dash salt
1 teaspoon vanilla
3 (16 ounce) cans tiny whole
   beets, quartered (reserve
   liquid)

Place sugar, cornstarch, vinegar, cloves, ketchup, oil, salt and vanilla in a large shallow skillet. Mix well. Add beets and 1½ cups beet liquid. Cook over medium heat for 3 minutes, stirring constantly until thickened. Serve hot or cold. Keeps well in a glass jar in refrigerator. Delicious served on a mound of cottage cheese as a salad. Serves 10-12.

Mrs. James Kelly Wallace

Broccoli with Horseradish Sauce

4 Tablespoons butter, melted
¾ cup mayonnaise
1 Tablespoon horseradish
1 Tablespoon grated onion
¼ teaspoon salt

¼ teaspoon dry mustard
Dash red pepper
2 (10 ounce) packages frozen
   broccoli spears or 1 head
   fresh broccoli

Combine first 7 ingredients and refrigerate until ready to use. Cook broccoli by package directions. If using fresh broccoli, cut into spears and scrape the spear ends with a potato peeler. Cook in boiling, salted water 8 minutes. Do not overcook. Broccoli should be crisp. Drain and lightly salt. Serve with a spoonful of sauce on top. Sauce will keep for several months in the refrigerator and may be used as desired. Serves 6.

Mrs. Clyde X. Copeland, Sr.

Brussels Sprouts with Hot Bacon Dressing

2 eggs
¼ cup sugar
⅔ cup white vinegar
⅓ cup water
½ teaspoon dry mustard
1 teaspoon salt

¼ teaspoon pepper
12 strips bacon, halved
   crosswise
1 Tablespoon salt
6 (10 ounce) packages frozen
   Brussels sprouts, thawed

In a screw top jar beat eggs lightly with a fork; add sugar, vinegar, water, dry mustard, salt and pepper. Shake to blend and place covered jar in refrigerator. About 1 hour before serving fry bacon and drain on paper towel. Remove all but 4 Tablespoons grease. Reduce heat to low, shake jar mixture and add to skillet. Stir until sauce is thick. Set aside. Cook Brussels sprouts in boiling, salted water about 8 minutes and drain. Serve with warm sauce poured over them and garnish with crumbled bacon. Serves 8-10.

Mrs. Henry H. Mounger

Hot Cabbage Creole

2 slices bacon
1 large onion, chopped
1 large green pepper, chopped
1 (28 ounce) can whole tomatoes,
   chopped (reserve juice)

1 head cabbage, chopped
2 teaspoons salt
¼ teaspoon pepper
Cayenne pepper
⅓ cup vinegar

Cut up bacon and fry in large pan. Add onion and green pepper and sauté with bacon. Add tomatoes and juice. Stir. Add cabbage, salt and pepper. Sprinkle lightly with cayenne pepper. Add vinegar. Bring to a boil and cover. Simmer for 45 minutes. Serves 8.

Mrs. C. Lee Lott, Jr.

Carrot Ring Soufflé

12 medium carrots, cooked and
  mashed
½ to 2 Tablespoons prepared
  horseradish
½ cup mayonnaise

2 Tablespoons finely minced
  onion
3 eggs, well beaten
½ teaspoon salt

Mix all ingredients and pour into lightly oiled ring mold. Place in pan of hot water and bake at 350°F for 40 minutes. Turn out on serving platter and fill center with cooked fresh English peas or creamed mushrooms. Serve immediately. Serves 8.

Mrs. Louis J. Lyell

Julienne Carrots with Walnuts

3 pounds carrots
Salt
2 Tablespoons sliced green
  onion and tops

½ cup butter or margarine,
  softened
2 (3¼ ounce) packages black or
  English walnuts, broken

Scrape carrots and remove ends. Cut carrots into julienne strips. In saucepan heat 1 inch salted water (½ teaspoon salt to 1 cup water) to boiling. Add carrots and onion. Cover. Heat to boiling; reduce heat and simmer until tender, about 25 minutes. Drain carrots. Toss with butter and walnuts. Season to taste. Serve warm. This may be made a day or two in advance and reheated. Serves 12.

Mrs. Lewis Wright, Metairie, Louisiana

Cauliflower Duchesse

1 medium head cauliflower
4 Tablespoons butter
3 Tablespoons white vinegar
1 Tablespoon sugar

2 Tablespoons chopped pimiento
2 Tablespoons chopped green
  pepper
¼ teaspoon salt

Trim cauliflower and pierce end of stalk several times with knife. Boil whole head in salted water, covered, until tender (about 15-20 minutes). Drain. Mix remaining ingredients and heat to boiling. Transfer cauliflower to serving dish and pour sauce over it. Serve immediately. Serves 6.

Mrs. Robert W. Graves

Variation: Make TANGY CAULIFLOWER SAUCE by combining ½ cup mayonnaise, ½ teaspoon grated onion or onion flakes and 1 teaspoon prepared mustard. Spread over cooked cauliflower head and sprinkle with ½ cup grated Cheddar cheese. Heat in 350°F oven until cheese is melted. Serve immediately.

Mrs. H. Henry Hederman, Jr.

Creamed Celery with Water Chestnuts

4 cups sliced celery
½ teaspoon salt
¼ cup slivered almonds
½ cup sliced water chestnuts
½ cup drained, canned sliced
  mushrooms
3 Tablespoons flour

5 Tablespoons margarine,
  divided
½ cup milk
1 cup chicken broth
½ cup grated Parmesan cheese
½ cup crushed Ritz crackers

Cook celery and salt in water to cover for 5 minutes. Drain. In a bowl mix celery with almonds, water chestnuts and mushrooms. Stir flour into 3 Tablespoons melted margarine and cook until well blended. Add milk and chicken broth and stir until thickened. Combine cream sauce with celery mixture. Place mixture in buttered 8 x 8-inch casserole dish. Cover with Parmesan cheese. Melt remaining margarine and add cracker crumbs. Sprinkle over cheese. Bake at 350°F until bubbly, about 30 minutes. May be prepared 1 day ahead. Particularly good with beef. Serves 8.

Mrs. Daniel H. Draughn

Shoe Peg Corn Casserole

2 Tablespoons butter
2 Tablespoons flour
½ pint whipping cream

1 (12 ounce) can shoe peg whole
  kernel white corn, drained
Salt and pepper to taste

Melt butter and blend in flour. Stir in the cream, corn, salt and pepper. Bake at 350°F for 30 minutes or until consistency is very creamy and thick. Stir occasionally. This dish is best served immediately. It tends to separate if reheated. Serves 4.

Mrs. William Dalehite, Jr.

Fried Corn

8 to 10 ears fresh corn
3 Tablespoons butter
½ cup half and half cream

Salt and pepper
Pinch sugar, if the corn is not
  garden fresh

The method of cutting the corn is most important. With a sharp knife slit each row of kernels in half. Then cut the top half off corn kernels and into a bowl. When all the kernels have been cut off, tilt the cob into the bowl and with the knife at an angle scrape the remaining juice from the kernels into the bowl. Heat butter in a heavy skillet until it foams. Quickly add the corn and stir rapidly until the corn milk thickens and the kernels begin to look clear. Add cream. Stir. Add salt, pepper and sugar if needed. Cook until thickened, about 10 minutes. Serve immediately. Serves 4-8.

Mrs. Herbert A. Kroeze, Jr.

Fresh Corn Loaf

2 cups fresh corn cut off cob
1 cup chopped fresh tomato
1 cup chopped onion
1 cup chopped green pepper
2 teaspoons salt
1/8 teaspoon cayenne pepper

1 cup yellow corn meal
1 cup grated Cheddar cheese
2 eggs
½ cup evaporated milk
½ cup water

Mix together corn, tomato, onion, green pepper, salt, pepper, corn meal and cheese. Combine well and let mixture sit for 30 minutes. Beat eggs; add to evaporated milk and water, mixing well. Then add egg mixture to vegetables. Pour into a greased 2-quart casserole or loaf pan and bake at 375°F for 1 hour. Serve hot or cold. This is great with ham sandwiches or as a picnic dish. Serves 6-8.

Mrs. John D. Adams

Corn, Limas and Tomatoes

1 medium onion, chopped
1 green pepper, chopped
Oil
1 (16 ounce) can whole kernel
    white corn, drained
1 (17 ounce) can lima beans,
    drained
1 (8 ounce) can tomato sauce

1 (16 ounce) can stewed
    tomatoes
1 Tablespoon Worcestershire
    sauce
Salt and pepper
Seasoned salt to taste
4 slices bacon

Cook onion and green pepper in a little oil until tender. Combine the corn, limas, tomato sauce, tomatoes, vegetables and seasonings in an 8 x 8-inch casserole. Lay bacon slices across top. Bake covered at 350°F for 1 hour. Uncover for last 10 minutes to crisp bacon. Serves 8.

Mrs. Paul H. Moore, Pascagoula, Mississippi

Variation: This dish may be made with fresh vegetables. Cover bottom of casserole with bacon slices. Then place over bacon a layer of fresh lima beans, a layer of sliced, peeled fresh tomatoes, chopped onion and green pepper, a layer of fresh white corn cut off cob, a second layer of tomatoes and a covering of bacon strips. Salt and pepper liberally between layers. Cover and bake as above for at least 1 hour or until limas are done.

———

CREAMED CORN Melt 3 Tablespoons each butter and bacon grease in heavy skillet. Grate 10 ears corn and measure corn. Add corn and water (to equal half the amount of corn) to skillet and season with salt and a liberal amount of pepper. Cook over low heat until thickened, about 45 minutes, stirring occasionally.

Escalloped Eggplant Pyramids

1 (1¼ pound) eggplant, cut in
 ½-inch slices
1 large or 2 medium fresh
 tomatoes, sliced
1 large onion, thinly sliced
¾ cup butter, melted, divided
½ teaspoon salt

½ teaspoon dried basil leaves
¼ pound Mozzarella cheese,
 sliced
½ cup Italian bread crumbs
2 Tablespoons grated Parmesan
 cheese

On a medium-size heatproof platter arrange eggplant slices; then stack a tomato slice and an onion slice on top of each eggplant slice. Drizzle with ¼ cup butter. Sprinkle with salt and basil. Bake covered in a preheated 450°F oven for 20 minutes. Cut Mozzarella cheese in thirds. Arrange on top of eggplant pyramids. Stir crumbs into remaining butter and sprinkle on top. Sprinkle with Parmesan cheese. Bake uncovered for 10 minutes or until cheese is bubbly. Serves 4.

Mrs. Raymond F. Grenfell

Eggplant Hollandale

½ cup chopped celery
¾ cup chopped onion
½ green pepper, chopped
2 Tablespoons butter
1 Tablespoon parsley flakes
1 clove garlic, mashed, or garlic
 salt to taste
Seasoned salt
Tabasco
Worcestershire sauce
2 large eggplants, peeled and
 diced

1 teaspoon sugar
1 large tomato, peeled and
 diced
1 (7 ounce) can shrimp or
 ½ pound peeled, cooked
 shrimp
1 cup bread crumbs, divided
 (preferably Progresso)
1 egg, beaten
3 Tablespoons grated Parmesan
 cheese

Sauté celery, onion and green pepper in butter. Add parsley, garlic and seasonings to taste. Cook eggplant in water seasoned with sugar until tender. Mix eggplant with sautéed vegetables, tomato, shrimp, ½ cup bread crumbs and egg. Place in casserole, top with remaining bread crumbs and Parmesan cheese and dot with additional butter. Cook 30 minutes at 350°F. Serve hot. Serves 8.

Mrs. James C. Hays

FRIED EGGPLANT   Peel and cut 3 pounds eggplant into julienne slices. Dredge in flour, dip into ¾ cup milk beaten with 2 eggs; then roll in ¾ cup cracker meal seasoned with ½ teaspoon each salt and pepper. Fry in deep fat for 5 minutes. Drain and dust with seasoned salt and Romano cheese.

Tomato-Eggplant Casserole

3 eggplants
3 slices bacon
1 small onion, minced
1 (28 ounce) can Progresso
   tomatoes or 10 to 12 fresh
   tomatoes, skinned
1 Tablespoon A-1 steak sauce

1 teaspoon sugar
2 teaspoons salt
½ teaspoon pepper
1 (5¾ ounce) can Dawn Fresh
   mushroom steak sauce
Progresso bread crumbs
Butter

Peel, slice and parboil eggplants until just tender. Drain. Fry bacon in large skillet and set aside. In same skillet sauté onion until clear. Add eggplant, tomatoes and remaining ingredients except bacon, bread crumbs and butter. Simmer until soft. Mash together. Adjust seasoning. Crumble bacon and add. Place in buttered casserole and cover with bread crumbs. Dot with butter. Bake at 350°F for 30 minutes. Can be made ahead and frozen. Serves 8.

Mrs. Donald Lutken

Ratatouille Supreme

½ cup olive oil
4 cups cubed peeled eggplant
4 cups cubed zucchini
½ cup green pepper cut in
   squares
¼ cup sweet red pepper cut in
   squares
½ cup chopped onion
2 Tablespoons chopped garlic
½ cup dry white wine

4 fresh tomatoes, peeled and
   quartered
Pinch thyme
1 bay leaf
1 teaspoon sweet basil
Pinch rosemary
1 Tablespoon salt
1 teaspoon white pepper
½ cup pitted small black olives
2 Tablespoons chopped parsley

In a large skillet heat the oil; sauté the eggplant and zucchini in it for 8 minutes. Add the peppers and onion and simmer uncovered for another 6 minutes. Add garlic and simmer 2 minutes. Add wine, tomatoes, herbs, salt, pepper and black olives and cook covered in a 350°F oven for 20 minutes or until eggplant is tender. Sprinkle with parsley and serve. Serves 8.

Mrs. Julian Henderson

FRIED OKRA   Wash 1 pound fresh okra and slice into ½-inch rounds or thaw 1 (10 ounce) package cut okra. Toss okra in plastic bag with ½ cup white corn meal seasoned with salt and pepper. Fry in hot oil in skillet, turning often and sprinkling with salt and pepper as needed. When lightly browned, remove with slotted spoon and drain on paper towels. To oven fry, spread prepared okra rounds in single layer on cookie sheet and bake at 350°F until tender and crisp.

Mirliton or Eggplant Casserole

4 mirlitons (or 1 large eggplant)
2 eggs
2 slices bread, crumbled
5 Tablespoons butter or bacon
  grease
2 onions, finely chopped
3 cloves garlic, finely chopped
½ cup chopped celery
1 cup chopped green pepper

Grated Velveeta cheese to taste
Salt
Pepper
Tabasco
Chopped parsley
1 pound small peeled, cooked
  shrimp
1 pound lump crab meat
Seasoned bread crumbs

Peel mirlitons; slice and remove seeds. Simmer in salted water until tender, about 10 minutes. Drain. Beat eggs and combine with bread. In butter or bacon grease sauté onions, garlic, celery and green pepper. Add mirlitons, egg mixture and cheese. Blend well with mixer. Add seasonings and parsley to taste, shrimp and crab meat. Place in a large baking dish or individual ramekins. Top with bread crumbs and bake at 350°F until browned, about 20 minutes. Serves 4-6.

Mrs. H. A. Whittington, Jr.

Baked Stuffed Mirlitons

8 small mirlitons
2 medium onions, chopped
2 cloves garlic, minced
3 Tablespoons bacon grease or
  shortening
⅔ cup chopped celery
½ cup chopped green pepper
⅔ cup chopped mushrooms
  (preferably fresh)
½ cup chopped parsley

1 bay leaf, crumbled
Dash thyme
¾ pound cooked shrimp
¾ pound bulk sausage (hot,
  optional), browned, drained
½ teaspoon Accent
1½ cups bread crumbs, divided
Salt and pepper
1 cup grated sharp Cheddar
  cheese

Parboil mirlitons about 20 minutes, or until tender. Cut in half and scoop out pulp. Set aside shells and pulp. Sauté onions and garlic in grease in heavy skillet until transparent. Add celery, green pepper, mushrooms, parsley, bay leaf and thyme; cook until tender. Cut up mirliton pulp; mix with shrimp, sausage, Accent and ½ cup bread crumbs. Combine with vegetables in skillet. Salt and pepper to taste. Fill shells with mixture, sprinkle with cheese and 1 cup buttered bread crumbs and bake in moderate oven at 350°F until crumbs are browned. Serves 16 as a vegetable or 8 as a luncheon main course.

Mrs. John F. Potter

For a ready supply of lemon juice to use in casseroles or iced tea, blend 1 lemon, sliced and seeded, and 3 Tablespoons water in blender. Will keep several weeks in refrigerator.

Eggplant Creole

1 onion, chopped
1 green pepper, chopped
½ cup butter
½ cup raw rice
1 large eggplant, peeled and
  chopped
1 (14 ounce) can tomatoes

¼ teaspoon basil
¼ teaspoon oregano
1 cup beef bouillon
½ teaspoon salt
½ teaspoon pepper
2 dashes Tabasco
1 cup grated sharp cheese

Sauté onion and green pepper in butter. Add rice and sauté until golden. Add all other ingredients except cheese. Bake in greased 2-quart casserole at 350°F for 30 minutes. Then sprinkle cheese on top and cook 30 minutes longer. Serve hot. Serves 6-8.

Mrs. Vernon H. Chadwick

Luncheon Mushrooms in Sour Cream

2 pounds fresh mushrooms
1 bunch green onions, chopped
½ cup butter
Juice of ½ lemon
2 teaspoons salt
Dash white pepper
Dash ground nutmeg

1 (8 ounce) carton sour cream
3 Tablespoons sherry or white
  wine (optional)
3 English muffins, split, or 6
  frozen puff patty shells
Parsley sprigs

Rinse, pat dry and slice thinly the mushrooms. Sauté onions in butter until wilted. Add mushrooms and sauté over medium heat 5 minutes. Add lemon juice, salt, pepper and nutmeg. With a wooden spoon fold in sour cream. Add sherry. Heat until warmed through. Serve on buttered toasted English muffin halves or in hot patty shells. Garnish with a sprig of parsley. Also makes a good stuffing for crêpes. Serves 6.

Mrs. J. George Smith

Gourmet Mushrooms and Noodles

½ cup butter
½ pound fresh mushrooms,
  sliced
¼ cup chopped onion
¼ cup sliced almonds

1 clove garlic, minced
1 (10½ ounce) can beef
  consommé
1 Tablespoon lemon juice
4 ounces medium noodles

Melt butter. Add mushrooms, onion, almonds and garlic. Cook 10 minutes over low heat. Add remaining ingredients and cook until noodles are tender, about 10 minutes. Great with roast and steak. Serves 4.

Mrs. John Mason, Jr., Birmingham, Alabama

Mushroom Soufflé

1 pound fresh mushrooms, sliced
5 Tablespoons butter, divided
½ cup chopped celery
½ cup chopped green onion
½ cup chopped green pepper
½ teaspoon salt
Pepper
Mayonnaise

6 slices white bread, trimmed,
  buttered and cubed
2 eggs, slightly beaten
1½ cups milk
1 (10½ ounce) can cream of
  mushroom soup
¼ cup dry vermouth
Bread crumbs, buttered

Sauté mushrooms in 3 Tablespoons butter. Sauté celery, onion and green pepper in 2 Tablespoons butter. Combine with mushrooms and season with salt and pepper. Add enough mayonnaise to moisten. Place ½ the bread cubes in buttered casserole. Pour mushroom mixture on top. Sprinkle remaining bread cubes over mushrooms. Combine eggs and milk and pour over all. Refrigerate at least 1 hour. Before baking, spoon mushroom soup mixed with vermouth over all. Sprinkle with bread crumbs. Bake at 325°F for 50-60 minutes. Serves 8.

Mrs. A. E. Blanton, London, England

Mushroom-Artichoke Casserole

3 cups fresh mushrooms, halved
½ cup sliced green onion and
  tops
5 Tablespoons butter or
  margarine, divided
2 Tablespoons flour
1/8 teaspoon salt
Dash pepper
¾ cup water

¼ cup milk
1 teaspoon instant chicken
  broth
1 teaspoon lemon juice
1/8 teaspoon ground nutmeg
1 (10 ounce) package frozen
  artichoke hearts, cooked and
  drained
¾ cup soft bread crumbs

Cook mushrooms and onion in 4 Tablespoons butter. With slotted spoon remove vegetables and set aside. Blend flour, salt and pepper into pan drippings. Add water, milk, instant chicken broth, lemon juice and nutmeg. Stir and cook until bubbly. Add all vegetables. Turn into 1-quart casserole. Combine bread crumbs and 1 Tablespoon melted butter. Sprinkle around edge. Bake at 350°F for 20 minutes. Serves 6.

Mrs. Richard L. Redmont, Jr.

SOUTHERN-STYLE GREENS   Boil for 20 minutes in 1 quart water 2 ham hocks, 1 or 2 teaspoons salt and ½ teaspoon crushed red pepper. Add 3 or 4 bunches fresh greens (turnip, mustard, collard) which have been washed well and tough stems removed. Cook slowly, covered, until tender. Correct seasoning. Meat may be removed from bone and shredded into greens.

Creamed Baked Mushrooms

⅓ cup butter, softened
1 Tablespoon each chopped
  parsley, Dijon mustard,
  grated onion
1 teaspoon salt
1/8 teaspoon cayenne pepper

1/8 teaspoon ground nutmeg
1½ Tablespoons flour
1 pound fresh mushrooms,
  thinly sliced
1 cup whipping cream

Blend butter with next 5 ingredients. Place a layer of mushrooms in the bottom of a 1½-quart casserole; dot with half the seasoned butter. Add another layer of mushrooms and top with remaining butter. Pour the cream over all and bake at 375°F for 40-50 minutes. Do not overcook as mushrooms may become greasy. Serves 4-6.

Mrs. William B. Wilson

Okra and Tomatoes

4 or 5 fresh medium tomatoes
  or 1 (16 ounce) can tomatoes
  and juice, chopped
1 pound okra

1 large onion, chopped
2 Tablespoons bacon grease
Salt and pepper

If using fresh tomatoes, peel and chop. Wash and slice okra into rounds about ½ inch thick. Sauté onion and okra in grease until browned. Add tomatoes, salt and pepper. Cover and cook slowly for 20 minutes. Add water if necessary to prevent sticking. If too juicy, uncover and cook a little longer. Serve hot. Serves 4-6.

Mrs. Herbert A. Kroeze, Jr.

Onion Casserole

9 to 10 medium onions, thinly
  sliced
1 Tablespoon salt
4 to 5 slices buttered toast,
  crust removed (preferably
  Pepperidge Farm)

½ pound American cheese,
  grated
1 egg
1 cup milk
1 teaspoon salt
¼ teaspoon pepper
1 teaspoon celery seed

Butter a flat 2-quart baking dish. Boil onions in salted water to cover until just tender, about 10 minutes. Drain. Line baking dish with toast. Cover with a layer of onions and cheese. Repeat layers of toast, onions and cheese. Beat egg slightly and add milk, salt, pepper and celery seed. Pour over casserole. (At this point, casserole can be covered with plastic wrap and stored in the refrigerator for the day.) Bake at 375°F for 40 minutes. Serve at once. Serves 8.

Mrs. David Mockbee

Onion Pie

CRUST:
Lump of butter size of an egg
Rounded teaspoon lard
Heaping teaspoon baking
  powder
Salt
Fairly heaping cup of flour (sift
  before measuring)
Cold sweet milk

1 egg yolk (optional)

FILLING:
3 large sweet Spanish onions
1 large Tablespoon butter
1 teaspoon flour
Salt and pepper
2 eggs
1 cup whipping cream

CRUST: Work together the softened butter, lard, baking powder, salt and flour. Add enough cold sweet milk to make a good firm dough. Well-beaten yolk of an egg may be added if desired. Line an 8-inch pie plate with rolled pastry. FILLING: Shave onions fine; fry in butter to a nice brown, really brown and much reduced. Add flour. Stir well; salt and pepper to taste. Beat the eggs till pretty light; mix with cupful cream; fold them into the fried onions gently till perfectly mixed. Pour into the crust and bake about 30 minutes or till brown and puffy at about 400°F. Serve at once. Serves 4.

Miss Eudora Welty

This is from a recipe Katherine Anne Porter gave me, which she got in France; these little pies are served hot at the wine festivals along with the bottle of wine.

Eudora Welty, America's first lady of letters, is a native of Jackson and a sustaining member of the Jackson Junior League. A noted short story writer and photographer, Miss Welty won the 1973 Pulitzer Prize for her novel THE OPTIMIST'S DAUGHTER.

Fried Onion Rings

1 cup beer
1 cup flour

2 large yellow or Bermuda
  onions
Vegetable oil

Mix beer and flour and allow to sit 3 or 4 hours (do not omit this step). Cut onions into rings of desired width. Dip rings into batter and fry in 375°F oil deep enough to cover the rings. As rings are removed from frying, drain on absorbent paper; then keep until ready to serve on a brown-paper lined pan in a 200°F oven. Though they dry out somewhat, the rings may be kept successfully up to an hour. They may be frozen after draining. Reheat frozen rings 5 minutes at 400°F. Serves 4-6.

Mrs. Ancel C. Tipton, Jr.

A teaspoon sugar for every 3 cups water used in cooking peas, carrots, cabbage, turnips or onions will improve the flavor.

Baked Stuffed Onions

6 medium white onions ·
1 (4 ounce) can mushrooms,
   stems and pieces, chopped
1 Tablespoon finely chopped
   pecans
3 Tablespoons butter

Salt
Pepper
1 cup beef consommé
Grated Cheddar cheese
Paprika

Peel onions and core, leaving shells about ½ inch thick. Reserve pulp. Cook cored onions in boiling water until barely tender. Chop raw onion pulp removed in coring. Sauté chopped onion, mushrooms and pecans in butter 10 minutes. Season to taste with salt and pepper. Stuff onions with mushroom mixture. Arrange onions close together in baking pan. Pour consommé around them. Bake at 300°F for 30 minutes. Sprinkle with grated cheese and paprika and continue to bake 30 minutes longer. Onions may be prepared 1 day ahead and refrigerated covered until time to add consommé and bake. Serves 6.

Mrs. O. B. Walton, Jr.

Shredded Potatoes au Gratin

6 medium white potatoes
2 cups shredded Cheddar cheese
6 Tablespoons butter, divided
2 cups sour cream

⅓ cup chopped onion
1 teaspoon salt
¼ teaspoon pepper

Boil potatoes in skins. Chill, peel and shred. Stir in cheese and 4 Tablespoons melted butter. Fold in sour cream, onion, salt and pepper. Place in greased casserole and dot with remaining butter. Bake at 350°F for 30 minutes. Serves 6-8.

Mrs. Robert Allen Smith

Sweet Potato Surprise Balls

4 large sweet potatoes
1 cup broken pecans
1 cup crushed corn flakes
1 Tablespoon flour
¾ cup sugar
2 Tablespoons milk

1 teaspoon ground cinnamon
1 teaspoon vanilla
Bourbon to taste
¼ teaspoon baking powder
Large marshmallows, halved
Cooking oil

Peel, slice and boil potatoes until done. Drain well and mash until smooth. Add remaining ingredients except marshmallows and oil and mix well. Chill for easier handling. Mold sweet potatoes around marshmallow halves; shape each into a ball and roll in additional crushed corn flakes. Refrigerate briefly to set. Fry in deep fat at 375°F about 3 or 4 minutes or until lightly browned. Drain well. Serves 8.

Mrs. Warren V. Ludlam, Jr.

Holiday Sweet Potatoes

½ cup margarine
6 sweet potatoes, cooked,
    peeled, sliced
1 teaspoon baking powder
1 teaspoon vanilla
1 teaspoon ground cinnamon

2 eggs
¾ cup sugar
¾ cup buttermilk
¾ cup chopped pecans
    (optional)
Marshmallows for topping

Add margarine to hot potatoes. Combine with next 6 ingredients in blender or with mixer. Stir in pecans, if desired. Place mixture in a greased 2-quart casserole dish and bake at 350°F for 30 minutes. Top with marshmallows during last 10 minutes of cooking. Serves 10-12.

Mrs. Jim Hendrick

Creole Stuffed Bell Peppers

16 large green peppers, divided
½ cup butter or margarine
2 cloves garlic, chopped
4 onions, chopped
1 cup chopped ham
1 cup water
1 cup tomato juice
1 (16 ounce) can tomatoes,
    chopped, and juice

2 eggs, well beaten
4 cups cracker crumbs
Salt and pepper to taste
1 teaspoon sugar
Bread crumbs
Melted butter or margarine
Dash paprika

Chop 4 of the green peppers, leaving in the seeds. Sauté chopped peppers in butter with garlic and onions until tender. Add ham, water, tomato juice and tomatoes. Cook until liquid is absorbed. Stir in eggs and cracker crumbs. Season to taste. Cut off tops and remove seeds from remaining 12 peppers. Parboil in water with sugar added until slightly tender, 5-10 minutes. Drain. Stuff with tomato mixture. Cover lightly with bread crumbs; sprinkle with butter or margarine and paprika. Bake at 350°F for 20 minutes or until very hot. Serves 12.

Mrs. Carl F. André

John McRae's Summer Vegetable Casserole

4 or more yellow summer
    squash
3 or 4 green tomatoes
1 small purple onion

Salt
McCormick's lemon-pepper
    seasoning
2 Tablespoons vegetable oil

Slice squash, tomatoes and onion and layer in casserole, sprinkling each layer lightly with salt and lemon-pepper seasoning. Pour oil over top. Bake uncovered at 300°F for 2 hours. Serves 4-6.

Mrs. Julius Ridgway

Spinach Timbales Provençal

2 (10 ounce) packages frozen
   chopped spinach
1 cup milk
2 Tablespoons butter
1 cup fine bread crumbs
2 Tablespoons grated onion
1 teaspoon salt

¼ teaspoon Tabasco
4 eggs, slightly beaten
4 small tomatoes
1 (14 ounce) can artichoke
   hearts
2 hard-boiled eggs, sieved
   (optional)

Cook spinach in salted water until just defrosted. Drain, squeezing out as much moisture as possible. Heat milk and butter in saucepan over medium heat until butter melts. *Do not boil.* Add bread crumbs, onion, salt and Tabasco to milk. Add beaten eggs and spinach and stir until well blended. Grease 8 timbale molds or custard cups with additional butter. Peel tomatoes and cut in half; place one tomato half in each mold, cut side up. Drain artichokes and cut in half; place ½ artichoke heart on each tomato in molds. Spoon spinach mixture over artichokes until mold is full. Place molds in a large baking pan and add boiling water ¾ up the side of the mold. Bake at 350°F for 25-30 minutes or until set. Turn out and serve sprinkled with sieved egg, if desired. Serves 8.

Mrs. G. G. Mazzaferro

Spinach Casserole

4 (10 ounce) packages frozen
   chopped spinach
10 Tablespoons butter, divided
8 Tablespoons flour
2 cups milk
1 onion, chopped
1 teaspoon celery salt
1 teaspoon garlic salt
1 teaspoon salt

¾ (6 ounce) roll Jalapeño
   cheese
2 (14 ounce) cans artichoke
   hearts, drained and
   quartered
1 cup raw brown rice, cooked
1 cup herb-seasoned stuffing
2 (8 ounce) cans sliced
   mushrooms, drained
Bread crumbs, buttered

Cook spinach according to package directions. Drain and reserve 1 cup spinach liquid. Melt ½ cup butter in a saucepan. Add flour, stirring until smooth. Add spinach liquid and milk slowly, stirring to avoid lumps. Cook until thick and smooth. Sauté onion in remaining 2 Tablespoons butter until tender. Add onion to sauce mixture. Add seasonings. Cube cheese and add to sauce, stirring until cheese melts. Add artichoke hearts, brown rice, stuffing and mushrooms. Combine sauce with spinach. Serve immediately or place in a 3-quart flat casserole, top with bread crumbs and bake at 350°F until bubbling. Recipe may be halved. Serves 12-16.

Mrs. Henry Tyler

Spinach Roll

2 pounds fresh spinach or
   3 (10 ounce) packages frozen
   chopped spinach
¼ cup seasoned bread crumbs
1 teaspoon salt
Pinch pepper
Pinch ground nutmeg
3½ Tablespoons butter, divided
4 eggs, separated
6 teaspoons grated fresh
   Parmesan cheese, divided

6 teaspoons grated Gruyère
   cheese, divided
¾ pound fresh mushrooms,
   sliced
2 teaspoons flour
½ teaspoon salt
¼ teaspoon pepper
¾ cup whipping cream
2 teaspoons chopped parsley

Cook spinach; drain and chop. Butter a 15 x 10-inch pan and line with wax paper. Butter paper and sprinkle with bread crumbs. Squeeze out excess water in spinach and place in a bowl. Add salt, pepper and nutmeg along with 2 Tablespoons melted butter. Beat in egg yolks one at a time. Beat egg whites until stiff; fold into spinach mixture. Spoon into prepared pan and smooth evenly. Sprinkle 4 teaspoons Parmesan cheese and 4 teaspoons Gruyère cheese over top. Bake at 350°F for 30 minutes. Meanwhile make the filling. Sauté mushrooms in remaining butter. Sprinkle with flour, salt and pepper. Stir in the cream and parsley and mix until thickened. When the roll is baked, place a sheet of buttered wax paper, buttered side down, over the roll. Invert onto a warm cookie sheet. Cool for 5 minutes. Then carefully remove wax paper. Spread mushroom mixture over hot spinach roll. Roll up jelly roll fashion along the 15-inch side. Ease onto a warm platter and sprinkle with remaining cheese. Serves 12.

Mrs. James Keeton

Spinach Ring

3 Tablespoons butter
3 Tablespoons flour
1 cup milk
⅓ teaspoon ground nutmeg
1 teaspoon grated onion
1 Tablespoon lemon juice
2 eggs, well beaten

1 teaspoon salt
2½ cups chopped, cooked
   fresh spinach or
   3 (10 ounce) packages
   frozen chopped spinach,
   cooked and drained

Melt butter, stir in flour and cook for 1 minute. Add warmed milk and stir until thickened. Add remaining ingredients. Pour into well-buttered 1-quart ring mold. Place in a pan of hot water and bake at 375°F until firm, at least 40 minutes. Unmold and fill center with buttered cauliflower florets, artichoke hearts or any vegetable desired. For Christmas, garnish outside of ring with small whole beets to give a wreath effect. Serves 8-10.

Mrs. Sherwood Wise

Spinach-Potato Pancakes

1¾ cups milk
2 teaspoons salt
1/8 teaspoon ground nutmeg
1 cup plus 1 Tablespoon flour
2 Tablespoons butter, melted
½ pound potatoes, peeled and
    finely grated

3 eggs, slightly beaten
½ teaspoon sugar
1 (10 ounce) package frozen
    chopped spinach, thawed
    and squeezed dry
½ onion, finely grated

Mix all ingredients well. The first 5 ingredients may be mixed in a blender and then combined with the others. Melt 1 Tablespoon additional butter in electric skillet or on griddle and when hot, spoon on pancake batter. Cook several minutes on each side or until pancakes are nicely browned. Add more butter to skillet as it becomes necessary while cooking remaining pancakes. Small pancakes are the prettiest. Serves 12-14.

Mrs. Clyde Copeland, Jr.

Butternut Squash Soufflé

2 pounds butternut or acorn
    squash
2 Tablespoons water
3 Tablespoons butter
4 Tablespoons flour
1 cup milk
½ teaspoon ground ginger

1 teaspoon ground cinnamon
¼ teaspoon salt
1 cup sugar
½ cup orange juice
4 eggs, separated
3 egg whites

Cut squash into chunks and remove seeds. Place chunks in a baking dish with the water and bake covered at 350°F until tender. Peel and mash well with a fork; then whip until smooth. In a heavy pan melt butter; add flour and milk. Cook until thick. Add ginger, cinnamon, salt, sugar and orange juice. Mix with puréed squash. When warm, mix in egg yolks. Beat all 7 egg whites until stiff but not dry. Fold into squash mixture. Spoon into a buttered 2-quart soufflé dish and place in a preheated 325°F oven in a pan filled with water halfway up the dish. Bake for 1½ hours. Test for doneness with a straw as for a cake. Serve immediately. Will stay puffy about 30 minutes. Serves 8.

Mrs. Herbert A. Kroeze, Jr.

NEW POTATOES   In skillet or large saucepan melt ½ cup butter. Cover bottom of pan with peeled small new potatoes. Cover and turn heat to low. Cook potatoes in butter until tender, about 20-30 minutes. Shake pan and turn potatoes occasionally. Salt and pepper as they cook. Serve sprinkled with chopped parsley.

Spinach-Stuffed Squash

4 yellow crookneck squash
Melted butter
Salt and pepper
Grated Parmesan cheese

SPINACH STUFFING:
½ cup chopped onion
½ cup butter or margarine

2 (10 ounce) packages frozen
   chopped spinach, cooked
   and drained
1 teaspoon salt
1 cup sour cream
2 teaspoons red wine vinegar
Bread crumbs

Cook whole squash in boiling, salted water for about 10 minutes or until tender. Very carefully cut into halves and scoop out seeds. Sprinkle each shell with butter, salt, pepper and Parmesan cheese. *SPINACH STUFFING:* Sauté onion in butter until tender. Add spinach, salt, sour cream and vinegar and blend well. Stuff each squash shell with spinach mixture. Sprinkle each with additional Parmesan cheese and bread crumbs; dot with butter. Bake in 350°F oven for 15 minutes or until hot enough to serve. Serves 8.

Mrs. Clyde Copeland, Jr.

Zucchini and Artichokes

4 zucchini, sliced in ¼-inch
   rounds
1 large onion, thinly sliced
2 Tablespoons butter or
   margarine
2 Tablespoons flour
1½ cups milk, warmed
1 teaspoon salt
White pepper to taste
1 cup grated Swiss cheese

1 (4 ounce) can sliced mushrooms,
   drained, or 6 ounces fresh
   mushrooms, sliced and
   sautéed in 2 Tablespoons
   butter
1 (10 ounce) package frozen
   artichoke hearts, cooked and
   quartered, or 1 (14 ounce)
   can artichoke hearts, drained
   and quartered
Cracker crumbs
Grated Parmesan cheese

Cook zucchini and onion in boiling, salted water until tender, about 10 or 15 minutes. Drain. Melt butter in saucepan. Stir in flour and blend well. Add milk all at once and stir until thickened. Season with salt and pepper. Remove from heat and stir in cheese until melted. Arrange zucchini, mushrooms and artichoke quarters in a 7 x 11-inch casserole. Pour cheese sauce over vegetables. Sprinkle with cracker crumbs and Parmesan cheese. Heat at 350°F for 20 minutes or until bubbly. Serves 8.

Mrs. Robert C. Travis

ELEGANT PEAS Combine 1 (16 ounce) can early peas (drained), 1 cup sour cream, ½ cup chopped chives, 1 teaspoon curry powder, salt and pepper to taste. Chill. Serves 4.

Squash with Almonds

8 to 10 yellow squash, sliced
1 large onion, thinly sliced
2 teaspoons salt
¼ teaspoon pepper

1 cup whipping cream
¼ cup slivered almonds,
   toasted
½ cup bread crumbs, buttered

Cook squash in water to cover with onion, salt and pepper. Drain well. Mix with cream. Add more salt if needed. Stir in almonds. Spoon into baking dish. Spread crumbs on top. Bake at 325 °F for 30-35 minutes or until set. Serves 8.

Mrs. John Baxter Burns, III

Zucchini Lasagne

2 medium zucchini squash,
   peeled and sliced
Salt and pepper
Thyme

2 Tablespoons tomato sauce,
   divided
½ cup cottage cheese
Grated Parmesan or Romano
   cheese

Cook zucchini in salted water to cover until tender. Drain. In a small oven-proof casserole place ½ the cooked zucchini. Sprinkle with salt, pepper and a little thyme. Spoon over the squash 1 Tablespoon tomato sauce and the cottage cheese. Repeat zucchini, seasonings and tomato sauce. Top with grated cheese. Bake uncovered at 350°F for 20 minutes or until bubbling. Serves 2.

Mrs. W. Edward Ellington

Zucchini Boats with Fresh Mushrooms

8 (¼ pound) or 2 (1 pound)
   zucchini
1 Tablespoon minced onion
1 Tablespoon olive oil
1¼ cups chopped fresh
   mushrooms

½ cup grated Parmesan or
   Gruyère cheese, divided
1/8 teaspoon marjoram, basil
   or thyme
Salt and ground pepper to taste
4 strips bacon, halved

Wash well and trim off ends of unpeeled zucchini. Cut in half lengthwise (if using large zucchini, also cut in half crosswise) and scoop out seeds, being careful *not* to break shells. Drop zucchini into boiling water to cover. Cover and simmer 8 minutes. Carefully remove and drain upside down on rack. In skillet, sauté onion in olive oil until tender and set aside. Add mushrooms to skillet and sauté until tender. Combine mushrooms, onion, ¼ cup grated cheese, marjoram, salt and pepper. Mix gently. Spoon mixture into each zucchini shell and sprinkle with remaining cheese. Top with a strip of bacon. Place stuffed zucchini boats side by side in well-greased shallow baking dish. Bake at 350°F for 15 minutes or until bacon is browned. May be prepared early in the day and reheated in moderate oven. Serves 8.

Mrs. Reuel May, Jr.

Continental Squash

10 to 12 yellow squash
Salt and pepper
Sugar
1½ pounds bacon
8 green onions with tops,
   chopped
1½ large onions, chopped
1½ Tablespoons chopped parsley

1 green pepper, chopped
1 cup grated Parmesan cheese
1 cup seasoned bread crumbs
1 Tablespoon chicken stock base
1 Tablespoon sugar
Dash white pepper
Dash paprika
Chopped chives

Slice squash and cook in water seasoned with salt, pepper and sugar until almost done. Drain. Fry bacon, remove and crumble. Sauté remaining vegetables in some of the bacon grease. Drain. In a large bowl add the bacon and the vegetables to the squash. Mix. Add remaining ingredients except chives. Mix well. Use no salt until all ingredients are combined, then taste for seasoning. (The Parmesan cheese is usually salty enough for the entire casserole.) Place mixture in buttered baking dish. Top with chives, additional bread crumbs and paprika. Bake at 350°F until bubbly and brown on top, about 25-30 minutes. Serves 8.

Mrs. C. Chunn Sneed, Gulfport, Mississippi

Squash Boats with Lagniappe of Acorn Squash Seeds

2 medium acorn squash
Butter
4 teaspoons sugar (or equivalent
   artificial sweetener)

¼ teaspoon ground cinnamon
   or nutmeg

Slice each squash into 2 boats and with sharp-edged spoon scoop out seeds and central fiber. Separate seeds from fiber and reserve to make TOASTED SQUASH SEEDS. Place a slice of butter in center of each boat and sprinkle with sugar and cinnamon. Place squash halves in shallow baking dish. Each half may be wrapped in foil. Bake at 400°F for about 45 minutes or until tender (depending on size of squash). Serves 4.

TOASTED SQUASH SEEDS

Squash seeds
1 Tablespoon cooking oil

1 teaspoon salt

Spread seeds evenly over a shallow pan that has been smeared with oil. Salt them lightly and bake in a slow 250°-300°F oven until crisp and brown. Stir from time to time. Seeds will keep several weeks. They are nutritional and make a nice hors d'oeuvre served with tomato juice before dinner. Seeds can be stored in small baby food jars to be given as gifts. Pumpkin seeds may be toasted also.

Mrs. Patrick H. Scanlon

Cherry Tomatoes in Cream

3 Tablespoons butter
3 Tablespoons brown sugar
½ teaspoon salt

1 quart cherry tomatoes
1 pint whipping cream

Melt butter, sugar and salt in heavy skillet. Add washed tomatoes. Stir with wooden spoon. When tomatoes begin to split open, add cream. Serve hot in individual ramekins. Serves 4-6.

Mrs. Donald Hall, Shreveport, Louisiana

Baked Stuffed Tomatoes

10 ripe medium tomatoes
1 bunch green onions with
    tops, chopped
2 cloves garlic, crushed
¼ cup butter
¼ cup olive oil
1 Tablespoon oregano
½ teaspoon thyme
½ teaspoon crushed red pepper

½ teaspoon basil
2 bay leaves
2 (3 ounce) cans mushrooms,
    stems and pieces, chopped
    (reserve liquid)
Salt to taste
1 cup Italian seasoned bread
    crumbs
½ cup grated Parmesan cheese

Cut stem end off tomatoes; scoop out pulp with spoon, chop and reserve. Turn shells upside down to drain. Sauté onions and garlic in butter and oil until soft; add oregano, thyme, red pepper, basil, bay leaves and mushrooms with liquid and cook 5 minutes. Add tomato pulp and· salt. Simmer 20-30 minutes. Remove bay leaves. Add bread crumbs and cheese and stir well. Stuff mixture into tomato shells and top with extra cheese. Bake at 350°F until hot, about 20-30 minutes. Serves 10.

W. T. Phelps, Sr.

Tomatoes Stuffed with Spinach Rockefeller

6 large tomatoes
4 Tablespoons butter
½ cup finely chopped onion
2 (10 ounce) packages frozen
    chopped spinach, cooked
    and drained

1 Tablespoon Accent
½ teaspoon thyme
1 teaspoon salt
½ cup seasoned bread crumbs
2 eggs, slightly beaten
¼ cup grated Parmesan cheese

Peel tomatoes; remove stem end and scoop out seeds. Turn upside down to drain. Melt butter; add onion and cook until tender. Add spinach, seasonings and bread crumbs; mix well. Add eggs and cook, stirring constantly, until well combined. Stuff tomatoes with spinach mixture, sprinkle cheese over top and dot with additional butter. Bake in a 350°F oven 10 minutes or until brown on top and thoroughly heated. Serves 6.

Mrs. A. Arthur Halle, Memphis, Tennessee

Whipped Turnip Puff

4 cups mashed cooked turnips
2 cups soft bread crumbs
½ cup butter, melted
2 Tablespoons sugar

2 teaspoons salt
¼ teaspoon pepper
4 eggs, slightly beaten

Mix all ingredients together thoroughly. Spoon into a greased 1½-quart casserole and brush the top with a little additional melted butter. Bake at 375°F for 1 hour. Turnips may be prepared ahead but do not freeze. Serves 8.

Mrs. Jack M. McLarty

This is an excellent Thanksgiving dish.

Turnip Greens Casserole

1 (15 ounce) can Bush's chopped
   turnip or mustard greens,
   drained
1 teaspoon sugar
Salt and pepper to taste
½ (10½ ounce) can cream of
   mushroom soup

½ cup mayonnaise
2 Tablespoons wine vinegar
1 teaspoon horseradish
2 eggs, slightly beaten
Bread crumbs
Grated Cheddar cheese

Blend all ingredients together except crumbs and cheese. Spoon into casserole, cover top with bread crumbs and cheese and bake 1 hour at 350°F. This dish multiplies well for a big crowd. Serves 6-8.

Mrs. Mendell M. Davis

Turnip Casserole

1½ pounds turnips, peeled and
   thinly sliced
2 Tablespoons butter
1 onion, thinly sliced
⅔ cup chopped green pepper
⅓ cup chopped celery

2 Tablespoons flour
1 cup milk
½ cup grated sharp cheese
Salt and pepper to taste
3 Tablespoons bread crumbs

Cook turnips in boiling, salted water to cover until just tender. Drain. Sauté in butter the onion, green pepper and celery until tender. Sprinkle with flour and cook 1 minute. Add milk and stir until thickened. Stir in cheese, salt and pepper. Combine cheese sauce with turnips, place in baking dish and top with crumbs. Brown under broiler. May be prepared ahead and run under broiler just before serving. Very good with game. Serves 4.

Mrs. Robert Ratelle

Desserts

Cookies

Ladyfingers

6 eggs, separated
½ cup sugar
1 teaspoon vanilla (or almond
  extract, if desired)

Dash salt
⅔ cup sifted flour (sift twice,
  then measure)
1¼ cups powdered sugar

Place egg yolks in mixing bowl and beat until thick. Add sugar slowly while continuing to beat until very light and thick. Add vanilla and beat well. In another bowl beat the egg whites with salt until soft peaks are formed. Spoon ¼ of the egg whites and sift ¼ of the flour over the egg yolk mixture; fold in. Repeat this process until all the whites and the flour have been folded in. Place batter into a pastry bag and squeeze out finger shapes about 3 inches long and 1 inch wide; space 1 inch apart on greased and floured cookie sheets. Sift the powdered sugar over the fingers making a layer about 1/16 inch deep. Hold the baking sheet upside down over the sink and tap gently to remove excess sugar. (The ladyfingers will not fall off.) Bake 20 minutes at 300°F in upper third of oven. Remove immediately. Ladyfingers may be frozen. Makes 24-30 ladyfingers.

Mrs. G. G. Mazzaferro

Madeleines

2 eggs, at room temperature
1/8 teaspoon salt
⅓ cup sugar
½ cup sifted flour

1 teaspoon grated lemon rind
  (optional)
½ cup clarified butter, melted
  and cooled

Grease and flour well 12 madeleine shells. Beat eggs with salt until frothy; then gradually beat in sugar. Beat the mixture at high speed until very thick and lemon colored, about 15-20 minutes. Fold in the flour, 2 Tablespoons at a time, and the lemon peel, if desired. Add butter, 1 Tablespoon at a time, and fold it in quickly. Fill shells about ¾ full and bake in a preheated 400°F oven for 8-10 minutes or until golden. Remove from shells to wire rack to cool. Makes 12 madeleines.

Mrs. Lawrence Long

To clarify butter, melt it in a saucepan over moderate heat. Skim off the foam. Strain the clear yellow liquid or clarified butter into a bowl, leaving the milky residue in the bottom of the pan to be discarded. Or place melted butter in refrigerator to harden. Clarified butter will solidify and separate from milky residue which can then be poured off.

Almond Macaroons

1 (8 ounce) can almond paste
¾ cup sugar
Pinch salt

3 egg whites
½ teaspoon almond extract

Break up and mash almond paste to soften; add other ingredients alternately and beat well. Line a cookie sheet with brown paper or foil. Squeeze small amounts of dough through a pastry tube or drop from a teaspoon 2 inches apart onto cookie sheet. Smooth tops with pastry brush moistened with water. Bake at 350°F for 15-20 minutes or until golden and puffed. May be stored indefinitely in an airtight tin or freezer. Makes 40-50 macaroons.

Mrs. Faser Triplett

Gingerbread Boys

1 cup shortening
1 cup sugar
½ teaspoon salt
1 cup molasses
2 Tablespoons white vinegar
1 egg, beaten

5 cups flour
1½ teaspoons baking soda
1 Tablespoon ground ginger
1 teaspoon ground cinnamon
1 teaspoon ground cloves

Cream shortening, sugar and salt. Stir in molasses, vinegar and egg. Sift together and add the remaining ingredients. Chill mixture overnight. Divide dough into fourths. Roll one part of dough at a time on floured board 1/8 inch thick. Refrigerate remainder. Cut out gingerbread boys with sharp cookie cutter. Place on greased cookie sheets and bake at 375°F about 6 minutes. Cool slightly and remove. Decorate as desired. Cookies will keep several months in airtight container and indefinitely in freezer. Makes 55-65 boys.

Mrs. Charles Wesley Robinson, New Orleans, Louisiana

Christmas Casserole Cookies

2 eggs
1 cup sugar
1 cup chopped walnuts
1 cup snipped dates

1 cup flaked coconut
1 teaspoon vanilla
¼ teaspoon almond extract

Beat eggs well. Gradually add sugar and beat until fluffy. Stir in the remaining ingredients in the order given. Turn into an ungreased 2-quart casserole. Bake at 350°F for 30 minutes. Remove from oven and while hot stir well with a wooden spoon. Cool. Form into small balls and roll in additional sugar. Makes about 3 dozen balls.

Mrs. William E. French

This is a good recipe for children to help with during the Christmas season. Also the cookies make an attractive sweet on a party table.

Berlin Croncler

1 pound butter
4 cups flour, sift after measuring
2¼ cups sugar, divided
4 egg yolks, beaten

Yolks of 4 hard-boiled eggs,
mashed
1 egg white
¼ cup finely chopped pecans

Cut together butter and flour as for pie crust. Add 2 cups sugar and both raw and cooked egg yolks and mix, kneading thoroughly. Form into a long roll and cut into lengthwise strips. Cut strips into small squares of equal size. Roll squares with hands into thin strips 4 or 5 inches long. Cross ends firmly, making a shape like a circle with the ends overlapping and extending downward. Dip one side of the cookie into unbeaten egg white. Then dip into a mixture of pecans and ¼ cup sugar. Place on greased cookie sheet and bake at 350°F until light brown. Keeps well in a cookie tin. Makes 12 dozen cookies.

Mrs. Herbert A. Kroeze, Sr.

A favorite Christmas cookie.

Stained-Glass Cookies

¾ cup shortening (part butter
or margarine)
1 cup sugar
2 eggs
1 teaspoon vanilla
2½ cups flour
1 teaspoon baking powder
1 teaspoon salt

Cookie cutters of 2 sizes (the
smaller cutters should be ¼
to ½ inch smaller than the
larger)
8 packages Lifesavers (red,
green, butter rum, orange
show up well)

Mix shortening, sugar, eggs and flavoring. Blend in flour, baking powder and salt. Cover and chill at least 1 hour. Roll dough 1/8 inch thick and cut out cookies with larger cutters. Place cookies on baking sheet that has been covered with foil. Then use small cutters to cut out a section from the cookie (small bell shape within larger bell, etc.). Crush candy into small pieces and fill in cut-out areas, making sure there is enough crushed candy to spread into corners. (When first making this recipe, try just a few cookies first to find the right amount of crushed candy to use. Too much will bleed over onto dough.) Make hole in top of each cookie with plastic straw. Bake at 375°F for 7-9 minutes or until dough is light brown and candy has melted. (If candy does not completely cover center of cookie, spread candy out quickly while still soft with a *metal* spatula.) Cool completely on baking sheet and remove *gently*. String with ribbon for hanging. When hanging on Christmas tree, place cookie in front of lights for a stained-glass effect. Different colored candies can be mixed together or only one color used for different effects. Cookies also look festive on dowel tree for kitchen decoration. Heart-shaped cookies make cute Valentines. Makes about 70 cookies.

Mrs. William P. Furr, Jr.

Great Grandmother Doty's Sugar Cookies

1 cup butter or margarine,
softened
2 cups sugar
3 eggs

2 teaspoons vanilla
4 cups sifted flour
2 teaspoons baking powder

Cream butter and sugar. Add eggs and beat until fluffy. Add vanilla, flour and baking powder. Refrigerate until dough is quite firm. Roll about ¼ of dough out at a time on a floured board. Roll about 1/8 inch thick. Do not overwork dough or it will stick to the board. Cut out cookies with cookie cutter and bake on cookie sheet in preheated 325°F oven about 10 minutes or until light brown. May be sprinkled with colored or plain sugar before baking. For holiday cookies cut out with Christmas or gingerbread cutters. Makes about 80 (2 inch) round cookies.

Mrs. Arthur W. Doty

Nut Macaroons

3 egg whites
1 cup sugar
½ teaspoon cream of tartar

8 ounces ground pecans
½ teaspoon vanilla

Beat egg whites until stiff, adding sugar and cream of tartar gradually. Fold in nuts and vanilla. Grease and lightly flour cookie sheet. Drop macaroons from spoon onto baking sheet. Bake at 300°F for 20 minutes. Makes 50 cookies.

Mrs. Carl Fox, III

Martha Fox's Christmas Fruit Cake Cookies

1 cup butter or margarine,
softened
1½ cups sugar
3 eggs, separated
3 cups flour, divided
½ pound candied cherries,
finely chopped
½ pound candied pineapple,
finely chopped

½ pound white raisins
1 quart shelled pecans, finely
chopped
1 teaspoon ground cinnamon
1 teaspoon ground nutmeg
½ teaspoon salt
1 teaspoon vanilla
1 teaspoon baking soda, dissolved
in a little water

Cream butter; add sugar, then beaten egg yolks. Sprinkle some of the flour over the fruit and pecans. Add spices and salt to remaining flour. Combine butter, fruit and flour mixtures. Add vanilla and soda. Beat egg whites until stiff and fold in. Drop scant teaspoonfuls on greased cookie sheet and bake at 350°F for 10-15 minutes. Batter may be prepared several weeks ahead. Freezes well before and after baking. Yields 125-150 cookies.

Mrs. M. E. Ragsdale, Canton, Mississippi

This 100-year-old recipe was Mrs. Fox's mother's recipe.

Brown Sugar Confections

2 egg whites
2 cups brown sugar
2 Tablespoons flour

¼ teaspoon salt
2 cups chopped pecans or
  walnuts

Beat egg whites to a stiff froth. Continue beating and adding sugar gradually. When all sugar has been incorporated, sift the flour and salt over egg white mixture and fold in completely. Fold in nuts. Drop by spoonfuls on a greased cookie sheet at least 2 inches apart. Bake in 325°F oven about 15 minutes. Makes 4 dozen cookies.

Mrs. Rabian D. Lane

Shortbread

1 pound butter, softened (do
  not substitute)

1¼ cups sugar
6 cups flour

Cream butter and sugar. Add flour one cup at a time. Press into ungreased 9 x 15-inch jelly-roll pan. Use rolling pin to flatten the dough neatly. Dough may be stamped with a cookie stamp. Bake at 325°F for 35-45 minutes. Cut into squares or fingers as desired while hot. Let cool in pan. Keeps well if tightly covered; do not freeze. Makes 25-30 cookies.

Mrs. Michael T. McRee

Heavenly Hash Brownies

4 eggs, beaten
2 cups sugar
1½ cups flour
1 teaspoon vanilla
1 cup margarine

⅓ cup cocoa
1½ cups pecans, chopped
1 (6¼ ounce) bag miniature
  marshmallows

Combine eggs, sugar, flour and vanilla. Melt margarine and add cocoa. Add to egg mixture and beat well. Add nuts. Bake in 9 x 13-inch pan at 350°F for 25-30 minutes. As soon as cake is taken from oven, cover with marshmallows. Return pan to oven until marshmallows are slightly melted. Pour CHOCOLATE FROSTING over marshmallows and cool before cutting. Makes 48 brownies.

CHOCOLATE FROSTING

½ cup margarine, melted
⅓ cup milk
3 Tablespoons cocoa

1 (1 pound) box confectioners'
  sugar
1 teaspoon vanilla

Combine margarine, milk and cocoa. Beat in sugar and vanilla.

Mrs. Fred Weathersby

Cook's Brownies

4 (1 ounce) squares unsweetened
  chocolate
¾ cup butter (do not substitute)
4 eggs

2 cups sugar
1 cup sifted flour
1 teaspoon vanilla
1 cup chopped pecans

Melt chocolate and butter together; cool. Beat eggs. Add sugar, flour, chocolate mixture, vanilla and pecans. Pour into 2 greased and floured 7 x 7-inch pans. Bake at 325°F for 30 minutes. Do not let brownies get too done; they should be moist. Yields 12 brownies.

Mrs. Cooper Campbell, Jr.

Florentines

¼ cup whipping cream
⅓ cup sugar
¼ cup butter
1 cup sliced almonds (grind ½
  cup in blender)
2 Tablespoons flour

½ cup candied orange peel,
  chopped
¼ teaspoon almond extract
¼ pound semisweet chocolate,
  melted

Combine cream, sugar and butter in pan and cook, stirring until butter melts. Turn heat to medium high and bring to a boil. Remove from heat and add all other ingredients except chocolate. Drop by Tablespoons on greased and floured cookie sheets. Leave plenty of room between cookies, for they spread when baked. Bake at 350°F for 10-12 minutes or until edges are slightly brown. Cool a minute or two. Remove to rack or wax paper. When completely cool, turn upside down and coat with melted chocolate. Makes about 24 cookies.

The Editors

Grandmother's Ice Box Cookies

1½ cups butter or margarine,
  softened
1 cup sugar
2 cups brown sugar
3 eggs

½ pound chopped nuts
4½ cups flour
1 teaspoon salt
1 teaspoon baking soda
1 teaspoon ground cinnamon

Cream margarine and sugars. Beat in eggs; stir in nuts. Sift flour with salt, soda and cinnamon and add to mixture. Form into a ball of dough. Chill dough and shape into 10 or 12-inch rolls that are 1 inch in diameter. Wrap in wax paper and aluminum foil and store in freezer. When frozen, slice thinly and bake at 350°F for 8-10 minutes. Rolls may be prepared and kept for months in the freezer, using as needed. Yields 3 dozen cookies per roll.

Mrs. Tom Abernethy, Jr.

Keep in freezer for children and grandchildren to slice and bake.

Coconut Macaroons

½ cup Eagle Brand condensed
    milk
2 cups flaked coconut

1 teaspoon vanilla
2 egg whites

Mix milk, coconut and vanilla. Beat egg whites until stiff and fold into coconut mixture. Spoon onto greased cookie sheet. Bake in preheated 350°F oven for 10-15 minutes. Makes 4 dozen cookies.

Mrs. Ralph Avery

Lou's Lace Cookies

½ cup flour
¼ teaspoon baking powder
½ cup sugar
⅓ cup plus 1 Tablespoon
    melted butter

¾ cup quick-cooking rolled
    oats
2 Tablespoons whipping cream
2 Tablespoons light corn syrup
1 Tablespoon vanilla

Sift together in a bowl the flour, baking powder and sugar. Add the remaining ingredients and mix until well blended. Drop on an ungreased cookie sheet about 4 inches apart, using a ¼-teaspoon measure. Bake at 325°-350°F for 8-10 minutes or until light brown. Let stand 15 seconds before removing from cookie pan with spatula. If the cookies harden before they are all removed, run the pan back in the oven for 3-4 seconds and then remove them. Makes about 4 dozen cookies.

Mrs. D. C. Latimer

Chocolate Chip Blond Brownies

1 cup sifted flour
½ teaspoon baking powder
1/8 teaspoon baking soda
½ teaspoon salt
½ cup chopped nuts
⅓ cup butter or margarine

1 cup packed brown sugar
1 egg, slightly beaten
1 teaspoon vanilla
½ (6 ounce) package semisweet
    chocolate chips

Sift together flour, baking powder, soda and salt. Add nuts; mix well and set aside. Melt butter in saucepan and remove from heat. (If margarine is used, add 1 Tablespoon hot water.) Add brown sugar and beat well. Let cool. Add egg and vanilla and blend. Add flour mixture, a small amount at a time, mixing well after each addition. Spread in greased 8 x 8-inch pan. Sprinkle chocolate chips over top. Bake at 350°F for 20-25 minutes. Do not overbake. Cool in pan and cut in squares. If doubling recipe, bake in 9 x 12-inch pan. Makes 48 squares.

Mrs. R. Baxter Brown

Almond Crescent Cookies

2 cups whole almonds, divided
1¼ cups flour
¼ cup sugar

1 cup butter, softened
1 teaspoon vanilla
1 cup powdered sugar

Measure 1⅔ cups almonds. Grind finely in blender or with food processor or meat grinder. Finely chop remaining almonds and set aside. Mix flour, sugar and ground almonds. With fingers work in butter and vanilla until mixture pulls away from side of bowl. Chill 1 hour. Roll dough into balls, then into rolls; form crescents. Press tops of crescents into chopped almonds. Bake on ungreased cookie sheet at 350°F for 12-15 minutes or until lightly browned. Cool on pan about 10 minutes. While still warm, roll in powdered sugar. Yields 25-30 cookies.

Mrs. Richard L. Redmont, Jr.

Mae Travis's Jelly Cookies

1½ cups butter, softened
1 cup sugar
3 egg yolks

3 cups sifted flour, or more
1½ teaspoons vanilla
Jelly or jam

Cream butter. Beat in sugar. Add egg yolks, flour and vanilla. Mix well. Roll dough into little balls. Place on ungreased cookie sheet. Make a thumb print in the center of each. Fill with jelly (strawberry jam is especially good). Bake a few at first. If they spread out too much, add a little more flour to dough. Bake at 400°F until light brown on edges. Watch carefully. Do not let them burn. Makes 8-10 dozen.

Mrs. Robert C. Travis

Florence's Toffee-Chocolate Squares

Graham crackers
1 cup dark brown sugar
1 cup butter

1 (11¾ ounce) package milk
    chocolate chips
1 cup ground pecans

Line a pan (at least 10 x 15 inches in size) with foil on bottom and sides. Line this with separated rectangular graham crackers (not crumbs) placed side by side. Simmer together for 3 minutes the sugar and butter. Pour mixture quickly over crackers and bake in preheated 400°F oven 5 minutes. Remove from oven. Sprinkle chocolate chips over all, spreading to cover as they melt. Sprinkle pecans over top. Cool and cut into squares. Makes about 75 squares.

Mrs. T. Arnold Turner, Jr.

Variation: Add finely chopped nuts and 1 teaspoon vanilla to simmered sugar-butter mixture. Pour over crackers. Bake at 350°F for 10-12 minutes. Delete chocolate. Almonds can be used.

Mrs. Wade Creekmore, Jr.

Chocolate Drops

6 eggs
1 (1 pound) box powdered
   sugar
3 cups sifted flour

4 Tablespoons cocoa
1 Tablespoon ground cinnamon
½ Tablespoon ground nutmeg
¼ Tablespoon ground cloves

Beat eggs for 10 minutes. Add sugar and beat for 10 minutes more. Fold in flour, cocoa and spices, stirring well. Drop onto greased cookie sheet and let stand at room temperature overnight. Bake in the morning at 400°F for 10 minutes. Makes 8 dozen cookies.

Mrs. Carl Fox, Jr.

Whole Wheat Molasses Cookies

¼ cup butter or margarine
¼ cup turbinado or granulated
   sugar
½ cup molasses
½ teaspoon salt
2 teaspoons baking soda

1 teaspoon ground ginger
1 teaspoon ground cinnamon
¼ teaspoon ground cloves
1½ cups whole wheat flour
2 Tablespoons vinegar

Melt butter with sugar and molasses in small saucepan over low heat. Cool. Combine salt, soda and spices with flour in bowl. Stir in butter mixture and add vinegar. Drop by teaspoonfuls onto greased cookie sheet. Bake 7 minutes at 350°F. May be prepared several days in advance. Yields 30 cookies.

Mrs. Cecil A. Ford

Scotch Bars

½ cup margarine, softened
¼ cup sugar
¼ cup light brown sugar
½ teaspoon vanilla
1 egg yolk
½ cup sifted flour
½ cup rolled oats

ICING:
2 (1 ounce) squares
   unsweetened chocolate
1½ Tablespoons margarine
1½ cups confectioners' sugar
Pinch salt
3½ Tablespoons milk
1½ teaspoons vanilla

Cream margarine and sugars. Add vanilla and egg yolk and beat until light. Stir in flour and oats and pour into a greased 8 x 8-inch baking pan and bake 25-30 minutes at 300°F. Ice when cool. *ICING*: Melt chocolate and margarine in double boiler. Turn off heat and add other ingredients, beating quickly until smooth. Spread over uncut pastry. Let icing become firm in the refrigerator before cutting into squares. Makes 16 squares.

Mrs. Edward H. Nicholson

Potato Chip Cookies

1 cup butter, softened (do not
  substitute)
½ cup sugar

1 teaspoon vanilla
1½ cups sifted flour
½ cup crushed potato chips

Cream butter and sugar; add vanilla, flour and potato chips. Drop by ½-teaspoonfuls on ungreased cookie sheet. Bake 10-12 minutes at 350°F. Makes 4 dozen cookies.

Mrs. Alexander Endy

Peanut Butter Cup Tarts

36 Reese's milk chocolate
  peanut butter cups

1 (15 ounce) roll refrigerated
  peanut butter cookie dough

Refrigerate candies so paper will peel off easily. Unwrap each. Follow slicing instructions on peanut butter cookie wrapper and quarter each slice. Place each piece in a greased miniature muffin cup. Place in preheated 350°F oven 8-10 minutes or just until cookie puffs up and is barely done. Remove from oven and *immediately* push a candy cup into each cookie-filled muffin cup. The cookie will deflate and form a tart shell around the peanut butter cup. The heat of the cookie will melt the chocolate topping. Let pan cool; then refrigerate until the shine leaves the chocolate. Remove from refrigerator and gently lift each tart from the cup with the tip of a knife. Makes 36 cookies.

Mrs. Dick B. Mason, III

Russian Rocks

1 cup butter, margarine or
  Crisco
1 cup sugar
1 cup brown sugar
½ cup light corn syrup
3 eggs or 6 egg yolks
½ teaspoon baking soda
½ cup buttermilk

3½ cups flour
1 (16 ounce) box dates, chopped
1 Tablespoon ground cinnamon
1 teaspoon ground cloves
1 teaspoon ground nutmeg
1 to 1½ teaspoons vanilla
Pinch salt
4 cups pecans, broken

Cream butter and sugar. Add corn syrup. Beat in eggs. Mix soda with buttermilk and add. Sprinkle a little flour over dates; then mix remaining flour with spices and add. Add vanilla and salt to butter mixture, then pecans and dates. Blend well. Drop on foil or greased pan. Bake at 350°F about 15 minutes. Makes about 150-160 cookies.

Mrs. James S. Ricks

This is an old Southern recipe which has been in my family for at least 3 generations.

Oat Cakes
(Canadian version of the Scotch favorite)

2 cups flour
¾ cup sugar
¾ teaspoon salt
¾ teaspoon baking soda

¾ teaspoon ground nutmeg
2 cups quick-cooking rolled oats
1 cup Crisco or lard
⅓ cup cold water

Measure and sift into a bowl the first 5 ingredients. Mix in rolled oats. Cut in Crisco and blend in water (enough to make a workable stiff dough). Roll out on a floured board ¼ inch thick. Cut into squares or cut out rounds with cookie cutter. Bake at 375°F for 15 minutes or until just brown. Recipe makes a not-too-sweet cookie. They are delightful served on a dessert tray with cheese. Makes 12 dozen (1 inch) squares.

Mrs. Warren N. Bell

Nut Butter Balls

1 cup butter or margarine,
   softened
¼ to ½ cup sugar
½ teaspoon salt
1 teaspoon almond extract

2 teaspoons vanilla
2 cups sifted flour
1 to 2 cups finely chopped nuts
Powdered sugar

Cream butter and sugar. Add salt, almond and vanilla extracts, flour and nuts. Mix well. Refrigerate until easy to handle. Preheat oven to 350°F. With fingers shape dough into 1-inch balls. Place on ungreased cookie sheet. Bake 10-12 minutes or until brown. While cookies are warm, roll in powdered sugar. Makes 3 dozen cookies.

Mrs. Alvin E. Brent, Jr.

Peanut Blossoms

1⅓ cups flour
1 teaspoon baking soda
½ teaspoon salt
½ cup sugar
2 Tablespoons milk
½ cup brown sugar

½ cup shortening
½ cup peanut butter
1 egg
1 teaspoon vanilla
48 milk chocolate kisses

Combine all ingredients except candy in a large mixing bowl. Mix on lowest speed of mixer until dough is formed. Shape dough into small balls using a rounded teaspoonful for each. Roll balls in additional sugar. Place balls on ungreased cookie sheets. Bake at 375°F for 10-12 minutes. Immediately top each cookie with a candy kiss. Press down firmly so cookie cracks around edge. Yields about 4 dozen cookies.

Mrs. J. A. Crellin

Candy

Yellow Divinity

2 cups sugar
½ cup light Karo
½ cup milk

2 egg yolks
1 cup nuts, chopped
1 teaspoon vanilla

Combine sugar, Karo and milk and cook over low heat until mixture reaches the hard ball stage (248°F on candy thermometer). While syrup is cooking, beat egg yolks. Add hot syrup to eggs slowly, beating until slightly cool. Add nuts and vanilla. Drop by spoonfuls on wax paper. Makes 16-20 pieces.

Mrs. Alvin E. Brent, Jr.

Skillet Fudge

2 ounces unsweetened chocolate
2 cups sugar
½ teaspoon salt
⅓ cup light Karo

½ cup milk
1 teaspoon vanilla
2 Tablespoons butter
1 cup chopped nuts (optional)

Place first 5 ingredients in large cold iron skillet. Let come to a full rolling boil and cook to 236°F on candy thermometer, stirring constantly with a wooden spoon. Set aside to cool to lukewarm (110°F) without stirring. Add butter and vanilla. Beat with mixer for 8 minutes on low speed. Add nuts, if desired. Pour into buttered dish or pan and score. When cool, cut into squares. Makes about 1¼ pounds candy.

Mrs. W. W. Ford, Jr.

Broken Glass Candy

Powdered sugar
3¾ cups sugar
1¼ cups light Karo
1 cup water
Food coloring

1 teaspoon oil flavoring
(available at pharmacy in
flavors such as cinnamon,
anise, wintergreen,
spearmint, lime)

Sprinkle powdered sugar on 2 (11 x 15 inch) cookie sheets. Combine sugar, Karo and water in heavy saucepan and stir over medium heat until sugar dissolves. Continue to cook, without stirring, until syrup reaches 290°F on candy thermometer. Remove from heat and add food coloring to desired intensity and the desired oil flavoring. Pour onto cookie sheets, cool and break into small pieces. Makes 2¼ pounds candy.

Mrs. Robert Rall

Candy looks pretty in apothecary jars. Make several batches, using a different flavor and color for each. Mix red and green candy in jars for Christmas gifts!

Caramel Candy

2 cups sugar
2 cups whipping cream
2 cups chopped pecans
1¾ cups light corn syrup

½ cup butter
Pinch salt
1 teaspoon vanilla

Mix first 5 ingredients together and cook slowly in heavy 4-quart boiler (or pot large enough to keep from boiling over) to firm ball stage (238°F on candy thermometer). Add salt and vanilla. Pour in buttered 9 x 12-inch pan and let cool. This will take several hours. When cool, cut in squares and wrap in wax paper. Will keep for several weeks. Makes about 9 dozen pieces.

Mrs. Robert C. Cannada

Divinity

1 cup boiling water
¾ cup light Karo
3 cups sugar
Pinch salt

2 egg whites
1 cup chopped pecans
1 teaspoon vanilla

Cook water, Karo, sugar and salt to the soft ball stage (234°F on candy thermometer). Add ½ of the syrup, a Tablespoon at a time, to well-beaten egg whites beating constantly. Continue cooking remaining syrup until it reaches the crack stage (270°F). Pour into egg mixture and continue beating until high gloss changes to dull. Fold in pecans and vanilla and drop by the spoonful on wax paper. Have boiling water ready in case candy sets up too fast. Add 2 or 3 drops to make it creamy as it is spooned onto wax paper. Makes 48 pieces.

Mrs. Phillip B. Lawrence

Chocolate Truffles

1 (12 ounce) package semisweet
  chocolate chips
3 Tablespoons milk
3 egg yolks

¾ cup butter, cut into pieces
1 Tablespoon brandy (optional)
Chocolate shot, nonpareil
  decors or cocoa

In top of double boiler melt chocolate chips with milk. Beat with electric beater until smooth. Continue beating the chocolate as the egg yolks are added, one at a time. Remove pan from hot water and beat in butter, a few pieces at a time, until completely blended. Continue beating 2-3 more minutes. Add brandy, if desired. Let chocolate sit for 4-5 hours to cool. Chocolate may be cooled more quickly by placing in refrigerator. When workable, roll into balls about the size of large marbles. Roll in chocolate shot, colored candy dots or cocoa to coat. Refrigerate. Serve in tiny paper cups. Yields 50 truffles.

Mademoiselle Marie Rose Tizon

Peanut Brittle

¾ cup water
3 cups sugar
1 cup light Karo

1 quart shelled, raw peanuts
3 teaspoons baking soda

Combine water, sugar and Karo in heavy saucepan. Cook until sugar is dissolved. Add peanuts. Continue cooking until syrup reaches hard crack stage (285 °F on candy thermometer). Remove from heat and carefully blend in soda, stirring hard about 3 minutes. Pour on slightly greased cookie pan with sides. Pat gently to break bubbles. When cool, break into pieces. Store in airtight container. Will keep up to a month. Pecans may be substituted for peanuts. Makes about 3 pounds candy.

Lem O. Smith, Jr.

G. G.'s Fudge Candy

½ cup margarine
1 (13 ounce) can evaporated
   milk
4½ cups sugar
3 (5 ounce) Hershey bars

1 pint marshmallow creme
2 quarts pecans, chopped fine
   or broken in pieces
1 teaspoon vanilla
Pinch salt

Bring margarine, milk and sugar to boil and boil for 3 minutes, stirring constantly (total time is approximately 20 minutes). Remove from heat and add Hershey bars, marshmallow creme, pecans, vanilla and salt. Drop by teaspoonfuls on wax paper to harden or pour into 2 greased Pyrex dishes, 1½ and 3 quarts in size. It is necessary to work quickly as candy will harden as it cools. If kept more than one week, refrigerate. Makes 60-70 pieces.

Mrs. Joseph L. Speed

Apricot Roll

2 cups sugar
1 cup milk
12 ounces dried apricots,
   chopped fine

1 Tablespoon butter
2 cups chopped pecans
1 teaspoon vanilla
Dash salt

Boil sugar and milk mixture until it thickens (236 °F on candy thermometer), stirring constantly. Add apricots and boil until they melt into the syrup and mixture reaches about 230 °F on candy thermometer. Remove from heat and beat hard. Add butter, pecans, vanilla and salt. Beat candy until it begins to harden. Pour onto a wet, smooth cloth and roll to desired diameter. Cool; then store in refrigerator. Cut in thin slices to serve. Makes a 2-pound roll.

Mrs. Ancel C. Tipton, Sr., Natchez, Mississippi

Variation: For Christmas candy, add a few chopped red and green candied cherries with the pecans.

Caramel Fudge

6 cups sugar, divided
2 cups whipping cream
½ cup butter

2 cups pecans, chopped
2 teaspoons vanilla

Cook 4 cups sugar and cream to boiling point. Caramelize the remaining 2 cups sugar and add to sugar and cream mixture. Cook until mixture reaches soft ball stage (238°F on candy thermometer). Remove from heat. Add butter, pecans and vanilla. Beat until thick. Drop by spoonfuls on wax paper or pour into buttered pan and cut when cool. Makes approximately 70 pieces.

Mrs. J. L. Knight, Louisville, Mississippi

Cathedral Windows

4 Tablespoons butter
1 (12 ounce) package semisweet
    chocolate chips
2 eggs, well beaten

1 (10½ ounce) package colored
    marshmallows
1 cup chopped pecans (optional)
Powdered sugar

Melt butter and chocolate in top of double boiler. Cool. Beat in eggs. Fold in marshmallows and pecans, if desired. Pour into a 9 x 5-inch loaf pan lined with foil. Cover with powdered sugar and chill until firm. Remove from pan and slice very thin to serve. Freezes well. Makes 1 loaf candy.

Mrs. McKamy Smith

This candy is easy for children to make and very tasty.

Toffee-Butter Crunch

1 cup butter or margarine
1½ cups sugar
3 Tablespoons water
1 Tablespoon light corn syrup
1 cup coarsely chopped
    blanched almonds, toasted

4 (4½ ounce) milk chocolate
    candy bars, melted, divided
1 cup finely chopped blanched
    almonds, toasted, divided

In large saucepan melt butter. Add sugar, water and corn syrup. Cook over medium heat, stirring occasionally to hard crack stage (300°F). Quickly stir in the coarsely chopped almonds. Spread while hot onto well-greased 9 x 13-inch flexible metal pan. Cool thoroughly. Turn out on wax paper. Spread with half the chocolate; sprinkle with half the finely chopped almonds. Cover with wax paper. Flip to other side. Spread with remaining chocolate and sprinkle with remaining almonds. Chill to firm. Break into pieces. Yields 24 pieces.

Mrs. Julian Henderson

Candied Popcorn

½ cup sugar
¾ cup light Karo
¾ cup peanut butter

1 teaspoon vanilla
1 gallon popped corn, salted

Combine sugar and Karo. Boil until sugar dissolves. Remove from heat. Add peanut butter and vanilla. Pour over popcorn and mix well. Makes 1 gallon candied popcorn.

Mrs. John Baxter Burns, III

Peanut Butter Balls

1 cup margarine
½ cup crunchy peanut butter
½ cup chopped peanuts
1 cup flaked coconut
2¼ cups crushed graham
    crackers

1 teaspoon vanilla
1 (1 pound) box powdered sugar
1 (12 ounce) package semisweet
    chocolate chips
⅔ cup grated paraffin

Melt margarine. Add other ingredients except chocolate chips and paraffin. Form into small balls and chill. Melt chocolate and paraffin in double boiler over hot water. Using 2 forks, dip balls into chocolate. Place on wax paper to dry. Yields 100 balls.

Mrs. Torrance Sneed, Balboa, Canal Zone

Chocolate Covered Candy

2 pounds powdered sugar
1 (14 ounce) can condensed
    milk
½ cup butter, softened
½ cup chopped pecans
    (optional)
Flavorings (peppermint, lemon,
    brandy) total amount used to
    equal 1 Tablespoon

1 (12 ounce) package
    unsweetened or milk
    chocolate chips
1 (12 ounce) package
    butterscotch chips
⅔ cake paraffin

Mix sugar, milk and butter. Add pecans, if desired. Separate mixture equally into bowls according to number of flavorings desired. Add 1 flavoring to each bowl. Roll mixture into small balls. Place on wax paper. Refrigerate. Melt chocolate and butterscotch chips with paraffin in double boiler. Dip balls into chocolate mixture with toothpick. Cool on wax paper. Yields 75-100 balls.

Mrs. Lewis Lipscomb

Peanut Butter Candy

½ cup crunchy peanut butter
⅓ cup honey
¾ cup wheat germ

1 Tablespoon instant non-fat
dry milk

Mix all ingredients together. Drop by teaspoonfuls onto large plate. Store in refrigerator. For harder candy place in freezer ½ hour before serving. May be prepared in advance. Freezes well. Yields 10-12 pieces.

Mrs. E. B. Robinson, Jr.

Nutritious and children love it!

Orange Pralines

2 cups sugar
¾ cup half and half cream
¼ teaspoon salt
2½ Tablespoons light Karo
Juice and grated rind of 1 orange

4 Tablespoons butter
1 teaspoon vanilla
Few drops orange food coloring
(optional)
2 cups chopped pecans

Place sugar, cream, salt and Karo in saucepan and stir constantly until mixture boils. Add orange juice slowly and continue cooking until mixture reaches soft ball stage (240°F on candy thermometer). Add orange rind and cook until it again reaches 240°F. Add butter, vanilla and food coloring. Cool. Beat until mixture holds its shape. Add pecans. Drop on wax paper. Store in tin or plastic container. Makes about 1¼ pounds candy.

Mrs. W. W. Ford, Jr.

Fruit Drops

2 cups sugar
½ cup light brown sugar
1½ cups milk
3 Tablespoons butter
3 Tablespoons light Karo
Pinch salt

1 teaspoon vanilla
1 (7 ounce) package flaked
coconut
½ cup maraschino cherries,
quartered
½ cup chopped pecans

Cook sugars, milk, butter, Karo and salt quickly to dissolve sugar. Reduce heat and cook slowly to soft ball stage (238°F on candy thermometer). Remove from heat, add vanilla and beat briefly until smooth and cooler, about 1½ minutes. Add coconut, cherries and pecans. Drop on wax paper or form into balls with hands. Mixture may separate while cooking, but will become smooth when beaten. Makes 50 pieces.

Mrs. J. L. Knight, Louisville, Mississippi

Party Mints

1 (1 pound) box powdered
   sugar
5 Tablespoons butter, softened

2 Tablespoons evaporated milk
12 drops oil of peppermint
Food coloring as desired

Mix ingredients well and press into rubber candy molds. Pop out of molds immediately. Makes 50 mints.

Mrs. Ralph Godwin

With the wide availability of candy molds, these mints can be made for every occasion.

Cakes

Angel Food Cake

1¼ to 1½ cups egg whites
1¼ teaspoons cream of tartar
¼ teaspoon salt

1 teaspoon vanilla
1½ cups sugar, divided
1 cup flour

Beat the egg whites, cream of tartar, salt and vanilla until mixture holds a peak. Continue beating, adding ½ cup sugar a little at a time. Sift together the flour and remaining sugar; then sift again over the egg whites. Fold in by hand. Rinse a 10-inch angel food cake pan with water and drain. Spoon cake batter into pan and bake at 375 °F for 30 minutes. When cake is done, immediately turn pan upside down to keep cake from falling. Remove cake from pan when cool. Serves 12.

Mrs. Ralph Avery

Note: To make a chocolate angel food cake, substitute ¼ cup cocoa for ¼ cup flour.

Devil's Food Cake

¾ cup butter, softened
2 cups sugar
2 eggs
2¼ cups cake flour
¾ cup cocoa

1 teaspoon salt
2 teaspoons baking soda
2 cups buttermilk
1 Tablespoon vanilla

Cream butter and sugar together. Add eggs one at a time. Sift together flour, cocoa, salt and soda. Add alternately with buttermilk to creamed mixture. Add vanilla and beat at medium speed for 2½ minutes. Bake in 3 (8 inch) cake pans lined with greased wax paper at 350 °F for about 30 minutes or until done. Frost, if desired, with Seven Minute Icing (see Index). Serves 12.

Mrs. Gus Primos

Golden Gate Cake

¾ cup butter, softened
1½ cups sugar
2 cups cake flour
2½ teaspoons baking powder
¾ teaspoon salt

1 cup egg yolks (about 12)
¾ cup milk
¾ teaspoon lemon extract
¾ teaspoon orange extract

Cream butter and sugar. Sift together flour, baking powder and salt. Add egg yolks to creamed mixture, beating well; add flour mixture and milk alternately. Add flavorings. Bake in a greased and floured 12 x 9-inch pan at 350°F for 35 minutes. Use as base for a Baked Alaska or any trifle dessert or serve iced with Chocolate Fudge Icing or Caramel Icing. Serves 12.

Mrs. A. Y. Brown, Jr., Memphis, Tennessee

This is a great recipe for using egg yolks left over from making meringues.

Chocolate Fudge Icing

2 cups sugar
½ cup cocoa
½ cup milk

6 Tablespoons margarine
2 Tablespoons light corn syrup
1 teaspoon vanilla

Mix sugar, cocoa, milk, margarine and corn syrup. Slowly bring to a full boil. Let boil for 1 minute. Add vanilla. Cool and beat with mixer until mixture is of spreading consistency. Spread quickly. Sufficient to ice a 2-layer (9 inch) cake or 1 (9 x 13 inch) sheet cake.

Mrs. Zach Taylor, Jr.

Caramel Icing

1 teaspoon baking soda
  (1¼ teaspoons)
2 cups sugar (2½ cups)
¾ cup butter (1 cup)
½ cup buttermilk (¾ cup)

1 Tablespoon light corn syrup
  (1¼ Tablespoons)
12 large marshmallows (15)
1 teaspoon vanilla (1¼ teaspoons)

Mix first 5 ingredients together in heavy pot and place over low heat, stirring until completely dissolved. When hot, add marshmallows. Cook until candy thermometer reaches 238°F. Remove from heat. Add vanilla and beat until cloudy. Place pot in pan of hot water to keep at spreading consistency, if desired. Icing is sufficient for 1 (9 x 12 inch) sheet cake, a 2-layer (9 inch) cake or about 44 cupcakes. Proportions in parentheses will ice about 55 cupcakes.

Mrs. Robert Cannada

Yellow Sponge Cake

12 egg yolks
½ cup water
1¾ cups sugar, divided
2½ cups flour

⅓ teaspoon salt
2 teaspoons baking powder
1 to 2 teaspoons vanilla

Beat egg yolks and water with electric beater until lemon-colored. Add ½ cup sugar and continue beating until light yellow. Sift together the remaining sugar, flour, salt and baking powder. Fold dry ingredients and vanilla into egg yolk mixture. Bake in a greased and floured tube pan at 375°F for about 30 minutes or until done. Remove from pan when cool. Serves 12.

Mrs. Ralph Avery

Cheese Cake with Apricot Sauce

½ cup graham cracker crumbs
2 pounds cream cheese,
    softened
4 eggs
1¾ cups sugar

Juice and grated rind of 1 lemon
1 teaspoon vanilla
Strawberries, blueberries or
    other fruit or berries

Preheat oven to 325°F. Butter the inside of an 8-inch wide soufflé dish and sprinkle with graham cracker crumbs until coated. (Do not use a springform pan.) Shake out the excess crumbs. Set aside. Place the cream cheese, eggs, sugar, lemon juice and rind and vanilla in a bowl. Start beating with electric beater at low speed and, as the ingredients blend, increase the speed to high. Continue beating until thoroughly blended and smooth. Scrape batter into prepared dish and shake gently to level the mixture. Set the dish inside a slightly wider pan and fill larger pan with boiling water to a depth of about ½ inch. Do not let the edge of the soufflé dish touch the rim of the larger pan. Place in oven and bake 1½ hours. Turn off oven heat and let cake sit in oven 20 minutes longer. Lift soufflé dish out of water and place on a rack. Let dish stand until cake reaches room temperature. Invert a plate over the cake and carefully turn both upside down to unmold the cake. Invert a cake plate over the bottom of the cake and carefully turn this upside down so that the cake comes out right side up. Garnish with berries or fruit and spoon APRICOT SAUCE over all. Makes 12 or more servings.

APRICOT SAUCE

1 (10 ounce) jar apricot jam
¼ cup sugar
¼ cup water

1 Tablespoon rum, Cognac or
    kirsch

Combine jam, sugar and water in a small saucepan and stir over low heat until blended and smooth. Push the sauce through a small sieve with a spoon. Let cool and stir in the rum. Makes 1½ cups sauce.

Maurice Reed, Jr.

Praline Cheese Cake

1 cup graham cracker crumbs
3 Tablespoons sugar
3 Tablespoons margarine,
  melted
3 (8 ounce) packages cream
  cheese, softened
1 ¼ cups packed dark brown
  sugar

2 Tablespoons flour
3 eggs
1 ½ teaspoons vanilla
½ cup finely chopped pecans
Maple syrup
Pecan halves (optional)

Preheat oven to 350 °F. Combine crumbs, sugar and margarine; press into bottom of a 9-inch springform pan. Bake for 10 minutes. Combine cheese, sugar and flour, beating with electric mixer at medium speed until well blended. Add eggs, one at a time, mixing well after each addition. Blend in vanilla and nuts. Pour mixture over crumbs. Bake 50-55 minutes. Cool and loosen cake from rim of pan. Chill. Brush with maple syrup and garnish with pecan halves, if desired. Serves 10-12.

Mrs. Richard L. Redmont, Jr.

Chocolate Ripple Cheese Cake

1 cup flour, divided
1 cup plus 2 Tablespoons sugar
¼ teaspoon salt
½ cup butter
3 (1 ounce) packets premelted
  unsweetened chocolate

3 (8 ounce) packages cream
  cheese, softened
2 teaspoons vanilla
6 eggs
1 cup sour cream

Preheat oven to 400 °F. Combine ¾ cup flour, 2 Tablespoons sugar and salt. With pastry blender or fork cut butter into flour mixture until fine; stir in 1 packet chocolate. Press mixture in bottom of a 9-inch springform pan. Bake 10 minutes. Remove from oven; turn oven to 475 °F. In large bowl beat at low speed cream cheese and remaining 1 cup sugar until smooth; blend in remaining ¼ cup flour and vanilla. Add eggs one at a time, beating well after each. Beat in sour cream. In small bowl combine 1 ½ cups cheese mixture with remaining 2 packets chocolate. Pour ½ the plain cheese mixture over crust. With circular motion drizzle half the chocolate mixture on top. Repeat sequence. With a spatula cut through mixture to marbleize it. Bake at 475 °F for 12 minutes; turn oven down to 200 °F and bake 1 hour longer. Remove from oven. Cool 2-3 hours. Refrigerate 8 hours. To cut, use sharp knife which has been run under hot water. Cracks in top are characteristic. Should be made the day before. Serves 12.

Mrs. McWillie Robinson, Jr.

Cheese Cake with Strawberry Glaze

COOKIE CRUST:
1 cup sifted flour
¼ cup sugar
1 teaspoon grated lemon rind
Scrapings from small vanilla
    bean
1 egg yolk, beaten
½ cup butter, softened

FILLING:
1¼ pounds cream cheese
¾ cup sugar
1¼ Tablespoons flour

¾ teaspoon vanilla
¾ teaspoon grated orange rind
2 Tablespoons sour cream
2 Tablespoons milk or cream
4 egg yolks

STRAWBERRY GLAZE:
2 pints fresh strawberries,
    divided
¾ cup sugar
1½ Tablespoons cornstarch
Juice of ½ lemon
5 drops red food coloring

COOKIE CRUST: Mix the ingredients by hand. Pat into bottom of springform pan. Bake in 400°F oven for 10 minutes. Cool. FILLING: Cream cheese until softened. Beat in next 6 ingredients. Add egg yolks one at a time, beating well after each. Pour into springform pan over crust. Bake at 500°F for 6 minutes; then reduce heat to 200°F and cook for 30 minutes more. Do not overcook. Cool and refrigerate. Leave in springform pan until chilled; then unmold. STRAWBERRY GLAZE: Pour 1 cup strawberries in blender. Blend on high. Place sugar and cornstarch in shallow pan; add strawberry purée slowly; then add lemon juice and red food coloring. Cook until thick. Do not overcook. Arrange remaining whole or halved strawberries on top of cake and pour glaze over all. Decorate with more whole strawberries or mint leaves. Serves 12.

Mrs. James Savage, Jr.

Beautiful!

Applesauce Cake

⅔ cup butter, softened
1½ cups sugar
2 eggs
1 cup unsweetened applesauce
2 cups flour
1 teaspoon baking soda
1 teaspoon ground cinnamon

1 teaspoon ground nutmeg
2 cups chopped dates
2 cups chopped pecans
1 cup raisins
1 (9 ounce) package condensed
    mincemeat

Cream butter and sugar. Add eggs, beating them into mixture. Add applesauce. Sift together flour, soda, cinnamon and nutmeg; add to applesauce mixture. Mix dates, pecans, raisins and mincemeat; fold into batter. Mix well and pour into a 9-inch greased and floured tube pan. Bake in a preheated 350°F oven for 60-75 minutes. Serves 15.

Mrs. Richard L. Blount

Quick Applesauce Cake

¼ cup sugar
2 teaspoons ground cinnamon
½ cup margarine, softened
3 eggs

1 (16 ounce) can applesauce
1 (18½ ounce) package yellow
cake mix

Blend sugar and cinnamon. Grease a 10-inch bundt or tube pan and dust with 1 Tablespoon sugar-cinnamon mixture, reserving remainder for cake. Blend margarine, eggs, applesauce and cake mix until moistened. Reserve 1½ cups batter. Pour remaining batter into pan. Sprinkle with remaining sugar-cinnamon mixture; then top with reserved batter. Bake at 350°F for 35-45 minutes or until done. Cool cake in pan for 15 minutes; then invert on serving plate. Serves 12.

Mrs. John Rivers

Christmas Fruit Cake

2¼ cups butter, softened
3 cups sugar
9 eggs, well beaten
¾ cup coffee
¾ cup sherry or a Mogen
   David wine
1½ teaspoons baking soda,
   dissolved in water
6 cups flour
1½ teaspoons salt
1½ teaspoons each ground
   nutmeg, ground cloves,
   ground cinnamon

26 slices candied pineapple,
   mixed colors
3 (12 ounce) packages candied
   cherries, red and green
1 pound golden seedless raisins
2 pounds chopped dates
2 pounds English walnuts in the
   the shell, shelled
2 pounds blanched almonds in the
   shell, shelled
1½ quarts shelled pecans
¾ cup light corn syrup
6 Tablespoons water

Grease 2 (9 inch) tube pans and 2 (10½ x 3½ inch) loaf pans and line each with well-greased brown paper. Cream together butter and sugar. Add eggs and beat 5 minutes. Add coffee, wine and soda. Sift dry ingredients together and add. Reserve some pineapple and cherries for top decoration. Chop remaining fruit and dredge with extra flour. Carefully mix all the fruit into the batter. Reserve some halved nuts for decoration. Chop remaining nuts and add to batter. Pour batter in pans and place in cold oven. Keep a pan of water on oven rack under cakes to prevent drying. Bake loaf cakes at 250°F for about 3 hours and tube cakes for about 5 hours. Cakes are done when a cake tester inserted in center comes out clean. Cool thoroughly in pans. Bring corn syrup and water to a rolling boil. Cool to lukewarm. Brush glaze on tops of cooled cakes. Decorate as desired with reserved fruits and nuts. Brush tops with glaze. Store, well wrapped, in refrigerator. Makes 4 cakes.

Mrs. Robert G. Barnett

White Fruit Cake

1½ cups butter or margarine
2 cups sugar
6 eggs
½ cup plus 4 Tablespoons
    whiskey, divided
1 teaspoon vanilla
1 teaspoon ground nutmeg

1 teaspoon ground cinnamon
2 teaspoons baking powder
4 cups sifted flour, divided
1 pound candied pineapple, diced
½ pound whole candied cherries
1 pound shelled pecans
1 pound white raisins

Cream butter and sugar. Beat in eggs, one at a time; then add ½ cup whiskey and vanilla. Mix spices and baking powder with 3 cups flour and add to mixture. Dredge with remaining flour the pineapple, cherries, pecans and raisins; add to batter. Bake in 2 (9 x 5 inch) loaf pans or 1 (10 inch) tube pan which has been lined with heavy paper and greased. (Paper bags may be used.) Bake 2 hours at 250°F or 275°F, depending on heat control. This cake must not be baked dry. While cake is still hot, pour remaining whiskey over each loaf. Cover cakes with dish towel while they cool. Do not remove from pans until cold. Serves 20.

Mrs. Luther Flowers

Dark Fruit Cake Loaves

2 cups margarine, softened
7 cups sugar
12 medium eggs
1 teaspoon baking soda
1 cup buttermilk
2 (18 ounce) jars apple jelly or
    apple butter
2 pounds prepared mincemeat
1 Tablespoon salt
4 Tablespoons vanilla

2½ cups nuts
2½ pounds candied pineapple
3 pounds dates
2½ pounds candied orange peel
2½ cups raisins
2 (11 ounce) boxes currants
4¼ cups flour, divided
2 teaspoons ground allspice
2 teaspoons mace
½ teaspoon ground cloves

Cream margarine, sugar and eggs. Dissolve soda in buttermilk and add to creamed mixture. Add jelly, mincemeat, salt and vanilla. Finely chop nuts and fruits and dredge in ¼ cup flour. Combine spices and remaining flour, mix with fruits and nuts in a large bowl and blend in creamed mixture, using hands to mix. Fill 10 to 12 (7½ x 3½ inch) loaf pans within an inch of the top. Bake at 275°F for 2½ hours. Cake will be very moist. If too moist, bake 5-10 minutes longer. Wrap and store for at least a month, preferably longer. Makes 10-12 cakes.

Mrs. W. P. Robinson, Tulsa, Oklahoma

If raisins are heated in the oven before being added to cakes or muffins, they will be more evenly distributed.

Christmas Nut Cake

1 cup butter, softened
2 cups sugar
6 eggs
4 cups flour
2 pounds raisins
1 quart chopped pecans

1 teaspoon baking soda
1 teaspoon ground allspice
1 teaspoon ground cinnamon
1 teaspoon ground nutmeg
1 cup bourbon

Cream together the butter and sugar; beat in eggs one at a time. Mix flour, raisins, pecans and soda and fold into butter mixture. Add spices; then slowly add bourbon. Batter will be very stiff. Grease and flour 1 large or 2 small tube pans. Cut brown paper to fit the bottom and grease it. Place a pan of water on the lower shelf of oven below the cake. Bake cake at 275°F for 2 hours for a large cake or 1 hour for small ones or until done. Cake is done when a straw comes out of the middle clean. Cool cake and remove from pan. Leave cake inverted with brown paper on top until ready to cut. If cake becomes dry, pour more bourbon over it. Prior to baking, cake may be decorated with candied fruits and nuts and brushed with light corn syrup for added gloss. Serve with Whiskey Sauce (see Index). Serves 10.

Mrs. George S. Yerger, Jr., Tallulah, Louisiana

Fig Preserves Cake

CAKE:
2 eggs, beaten
2 cups sugar
1 cup buttermilk
1 cup oil
2 cups flour
1 teaspoon ground cinnamon
1 teaspoon ground nutmeg
1 teaspoon baking soda
1 teaspoon vanilla
1 teaspoon salt
2 cups chopped pecans

2 cups drained fig preserves, cut in small pieces

SAUCE:
½ cup buttermilk
½ cup sugar
1 Tablespoon light corn syrup
½ cup butter
¼ cup Marsala, rum or sherry wine (if using sherry, add 1 teaspoon almond flavoring)

CAKE: Beat together eggs, sugar, buttermilk and oil. Cream in the flour. Add spices, soda, vanilla, salt and pecans. Fold in figs. Grease and flour a tube or bundt pan. Pour batter into pan. Bake at 350°F for 1 hour. Let cake cool in pan. *SAUCE:* Bring buttermilk, sugar and corn syrup to a boil, stirring constantly. Remove from heat and add butter, stirring until melted. Add flavoring. Pour sauce over cake while still in pan. Let soak overnight. Turn out the next day. Serves 15.

Mrs. Wildridge Thompson

Japanese Fruit Cake

WHITE CAKE LAYER:
¾ cup shortening
1½ cups sugar
1½ teaspoons vanilla
2¼ cups sifted cake flour
3 teaspoons baking powder
1 teaspoon salt
1 cup skim milk
5 egg whites, stiffly beaten

FRUIT CAKE LAYER:
⅓ cup butter, softened
1 cup sugar
2 eggs
1¾ cups flour
1½ teaspoons baking powder
½ teaspoon salt
1 teaspoon ground cloves
1 cup milk

¼ cup raisins, chopped
½ cup candied cherries, chopped
½ cup coarsely chopped pecans, toasted

FILLING:
1 cup golden raisins
3 cups sugar
Sections of 6 oranges, chopped fine
2 Tablespoons butter
8 egg yolks, well beaten
1 cup grated coconut, fresh or canned
1 (8 ounce) can crushed pineapple, drained

½ cup chopped pecans, toasted
½ cup maraschino cherries, halved

WHITE CAKE LAYER: Cream shortening to soften. Gradually add sugar and beat until light and fluffy. Add vanilla. Sift flour with baking powder and salt and add to creamed mixture, alternating with the milk. Begin and end with the flour mixture and beat after each addition. Fold in egg whites. Pour batter into 2 (9 inch) cake pans which have been foil or paper-lined, then greased and floured. Bake in a preheated 375°F oven for 18-20 minutes or until done. Cool. *FRUIT CAKE LAYER:* Cream butter and sugar; then add eggs, one at a time, beating until smooth. Add sifted dry ingredients, alternating with the milk. Fold in fruit and pecans. Pour into 1 (9 inch) cake pan which has been foil-lined, greased and floured. Bake in a preheated 350°F oven for 25-30 minutes or until done. Cool. With a sharp knife split the cake to make 2 layers. *FILLING:* Place first 5 ingredients in top of double boiler and cook over boiling water, stirring constantly, until thickened, about 20 minutes. (It may be necessary to add a small amount of cornstarch if the oranges are very juicy.) Add the coconut and crushed pineapple. Cook until thickened again, about 10 minutes. Cool. To assemble cake, place 1 fruit cake layer on bottom and spread with filling. Top with a white cake layer and spread with filling. Repeat this sequence one more time. Sprinkle pecans and cherries over top layer of cake after it has been spread with filling. Spread remaining filling around sides of cake. This cake makes a very special holiday dessert. Serves 20.

Mrs. John Disepo, Clinton, Mississippi

For a very white cake, add 1/8 teaspoon cream of tartar per layer to cake batter.

Grandmother's Coconut Cake

¾ cup shortening
2 cups sugar
1½ teaspoons vanilla
½ teaspoon almond extract
3 cups sifted cake flour

3 teaspoons baking powder
pinch of salt
1 cup milk
6 egg whites

Soften shortening. Gradually add sugar and cream. Add flavorings. Sift flour, baking powder and salt and add alternately to sugar mixture with the milk, ending with the flour. Add egg whites one at a time and beat well. Place in 3 paper-lined and greased 9-inch cake pans and cook at 350°F for 25 minutes. Cool. Spread plenty of COCONUT ICING between layers; then ice entire cake. Serves 16-20.

COCONUT ICING

2 cups sugar
2 coconuts, peeled and grated
¾ cup liquid (½ water, ½ coconut milk)
1 Tablespoon light corn syrup

2 egg whites, stiffly beaten
6 large marshmallows
1 teaspoon almond extract
½ teaspoon salt

Cook sugar, liquid, and corn syrup over low heat stirring til sugar is dissolved. Cover 2 to 3 minutes. It is in the rolling boil stage when uncovered. Cook mixture til candy thermometer reads 238°F. Add marshmallows and beat. Fold in stiffly beaten egg whites and ½ grated coconut. Add flavoring. Ice between layers then insert toothpicks to hold layers while icing top. Sprinkle remaining coconut over icing and gently press in icing while hot. Cool. Wrap well and refrigerate.

Mrs. J. George Smith

Apple Dumpling Cake

2 cups flour
2 cups packed brown sugar
½ cup butter or margarine, softened
1 cup chopped nuts
1 to 2 teaspoons ground cinnamon
1 teaspoon baking soda

½ teaspoon salt
1 cup sour cream
1 teaspoon vanilla
1 egg, beaten
2 cups finely chopped, peeled apples
Whipping cream, whipped

Preheat oven to 350°F. In large bowl combine first 3 ingredients. Blend with mixer at low speed until crumbly (can use food processor). Stir in nuts. Press 2¾ cups crumb mixture into an ungreased 13 x 9-inch pan. To remaining mixture add cinnamon, soda, salt, sour cream, vanilla and egg. Blend well. Stir in apples. Spoon evenly over crumb layer. Bake 25-35 minutes or until toothpick inserted in center comes out clean. Cut into squares and serve with whipped cream. Can be served warm or cold. Serves 12-15.

Mrs. George A. Wilkinson

Delicate White Cake with Lemon Filling

WHITE CAKE:
½ cup shortening
1½ cups sugar
2¼ cups sifted cake flour
4 teaspoons baking powder
½ teaspoon salt
½ cup milk
½ cup water
1¼ teaspoons vanilla

5 egg whites, stiffly beaten

LEMON FILLING:
5 egg yolks
1 cup sugar
½ cup lemon juice
2 Tablespoons grated lemon rind

Confectioners' sugar

WHITE CAKE: Cream shortening; add sugar gradually and cream thoroughly. Sift flour, baking powder and salt together and add to sugar mixture alternately with the milk and water mixed. Add vanilla and fold in egg whites. Pour into 2 well-greased and floured 8-inch cake pans. Bake at 350°F for 30-35 minutes. Cool. Remove from pans. *LEMON FILLING:* Beat egg yolks and add remaining ingredients. Place mixture in top of double boiler and cook over hot water until thick. Let filling cool; then spread between cake layers. Dust cake with confectioners' sugar. Serves 15.

Mrs. Charles North

Boston Cream Pie

CAKE:
8 eggs, separated
2 cups sugar
2 teaspoons vinegar
2 cups cake flour

CUSTARD FILLING:
1 cup sugar

3½ Tablespoons flour
4 egg yolks
Pinch salt
3 cups milk, scalded
1 teaspoon vanilla
1 cup whipping cream, whipped
Confectioners' sugar

CAKE: Beat egg whites until dry. Add sugar slowly and beat until stiff. In separate bowl beat yolks until creamy; add vinegar. Fold yolks into egg whites. Fold in flour. Pour into 3 greased and floured 9-inch cake pans and bake at 350°F for 20 minutes or until done. *CUSTARD FILLING:* Beat sugar, flour, egg yolks and salt together for 5 minutes. Add milk a little at a time while continuing to beat. Place mixture in heavy saucepan and cook until thick. Cool; add vanilla and fold in whipped cream. Cut cakes in half horizontally and spread custard filling in the middle of each. Top with sifted confectioners' sugar. Freezes well. Yields 3 cakes, each serving 12.

Mrs. Joe Dehmer, Jr.

QUICK COCONUT ICING   Mix together 1 (8 ounce) carton sour cream, 2 cups sugar and 2 (6 ounce) packages frozen grated coconut. Let sit at room temperature about 30 minutes. Sprinkle an additional package coconut over top of frosted cake. Icing will frost a 3-layer (9 inch) cake.

Chocolate Cups

CUPCAKES:
1½ cups flour
1 cup sugar
¼ cup cocoa
1 teaspoon baking soda
½ teaspoon salt
½ cup oil
1 Tablespoon vinegar
1 teaspoon vanilla
1 cup warm water

FILLING:
1 (8 ounce) package cream cheese, softened
⅓ cup sugar
1 egg, beaten
1/8 teaspoon salt

Chocolate chips and nonpareil decors

CUPCAKES: Combine flour, sugar, cocoa, baking soda and salt in a large mixing bowl. Add remaining ingredients and mix well. *FILLING:* Beat together cream cheese, sugar, egg and salt until creamy. Pour cupcake batter into paper-lined muffin pans about ½ full. (Miniature muffin pans are best.) Place a small dollop of the filling mixture on each cupcake. Add a few chocolate chips to each and sprinkle with nonpareil decors. Bake at 350°F for 20-25 minutes. Serves 12.

Mrs. David Trigiani

Fresh Apple Cake

1 cup cooking oil
2 cups sugar
3 eggs, well beaten
2½ cups flour
2 teaspoons baking powder
1 teaspoon baking soda
1 teaspoon salt

1 teaspoon ground cinnamon
1 teaspoon ground nutmeg
1 teaspoon vanilla
4 cups chopped, peeled Delicious apples
1 cup ground pecans (optional)

Combine oil and sugar. Beat in eggs. Sift together dry ingredients and add to egg mixture. Fold in vanilla, apples and pecans. Bake in a 13 x 9-inch pan at 325°F for 55 minutes. Cool and ice cake with VANILLA CREAM CHEESE ICING. Cake will keep moist and fresh for days. Serves 12.

VANILLA CREAM CHEESE ICING

1 (1 pound) box confectioners' sugar
1 (8 ounce) package cream cheese

½ cup margarine
2 teaspoons vanilla
1 cup chopped pecans

Have all ingredients at room temperature. In a large bowl with mixer at low speed beat sugar, cream cheese and margarine until smooth. Add vanilla; then stir in pecans.

Mrs. Carolyn Powell

Apple Cake with Brown Sugar Icing

1 cup cooking oil
2 cups sugar
3 eggs, well beaten
1 Tablespoon vanilla
2½ cups flour

1 teaspoon baking soda
2 teaspoons baking powder
1 teaspoon salt
1 cup chopped pecans
3 cups chopped, peeled apples

Cream well the oil, sugar and eggs. Add vanilla. Sift dry ingredients together and blend into creamed mixture. Fold in pecans and apples. Pour into well-greased bundt pan and bake at 350°F for 55-60 minutes. Remove cake from pan and cool. Ice with BROWN SUGAR ICING. Serves 15.

BROWN SUGAR ICING

1 cup light brown sugar
½ cup butter

¼ cup evaporated milk
1 teaspoon vanilla

Bring the first 3 ingredients to a boil, stirring constantly. Remove from heat immediately and stir in vanilla. Beat with a spoon until the icing is cool. Pour over cake.

Mrs. Leland R. Speed

Orange-Glazed Carrot Cake

CAKE:
2 cups sugar
1¼ cups salad oil
2 cups sifted flour
2 teaspoons baking powder
2 teaspoons ground cinnamon
1 teaspoon baking soda
1 teaspoon salt
4 eggs
3 cups grated carrots

1 cup finely chopped pecans

ORANGE GLAZE:
1 cup sugar
¼ cup cornstarch
1 cup fresh orange juice
1 teaspoon lemon juice
2 Tablespoons butter
2 Tablespoons grated orange rind
¼ teaspoon salt

CAKE: In a bowl combine thoroughly the sugar and salad oil. Sift together the dry ingredients. Stir ½ the dry ingredients into the sugar mixture. Mix in the remaining dry ingredients alternately with the eggs, adding them one at a time and beating well after each addition. Stir in carrots and pecans. Pour mixture into a lightly oiled 10-inch tube pan. Bake at 350°F for 70 minutes or until cake tests done. Let the cake cool to the touch in an upright position. Remove from pan and let cool completely. *ORANGE GLAZE:* In a saucepan mix sugar and cornstarch. Gradually add juices. Stir mixture until smooth. Add butter, orange rind and salt. Cook mixture over low heat, stirring constantly, until glossy and somewhat thickened. Let cool completely. Split cake into 3 layers. Spread each layer with *ORANGE GLAZE*; then reassemble the cake. Cake is better the second day. Serves 16.

Mrs. Cassius L. Tillman, Sr., Natchez, Mississippi

Ree's Raisin Cake

1 cup raisins
2½ cups water
⅓ cup plus 1 Tablespoon Crisco
1 teaspoon baking soda
2 cups flour

1 cup sugar
1 teaspoon each ground cinnamon,
  ground allspice, ground cloves
½ teaspoon salt
½ cup chopped nuts

Cook raisins in water for 20 minutes. Drain off liquid, reserving 1 cup. To the warm liquid add Crisco and soda. Stir to dissolve. Sift dry ingredients together; add Crisco mixture, nuts and cooked raisins and blend well. Bake in greased and floured 8 x 8-inch cake pan at 375°F for 35-40 minutes. Use cake tester to check for doneness. Remove cake from pan when slightly cool. Cool completely and frost cake with CHOCOLATE BUTTER ICING or PENUCHE ICING. Serves 8.

CHOCOLATE BUTTER ICING

3 Tablespoons butter, melted
2 Tablespoons milk
Confectioners' sugar

2 Tablespoons cocoa
¼ teaspoon vanilla

Combine butter and milk. Beat in enough sugar to create a good spreading consistency (about ½ cup). Add cocoa and vanilla.

PENUCHE ICING

6 Tablespoons butter, melted
1 cup dark brown sugar
¼ cup milk

1½ teaspoons vanilla
Dash salt
Confectioners' sugar

Mix butter and sugar until sugar is dissolved. Add milk, vanilla, salt and confectioners' sugar until mixture is of spreading consistency.

Mrs. Howard Nichols

This is a very old recipe. It was commonly known as the "milkless, eggless and butterless" cake during the War years.

Chocolate Angel Goodie

1 angel food cake
7 (1.05 ounce) Hershey bars
  with almonds

1 (1 ounce) square unsweetened
  chocolate
1 cup whipping cream, whipped

Buy or prepare (see Index) angel food cake. Melt Hershey bars and chocolate together. Let chocolate cool and mix with whipped cream. Ice cake with mixture and refrigerate. Serves 16.

Mrs. Henry Barksdale

Lemon-Coconut Angel Food Cake

1 angel food cake
2 Tablespoons grated lemon
 rind
½ cup lemon juice
3 eggs, beaten
¾ cup butter or margarine,
 softened

1 cup sugar
3 cups whipping cream, whipped,
 divided
1½ cups grated coconut, divided
3 or 4 Tablespoons confectioners'
 sugar

Buy or prepare (see Index) angel food cake. In top of double boiler combine lemon rind, lemon juice, eggs, butter and sugar. Place over simmering water and cook, stirring constantly, about 10-12 minutes or until mixture coats metal spoon. Let cool completely. Fold in ⅓ of the whipped cream and 1 cup coconut. Chill. With a serrated knife cut cooled cake crosswise into 3 layers. Place first layer on cake plate and spread with ½ the lemon filling. Top with middle layer and spread with remaining filling. Place last layer on top and frost entire cake with remaining whipped cream sweetened with confectioners' sugar. Sprinkle all over with remaining coconut. Refrigerate overnight before serving. Makes 12 large servings.

Mrs. Arthur W. Doty

Blackberry Jam Cake

1 cup butter, softened
2 cups sugar
6 eggs
1 cup buttermilk
1 teaspoon baking soda

3 cups sifted flour
3 teaspoons each ground
 cinnamon, ground allspice,
 ground cloves
2 cups seedless blackberry jam

Cream butter and sugar. Beat in eggs one at a time; then add buttermilk in which soda has been dissolved. Stir in all dry ingredients and add jam. Bake in 3 greased and lightly floured 9-inch cake pans at 325°F for 25-30 minutes. Cool and remove from pans. Frost each layer and entire cake generously with CONFECTIONERS' SUGAR ICING. Freezes well. Serves 16-20.

CONFECTIONERS' SUGAR ICING

¾ cup butter, softened
6 cups confectioners' sugar
3 egg yolks

1½ teaspoons vanilla
6 Tablespoons whipping cream

Cream together butter and sugar. Beat in egg yolks, then vanilla and cream until icing is smooth.

Mrs. Gerrit Maris

One cup cake flour equals 1 cup all-purpose flour minus 2 Tablespoons.

Pumpkin Cake

4 eggs, beaten
2 cups sugar
1 cup cooking oil
2 cups self-rising flour
2 teaspoons baking soda

1 teaspoon baking powder
2 teaspoons ground cinnamon
½ teaspoon salt
1 cup canned pumpkin

Mix well the eggs, sugar and oil. Sift dry ingredients together and add. Beat 3 minutes on medium speed of electric mixer; add pumpkin. Bake in 3 greased and floured 9-inch cake pans at 300°F for 40-45 minutes. Cool and remove from pans. Frost cake with CREAM CHEESE ICING and refrigerate until icing is set. Will keep in refrigerator for at least 1 week. Freezes well. Serves 16.

CREAM CHEESE ICING

1 (8 ounce) package cream
  cheese, softened
½ cup margarine, softened
½ teaspoon vanilla

1 (1 pound) box confectioners'
  sugar
½ cup chopped nuts
Milk

Cream together cream cheese and margarine. Add vanilla, sugar and nuts, blending until smooth. Add milk to thin, if necessary.

Mrs. Donald L. Seago

Orange Kiss-Me-Cake

CAKE:
1 large orange
1 cup seedless raisins
½ cup pecans
2 cups flour
1 teaspoon baking soda
1 teaspoon salt
1 cup sugar
½ cup shortening

1 cup milk, divided
2 eggs

TOPPING:
1 teaspoon ground cinnamon
⅓ cup sugar
½ cup chopped pecans
⅓ cup reserved orange juice

CAKE: Juice the orange and reserve juice for TOPPING. Remove the seeds. Grind the orange, raisins and pecans with meat grinder. Set aside. Sift together flour, soda, salt and sugar. Add shortening and ¼ cup milk to dry ingredients. Beat for 2 minutes. Add eggs and remaining milk. Beat 2 minutes. Combine creamed and orange mixtures. Pour into a greased 9 x 13-inch pan. Bake at 350°F for 45 minutes. TOPPING: Mix cinnamon, sugar and pecans. While cake is still warm and in the pan, drip orange juice over top. Then sprinkle with cinnamon mixture. Broil slightly to melt topping. Serve as a dessert with sweetened whipped cream or hot for a breakfast coffee cake. Serves 12.

Mrs. Sherwood Wise

Pineapple-Butternut Cake

CAKE:
1½ cups sugar
¾ cup shortening
3 eggs
1 cup milk
2 teaspoons butternut
   flavoring
2¼ cups cake flour
1 teaspoon salt
3 teaspoons baking powder

FILLING:
1 (20 ounce) can crushed pineapple
3 Tablespoons cornstarch
½ cup margarine
1 cup sugar
1 Tablespoon butternut flavoring
1 cup flaked coconut
1 cup chopped pecans
½ cup maraschino cherries, cut
   in half

CAKE: Cream sugar and shortening. Add eggs one at a time and beat after each addition. Add milk and flavoring. Mix in dry ingredients. Beat on high speed for 2 minutes. Bake at 325 °F for 30 minutes in 2 greased and floured 9-inch cake pans. *FILLING:* Cook the first 5 ingredients until thick. Add coconut, pecans and cherries. Spread filling between layers; then ice entire cake. Serves 12.

Mrs. Ward T. McCraney, Jr.

Banana Nut Cake

¾ cup butter or margarine,
   softened
2 cups sugar
3 large eggs
4 medium bananas
1 teaspoon baking soda

½ cup nuts, finely chopped
3 cups flour
½ teaspoon salt
2 teaspoons baking powder
½ cup buttermilk

Cream butter and sugar well. Add eggs one at a time, beating thoroughly after each addition. Mash bananas and mix in the baking soda. Add to creamed mixture. Add nuts. Sift flour with salt and baking powder. Add to banana mixture, alternating with buttermilk. Beat until smooth. Grease 4 (8 inch) cake pans and pour batter into them. Bake at 350 °F for 30 minutes. Cool. Frost with BOILED ICING. May be prepared 1 day in advance. This is a very large, moist cake. Serves 20.

BOILED ICING

2 cups sugar
¼ cup light Karo

½ cup boiling water
4 egg whites, stiffly beaten

Mix sugar with Karo; add to the boiling water and stir over medium heat. When the sugar has completely dissolved, remove from heat and cool; then pour very slowly into stiffly beaten egg whites, beating constantly. Continue to beat until icing is stiff enough to spread.

Mrs. Don T. Caffery, Franklin, Louisiana

Pineapple Cake

1 (18½ ounce) box Duncan
Hines Butter Recipe Golden
cake mix
1 (11 ounce) can mandarin
oranges with juice
4 eggs

1½ cups cooking oil
1 (15½ ounce) can crushed
pineapple with juice
1 (3½ ounce) box vanilla instant
pudding mix
1 (13½ ounce) carton Cool Whip

Beat first 4 ingredients together until well blended. Bake in 3 foiled-lined, greased 9-inch cake pans at 350°F for 20-25 minutes. Cool thoroughly. Combine pineapple with juice and pudding mix. Fold into thawed Cool Whip. Spread between layers and ice top and sides of cake. Refrigerate overnight. Keeps for days in refrigerator. Serves 16-20.

Mrs. Richard McRae, Jr.

White Chocolate Cake

1 cup butter, softened
2 cups sugar
4 eggs, separated
1 teaspoon vanilla
¼ pound white chocolate or
almond bark, melted

2½ cups cake flour
1 teaspoon baking powder
1 cup buttermilk
1 cup chopped pecans
1 cup flaked coconut

Cream butter and sugar. Beat in egg yolks; add vanilla and melted chocolate. Sift together flour and baking powder; add to chocolate mixture alternately with buttermilk. Fold in stiffly beaten egg whites. Stir in pecans and coconut. Bake in 2 greased and floured 9-inch cake pans at 350°F for 45 minutes. Cool, remove from pans and ice with WHITE ICING or WHITE CHOCOLATE ICING. Serves 15.

WHITE ICING

2 cups sugar
1 cup butter, melted
1 teaspoon vanilla

1 (5.33 ounce) can evaporated
milk

Mix ingredients and let stand 1 hour. Stir occasionally. Cook to the soft ball stage (238°F). Beat until batter is of spreading consistency.

WHITE CHOCOLATE ICING

½ cup plus 2 Tablespoons
sugar
6 Tablespoons evaporated milk
¼ cup butter or margarine

2 cups white chocolate broken
into small pieces
1½ teaspoons vanilla
Slivered almonds, toasted

Combine ingredients, except almonds, in top of double boiler and stir over hot water until melted. Blend until smooth. Ice cake immediately. Garnish with almonds.

Mrs. Edna Mills

Janie's Chocolate Pound Cake

1 cup butter, softened
½ cup Crisco
3 cups sugar
5 eggs, beaten
3 cups cake flour

½ teaspoon baking powder
½ teaspoon salt
5 Tablespoons cocoa
1 cup milk
1 Tablespoon vanilla

Cream butter, Crisco and sugar until fluffy. Add eggs. Mix well. Sift dry ingredients. Add to butter mixture alternately with milk and vanilla. Grease and flour a 10-inch tube pan; then pour in batter. Bake at 300°F for 1½-2 hours. Cool 5 minutes before removing from pan. Freezes well. Serves 15.

Mrs. Stuart Robinson

My Own Chocolate Cake

CAKE:
1 (4 ounce) package plus
   2 squares German's sweet
   chocolate
1½ (1 ounce) squares
   unsweetened chocolate
½ cup boiling water
1 cup butter or margarine,
   softened
2¼ cups sugar
4 eggs, separated
2½ cups flour

½ teaspoon salt
1 teaspoon baking soda
¾ cup buttermilk
1 teaspoon vanilla

CHOCOLATE GLAZE:
1 (1 ounce) square unsweetened
   chocolate
1 teaspoon margarine
2 Tablespoons boiling water
1 cup confectioners' sugar

CAKE: Melt chocolates over hot water. Add the boiling water and blend well. Cream butter and sugar. Add melted chocolate and beaten egg yolks. Blend just until well mixed. Sift together flour, salt and soda. Add to chocolate mixture alternately with buttermilk and vanilla. Fold in stiffly beaten egg whites. Pour batter into 3 (9 inch) cake pans which have been foil-lined, greased and floured. Bake at 350°F for 25 minutes. Cool and remove cake from pans. Make DIVINITY ICING. Frost cake between layers with icing; then ice entire cake. *CHOCOLATE GLAZE:* Melt the chocolate and margarine over hot water. Add the boiling water and sugar and beat until smooth to make a thin glaze. Drizzle glaze over edge only of iced cake. Cake layers freeze well unfrosted. Serves 16.

DIVINITY ICING

3 egg whites
¾ cup sugar

⅓ cup light Karo
¼ teaspoon cream of tartar

Place all ingredients in top of a double boiler. Cook, beating constantly, over hot water for 7-10 minutes or until mixture is of spreading consistency.

Mrs. Stewart H. Bridgforth, Pickens, Mississippi

Fluffy Gingerbread

GINGERBREAD:
½ cup butter or shortening, softened
½ cup packed brown sugar
2 eggs, well beaten
2 cups sifted flour
1½ teaspoons baking soda
½ teaspoon salt
1 teaspoon ground cinnamon
½ teaspoon ground cloves
¾ cup molasses
1 cup boiling water

TOPPING:
½ cup brown sugar
¼ cup flour
2 teaspoons ground cinnamon
½ to 1 cup chopped nuts
¼ cup butter, softened

GINGERBREAD: Cream together the butter and brown sugar. Beat in the eggs; then blend in remaining ingredients. Bake in an 8 x 11-inch pan at 350°F for about 40 minutes. During the last 10 minutes of baking, spread *TOPPING* over the gingerbread. Make *TOPPING* by combining ingredients. Serve with whipped cream, if desired. Serves 8.

From LET'S COOK SOMETHING NICE, published by the
Women's Auxiliary, St. Andrew's Episcopal Church, 1949

Selma's Virginia Pound Cake

1 cup butter, softened
½ cup Crisco
3 cups sugar
5 eggs
3 cups cake flour
1 cup milk
1 teaspoon vanilla
1 teaspoon almond extract
½ teaspoon baking powder

Cream together butter and Crisco. Add sugar and continue to cream until perfectly smooth, about 10 minutes. Add eggs one at a time, beating until well blended. Add cake flour a little at a time. Slowly add milk, then flavorings. Add baking powder *last*. (This is a lighter and better blended mixture if electric mixer is used.) Grease and flour a large bundt pan (or line with foil and grease and flour a large tube pan or a small tube pan and a loaf pan). Pour cake batter into pans and place in a cold oven. Turn temperature to 325°F or 350°F and bake for 1 hour and 15 minutes. Do not jar cake or remove from oven too soon. Cool slightly and remove from pan. Can be served as a base for strawberry shortcake. Toasted pound cake slices spread with butter make an excellent breakfast treat. Freezes well. Serves 15.

Mrs. Patrick H. Scanlon

Variation: Substitute 1 teaspoon rum extract and 1 teaspoon coconut extract for the above extracts and add 1 (3½ ounce) can flaked coconut to the batter. Bake at 325°F for 1½ hours. Make a glaze by dissolving ½ cup sugar in ¼ cup water and boiling mixture for 3 minutes. Add 1 teaspoon almond extract and brush glaze over cooled cake with pastry brush.

Mrs. Clyde X. Copeland, Sr.

Blueberry Pound Cake

1 cup butter, softened
2 cups sugar
4 eggs
1 teaspoon vanilla
3 cups flour, divided

½ teaspoon salt
1 teaspoon baking powder
1 pint fresh blueberries or
  2 cups canned blueberries,
  drained and rinsed

Cream butter and sugar. Add eggs one at a time and beat until light and fluffy. Add vanilla. Sift 2 cups flour, salt and baking powder together. Add sifted ingredients to creamed mixture and beat. Dredge berries in remaining flour. Fold berry mixture gently into creamed mixture. Pour mixture into a tube pan which has been buttered and coated with sugar. Bake in preheated 325 °F oven for 1 hour and 15 minutes. Serves 15.

Mrs. G. G. Mazzaferro

Minnehaha Cake

CAKE:
4 eggs, separated
1 cup butter, softened
2 cups sugar
3 cups sifted flour
1 cup milk
3 teaspoons baking powder
Pinch salt
1½ teaspoons almond extract

FILLING:
1 cup raisins, puffed and chopped
1 cup grated coconut, divided
1 cup chopped pecans
½ teaspoon almond extract
1 recipe SEVEN MINUTE ICING

1 recipe SEVEN MINUTE ICING

CAKE: Beat egg whites until stiff. Set aside. Cream butter and sugar until fluffy; then beat in egg yolks. Add flour and milk alternately to creamed mixture. Add baking powder and salt with the last addition of flour. Fold in almond extract and egg whites. Bake at 350 °F for 35 minutes in 2 greased and floured 8 x 8-inch cake pans. Cool and remove from pans. *FILLING:* Puff raisins by steaming in a colander 2 hours. Reserve ½ cup coconut; mix all other filling ingredients with SEVEN MINUTE ICING. Use filling between layers and on top of cooled cake. Ice top and sides of cake with a second recipe of SEVEN MINUTE ICING and sprinkle reserved ½ cup coconut on top. Cake is better if prepared the day before. Serves 12.

SEVEN MINUTE ICING

2 egg whites
1½ cups sugar
5 Tablespoons water

¼ teaspoon cream of tartar
1½ teaspoons light corn syrup
1 teaspoon vanilla

Place ingredients except vanilla in top of double boiler and beat until thoroughly blended. Place over rapidly boiling water. Beat constantly with rotary beater for 7 minutes. Remove from heat and add vanilla. Continue beating until mixture reaches spreading consistency.

Mrs. August J. Stone, Jr.

Apricot-Glazed Pound Cake

3 cups sugar
1 cup margarine, softened
6 eggs, separated
3 cups cake flour

1 cup whipping cream
2 teaspoons vanilla
1 teaspoon almond extract

Cream sugar and margarine. Add egg yolks slowly, beating well. Add egg whites and cream well. Add flour and cream alternately. Add flavorings. Bake in lightly greased tube pan at 325°F for about 1 hour 15 minutes. Remove from oven and let sit for 10 minutes. Remove from pan and spread APRICOT GLAZE over warm cake. Serves 15.

APRICOT GLAZE

½ cup apricot nectar
2 cups confectioners' sugar

1 Tablespoon butter

Heat nectar. Add sugar and stir until dissolved. Add butter; stir until melted.

Mrs. C. L. Buford, Edwards, Mississippi

Italian Cream Cake

5 extra large eggs, separated
2 cups sugar, divided
½ cup butter
½ cup margarine
½ teaspoon salt
1½ teaspoons vanilla

1 teaspoon baking soda
1 cup buttermilk
2 cups flour
1 cup finely chopped pecans
1 (3½ ounce) can flaked coconut

Have all ingredients at room temperature. Beat egg whites until they form soft peaks. Slowly add ½ cup sugar and beat until consistency of meringue. Set aside. Cream butter, margarine, remaining sugar, salt and vanilla, adding egg yolks one at a time until consistency of whipped cream. Stir baking soda into buttermilk. Add this mixture alternately with flour to butter mixture, beginning and ending with the flour. Fold in egg white mixture, then pecans and coconut. Pour batter into 3 (9 inch) cake pans, the bottoms of which have been greased and floured. Bake at 325°F for approximately 40 minutes. Cool and remove from pans. Frost layers and sides of cooled cake with ITALIAN CREAM FROSTING. Cake should be refrigerated if not eaten the day it is made. Serves 16-20.

ITALIAN CREAM FROSTING

¾ cup butter
12 ounces cream cheese
1½ teaspoons vanilla

1½ (1 pound) boxes powdered
 sugar

Have ingredients at room temperature. Beat ingredients together to the consistency of whipped cream.

Mrs. James L. Young, Madison, Mississippi

Brown Sugar Pound Cake

1½ cups Crisco
1 pound brown sugar
½ cup sugar
5 eggs, separated
3 cups flour

½ teaspoon baking powder
½ teaspoon salt
1 cup milk
1 cup chopped pecans
1 teaspoon vanilla

Cream Crisco. Add sugars and beat well. Beat in egg yolks one at a time. Sift flour with baking powder and salt. Add flour mixture alternately with milk. Add pecans and vanilla. Fold in stiffly beaten egg whites. Bake in greased and floured tube pan for 1½ hours in preheated 325°F oven. Serves 15.

Mrs. Donald Parsons

French Chocolate Torte

5½ ounces semisweet chocolate
1½ cups pecans, pulverized
2 Tablespoons flour

¾ cup butter, softened
¾ cup sugar
6 eggs, separated

Melt chocolate in top of double boiler set over hot water. Let chocolate cool to room temperature. Stir together pulverized pecans and flour. With electric mixer cream together butter and sugar until mixture is light and fluffy. Add 6 egg yolks, one at a time, beating well after each addition. Stir in the melted chocolate and the pecan mixture. Beat egg whites to stiff peaks and fold them gently but thoroughly into egg yolk mixture. Pour batter into a 10-inch cake pan which is 2 inches deep. (To remove cake easily, cover bottom of pan with foil; then grease and flour it.) Bake in a preheated oven at 350°F for 30 minutes or until cake tests done. Let cake cool. Turn cake out of pan and frost it thickly with CHOCOLATE WHIPPED CREAM FROSTING. Chill the cake for at least 2 hours before serving. Serves 12.

CHOCOLATE WHIPPED CREAM FROSTING

¼ cup hot water
1 Tablespoon instant espresso
  coffee
¼ cup sugar

3½ ounces semisweet chocolate,
  grated
2 egg yolks
1 cup whipping cream

In a saucepan combine water and coffee. Add sugar and chocolate and cook mixture over moderate heat, stirring, until the chocolate is melted and sugar is dissolved. Let mixture cool, stirring occasionally, for 5 minutes. Add egg yolks, one at a time, beating well after each addition. Let mixture cool to room temperature. Whip cream until stiff and fold into the chocolate mixture. Chill frosting for 20 minutes or until it is of spreading consistency. Makes 1½ cups frosting.

Mrs. Richard L. Redmont, Jr.

This torte may be made in a 9 x 13-inch cake pan and cut into small squares to be used as pick-up desserts. Adjust baking time to 20 minutes.

Fudge Cake

CAKE:
1 cup butter
4 (1 ounce) squares unsweetened
   chocolate
4 eggs, beaten
2 cups sugar
2 Tablespoons milk
¼ teaspoon salt

1 cup sifted flour
1 cup broken nuts

ICING:
1 Tablespoon butter, melted
2 Tablespoons cocoa
1 cup powdered sugar
1 egg white

CAKE: Melt butter and chocolate together. Cool slightly. Combine eggs, sugar, milk and salt; add flour and nuts. Mix well. Add chocolate and butter mixture. Bake in well-greased 10½ x 15½-inch pan at 350°F for 24 minutes. Cake should be extremely moist. ICING: Beat together all ingredients. Ice cake immediately while hot. Serve plain or topped with ice cream. Serves 16-20.

Mrs. Howard Nichols

Shortcake

1 cup flour
½ cup sugar
½ teaspoon salt
2 teaspoons baking powder
1 Tablespoon shortening

1 Tablespoon butter
½ cup milk
Fresh strawberries
Vanilla ice cream

Sift dry ingredients together and cut in shortening and butter. Add milk, mixing in well with a spoon. Pour mixture into an 8-inch pie plate. Dot with additional butter and sprinkle with additional sugar. Bake at 400°F for 20 minutes. Serve warm topped with strawberries and vanilla ice cream. Serves 6.

Mrs. Benjamin F. Bracy

Pies

No-Roll Pastry Shell

1½ cups sifted flour
1½ teaspoons sugar
1 teaspoon salt

½ cup Wesson oil
2 Tablespoons cold milk

Sift dry ingredients into a 9-inch pie pan. Combine oil and milk and beat with a fork. Pour over flour mixture. Mix with fork until flour is dampened. With fingers press pastry evenly and firmly against bottom and sides of pan. Partly cover rim and flute edge, pinching lightly with fingers. Prick entire surface with fork. Bake at 425°F for 12-15 minutes or until brown. Yields 1 (9 inch) crust.

Mrs. Cecil F. Heidelberg, III

Pie Crusts

BASIC PIE CRUST

2 cups flour
1 teaspoon salt

⅔ cup shortening
¼ cup cold water

Sift flour and salt into a bowl. Cut shortening into flour until mixture is the consistency of coarse meal. Add water, mixing until dough forms a ball. Roll between 2 sheets of wax paper or on lightly floured pastry cloth or board. For baked shell, prick with a fork and cook 10-12 minutes at 450°F. Yields 2 (9 inch) crusts.

FLAKY PASTRY

5 cups flour
1 Tablespoon brown sugar
¼ teaspoon baking powder
1½ teaspoons salt

2 cups shortening
1 Tablespoon vinegar
1 egg, beaten
Water

Sift dry ingredients together. Cut shortening into dry ingredients until mixture is the consistency of coarse meal. Combine vinegar and egg and add enough water to make 1 cup liquid. Add liquid to dry ingredients and mix until dough forms a ball. Divide dough and pat out with hands into desired shape on floured pastry cloth or board or on floured sheet of wax paper. Smooth with rolling pin. For baked shell, prick with a fork and cook at 450°F for 12-15 minutes. Keeps several months in freezer tightly wrapped. Yields 5 or 6 (9 inch) crusts.

COOKIE CRUMB CRUST

1½ cups graham cracker,
    chocolate wafer, ginger
    snap or zwieback crumbs
¼ cup powdered sugar

Melted butter (6 Tablespoons with
    graham cracker crumbs;
    ¼ cup with other cookie
    crumbs)

Cookies may be crushed with rolling pin, in blender or in food processor. Mix sugar and melted butter with cookie crumbs. Press mixture on sides and bottom of 9-inch pie pan. Bake at 350°F for 10-15 minutes. Cookie selection depends on choice of filling. Chopped nuts or ½ teaspoon ground cinnamon may be added to crust mixture before baking. Yields 1 (9 inch) crust.

SESAME SEED PASTRY

½ cup boiling water
1 cup shortening
3 cups flour

2 teaspoons salt
1 teaspoon baking powder
¼ cup sesame seeds

Pour boiling water over shortening and stir until shortening melts and mixture is cold and creamy. Sift flour with salt and baking powder. Stir flour mixture into shortening. Add seeds. Form a ball, cover and chill. Roll 1/8 inch thick on lightly floured board. For baked shell, prick with fork and cook at 450°F for 15 minutes. Yields 4 (9 inch) crusts or 12 tart shells.

Peach Cobbler

PASTRY:
1 cup flour
¼ teaspoon salt
½ cup shortening
3 Tablespoons ice water

FILLING:
½ cup butter

9 ripe peaches, peeled and sliced
1½ cups water
1½ cups sugar
2 Tablespoons flour
Dash ground cinnamon or nutmeg
Pinch salt

PASTRY: Combine first 3 ingredients with pastry blender; add ice water. Form dough. Wrap in wax paper and chill. Roll out pastry and cut into strips. Reserve enough strips to lattice top of cobbler. Place remaining strips on cookie sheet and bake at 450°F for 10 minutes or until crisp. FILLING: Mix first 3 ingredients in saucepan and let come to a boil. Reserve a little sugar for top of cobbler; then blend sugar, flour, cinnamon or nutmeg and salt and stir into boiling mixture until dissolved. Grease an 8½ x 9½-inch baking dish. Place ½ the peach mixture in dish; then top with cooked pastry strips. Add remaining peach mixture and lace uncooked pastry strips over top. Sprinkle with reserved sugar. Bake at 375°F for 35-40 minutes. Delicious served warm with cream. Serves 8.

Mrs. Chick Warner, Vicksburg, Mississippi

Concord Grape Pie

Pastry for 2-crust (9 inch) pie
Concord grapes
⅔ cup sugar

1 Tablespoon cornstarch
1 egg, lightly beaten

Prepare 1 (9 inch) unbaked pie shell. Separate hulls and pulp of Concord grapes until there are 1½ cups packed hulls. Be careful to catch the juice. Simmer the pulp for about 15 minutes; push it through a colander to remove seeds. Mix sugar and cornstarch. Add egg, pulp and hulls. Cook on low heat, stirring frequently, until thickened. Pour filling into pie shell. Roll out the remaining pastry and cut into strips. Cover pie with strips in lattice form and bake at 425°F for 10 minutes; reduce heat to 325°F and cook until center begins to bubble. Serves 8.

Mrs. Henry Toler

Since Concord grapes are so seldom available, the grapes may be prepared, the pulp simmered with ½ the sugar, the seeds removed, and the pulp and hulls frozen for use later. When thawed, add the other half of the sugar.

The amount of cornstarch needed depends on the amount of juice. If the mixture is not thick enough, dissolve additional cornstarch in a little water and add to filling mixture; add a bit of water if filling is too thick.

Pecan Pie

1 (9 inch) pie shell, partially
   baked
½ cup butter
1¼ cups sugar

½ cup light corn syrup
3 eggs, slightly beaten
1 teaspoon vanilla
1½ cups pecans

Prepare partially baked pie shell. (Bake for 3 or 4 minutes.) Cook next 3 ingredients over low heat until butter melts. Do not let mixture boil. Cool slightly. Stir in eggs and mix well. Add vanilla and pecans. Pour filling into pie crust. Bake at 375°F for 40-45 minutes. Pie should still be soft in the center when removed from oven. Serves 6-8.

Mrs. Michael E. Jabaley

Pecan Cream Pie

1 (9 inch) pie shell, baked
1¾ cups sugar, divided
1 cup whipping cream

4 eggs, separated
1 cup pecans, toasted (coarsely
   chopped, if desired)

Prepare baked pie shell. Cook 1 cup sugar and cream in a heavy saucepan for 12 minutes, stirring occasionally. Beat egg yolks. Stir a little of the hot mixture into yolks; then return yolks to pan and continue cooking and stirring another 2 minutes. Remove from heat. Add pecans and pour into pie shell. Make meringue by beating egg whites until stiff. Add remaining sugar gradually, beating until glossy. Cover pie with meringue and bake at 325°F for about 20 minutes. Cool before slicing. This pie is best made and eaten the same day. Serves 8.

Mrs. G. B. Shaw

Harvest Apple Pie

Pastry for 2-crust (9 inch) pie
6 medium apples, peeled,
   cored and sliced
1 Tablespoon cornstarch
½ teaspoon salt
3 Tablespoons butter, melted
1 teaspoon ground cinnamon

3 Tablespoons sugar
⅓ cup light corn syrup
½ cup light brown sugar
3 Tablespoons light corn syrup
¼ cup chopped nuts
2 Tablespoons flour
2 Tablespoons butter, softened

Fill pastry-lined 9-inch pie pan with apples. Combine next 6 ingredients and pour over apples. Cover with top crust and bake at 425°F for 30-45 minutes. Combine remaining ingredients and spread over crust. Return to oven for 10 minutes or until topping is bubbly. Serves 8.

Mrs. Richard L. Redmont, Jr.

Lemon Rub Pie

1 (9 inch) pie shell, unbaked
½ cup butter, softened
2 cups sugar
5 eggs

Juice and grated rind of
3 lemons
3 Tablespoons flour

Prepare unbaked pie shell. Cream together butter and sugar until well blended. Add eggs and beat well. Add lemon juice, rind and flour, mixing well. Pour filling into pie shell and bake at 300°F for 30-45 minutes or until top browns and pie is set. Serves 8.

Mrs. James R. Galyean, III

Chocolate Chess Pie

1 (9 inch) pie shell, unbaked
1½ cups sugar
3 Tablespoons cocoa
¼ cup margarine, melted
2 eggs, slightly beaten
1/8 teaspoon salt

1 (5.33 ounce) can evaporated
milk
1 teaspoon vanilla
½ to ¾ cup chopped pecans
(optional)

Prepare unbaked pie shell. Mix sugar, cocoa and margarine. Stir well. Add eggs and beat with electric mixer for 2½ minutes. Add salt, milk and vanilla. Stir in pecans, if desired. Pour filling into pie shell. Bake at 350°F for 35-45 minutes. Serves 6-8.

Mrs. E. E. Laird, Jr.

Cheese Pie

1 (9 inch) graham cracker crust
4 (3 ounce) packages cream
cheese, softened
2 eggs
¾ cup sugar

2 teaspoons vanilla or
½ teaspoon almond extract
1 cup sour cream
3½ Tablespoons sugar
1 teaspoon vanilla

Prepare pie crust. Combine cream cheese, eggs, ¾ cup sugar and 2 teaspoons vanilla or almond extract and beat until light and fluffy. Pour filling into pie crust and bake at 325°F for 28 minutes. Remove from oven; cool. Mix sour cream, 3½ Tablespoons sugar and 1 teaspoon vanilla and spread on top of pie. Bake at 325°F for 10 minutes. Cool; refrigerate for several hours before serving. Serves 6.

Mrs. Kye Bethany

This pie is as rich as cheese cake but creamier.

Becky's Custard Pie

1 (10 inch) pie shell, unbaked
2 eggs
6 egg yolks
1 cup plus 2 Tablespoons sugar
1 Tablespoon flour

¼ cup butter, softened
¼ teaspoon salt
2 cups milk
2 teaspoons vanilla

Prepare unbaked pie shell. Beat eggs and yolks with mixer. Add sugar and flour and mix well. Beat in butter and salt. Mix in milk and vanilla. Pour mixture into pie shell and cook at 350°F for about 35 minutes or until center of pie is firm. Serves 8.

Mrs. Gus Primos

Old Fashioned Coconut Pie

1 (9½ inch) pie shell, unbaked
1½ cups sugar
2 eggs
½ teaspoon salt
½ cup margarine, softened

¼ cup flour
½ cup milk
1½ cups grated fresh coconut,
   divided

Prepare unbaked pie shell. Beat together sugar, eggs and salt until lemon-colored. Add margarine and flour and blend well. Beat in milk; fold in 1 cup coconut. Pour filling into pie shell. Top with remaining coconut and bake in 325°F oven for 1 hour. Serves 8.

Mrs. J. L. Knight, Louisville, Mississippi

Chess Pie

1 (9 inch) pie shell, unbaked
½ cup butter or margarine,
   melted
1½ cups sugar

3 eggs
1 teaspoon vanilla
Pinch salt
¾ Tablespoon vinegar

Prepare unbaked pie shell. Mix butter and sugar and simmer slowly, stirring, for 5 minutes. Remove from heat and let cool slightly, stirring constantly. Add eggs, one at a time, beating well. Add vanilla, salt and vinegar; mix well. Pour filling into pie shell and bake at 400°F for 15 minutes; reduce heat to 350°F and bake for 20-30 minutes. Shake pie gently. It is done when center quivers slightly. Do not try to double recipe. Pie keeps well in the refrigerator overnight. Can freeze and reheat. Pie may be cut in slivers for finger desserts. Serves 6-8.

Mrs. Raymond S. Martin, Jr.

This is an old-fashioned recipe from my mother's home, Mayfair Farm, Kentucky.

Sour Cream Pie

Pastry for 2-crust (8 inch) pie
1 cup sugar
1 cup sour cream

1 cup raisins, dusted with
1 Tablespoon flour
1 teaspoon vanilla

Prepare but do not bake 1 (8 inch) pie shell. Combine remaining ingredients. Pour filling into pie shell and cover with top crust. Bake at 350°F for 30 minutes or until done. Serves 6.

Mrs. Ralph G. Sharp

This recipe was found by an ancestor in the old Revolutionary village of Stillwater, New York, where the Battle of Saratoga was fought.

Sweet Potato Custard Pie

1 (10 inch) pie shell, unbaked
1 small sweet potato
½ cup margarine
1½ cups sugar
1 Tablespoon sifted flour

1 teaspoon vanilla
1 teaspoon lemon extract
3 eggs
1 (5.33 ounce) can evaporated
milk

Prepare unbaked pie shell. Peel and boil potato. Drain and mash with margarine. Beat in sugar, flour, vanilla and lemon extract. Add eggs, one at a time, beating well after each. Add milk; beat well. Pour filling into pie shell and bake at 350°F for 45 minutes or until done. Serves 8.

Mrs. Lloyd Brannon, Laurel, Mississippi

Chocolate Pie with Meringue

1 (9 inch) pie shell, baked
¼ cup cocoa
1½ cups sugar, divided
¼ teaspoon salt
2 Tablespoons flour

1 cup milk
4 eggs, separated
¼ cup butter
1 teaspoon vanilla

Prepare baked pie shell. Mix cocoa, 1 cup sugar, salt and flour. Add milk. Cook in a heavy pan over low heat until almost boiling, stirring constantly. Remove from heat. Add a spoonful of hot mixture to the beaten egg yolks, stirring. Repeat 8 times; return egg mixture to the chocolate mixture. Cook until very thick in top of double boiler or in heavy pan on low heat that never lets mixture boil. Add butter and stir. Add vanilla. Pour filling into pie shell. Make meringue by beating egg whites until stiff. Add ½ cup sugar and beat until glossy. Spread on top of pie. Bake at 350°F until meringue is lightly browned. Cool and serve. Serves 8.

Mrs. Herbert A. Kroeze, Jr.

Frozen Lime Pie

CRUST:
1⅔ cups crushed chocolate-
    covered graham crackers,
    divided
⅓ cup butter or margarine,
    melted

FILLING:
2 eggs, separated
1 (14 ounce) can condensed milk
1 Tablespoon grated lime rind
⅔ cup fresh lime juice
4 drops green food coloring
¼ cup sugar

CRUST: Crush graham crackers between 2 pieces of wax paper; combine 1⅓ cups crumbs with butter or margarine and press mixture evenly on bottom and sides of a 9-inch pie plate. Reserve remaining ⅓ cup crumbs. FILLING: Beat egg yolks until thick; combine with condensed milk. Mix together lime rind, juice and food coloring. Combine juice with milk mixture and mix well. Beat egg whites until stiff. Continue to beat, adding sugar gradually, until very stiff. Fold egg whites into lime mixture. Pour filling into prepared pie shell. Sprinkle with reserved cracker crumbs. Freeze for at least 6 hours before serving. Serves 8.

Mrs. H. Henry Hederman

Orange Chiffon Pie

1 envelope unflavored gelatin
¾ cup sugar, divided
1/8 teaspoon salt
2 eggs, separated
½ cup cold water

1 (6 ounce) can frozen orange
    juice concentrate
1 cup whipping cream, whipped
8 lady fingers
Orange sections

Mix gelatin, ½ cup sugar and salt in medium saucepan. Beat together egg yolks and water; stir into gelatin mixture. Place over low heat; stir constantly until gelatin dissolves and mixture thickens slightly, about 5 minutes. Remove pan from heat. Add frozen orange juice concentrate and stir until melted. Mixture should mound slightly when dropped from spoon (if not, chill a few minutes). Beat egg whites until stiff, but not dry. Gradually add remaining sugar to egg whites and beat until very stiff. Fold into gelatin mixture. Fold in whipped cream. Split lady fingers. Cut ends off enough lady fingers to line sides of a 9-inch pie plate. (They should extend above the rim of pie plate to hold the filling.) Line bottom of pie plate with remaining lady fingers and ends. Pile orange chiffon mixture into pie shell. Chill until firm. Do not freeze. Garnish with additional whipped cream and orange sections. Serves 6.

Mrs. John A. Jenkins, Jr.

Variation: Spoon chiffon mixture into individual dessert dishes. Serve immediately or chill until firm. Garnish with whipped cream and orange sections.

Pink Squirrel Pie

24 almond macaroons, crushed
3 Tablespoons butter, melted
24 marshmallows
¾ cup milk
Red food coloring

1½ ounces crème de noyaux
   liqueur
1½ ounces white crème
   de menthe
2 cups whipping cream, whipped

Combine macaroons and butter. Press into a 9-inch pie plate and bake at 350°F for about 5 minutes. In the top of a double boiler set over boiling water melt marshmallows in milk. Cool. Add food coloring and liqueurs. Fold whipped cream into marshmallow mixture. Pour filling into prepared pie shell. Chill or freeze. Garnish with additional whipped cream, if desired. Serves 6-8.

Mrs. Wilbur H. Knight

English-Toffee Glacé Pie

PASTRY SHELL:
½ (11 ounce) package pie crust
   mix
1 (1 ounce) square unsweetened
   chocolate, grated
¼ cup packed brown sugar
¾ cup chopped walnuts
2 Tablespoons water
1 teaspoon vanilla

FILLING:
1 quart chocolate or chocolate
   fudge ice cream

1 quart English-Toffee,
   Jamoca-almond-fudge or
   coffee ice cream

COFFEE WHIPPED CREAM:
1 cup whipping cream
2 teaspoons instant coffee
2 Tablespoons confectioners'
   sugar

Chocolate curls

PASTRY SHELL: Preheat oven to 375°F. In medium bowl mix well with a fork the pie crust mix, chocolate, sugar and walnuts. Add water and vanilla. Blend well. With moistened hands press mixture firmly on bottom and sides of well-buttered 9-inch pie plate. Bake 20 minutes. Cool. Freeze at least 1 hour before filling. FILLING: Let ice cream stand in refrigerator to soften slightly. Quickly fill bottom of pie shell with chocolate ice cream. Then top with English-Toffee ice cream, spreading evenly. Do not let ice cream melt. Freeze at least 2 hours. COFFEE WHIPPED CREAM: With rotary beater whip cream with coffee and sugar until just stiff. Cover top of pie with mixture, making swirls, or press it through a pastry bag with a #6 rosette tip. Decorate with chocolate curls. Store pie in freezer until serving time. To serve, let pie stand at room temperature 15 minutes for easier cutting. Makes 8-10 servings.

Mrs. Noel C. Womack, Jr.

Macadamia Nut Pie

1 (9 inch) pie shell, unbaked
3 large or 4 small eggs
⅔ cup minus 1 Tablespoon
    sugar
1 cup light corn syrup

2 Tablespoons butter, melted
1½ cups chopped macadamia
    nuts
1 teaspoon vanilla
Whipped cream (optional)

Prepare unbaked pie shell. Beat eggs with sugar. Add corn syrup and next 3 ingredients. Blend well. Pour into pie shell and bake on bottom rack of oven at 325°F for about 50 minutes. Serve with whipped cream, if desired. May be prepared a day ahead. Freezes well after cooking. Serves 6-8.

Mrs. Gibbs J. Fowler

Trilby's Rum Pie

5 (8 inch) thin graham cracker
    crumb crusts (use 4 recipes
    basic Cookie Crumb Crust,
    see Index)
12 egg yolks
1 cup sugar

2½ envelopes unflavored
    gelatin, softened in
    ½ cup water
½ cup rum
4 cups whipping cream
1 (1 ounce) square semisweet
    chocolate, grated

Prepare pie crusts. Cream together egg yolks and sugar. Place gelatin container in pan of hot water and stir until gelatin is dissolved. Add rum to gelatin. Combine gelatin and egg mixtures. Whip cream and fold into egg mixture. Pour filling into crusts. Garnish tops of pies with chocolate. Freeze. Serve frozen. Serves 30.

Mrs. Myron Lockey

Mile-High Raspberry Pie

1 (9½ inch) pie shell, unbaked
½ cup slivered almonds
1 (10 ounce) package frozen
    raspberries, thawed
3 egg whites

1 Tablespoon lemon juice
1 cup sugar
1 teaspoon almond extract
1 cup whipping cream, whipped

Prepare unbaked pie shell and press almonds into it. Bake until golden brown at 450°F, about 10-12 minutes. Mix raspberries, egg whites, lemon juice, sugar and almond extract and beat until very stiff. Fold in whipped cream. Spoon into pie shell and freeze at least 5 hours. Remove from freezer 15 minutes before serving. Serves 10-12.

Mrs. William H. Deterly, Jr.

Sugar Cream Pie

1 (10 inch) pie shell, baked
1 cup sugar, divided
2½ cups half and half cream
1 drop yellow food coloring
Dash salt

4 Tablespoons cornstarch
1 teaspoon vanilla
½ cup butter or margarine
Ground nutmeg

Prepare baked pie shell. Mix ¾ cup sugar, cream, food coloring and salt in saucepan. Cook to boiling point. Mix remaining sugar and cornstarch in another pan. Add boiling mixture gradually to pan mixture. Add vanilla. Add butter and return to heat; cook until thick. Pour into pie shell and sprinkle with nutmeg and a few extra pieces of butter. Bake at 325 °F for 20 minutes or until firm and lightly brown. Serves 6-8.

Mrs. James L. Martin

Holiday Eggnog Pie

CRUMB CRUST:
1½ cups graham cracker
 crumbs
¼ cup sugar
¼ cup chopped almonds
1 teaspoon ground cinnamon
¼ cup butter, melted

FILLING:
1 envelope unflavored gelatin
¼ cup cold water
⅓ cup sugar
2 Tablespoons cornstarch
1/8 teaspoon salt

2 cups canned eggnog
1½ (1 ounce) squares
 unsweetened chocolate,
 melted
1 teaspoon vanilla
2 Tablespoons rum
1 cup whipping cream, whipped

TOPPING:
¼ cup confectioners' sugar
1 to 4 Tablespoons rum
1 cup whipping cream, whipped

Chocolate curls (optional)

CRUMB CRUST: Combine crust ingredients in a small bowl. Press the mixture on bottom and sides of a buttered 10-inch pie pan. *FILLING:* Sprinkle gelatin over water to soften. Mix sugar, cornstarch and salt in top of a double boiler. Gradually stir in eggnog. Cook over hot, not boiling, water, stirring constantly until thickened. Remove from heat and stir in softened gelatin until dissolved. Divide filling in half. Add melted chocolate and vanilla to one half. Set aside. Allow remaining half to cool; then fold in rum and whipped cream. Pour the rum-flavored mixture into the pie shell. Let set in refrigerator. Pour chocolate mixture on top. Chill at least 6 hours or overnight. Several hours before serving make *TOPPING* by folding sugar and rum into whipped cream. Pipe onto top of pie with a pastry tube or swirl on top. Sprinkle with chocolate curls, if desired. Chill before serving. Serves 6-8.

Mrs. William H. Wallace

Impossible Pie

In blender place 1 cup sugar, 4 eggs, 2 cups milk, ½ cup melted margarine, ½ cup flour, 1 teaspoon vanilla and 1 cup flaked coconut. Blend for 1 minute. If blender will not contain all the mixture, add as much milk as it will hold, blend ingredients and stir in remaining milk. Pour mixture into a 10-inch pie pan. Bake 1 hour at 350°F or until set. The pie makes its own crust as it bakes. Serves 8.

Mrs. Thomas A. Rhoden

Sibyl's Buttermilk Pie

1 (9 inch) pie shell, unbaked
½ cup butter, softened
2 cups sugar
3 Tablespoons flour

3 eggs, beaten
1 cup buttermilk
1 teaspoon vanilla
Dash ground nutmeg

Prepare unbaked pie shell. Cream butter and sugar together with mixer. Add flour and eggs and beat well. Stir in buttermilk, vanilla and nutmeg. Pour filling into pie shell. Bake on lower rack of oven at 350°F for 45-50 minutes. Place on wire rack and let cool completely before serving. Serves 6-8.

Mrs. Isaac Coe

Pumpkin Pie with Praline Topping

1 (9 inch) pie shell, unbaked
   and chilled
½ cup sugar
1 Tablespoon flour
½ teaspoon salt
1 teaspoon ground ginger
1 teaspoon ground cinnamon
¼ teaspoon ground nutmeg
1/8 teaspoon ground cloves
¼ cup margarine, softened

1½ cups canned pumpkin
½ cup unsulphured molasses
3 eggs
1 cup evaporated milk

TOPPING:
2 Tablespoons margarine
¼ cup packed brown sugar
½ cup chopped pecans

½ pint whipping cream, whipped

Prepare unbaked pie shell. Mix sugar, flour and spices. Blend in margarine, pumpkin and molasses. Beat in eggs, one at a time. Stir in milk. Pour into pie shell. Bake in 350°F oven 1 hour or until tip of knife inserted in center comes out clean. Cool. *TOPPING:* Stir margarine and sugar in small skillet over medium heat until bubbly. Add pecans and cook 2 minutes, stirring constantly. Remove from heat and pour onto foil. Cool. Crumble into small pieces. Spoon whipped cream over cooled pie. Sprinkle *TOPPING* over whipped cream. Serve cold. Serves 6-8.

Mrs. G. G. Mazzaferro

Chocolate Ice Box Pie

1 (9 inch) pie shell, baked
1 (14 ounce) can condensed
   milk
2 (1 ounce) squares
   unsweetened chocolate

¼ teaspoon salt
½ cup water
½ teaspoon vanilla
1 cup whipping cream, whipped

Prepare baked pie shell. Cook first 3 ingredients in top of double boiler over hot water until thick. Add water slowly and let thicken again. Stir in vanilla. Pour in pie shell; refrigerate. Serve cold with whipped cream on top. Serves 6-8.

Mrs. Wilfred Cole

An adaptation of Toddle House chocolate pie. Remember how good it was?

Special Lemon Pie

5 (9 inch) or 4 (10 inch) pie
   shells, unbaked
1 cup butter, softened
6 cups sugar

1 dozen eggs, separated
1½ cups milk
4 Tablespoons flour
Juice of 8 or 9 lemons

Prepare unbaked pie shells. Cream together well the butter and sugar. Set aside. Beat egg yolks; add milk and mix well. Add flour. Gradually add this mixture to creamed butter and sugar. Beat egg whites until stiff peaks form. Fold egg whites into butter mixture and add lemon juice. Pour filling into pie shells. Cook at 325 °F for 40-45 minutes. This recipe may be halved to make 2 (10 inch) pies. Serves 40.

Mrs. Thurman B. Oliver, Grenada, Mississippi

Tilghman's French Apricot Tarts

1 recipe Sesame Seed Pastry
   (see Index)
1 (12 ounce) jar apricot
   preserves
36 canned apricot halves

¼ cup red raspberry preserves
1 Tablespoon apricot juice
Sweetened whipped cream,
   flavored with vanilla

Prepare 12 baked (5 inch) tart shells from Sesame Seed Pastry. Spread a thin coating of apricot preserves on bottom of each tart shell. Drain apricot halves well and place 3 halves in each shell. Combine raspberry preserves and apricot juice and melt over low heat. Glaze top of apricots with preserves mixture. Refrigerate to set glaze. With pastry tube make rosette ring of whipped cream around edge of fruit or spoon it around tart. Serves 12.

Mrs. Lewis Prosser, Shreveport, Louisiana

Ice Creams

Christmas Eggnog Ice Cream

4 cups milk
8 eggs, beaten
2¼ cups sugar
½ teaspoon salt
4 cups whipping cream

10 Tablespoons brandy
2 Tablespoons vanilla
¾ teaspoon ground nutmeg
¼ teaspoon ground cinnamon

Warm milk; add eggs, sugar and salt. Cook, stirring constantly, until temperature reaches 155°F or until mixture coats the back of a spoon. Do not overcook. Remove from heat and add cream. Stir occasionally while mixture cools. In separate bowl combine brandy, vanilla, nutmeg and cinnamon. Beat flavorings into cooled custard mixture. Freeze in ice cream freezer. Pack to let ice cream set up. Makes 1 gallon ice cream.

Mrs. Charles G. Smith, Jr.

Ice cream is festive served from a punch bowl into cups or mugs.

Peppermint Ice Cream

½ pound peppermint stick
    candy, broken in pieces
16 large marshmallows

1 cup boiling water
1 pint whipping cream, whipped
1 cup half and half cream

In top of double boiler over hot water melt candy and marshmallows in boiling water. Chill in loaf pan or oblong Pyrex dish in freezer until slightly thickened. Blend whipped and half and half creams. Add to partially frozen mixture. Freeze, stirring once. Serves 10.

Mrs. Clarence Lott

A delicious and beautiful way to use Christmas candy canes.

Uncle Ed's Refrigerator Ice Cream

3 cups whipping cream
3 cups milk
3 cups sugar

Juice of 3 lemons
Juice of 3 oranges
3 bananas, mashed

Combine cream, milk and sugar. Stir until dissolved. Place in oblong or square freezer container. Freeze about ¾ hour or until mushy; then add juices and bananas. Mix well. Freeze until firm. Serves 12.

Mrs. Virgil L. Bigham, III

This ice cream was made and served by my great-uncle Edward Miller in Miller's Drug Store, Junction City, Kansas, from the early 1900's until around 1935.

Mint Sherbet

4 cups sugar
Large grocery bag fresh mint
  leaves, washed
7 cups water, divided
Juice of 4 lemons

2 (6 ounce) cans frozen orange
  juice concentrate, thawed
Dash green food coloring
1 pint whipping cream, whipped
2 egg whites, stiffly beaten

Heat the sugar, mint leaves and 2 cups water until sugar is dissolved. Simmer mixture for 30 minutes; then strain. Cool. Combine mint syrup with juices, remaining water and green food coloring. Place in freezer container and partially freeze. Fold together whipped cream and egg whites. Open freezer container and pour in cream mixture. Continue freezing until firm. Serve or pack in plastic containers and store in freezer. Makes 1 gallon sherbet.

Mrs. Charles Morris

Cinnamon Ice Cream

1¾ cups sugar, divided
6 Tablespoons water
1½ Tablespoons ground
  cinnamon

3 cups milk
1 egg, beaten
1 pint whipping cream
1 teaspoon vanilla

In a saucepan combine 1 cup sugar, water and cinnamon. Cook over low heat, stirring constantly, until mixture is smooth and the sugar dissolved. Set syrup aside. In top of double boiler scald milk. Stir in remaining sugar until it is dissolved and pour mixture slowly over egg, beating constantly. Return mixture to top of double boiler and cook over hot water until it thickens slightly. Chill and stir in cinnamon syrup. Add cream and vanilla. Freeze in electric freezer. Double the recipe for 1 gallon. Makes 2 quarts.

Mrs. T. Arnold Turner, Jr.

Caramel Ice Cream

2⅔ cups sugar, divided
2 Tablespoons flour
2 pints milk, divided

2 eggs, beaten
1 quart whipping cream

Mix 1 cup sugar with flour. Add to 1 pint milk and heat to boiling point. Mix small amount of hot milk with eggs; then return egg mixture to remaining hot milk. Caramelize 1 cup sugar (see Special Techniques chapter). Add to milk-egg mixture and cook slowly 10 minutes. Do not boil. Cool. Add remaining sugar, milk and cream. Freeze in ice cream freezer. Serve at least 2 hours after freezing. Serves 8.

Mrs. Herbert A. Kroeze

Uncooked Vanilla Ice Cream

2 cups sugar
1 (14 ounce) can Eagle Brand
   condensed milk
2 Tablespoons vanilla

Pinch salt
6 eggs, beaten
1 pint whipping cream
Milk

Mix sugar, condensed milk, vanilla, salt and eggs together. Add cream and mix well. Pour into 1-gallon capacity ice cream freezer and add enough cold milk to fill it ⅔ full. Freeze. Yields 1 gallon ice cream.

Mrs. Doug Elmore

Butter Pecan Ice Cream

2 cups brown sugar
1 cup water
¼ teaspoon salt
4 eggs, beaten
4 Tablespoons butter

2 cups milk
1 Tablespoon vanilla
2 cups whipping cream
1 cup chopped pecans, lightly
   toasted

In top of double boiler combine brown sugar, water and salt. Cook until sugar is melted. Add eggs; stir and cook over hot water until thickened. Stir in butter. Cool. Add milk and vanilla. Beat whipping cream and fold into mixture. Stir in pecans. Freeze in ice cream freezer. Makes ½ gallon ice cream.

Mrs. Edna Mills

Homemade Custard Ice Cream

3¾ cups sugar
5 Tablespoons flour
1¼ teaspoons salt
10 cups milk

10 eggs, well beaten
10 teaspoons vanilla
2 (14 ounce) cans condensed milk
1 pint half and half cream

Mix sugar, flour, salt and milk. Cook in top of double boiler over simmering water, stirring, until slightly thickened. Cover and cook 10 minutes more on low heat. Add hot milk mixture slowly to eggs, beating constantly. Return mixture to top of double boiler and cook over boiling water 5 minutes or until custard coats spoon. Cool. Add vanilla, condensed milk and cream. Freeze in ice cream freezer. Makes 1½ gallons ice cream.

Mrs. James L. Brown

PRALINE ICE CREAM   Crumble 12 pralines into custard. Omit 1 can condensed milk.

PEACH ICE CREAM   Add 1 quart crushed peaches cooked with 1¼ cups sugar. Add 2½ teaspoons almond extract and use only 5 teaspoons vanilla.

Lemon Ice Cream

1 pint half and half cream   2 cups milk
Juice of 5 large lemons   2 cups sugar
Grated rind of 2 lemons   Yellow food coloring

Mix ingredients and place in covered aluminum pan in freezer until slushy. Remove and place small amount at a time in blender. Blend until creamy. Return to a plastic container to freeze. Serve in stemmed compote with sprig of mint or in lemon shells with pulp removed. Excellent following seafood. Will keep indefinitely. Serves 6-8.

Mrs. Myron Lockey

Fig Ice Cream

1 cup sugar   2 egg whites, stiffly beaten
¼ cup water   1 quart crushed, peeled figs
1 Tablespoon vinegar   1½ cups milk
Pinch salt

Combine sugar, water, vinegar and salt and bring to a boil. Cook to the thread stage (230°F). Pour syrup slowly over egg whites, beating constantly until mixture is thick and smooth. Fold in figs and milk. Pour mixture into a container and freeze in refrigerator or use an electric ice cream freezer. One 29-ounce can apricots or any other fruit (crushed and pushed through a sieve) can be used in this recipe, the amount determined by the strength of the fruit. Makes 3 quarts ice cream.

Mrs. William H. Miller

Variation: Make EASY FIG ICE CREAM by blending in blender 3 cups peeled figs, ½ cup sugar, 4 teaspoons lemon juice and 1 teaspoon grated lemon rind. Fold mixture into ½ gallon vanilla ice cream. Pack in freezer containers and freeze. Makes about 3 quarts ice cream.

Mrs. Robert H. Thompson

Dessert Sauces

Bay Leaf Sauce

¾ cup brown sugar   6 bay leaves
2 Tablespoons flour   1 cup water
Juice of 1 lemon

Combine ingredients and cook slowly for 15 minutes. Strain. Use as sauce for bread pudding, pie or cake. Also good on chicken or ham. Makes 1½ cups sauce.

Mrs. William Hollingsworth, Jr.

Lemon-Raisin Sauce

1 Tablespoon cornstarch
½ cup sugar
¼ cup brown sugar
¼ teaspoon salt
Pinch ground ginger

1 cup hot water
Grated rind of 1 lemon
1 Tablespoon butter
3 to 4 Tablespoons lemon juice
1 cup seedless raisins

Combine cornstarch, sugars, salt and ginger. Add hot water and cook until thickened and clear. Add remaining ingredients and serve warm over ginger-bread or any loaf cake. Makes about 2¼ cups sauce.

Mrs. James N. McLeod

Praline Sauce

2 cups dark cane syrup
⅓ cup sugar
⅓ cup boiling water

1 cup chopped pecans or small
  pecan halves

Combine all ingredients and bring to a boil over medium heat. When mixture reaches a boil, remove from heat immediately. Cool and store in covered jar. Serve hot or cold over ice cream or cake. Makes 2½ cups sauce.

Mrs. Charles M. Head

Chocolate Sauce

2 (4 ounce) packages German's
  sweet chocolate
2 (1 ounce) squares unsweetened
  chocolate

½ cup sugar
¾ cup half and half cream,
  divided
½ teaspoon vanilla

In top of double boiler mix chocolates, sugar and ¼ cup cream. Cook over boiling water, stirring constantly, until smooth and thick. Remove from heat; gradually beat in remaining cream and vanilla. Serve warm. Makes about 2 cups sauce.

Mrs. J. T. Noblin

Whiskey Sauce

1½ cups sugar
1 (5.33 ounce) can evaporated
  milk

4 Tablespoons margarine
1 egg, beaten
3 Tablespoons whiskey

Combine all ingredients except whiskey in top of double boiler. Place over boiling water and cook, stirring well, until thick. Keep warm until serving time or make ahead and keep in the refrigerator. Do not add whiskey until just before serving. Good spooned over leftover fruit cake or pound cake and topped with whipped cream and a dash nutmeg. Makes 1½ cups sauce.

Mrs. Carl F. André

Finger Desserts

Mock Dobosch

With a bread knife slice a loaf-shaped prepared pound cake (about 5½ x 4½ inches in size) into 9 horizontal layers. Divide cake into 3 cakes of 3 layers each. Melt 1 (12 ounce) package semisweet chocolate chips in top of double boiler. Cool slightly and mix chocolate with 1 (8 ounce) carton sour cream. Spread chocolate mixture between each layer and on top of the 3 cakes. Sprinkle tops with finely chopped pecans (about ½ cup). Cut each cake into 12 small individual cakes. Trim the sides. Good for cocktail parties as a pick-up dessert. Freezes well. Makes 36 cakes.

Mrs. Joe Dehmer, Jr.

Wild Plum Tarts

½ cup butter, softened
1 (3 ounce) package cream
   cheese, softened
¾ teaspoon grated orange rind
¾ teaspoon grated lemon rind
1 cup sifted flour
1½ cups finely chopped pecans
½ pint wild plum jelly

Beat butter and cream cheese until smooth. Add orange and lemon rinds. Add flour slowly until well blended. Refrigerate 1 hour. Pinch dough into small balls. Place balls in miniature muffin tins and press dough into each to form shells. Place some nuts in bottom of each shell. Add about 1 teaspoon plum jelly to each and top with more nuts. Bake in preheated 400°F oven until dough is golden brown. Cool before removing. Makes 2½-3 dozen tarts.

Mrs. Dennis M. Ford

Buttermilk Orange Cupcakes

CUPCAKES:
½ cup butter or margarine,
   softened
1 cup sugar
2 eggs
1 teaspoon baking soda
2 cups flour
¼ teaspoon salt
⅔ cup buttermilk

ORANGE SAUCE:
Juice of 2 oranges
Grated rind of 1 orange
1 cup sugar

CUPCAKES: Cream butter and sugar, adding eggs one at a time. Sift in dry ingredients alternately with the buttermilk. Fill greased miniature muffin pans less than ½ full. Bake at 375°F for 12 minutes. *ORANGE SAUCE:* Mix and cook ingredients until sugar is dissolved. Spoon 1 teaspoon orange sauce over each cake when removed from oven but still in pans. After adding sauce, let cupcakes cool in pans; then remove. Serve warm or cold. Makes 60 cupcakes.

Mrs. R. Thomas Wolfe, Wilmington, North Carolina

Miniature Cheese Cakes

Butter
10 graham crackers, crushed
1 (8 ounce) package cream
    cheese, softened
¾ cup sugar

3 eggs, separated
1 (8 ounce) carton sour cream
2½ Tablespoons sugar
1 teaspoon vanilla

Butter the sides and bottoms of all 48 sections in 4 miniature muffin tins. Sprinkle with graham cracker crumbs and shake to coat. Beat together the cream cheese and sugar. Add egg yolks, one at a time, beating well. Beat the egg whites until very stiff and fold into cream cheese mixture. Spoon filling into muffin tins almost to the top and bake in upper third of a preheated 350 °F oven for 15 minutes. Remove from oven and cool. Cakes will sink in the middle. Mix together the sour cream, sugar and vanilla. Drop about 1 teaspoon sour cream mixture in the center of each little cake. Bake 5 minutes in 400 °F oven. Cool before removing from pans. To facilitate removal from pans, loosen sides with a sharp knife, hold pan perpendicular to counter top and ease out each tart with knife. Top each with a piece of fresh strawberry, a grape half or a drop of blueberry or cherry pie filling. Freezes well. Makes 48.

Mrs. J. A. Rowland, Jr.

Winfrey's Tart Shells

⅔ cup butter (do not substitute)
1½ cups flour
½ cup confectioners' sugar

½ teaspoon salt
2 Tablespoons water
½ teaspoon vanilla

Cut butter into flour, sugar and salt. Sprinkle water and vanilla over flour mixture. Form into dough and chill. Divide dough in half and roll out very thin, about 1/8 inch thick. Cut with a biscuit cutter. Place in miniature muffin tins. Prick and bake at 325 °F for 12-15 minutes or until delicately brown. Shells can be frozen or stored in cookie tin. Makes 4-5 dozen shells. To serve, fill with BERRY FILLING or LEMON FILLING (see Index).

BERRY FILLING

1 quart strawberries,
    blackberries or blueberries
1¼ cups water, divided
1 cup sugar

3 Tablespoons cornstarch
1 Tablespoon butter
Whipping cream, whipped

Mix 1 cup washed, hulled berries with 1 cup water and bring to a boil. Cook gently 15 minutes, covered. Strain, pressing juice out of berries. Return juice to saucepan and add sugar and cornstarch, mixed with remaining water to form a paste. Cook over low heat, stirring constantly, until thick and clear. Stir in butter. Cool. Fold in remaining berries or place 1 whole berry in tart shell and spoon sauce over berry. Top each tart with a dab of whipped cream.

Mrs. William F. Sistrunk, Jr.

Fruit Pastry Bites

Preheat oven to 400°F. Separate dough of 1 (12 ounce) box Pillsbury turnover pies (blueberry, cherry or apple) into 6 squares. Using kitchen shears, cut each square into 4 equal pieces, each about 1½ inches square. Place the squares on a large ungreased cookie sheet or 2 small ones. Cut off one end of the fruit filling package and squeeze about ½-1 teaspoon fruit filling in the middle of each square. Bake about 10 minutes or until pastry is golden brown. Remove from oven. Clip a very small corner from icing package; drizzle icing over fruit pastry. Serve warm. Yields 24 squares.

Mrs. John T. Moore

Gâteaux au Rum
(Rum Cakes)

1 angel food cake
1 cup butter, melted
1 egg white
2 Tablespoons light rum

1 (1 pound) box confectioners'
   sugar
2 cups finely chopped pecans

Buy or prepare (see Index) angel food cake. Slice horizontally through middle of cake; then make perpendicular slices 1 inch apart around cake creating 1 x 1 x 2-inch wedges. To cooled butter add unbeaten egg white and rum and beat in enough sugar to make mixture an easy spreading consistency. Spread mixture on all sides of cake wedge. Roll immediately in pecans. May be prepared ahead 3-4 days. Store in refrigerator in airtight container. Freezes well. Makes about 35 cakes.

Mrs. James H. Creekmore

Minnie's Miniature Fruit Cakes

1 pound candied cherries,
   halved
3 slices candied pineapple,
   chopped
1 pound chopped dates
2 cups pecan halves

1 cup flour
1 cup sugar
½ teaspoon salt
4 eggs, well beaten
1 cup butter, melted
Bourbon

Place fruit and pecans in bowl. Add flour and mix with hands. Add sugar and salt and mix. Add eggs and butter to fruit mixture. Spoon into greased and floured pan. If using a tube pan, bake at 250°F for 3½ hours. If using muffin tins (miniature or regular size), bake at 300°F for 40-50 minutes. Place cakes in tin and cover with a dish towel saturated with bourbon. This preserves flavor and keeps the cakes or cookies moist for up to at least 2 weeks. Makes 1 cake serving 24 or 6 dozen miniature cakes.

Mrs. Lester Alvis, Jr.

Children love to help stir these pretty Christmas cookies.

Desserts

Plum Pudding

1 pound dark raisins	½ pound slivered almonds
1 pound golden raisins	1 teaspoon each ground nutmeg,
2 pounds currants	ground cinnamon, ground
2 pounds dark brown sugar	allspice, ground cloves
2 cups Old London bread	1 teaspoon salt
crumbs	2 cups milk
2 cups flour	2 eggs, beaten
2 teaspoons baking soda	Sugar
2 pounds beef kidney suet,	2 Tablespoons brandy
ground	

In very large bowl mix first 11 ingredients; then add milk and eggs. Mix well. Pour into ovenproof bowls of desired sizes, packing down tightly. Fill to ½-1½ inches from the top. Make a tent over each bowl with plastic wrap and tie with a string. Place bowls on a rack in a roasting pan covering 2 eyes of the cooktop. Fill with water about ⅓ of the way up (about 1½-2 inches water). Cover pan, bring to boil, reduce heat and steam at a slow simmer for about 3 hours. Remove plastic and clean off bowls. Refrigerate until ready to use. Before serving, cover bowls with plastic wrap, tie and steam again for 1 hour. Invert bowl to remove. To serve, sprinkle a small amount of sugar into a depression made in the top of the pudding. Pour brandy into depression over sugar and flame it. Serve at once while flaming with PLUM PUDDING SAUCE or HARD SAUCE. May be made 4 or 5 weeks ahead of time. Recipe makes 2 large puddings or 4 smaller ones. Serves 50.

PLUM PUDDING SAUCE

1 cup sugar	1 Tablespoon butter
2 Tablespoons flour	Pinch salt
1 Tablespoon cold water	Brandy or bourbon to taste
1 cup boiling water	

In a saucepan mix sugar and flour. Add cold water. Pour boiling water over mixture. Cook over low heat until mixture thickens a bit; then blend in butter, salt and brandy. May be made a few hours before serving and reheated. Makes about 2 cups sauce.

HARD SAUCE

½ cup butter, softened	1 egg white
1 cup powdered sugar	Brandy or bourbon to taste

Cream butter and sugar with rotary beater. Beat in egg white and brandy or bourbon. Place into container from which it will be served. Refrigerate. May be made ahead. Makes about 1½ cups sauce.

Mrs. Harry G. Gwinnup

Strawberry Holiday Trifle

SPONGE CAKE:
1 cup sifted flour
1 teaspoon baking powder
¼ teaspoon salt
½ cup milk
2 Tablespoons butter or
  margarine
2 eggs
1 cup sugar
1 teaspoon vanilla

CUSTARD:
⅔ cup sugar
2 Tablespoons cornstarch
¼ teaspoon salt

2 cups milk
4 egg yolks, beaten
2 Tablespoons butter or
  margarine
1 teaspoon vanilla
1 teaspoon almond extract
1 cup whipping cream, whipped

3 pints fresh strawberries
3 Tablespoons sugar
¾ cup strawberry liqueur or
  wine
¾ cup sliced almonds
Powdered sugar
Whipping cream, whipped

SPONGE CAKE: Sift together flour, baking powder and salt. In saucepan heat milk and butter until butter melts. Keep hot. Beat eggs at high speed of mixer until thick and lemon-colored, about 3 minutes. Gradually add sugar, beating constantly for 4-5 minutes. Add dry ingredients and stir until just blended. Stir in hot milk and vanilla. Blend well. Divide batter between 2 greased and floured 8-inch cake pans. Bake at 350°F for 20 minutes or until done. Cool in pans 10 minutes; then remove and cool on rack. *CUSTARD:* Combine sugar, cornstarch and salt in saucepan. Stir in milk. Cook, stirring, over medium heat until thickened and bubbly. Stir some of hot mixture into egg yolks. Return egg yolks to mixture in pan, stirring constantly. Cook and stir 2 more minutes. Remove from heat. Stir in butter, vanilla and almond extract. Cover custard with plastic wrap and chill. Fold whipped cream into chilled custard. Set aside about 14 strawberries for garnish. Crush remaining berries to make 2 cups. Stir in sugar and set aside. Split cake layers in half to make 4 layers. Place first layer in bottom of 2½-quart soufflé dish or glass bowl and sprinkle with 3 Tablespoons liqueur. Spread with ⅔ cup crushed berries, cover with ⅓ of the custard and sprinkle with ¼ cup almonds. Repeat sequence 2 more times. Sprinkle last cake layer on cut side with remaining liqueur and place, cut side down, on top. Cover and refrigerate overnight. Just before serving sift a heavy covering of powdered sugar over the top. Garnish with whipped cream rosettes and reserved strawberries, halved. For Christmas, tint whipped cream green and simulate a wreath with whipped cream rosettes and strawberries. Makes a very festive dessert. Serves 15.

Mrs. Clyde Copeland, Jr.

Whip ½ pint whipping cream with 1 heaping Tablespoon vanilla ice milk or ice cream and powdered sugar to taste. The cream will take longer to whip but will not turn to butter. It will be increased in volume and will keep up to 2 days.

Pousse-Café Parfait

½ gallon vanilla ice cream
2 Tablespoons blackberry
  brandy or 3 Tablespoons
  blackberry jam
2 Tablespoons crème de cacao
  or 3 Tablespoons sweetened
  cocoa

2 Tablespoons crème de menthe
  or ½ teaspoon mint extract
2 Tablespoons orange curaçao or
  ½ teaspoon orange extract
Food colorings
1 cup whipping cream, whipped

Soften ice cream and divide into 4 equal portions. Blend into each portion a liqueur or flavoring. Add 3 or 4 drops of a different food coloring to each flavor. Spoon first flavor into bottom of a 2-quart mold or individual parfaits. Freeze slightly. Layer remaining portions into mold one at a time, freezing each slightly before adding next flavor. Freeze several hours or overnight. Before serving, garnish with whipped cream. Serves 6-8.

Mrs. Alvin E. Brent, Jr.

Christmas Snow Pudding

24 lady fingers
½ cup sherry wine
2 envelopes unflavored gelatin
1 cup cold water
12 egg whites

1 cup sugar
2 cups whipping cream, whipped
1 Tablespoon sugar
Maraschino cherries

Halve lady fingers lengthwise, dip in sherry and line bottom of 2 (9 x 13 inch) shallow Pyrex casseroles. Sprinkle gelatin over cold water in small saucepan. Place over low heat about 5 minutes until gelatin is dissolved, stirring constantly. Beat egg whites until stiff. Gradually add sugar. Continue to beat until very stiff. Fold in the gelatin that has been cooled slightly. Spread the egg white mixture over the lady fingers. Cover with plastic wrap and refrigerate until congealed, about 6 hours. Cut Snow Pudding into desired size squares and place on tray or dessert plates. Sweeten whipped cream with sugar. Ice top and sides of each square with whipped cream. Pour CUSTARD SAUCE over each serving and garnish with a cherry. Serves 10.

CUSTARD SAUCE

6 egg yolks
1 cup sugar
3 cups milk, scalded

1 teaspoon vanilla
1 Tablespoon dry sherry wine

Beat egg yolks and sugar together. Slowly pour in scalded milk, stirring constantly. Place mixture in top of double boiler and cook over simmering water until custard coats a spoon. Remove from heat. Cool and add vanilla and sherry. Refrigerate until serving time. Makes about 3½ cups sauce.

Mrs. Sherwood Wise

Boiled Custard

4 cups milk
6 eggs
1 cup sugar

2 teaspoons vanilla
or Brandy
nutmeg (optional)

Heat milk. Do not boil. Mix eggs and sugar with mixer or in blender. Add this to hot milk, stirring constantly. Cook until custard begins to thicken (5-7 minutes) on medium heat. Custard will thicken further as it cools. Add vanilla or Brandy to cooled custard. Sprinkle nutmeg. Delicious served as dessert or used in recipes calling for custard base. Makes 5 cups.

Mrs. Denny Terry

Crème Brulée

1 pint half and half cream
1 cup whipping cream
2 Tablespoons sugar

6 egg yolks, beaten
2 teaspoons vanilla
¾ cup light brown sugar

Heat creams but do not scald. Add sugar and stir until dissolved. Stir in egg yolks. Add vanilla. Pour into a 7½-inch ovenproof bowl or soufflé dish and place bowl in pan of water. Bake at 300°F for 50-60 minutes. Cool and chill thoroughly. Custard can be made the day before. At least 2 hours but no more than 4 hours ahead, sift brown sugar over top to cover custard completely. Preheat broiler to 350°F. Set custard in pan of ice and place about 6 inches below broiler. Move it around constantly to melt but not burn the sugar. Cool slightly and return to refrigerator to chill. Serve as is or topped with any fresh fruit. Serves 6-8.

Mrs. W. E. Walker, Jr.

Pots de Crème

3 cups whipping cream
½ cup sugar

1 Tablespoon vanilla
5 egg yolks

Begin 5 hours ahead. Preheat oven to 325°F and place 8 (5 ounce) or 10 (3 ounce) cups in baking pan filled with 1 inch water. Heat while preparing cream. In medium saucepan combine cream and sugar. Stir over moderate heat until sugar dissolves; do not allow to boil. Remove from heat and add vanilla. In another bowl beat egg yolks until fluffy. Gradually pour cream through strainer into egg yolks, stirring constantly. Pour into heated cups. Bake 25-30 minutes. Remove from oven and cool for 30 minutes. Cover and refrigerate until chilled. To serve, garnish with a dollop of whipped cream topped with a strawberry or grated chocolate. Serve with a fresh baked cookie or wafer. Serves 8-10.

Mrs. Paul G. Moak, Jr.

Kirsch Soufflé

1 quart fresh fruit (cherries or
 strawberries preferred)
11 Tablespoons sugar, divided
¾ cup kirsch, divided
1 envelope unflavored gelatin
3 Tablespoons water

4 eggs, separated
1 teaspoon vanilla
1 cup whipping cream, whipped
2 egg whites
½ to ¾ cup grated semisweet
 chocolate

Sprinkle fruit with 6 Tablespoons sugar and ¼ cup kirsch. Chill until ready to use. Soften gelatin in water; then dissolve over low heat. Set aside. Beat egg yolks until thick and light in color. Add vanilla and remaining kirsch. Stir gelatin into egg yolk mixture. Let sit for 20 minutes or until mixture begins to thicken. Fold whipped cream into egg yolk mixture. Beat the 6 egg whites until they hold a peak. Add remaining sugar gradually and beat until stiff. Fold into egg yolk mixture, mixing well. Place jar or other flat-bottomed displacement object in middle of a 2½-quart soufflé dish or a glass bowl of the same size. Pour ⅓ of the egg yolk mixture around jar, sprinkle with ½ the chocolate, add another ⅓ of the mixture and sprinkle with remaining chocolate. Top with remaining egg yolk mixture. Refrigerate at least 4 hours. To remove jar, run knife around jar, insert knife tip under bottom of jar and slowly twist jar out. Fill cavity with drained marinated fruit. Garnish with additional whipped cream and extra fruit, if desired. May be made 1 day ahead, adding fruit only 2 hours before serving. Serves 8.

Mrs. F. Dean Copeland, Atlanta, Georgia

Chocolate Rum Angel

1½ cups milk
2 eggs, beaten
½ cup sugar
¼ teaspoon salt
1 envelope unflavored gelatin
⅓ cup cold water

¾ cup semisweet chocolate chips
2 Tablespoons rum or rum
 flavoring
1½ cups whipping cream
1 (13 or 16 ounce) angel food cake
½ cup sliced almonds

Blend first 4 ingredients in top of double boiler and cook over simmering water, stirring, until mixture is of custard consistency and coats a spoon, about 10-15 minutes. Soften gelatin in cold water and add to hot custard, stirring to dissolve. Remove 1 cup of custard and add to chocolate chips. Stir until chocolate is melted. Set aside. When remaining custard is cool, add rum and chill until mixture just begins to thicken. Whip cream and fold into chilled custard. Tear cake into pieces and fold into custard. Pour mixture into springform pan or a 9 x 13-inch pan. Drizzle chocolate custard over top and sprinkle with almonds. Chill to set. If using springform pan, unmold. Cut into serving pieces and garnish each with additional sweetened whipped cream and a cherry. Serves 14-16.

Mrs. William F. Goodman, Jr.

Coupes Maxim

Peel and halve 6 fresh peaches (or use canned ones). Sprinkle peach halves with ¼ cup kirsch and a little sugar. Let stand at least 30 minutes. Place 1 peach half in each sherbet glass, top each with 2 scoops pistachio ice cream and cover with Raspberry Cardinal Sauce (see Index). Serves 12.

From the recipes of Mrs. J. E. Knighton

Praline Soufflé with Raspberry Sauce

1 cup egg whites (about 6), at room temperature
10 Tablespoons superfine sugar

Whipping cream, whipped
Fresh raspberries

Beat egg whites until frothy. Gradually beat in sugar until mixture is stiff and glossy. Do not overbeat. Fold in ½ cup PRALINE. Spoon meringue mixture into a buttered, sugared 2-quart soufflé dish. Set dish in a deep pan and pour boiling water halfway up the sides of the soufflé dish. Place on middle shelf of oven. Bake in preheated 350°F oven for 40 minutes or until a cake tester comes out clean. Remove dish from water and run a spatula carefully around the soufflé to loosen the edge. Soufflé will sink as it cools. When soufflé reaches room temperature, transfer to serving plate by turning plate upside down over soufflé dish and inverting. Spoon RASPBERRY CARDINAL SAUCE over soufflé and garnish with whipped cream and fresh raspberries, if available. Serves 6.

PRALINE

½ cup sugar
¼ cup water

½ cup chopped pecans

Place sugar and water in small, heavy saucepan. Heat, stirring until sugar dissolves. Continue to heat without stirring until mixture turns a pale caramel color. Stir in pecans and pour immediately onto an oiled cookie sheet. Cool completely. Break up candy into rough pieces; then pulverize in blender or food processor a little at a time until chunks are reduced to a powder. Serve praline as an ice cream topping or as a dessert garnish. Makes 1¼ cups praline.

RASPBERRY CARDINAL SAUCE

2 (10 ounce) boxes frozen raspberries, thawed
6 fresh strawberries (optional)

1 Tablespoon cornstarch
2 Tablespoons lemon juice
2 Tablespoons kirsch

Purée raspberries and juice with strawberries, if desired, in blender. Force through a sieve. Mix cornstarch with lemon juice and add to raspberry mixture. Bring to a boil and cook until slightly thick. Add kirsch. Will keep in refrigerator for weeks. Makes 2¼ cups sauce.

Mrs. Richard L. Redmont, Jr.

Apple Torte

½ cup margarine, softened
⅔ cup plus 4 Tablespoons
   sugar, divided
1½ teaspoons vanilla, divided
1 cup flour
1 (8 ounce) package cream
   cheese, softened

1 egg
½ teaspoon ground cinnamon
4 cups peeled, cored apple slices
¼ cup sliced almonds, or more
Whipping cream, whipped
1 Tablespoon Amaretto

Cream margarine, ⅓ cup sugar and 1 teaspoon vanilla; blend in flour. Spread crust mixture over bottom and 1½ inches up sides of a 9-inch springform pan. Cream cheese and 4 Tablespoons sugar; blend in egg and remaining ½ teaspoon vanilla. Spread cheese mixture evenly over crust. Combine remaining ⅓ cup sugar and cinnamon; toss apples in mixture. Spread over cheese layer. Sprinkle almonds on top. Bake at 450°F for 10 minutes. Reduce heat to 400°F and bake 25 minutes longer. Loosen from rim and cool before removing from pan. Best if made just before serving. Serve topped with whipped cream flavored with Amaretto. May be prepared the night before, refrigerated and then cooked before serving. Serves 10-12.

Mrs. Alvin E. Brent, Jr.

Almond Bavarians with Apricot Sauce

1 envelope unflavored gelatin
½ cup sugar, divided
1/8 teaspoon salt
2 eggs, separated

1¼ cups milk
½ teaspoon almond extract
1 cup whipping cream, whipped
Slivered almonds, toasted

In saucepan combine gelatin, ¼ cup sugar and salt. Mix together slightly beaten egg yolks and milk. Add to gelatin mixture and heat over low heat until gelatin is dissolved. Stir in almond extract and chill until mixture mounds slightly. Beat egg whites to soft peaks. Gradually beat in remaining sugar until stiff peaks form. Fold into gelatin mixture. Fold in whipped cream. Turn into 8 individual molds. Chill until set. Unmold. Top with APRICOT SAUCE and almonds immediately before serving. May be made a day ahead. Serves 8.

APRICOT SAUCE

1½ cups apricot nectar
½ cup sugar
1 teaspoon fresh lemon juice

½ cup dried apricot halves,
   quartered

In saucepan combine apricot nectar, sugar and lemon juice. Add apricots, cover and simmer 20-25 minutes or until apricots are tender. Pour into blender and purée for 30 seconds or until sauce is a smooth consistency. Chill.

Mrs. Charles H. Hooker, Jr.

Mousse à l'Orange
(Orange Mousse in Orange Halves)

3 Tablespoons Grand Marnier
Grated rind of 3 oranges
Grated rind of ½ lemon
1¾ cups fresh orange juice
½ cup plus 1 Tablespoon sugar, divided

6 eggs, separated
2 teaspoons cornstarch
Pinch salt
½ cup whipping cream, whipped
3 to 4 navel oranges, halved

Combine Grand Marnier, rinds and juice. Beat ½ cup sugar and egg yolks until pale yellow. Beat in cornstarch and juice mixture. Stir over moderate heat or in top of double boiler over hot water until mixture coats a spoon. *Do not overcook.* Remove from heat. Whip egg whites with salt and remaining Tablespoon sugar until stiff. Fold whites into hot orange mixture. Chill, stirring gently occasionally. Fold whipped cream into orange mixture. Scoop out orange halves and cut edges decoratively, if desired. Fill with orange mousse. Chill. Decorate with more whipped cream, candied violets, mint leaves or grated orange rind. Make and serve the same day. Serves 6-8.

Mrs. William B. Wilson

Spanish Cream or "Party"

1 envelope unflavored gelatin
3 cups milk
½ cup sugar
¼ teaspoon salt

3 eggs, separated
1 teaspoon vanilla
1 cup whipping cream, whipped
Maraschino cherries

Soften gelatin in milk for 5 minutes; then heat in top of double boiler over hot water. When hot, add sugar and salt, stirring until dissolved. Pour some of the hot mixture over beaten egg yolks and return yolks to milk mixture. Cook and stir until mixture coats spoon, about 3-5 minutes. Strain into bowl, add vanilla and cool. Lightly fold beaten egg whites into cooled custard and refrigerate to congeal. Serve in sherbet or other dessert dish topped with whipped cream sweetened with a little sugar and a cherry. This dessert congeals in 2 layers. The bottom is creamy and the top light and frothy. Good served with a simple cookie. Serves 8.

Mrs. Sam G. Cole, III

This recipe was used by my great grandmother, Mrs. Fred M. Jackson, of Birmingham, Alabama, for many years. Her home was a gathering place for family and friends. "Pa" Jackson always brought home company at mealtime. Once when a party was in the making, large quantities of Spanish cream were made. A snowstorm blew in at party time, preventing guests from coming. For days the family enjoyed this dessert and for many years thereafter it was referred to as "party." My grandmother, Mrs. R. L. Ezelle, brought this recipe of her mother's to Jackson in 1922, when the family moved here.

Cold Strawberry Soufflé

4 envelopes unflavored gelatin
2 cups sugar, divided
3 cups puréed strawberries,
  (about 3 pints), divided
8 eggs, separated

¼ cup fresh lemon juice
2 cups whipping cream
Red food coloring
Sliced, unblanched almonds,
  toasted

Extend depth of 2-quart soufflé dish or casserole by securing a 4-inch band of double-thickness aluminum foil around top. Mix gelatin and 1 cup sugar in saucepan; stir in 1½ cups strawberries. Mix in beaten egg yolks. Cook over medium heat, stirring constantly, just until mixture boils. Remove from heat. Stir in remaining strawberries and lemon juice. Place pan in refrigerator or in a bowl of ice and water, stirring occasionally, until mixture mounds slightly when dropped from a spoon, about 15-30 minutes. Meanwhile, beat egg whites until foamy. Beat in remaining sugar, a Tablespoon at a time, until egg whites are stiff and glossy. Fold strawberry mixture into meringue. Beat cream in chilled bowl until stiff and fold into meringue mixture. Fold in food coloring as needed. Carefully spoon into soufflé dish and swirl top; refrigerate. Just before serving, run edge of knife inside foil band and remove band. Garnish top and sides of soufflé with almonds. Serves 16.

Mrs. William H. Wallace

Chocolate Roll

5 large eggs, separated
1 cup sugar, divided
6 ounces dark sweet chocolate
3 Tablespoons coffee

Grated chocolate or cocoa
1 cup whipping cream, whipped
½ teaspoon vanilla
Sliced almonds, toasted

Beat into the egg yolks ¾ cup sugar and continue to beat well. Melt chocolate in saucepan with coffee. Stir over a low heat until dissolved. Do not let mixture get too hot. Cool the chocolate a little and beat into the egg yolk mixture. Beat egg whites until stiff and fold into chocolate mixture. Butter a 10 x 15-inch jelly-roll pan. Cover it with wax paper and butter it again. Spread the chocolate mixture evenly over wax paper. Bake at 375 °F for 10-15 minutes. Turn off heat, open oven door and let roll sit in oven another 5 minutes. Remove from oven and cover with a damp cloth. Cool and place in refrigerator for an hour. Remove cloth carefully and loosen roll from pan. Dust top of roll heavily with chocolate or cocoa. Turn out upside down on a piece of wax paper and carefully pull off the paper on top. Spread with whipped cream to which vanilla and remaining sugar have been added. Roll up like a jelly roll. Refrigerate. To serve, slice into pieces. Top each serving with a spoonful of additional whipped cream and a sprinkling of almonds. Can be made a day ahead. Serves 10.

Mrs. Duncan Briggs

Coconut Surprise

1 cup flour
½ cup butter, melted
½ cup chopped nuts
1 cup powdered sugar
1 (8 ounce) package cream
  cheese, softened

1 (13½ ounce) carton whipped
  topping, thawed, divided
1 (6 ounce) package frozen grated
  coconut
2 (3¾ ounce) packages French
  vanilla instant pudding
3 cups milk

Mix flour, butter and nuts; press into a 9 x 12-inch baking dish. Bake at 350°F for 20 minutes; cool. Cream sugar and cream cheese; fold in 1 cup whipped topping. Spoon on crust and sprinkle with ½ the coconut. Combine pudding and milk. Beat until thickened and spread over cream cheese layer. Cover with remaining whipped topping and coconut. Chill. Serves 15.

Mrs. Andrew Warriner

Variation: Substitute pistachio instant pudding for the French vanilla and delete the coconut. *Mrs. Thurman B. Oliver, Grenada, Mississippi*

Grape Juice Fluff

1 envelope unflavored gelatin
1 cup plus 3 Tablespoons grape
  juice
¾ cup sugar
Juice of 1 lemon

Juice of 1 orange
Pinch salt
2 egg whites, stiffly beaten
Chopped nuts
Whipping cream, whipped

Soften gelatin in 3 Tablespoons grape juice. Bring remaining grape juice to a boil. Stir in gelatin mixture until dissolved. Add sugar, juices and salt and stir. Remove from heat and let cool. When nearly congealed, fold in egg whites. Chill to congeal. Serve in parfait glasses with alternate layers of BOILED CUSTARD. Sprinkle nuts and whipped cream on top. Grape juice mixture and boiled custard can be made 1 or 2 days ahead. Serves 8-12.

BOILED CUSTARD

1 quart milk
⅓ cup sugar
1 Tablespoon flour

1 egg plus 4 egg yolks, beaten
1 teaspoon vanilla

Bring milk to scalding point. Mix sugar and flour and stir into milk. Add eggs very gradually to hot milk, stirring constantly. Custard can be cooked in top of double boiler or over direct heat in a heavy boiler. Cook custard until thick, stirring constantly with spatula. If it curdles, beat with rotary mixer and strain. When cool, add vanilla.

Mrs. Stewart H. Bridgforth, Pickens, Mississippi

This is unsurpassable as a dessert!

Robin's Chocolate Mousse

¾ cup butter, softened
1½ cups sugar
3 eggs, separated
1 Tablespoon brandy
½ teaspoon almond extract

½ pound semisweet chocolate
   chips, melted
¼ cup slivered almonds, toasted
2 cups whipping cream, whipped
Shaved chocolate

Cream butter until fluffy. Add sugar gradually, then egg yolks, brandy and almond extract. Add chocolate and almonds. Beat egg whites until stiff and fold into chocolate mixture. Fold in whipped cream. Freeze. Remove from freezer 30 minutes before serving. Garnish with extra whipped cream and shaved chocolate. Serves 10-12.

Mrs. T. Arnold Turner, Jr.

Rich Bourbon Dessert

4 dozen almond macaroons or
   Amaretti (Italian macaroons)
1 cup bourbon
2 cups butter, softened
2 cups sugar
1 dozen eggs, separated

4 (1 ounce) squares unsweetened
   chocolate, melted
1 teaspoon vanilla
1 cup chopped pecans
2 dozen lady fingers
1½ cups whipping cream, whipped

Soak the macaroons in bourbon. Cream butter and sugar together until light and fluffy. Beat egg yolks until light and blend into creamed mixture. Beat chocolate into butter mixture. Add vanilla and pecans. Whip egg whites until stiff but not dry and fold into chocolate mixture. Line a 10-inch springform pan around sides and bottom with split lady fingers. Alternate layers of chocolate mixture and soaked macaroons in the lined pan. Chill overnight. Remove sides of pan. Decorate with whipped cream. Slice and serve. Serves 16-20.

Mrs. R. Baxter Brown

Woodford Pudding

3 Tablespoons butter, softened
1 cup sugar
3 eggs
¾ cup flour
1 cup blackberry jam
1 teaspoon baking soda

3 Tablespoons buttermilk
½ teaspoon each ground cloves,
   ground allspice
½ cup raisins
½ to ¾ cup chopped nuts
Caramel sauce (optional)

Cream butter and sugar. Beat in eggs. Add other ingredients in order given, dissolving soda in buttermilk and folding in raisins and nuts. Bake in greased 9 x 13-inch pan at 350°F for 30 minutes or until done. Serve warm, topped with caramel sauce, if desired. Serves 8.

Mrs. Luther M. Thompson

This recipe belonged to Mrs. Hugh White, former first lady of Mississippi.

Princess Toffee Torte

24 lady fingers, split
1 envelope unflavored gelatin
½ cup cold water
1 (3 ounce) package vanilla
　　pudding and pie mix
1½ cups chopped English
　　Toffee or 5 Heath Bars,
　　chopped, divided

1 teaspoon vanilla
¾ teaspoon Kahlúa, brandy or
　　bourbon (optional)
4 cups whipping cream, whipped,
　　or whipped topping,
　　thawed, divided
2 to 3 cups frozen or fresh sliced
　　peaches (optional)

Cut 12 lady fingers into 2-inch lengths and stand them upright around the edge of a 9-inch springform pan, top crust side toward pan and cut side down. Line bottom of pan with lady finger halves. Soften gelatin in cold water. Prepare pudding mix by package directions. Add gelatin to hot pudding and stir until dissolved. Stir in 1¼ cups toffee pieces, vanilla and optional flavoring, if desired. Chill mixture until it starts to thicken. Fold ½ the whipped cream or topping into chilled pudding mixture. Fill prepared pan with alternate layers of pudding mixture and remaining lady finger pieces, ending with a pudding layer. Chill until firm. To serve, remove torte from pan and place on serving platter. Ring top edge of torte attractively with remaining whipped cream or topping and sprinkle with remaining toffee bits. Serve with sweetened peach slices, if desired. Serves 8-10.

Mrs. Troy E. Weathersby

Lemma Grantham's Nassau Pudding

2 (1 ounce) squares semisweet
　　chocolate
1½ cups milk
1 cup sugar
1 Tablespoon flour
½ teaspoon salt

3 Tablespoons butter
1 teaspoon vanilla
1 (13 or 16 ounce) angel food cake
3 Tablespoons bourbon, divided
1½ cups whipping cream
Grated chocolate

Melt chocolate with milk in top of double boiler set over hot water. Stir until smooth. Combine sugar, flour and salt; add chocolate mixture slowly to blend, return to top of double boiler and cook over hot water about 20 minutes, stirring until thick. Remove from heat and add butter and vanilla. Slice cake in thin slices. In 2-quart casserole place a layer of ½ the cake, sprinkle with 1 Tablespoon bourbon and cover with ½ the chocolate sauce mixture. Repeat layers one more time. Whip cream with remaining Tablespoon bourbon. Spread over top of cake and sprinkle with grated chocolate. Wrap in plastic wrap and freeze until firm. Remove from freezer about 10 minutes before serving to allow whipped cream to soften slightly. Serves 10-12.

Mrs. Stuart C. Liles

Tyrolean Angel Mold

¾ (5 x 9 inch) angel food cake
6 lady fingers
12 almond macaroons
3 egg whites
10 Tablespoons sugar, divided
2 cups whipping cream

1 teaspoon vanilla
½ teaspoon almond extract
Red, green or yellow food coloring
Blueberries, strawberries and
   peaches

Break into pieces the cake, lady fingers and macaroons. Beat egg whites until soft peaks form, adding 6 Tablespoons sugar gradually. In a separate bowl whip cream until stiff. Add flavorings and remaining sugar. Add food coloring. Fold together egg whites and whipped cream. Cover the bottom of a 3-quart springform pan with some of the cream mixture. Cover with some of the cake mixture. Repeat layers ending with cream. Do not stir. Freeze 12 hours. Serve on platter topped with additional whipped cream and garnished with fruit. Serves 12.

Mrs. Frank R. Briggs

Allison's Wells Special

1 cup good quality molasses
2 eggs
2 Tablespoons butter, softened
2 cups flour
1 teaspoon ground cinnamon
¼ teaspoon ground nutmeg

1 teaspoon baking soda
1 teaspoon vanilla
½ cup chopped pecans or walnuts
1 cup chopped, unpeeled apples
¼ cup raisins
Whipping cream, whipped

Cream the molasses, eggs and butter until light in color. Add and blend in well the flour, spices, soda and vanilla. Fold in nuts, apples and raisins. Bake in a greased and floured 7 x 11-inch baking dish at 350°F until done, about 25 minutes. Cake should be moist, but not dry. Cut in squares and serve with HOT SAUCE and a dab of whipped cream. Serves 8-10.

HOT SAUCE

1 cup brown sugar
½ cup water
1 Tablespoon butter

1 teaspoon vanilla
Rind of ½ orange, slivered
   (optional)

Combine ingredients in saucepan and cook until syrupy, about 15 minutes. Makes 1 cup sauce.

Mrs. John E. Fontaine, Sr.

Allison's Wells Resort of Way, Mississippi, founded 1879, was later owned and operated by the Wherry-Latimer-Fontaine family for three-quarters of a century. Famed for good food and quiet hospitality, it was the social center for the area. As home of the Allison Art Colony, it drew artists from far and near to its workshops. Allison's was destroyed by fire in 1963.

Chocolate Ice Box Dessert

1 cup crushed vanilla wafers
2 (1 ounce) squares unsweetened
    chocolate
⅔ cup butter
2 cups powdered sugar, sifted

1 cup chopped pecans
1 teaspoon vanilla
2 Tablespoons water
2 egg whites, stiffly beaten
½ gallon butter pecan ice cream

Spread crumbs on bottom of buttered 9 x 13-inch pan. Melt chocolate and butter together; cool and stir in sugar, pecans, vanilla and water. Fold in egg whites. Spread mixture over crumbs. Freeze 2 hours. Soften ice cream and spread on top. Sprinkle with additional cookie crumbs. Refreeze. Serves 12.

Mrs. John Crawford

Fabulous Lady Finger-Macaroon Dessert

1 cup butter, softened
1 cup sugar
2 teaspoons vanilla
6 eggs, separated
2 cups chopped pecans, toasted

18 lady fingers
24 stale almond macaroons, crushed
1 cup whipping cream
2 Tablespoons powdered sugar
1 teaspoon sherry wine (optional)

Cream butter and sugar and add vanilla. Beat egg yolks until lemon colored; then add to butter mixture and beat for 10 minutes on high speed. Beat egg whites until stiff and fold into butter mixture along with pecans. Line 2 (7 x 11 inch) Pyrex dishes with split lady fingers. Pour butter mixture into lined dishes. Sprinkle macaroons on top. Refrigerate mixture overnight. Whip cream with sugar and sherry, if desired, and top each serving with a spoonful. Serves 16.

Mrs. L. Arnold Pyle

Apricot Tortoni

⅓ cup chopped almonds
3 Tablespoons butter, melted
1⅓ cups vanilla wafer crumbs
1 teaspoon almond extract
3 pints vanilla ice cream,
    softened

1 (12 ounce) jar apricot preserves
1 cup whipping cream, whipped
4 Tablespoons sugar
1 teaspoon vanilla

Toast almonds in butter; then mix with crumbs and extract. Press a layer of ⅓ the crumb mixture on bottom of a 9-inch square baking dish. Spoon on a layer of ½ the ice cream; drizzle ½ the apricot preserves over top. Repeat layers of crumb mixture, ice cream and preserves one more time, ending with crumb mixture on top. Freeze several hours until firm. Remove dessert from freezer. Spread top with whipped cream flavored with sugar and vanilla. Cover with plastic wrap and return dish to freezer. Cut in squares to serve. May be prepared 5 days in advance, but add whipped cream 1 day ahead or when ready to serve. Serves 10-12.

Mrs. James B. Furrh, Jr.

Baked Alaska Tarts

2 cups biscuit mix
2 Tablespoons sugar
¾ cup half and half cream
2 pints vanilla ice cream
2 cups sliced fresh or frozen
    strawberries

4 egg whites
½ teaspoon cream of tartar
½ cup sugar
½ teaspoon vanilla

Mix biscuit mix, sugar and cream to form a soft dough. Beat vigorously for 20 strokes. Knead 8-10 times on a floured board. Roll out dough and cut into eight 6-inch circles. Prick and bake in 4-inch tart shell pans at 450°F for 10 minutes. Cool. Remove from pans. Place tart shells on baking sheet and fill with ice cream. Spoon strawberries over ice cream and place in freezer. Beat egg whites and cream of tartar until frothy. Gradually beat in sugar until stiff. Beat in vanilla. Cover berries with meringue, being sure to seal tarts completely. Bake in preheated 500°F oven for 3-5 minutes. Serve *immediately*. Serves 8.

Mrs. Robert H. Thompson, Jr.

Note: Eight frozen tart shells may be substituted for the pastry shells. Bake as directed and cool before filling.

Lady Gregory Trifle

1 (8 ounce) sponge cake
1 (10 ounce) jar strawberry or
    raspberry jam
1 (17 ounce) jar fruits for salad,
    drained

2 ounces Irish whiskey
1 cup whipping cream, whipped
Fresh fruit in season

Split sponge cake in half; spread each half with jam. Put halves together again and cut into small squares. Place cake squares in crystal bowl. Cut large pieces of fruits for salad in half and add fruit to bowl. Sprinkle with Irish whiskey and pour BOILED CUSTARD over all. Chill. Garnish with whipped cream and fresh fruit. Serves 8.

BOILED CUSTARD

1 pint milk
½ cup sugar
½ teaspoon flour

1 egg, beaten
½ teaspoon vanilla

In top of double boiler bring milk just to a boil. Blend sugar and flour; add to egg. Slowly add hot milk and vanilla to egg mixture; then return custard to top of double boiler. Cook over hot water until custard thickens slightly.

Mrs. Walker W. Jones, III

Pour 3 Tablespoons crème de cassis over individual servings of orange sherbet. Garnish with a sprig of mint.

Frozen Banana Split Dessert

1 cup milk chocolate chips
½ cup butter
2 cups confectioners' sugar
1½ cups milk
1 teaspoon vanilla
Graham cracker crumbs

4 or 5 bananas, sliced
½ gallon neopolitan ice cream or
　any other flavor
1 cup whipping cream, whipped
Chopped nuts

Melt together chocolate chips and butter. Add sugar and milk. Cook at a rolling boil for 8 minutes or until thick, stirring constantly. Add vanilla and cool. Cover bottom of 9 x 13-inch pan with graham cracker crumbs. Cover with bananas. Slice ice cream and place over bananas. Cover with cooled chocolate sauce. Freeze. Serve with whipped cream and sprinkle with chopped nuts. Serves 12-16.

Mrs. Roland F. Samson

Strawberry Ice Box Dessert

1 (12 ounce) package vanilla
　wafers, crushed
½ cup margarine, softened
1½ cups powdered sugar
2 eggs

1 quart fresh strawberries, halved
　& sugared
½ pint whipping cream, whipped
　& sweetened
½ cup chopped pecans (optional)

Place more than half the vanilla wafers in an 8 x 12-inch pan. Cream margarine and sugar; add eggs and beat well. Spread mixture over crumbs. Cover with strawberries, then whipped cream. Cover with remaining crumbs and pecans, if desired. Chill several hours or overnight. Serves 6-8.

Mrs. Don Bruce

Polar Creams in Chocolate Shells

2 (8 ounce) boxes semisweet
　chocolate
2 Tablespoons butter
2 eggs
1 cup brown sugar
⅔ cup butter, melted

½ cup crushed Heath candy bars
½ cup blanched, slivered almonds,
　toasted
1 teaspoon vanilla
1 cup whipping cream, whipped

Melt chocolate with butter and pour in bottoms of 16 paper muffin cups set in muffin tins. Paint chocolate up sides of paper cups, making a very thin chocolate coating. Chill thoroughly or freeze. Beat eggs until thick and light. Add sugar, blending until well dissolved. Add butter, candy, almonds and vanilla. Fold in whipped cream. Spoon into chocolate shells and freeze. Remove from freezer, peel off paper muffin cups and let sit 10 minutes before serving. Serves 16.

Mrs. William F. Goodman, Jr.

Mrs. Garland Lyell's Rum Bumble

1½ Tablespoons unflavored
  gelatin
2 Tablespoons cold water
6 Tablespoons boiling water
1 cup sugar

⅓ cup rum
4 Tablespoons whiskey
2 egg whites, stiffly beaten
1 pint whipping cream, whipped
Toasted almonds, chopped

Soften gelatin in cold water for 5 minutes. Add boiling water and stir to dissolve gelatin. Stir in sugar, rum and whiskey. As it cools and begins to thicken, beat well until frothy. Fold in the egg whites, then the whipped cream. Serve in sherbets with additional whipped cream and almonds on top. Can be made 1 or 2 days ahead; wrap with plastic wrap. Serves 6.

Mrs. Marianne McMullan

Coffee Tortoni

¼ cup chopped almonds
¼ cup flaked coconut
6 Tablespoons sugar, divided
1 Tablespoon instant coffee

1 teaspoon vanilla
3 drops almond extract
1 cup whipping cream, whipped
1 egg white

Toast chopped almonds and coconut in oven. Fold 4 Tablespoons sugar, the instant coffee and flavorings into the whipped cream. Beat egg white to soft peaks. Add 2 Tablespoons sugar and beat until stiff. Fold cream mixture into egg whites. Fold in the almond and coconut mixture, reserving a small amount to sprinkle on top of each serving. Mound into cupcake liners set in muffin tins. May be prepared and frozen several days in advance. Serve frozen. Serves 6.

Mrs. Anson Bob Chunn

Edith's Chocolate Fudge Pudding

1 cup butter or margarine
2 or 3 Tablespoons cocoa
2 cups sugar
4 eggs

1 cup flour
2 cups coarsely chopped pecans
2 teaspoons vanilla

Melt butter. Add cocoa and sugar. Beat in eggs one at a time. Stir in flour, pecans and vanilla. Butter a 9 x 13-inch baking dish. Place dish in a pan of water and bake at 300°F for 1½ hours. Serve warm or chilled with spoonful of whipped cream on top. This pudding is crisp on top and soft on the bottom. Serves 8-10.

Mrs. D. L. Simmons, Jr.

Variation: For a softer fudge pudding use only ½ cup sifted flour and 1 cup chopped pecans. Bake in a 7 x 11-inch baking dish set in a pan of water at 350°F for 1 hour and 10 minutes. Chill; serve upside down.

Mrs. Julian Lee Owen

Fruit Tart or Flan

FLAN SHELL:
¼ cup butter, softened
2 Tablespoons sugar
3 Tablespoons almond paste or
    ¼ cup ground almonds and
    ½ teaspoon almond extract
½ teaspoon grated lemon rind
1 egg white
¾ cup sifted flour

¼ cup currant jelly

ALMOND CUSTARD FILLING:
5 egg yolks

1 cup sugar
⅔ cup sifted flour
2 cups boiling milk
1 Tablespoon butter
2 teaspoons vanilla
¼ teaspoon almond extract
½ cup crushed almond macaroons

Fresh or canned fruits

APRICOT GLAZE:
¾ cup apricot preserves
3 Tablespoons water

FLAN SHELL: Grease and lightly flour an 8-inch cake or quiche pan. Cream together the butter, sugar, almond paste and lemon rind. Add egg white and beat well. Gradually add flour and continue to beat until smooth. Press dough into pan, patting it evenly onto the bottom and sides. Refrigerate for 1 hour; then bake at 300°F for 50 minutes. Cool for 15 minutes and remove from pan to completely cool. In a small saucepan boil the currant jelly until it is very sticky (about 228°F on candy thermometer). Paint the inside of the flan shell with the currant jelly glaze to waterproof it. Let glaze set for 5 minutes. *ALMOND CUSTARD FILLING:* Beat egg yolks, gradually adding sugar, until mixture is pale yellow. Beat in the flour, then the boiling milk in a thin stream. Pour mixture into saucepan and stir with a wire whisk over medium heat until it thickens. Turn heat to low and continue cooking and stirring for 2-3 minutes. Remove from heat, beat in butter and cool slightly before adding flavorings and macaroons. Spoon custard into prepared flan shell. Top flan with fruits. Use fresh fruits in season such as sliced banana rounds, seeded grape halves, peach slices, blackberries, blueberries and strawberry halves. For any season use thawed and drained frozen raspberries, apricot halves, canned peach slices, pineapple chunks, canned blueberries and maraschino cherries. Place raspberries in center of flan, filling a circle about 2 inches in diameter. Make concentric circles around raspberries, using a different fruit for each circle. *APRICOT GLAZE:* In saucepan heat preserves with water, stirring constantly until preserves melt. Strain or push through a sieve. Keep warm over hot water until ready to use. Brush or drip over top of fruit. Refrigerate flan until ready to serve. Serves 8.

Mrs. Clyde Copeland, Jr.

EASY BERRY COBBLER

Melt ½ cup butter in bottom of an 8 x 8-inch baking dish. Combine well 1 cup each Bisquick, sugar and milk. Pour mixture over butter in pan. Pour in 1 quart fresh fruit (blackberries, strawberries, peach slices or cut-up red plums). Bake at 350°F for 35-45 minutes. Serve topped with ice cream. Serves 6-8.

Baked Figs

Fill a baking dish tight with fresh figs, stems down. Sprinkle heavily with dark brown sugar and a little lemon juice. Prick figs with a fork and bake for about an hour at 300°F. Serve hot figs immediately in a bowl with the syrup and a spoonful sour cream. Use 6 or 7 figs per serving.

Mrs. Albert W. Lyle

Peach Clafouti

5 Tablespoons sugar, divided
3 cups sliced, peeled fresh
   peaches
1 cup milk
1 cup half and half cream
3 eggs

¼ cup flour
Pinch salt
1 teaspoon vanilla
Confectioners' sugar or vanilla
   ice cream

Sprinkle a well-buttered 1½-quart shallow, oval baking dish with 2 Tablespoons sugar. Distribute peaches over the sugar. In a blender blend milk, cream, eggs, flour and salt for 2 minutes. Add vanilla and remaining sugar. Blend mixture for a few seconds; then pour over fruit. Bake in preheated 375°F oven for 45-50 minutes or until puffed and golden. Sprinkle the clafouti with sifted confectioners' sugar or top with vanilla ice cream. Serve immediately. Serves 6.

Mrs. Zach Hederman, Jr.

Banana Pudding

3¾ cups milk
2 (3¼ ounce) packages vanilla
   pudding and pie mix
3 eggs, separated
3 teaspoons vanilla, divided
1 cup whipping cream, whipped

1 (3 ounce) package lady fingers
   or 1 (13 ounce) angel food
   cake, torn into small pieces
4 bananas, sliced thinly crosswise
¼ teaspoon ground nutmeg
⅓ cup sugar

In medium saucepan gradually blend milk and pudding mix. Add egg yolks and 1 teaspoon vanilla, beating with electric mixer until smooth. Cook, stirring constantly, until pudding comes to a full boil. Remove from heat, cover with foil or plastic wrap and cool thoroughly, about 20-30 minutes. Fold in whipped cream to which remaining vanilla has been added. Arrange ½ the lady fingers or cake in bottom of 2½-quart baking dish. Spoon ½ the pudding over cake and arrange ½ the bananas over pudding. Sprinkle layer with ½ the nutmeg. Repeat layers once more. Beat egg whites, gradually adding sugar, until stiff. Spoon meringue over cooled pudding and bake at 350°F for 7-8 minutes or until lightly browned. Serves 8.

Mrs. Sally C. Knight

Date Dessert

¼ cup flour
1 teaspoon baking powder
1 cup chopped pecans
1 cup chopped dates (not pre-chopped type)

4 egg whites
1 cup sugar
1½ teaspoons vanilla
1 cup whipping cream, whipped

Sift flour and baking powder over pecans and dates and toss well. Beat egg whites stiff, adding sugar gradually, then vanilla. Fold in date mixture. Bake in an 8 or 9-inch square pan that has been thoroughly greased and floured at 350°F for 40 minutes. Cut in squares and top generously with sweetened whipped cream. Serves 9.

Mrs. Profilet Couillard, Natchez, Mississippi

Ramada Inn Bread Pudding

6 eggs
1½ cups sugar
2 pints half and half cream
¼ teaspoon salt
2 teaspoons vanilla

6 dinner rolls, torn in small pieces
2 Tablespoons butter, diced
2 Tablespoons brown sugar
Ice cream (optional)

Beat eggs well; add next 4 ingredients and blend together well. Fold torn rolls into egg mixture. Pour custard mixture into ungreased 3-quart Pyrex baking dish and bake at 350°F for 1 hour. Sprinkle top of hot pudding with butter pieces, then brown sugar. Serve immediately, topped with ice cream, if desired. Can be prepared the same day, but do not bake until 1½ hours before serving. Serves 8.

Ramada Inn—Coliseum

Betty's Blueberry-Banana Dessert

¾ cup margarine
1½ cups self-rising flour
1 cup chopped pecans
1 (8 ounce) package cream cheese, softened
1 cup sugar

2 (1½ ounce) envelopes Dream Whip
5 ripe bananas, sliced
1 (16 ounce) can blueberry pie filling

Melt margarine in bottom of a 9 x 13-inch Pyrex dish and add flour and pecans. Mix well and spread over bottom of dish. Bake at 275°F for 1 hour. Cool. Beat together cream cheese and sugar. Prepare Dream Whip by package directions and fold into cream cheese mixture. Spread over crust. Top with bananas and cover with blueberry pie filling. Cover and chill in refrigerator. Cut into squares to serve. Serves 8-10.

Mrs. Guy M. Parker, Jr.

Queen's Bread Pudding

4 cups bread cubes, toasted
1 quart milk, heated
3 Tablespoons butter
4 eggs, separated
Dash salt

1¼ cups sugar, divided
1 teaspoon vanilla
2 teaspoons grated lemon rind
½ cup tart jelly (preferably
   currant)

Combine bread cubes, milk and butter. Allow to stand 10 minutes. Beat egg yolks and salt until light. Add 1 cup sugar and vanilla and beat until lemon-colored. Add bread mixture. Pour into a buttered 2-quart baking dish. Bake at 350°F for about 50 minutes. Cool slightly. Beat egg whites until foamy. Add remaining sugar gradually and beat until mixture stands in firm peaks. Fold in lemon rind. Spread jelly on pudding. Cover with meringue and bake 10-15 minutes longer or until meringue is golden brown. Serves 8-10.

Mrs. Sally C. Knight

Macaroon Dessert

36 almond macaroons
Bourbon
½ pint whipping cream

2 quarts almond toffee or coffee
   ice cream
Toasted almonds

Line a bowl or mold with macaroons, reserving a few for the top. Pour as much bourbon over macaroons as they will absorb. Place in refrigerator and chill. Whip cream stiffly, flavoring lightly with bourbon. Spoon ice cream over macaroons in bowl. Spread with whipped cream and sprinkle with toasted almonds and crumbled bourbon-soaked macaroons. Place in freezer. Serves 12-16.

Mrs. Thomas Mitchell Robinson

Louis's Chocolate Pudding

2 (1 ounce) squares unsweetened
   chocolate
1 cup sugar
1 Tablespoon flour

Pinch salt
1 cup milk
3 egg yolks, beaten
½ teaspoon vanilla

Melt chocolate on very low heat in heavy saucepan. In another saucepan mix sugar, flour and salt; add milk and heat until almost boiling. Add to melted chocolate. Take off heat; add small amount of milk mixture to egg yolks, stirring constantly. Return egg mixture to remaining milk, stirring constantly. Cook in top of double boiler until thick; do not allow to boil. Remove from heat and add vanilla. Chill before serving. Serves 4.

Mrs. Herbert A. Kroeze, Jr.

Variation: A meringue of the egg whites can be spread on top of pudding or may be folded into pudding. Can also use 3 whole eggs instead of 3 yolks.

English Toffee Squares

1 cup crushed vanilla wafers
1 cup chopped pecans
½ cup butter, softened
1 cup powdered sugar
3 eggs, separated

1½ (1 ounce) squares unsweetened
   chocolate, melted
½ teaspoon vanilla
Whipping cream, whipped

Mix vanilla wafer crumbs and pecans together. Using half the mixture, cover the bottom of a buttered 9 x 9-inch pan. Cream butter and sugar and beat in beaten egg yolks, melted chocolate and vanilla. Fold in stiffly beaten egg whites. Pour mixture over wafers and spread remaining crumbs on top. Refrigerate overnight. Cut in squares and serve with whipped cream. May be prepared several days in advance and kept in refrigerator or frozen. Serves 9.

Mrs. John R. Hutcherson

Lemon Cups

2 Tablespoons butter, melted
1 cup sugar
¼ cup flour
1/8 teaspoon salt

5 Tablespoons lemon juice
Grated rind of 1 lemon
3 eggs, separated
1½ cups scalded milk

Cream butter with sugar, flour and salt. Add lemon juice and rind. Set aside. Beat egg yolks well. Beat a little scalded milk into egg yolks; then return mixture to milk, beating constantly. Add to creamed mixture and mix well. Fold in stiffly beaten egg whites. Pour into greased custard cups or a greased shallow baking dish, placed in a pan of hot water. Bake in preheated 350 °F oven for 45 minutes. When baked, each dessert will have custard on the bottom and sponge cake on top. Serve hot or cold. Serves 8.

From the recipes of Mrs. Viola Moore

Fresh Strawberry Parfait

1 pint vanilla ice cream,
   softened
½ cup crushed vanilla wafers or
   almond macaroons
¼ cup finely ground nuts
½ teaspoon grated lemon rind

½ cup sugar
½ cup sliced strawberries, or more
1 egg white
½ cup sour cream
Whipping cream, whipped
Strawberries for garnish

Place a layer of ice cream in each parfait glass. Combine wafers, nuts and rind. Layer a spoonful of mixture on ice cream. Beat sugar, strawberries and egg white with electric mixer until soft peaks form, about 10 minutes. Gently fold in sour cream. Spoon a layer of strawberry mixture into parfait glasses. Repeat layers until glass is full. Freeze. Top with whipped cream and garnish with a strawberry. Serves 6-8.

Mrs. William H. Hight, Louisville, Mississippi

Fraises Romanoff

1 quart fresh strawberries
½ cup Grand Marnier
½ cup fresh orange juice
1 cup whipping cream

2 to 4 Tablespoons
  confectioners' sugar
½ teaspoon vanilla

Wash and hull berries. Place in a bowl with liqueur and orange juice; cover and chill for several hours, turning occasionally. Whip cream and add sugar, according to sweetness of berries, and vanilla. To serve, place berries and some of the juices in individual glass serving dishes or in a large glass serving bowl. Pipe whipped cream decoratively on top with pastry bag. Candied violets make an attractive garnish. Serves 6.

Mrs. William B. Wilson

Raspberry Mousse

1 (10 ounce) package frozen
  raspberries, thawed
¾ cup sugar
1 cup water, divided

1 envelope unflavored gelatin
1 cup whipping cream, whipped
3 Tablespoons kirsch

Blend raspberries in blender and strain to remove seeds. In a heavy saucepan stir sugar and ¾ cup water together. Boil without stirring until syrup registers 240°F on candy thermometer. Cool slightly. Soften gelatin in ¼ cup water and add to hot syrup. Stir until dissolved. Add syrup to raspberry purée and chill until syrupy, stirring occasionally. When mixture begins to thicken, fold in whipped cream that has been flavored with kirsch. Quickly spoon mousse into cups or sherbets and chill. To serve, top with additional whipped cream. Serves 6.

Mrs. Warren V. Ludlam, Jr.

Dessert Fondues

CHOCOLATE FONDUE

Break 3 (3 ounce) bars Toblerone chocolate into pieces. Combine with ½ cup whipping cream and 2 Tablespoons Cointreau in a saucepan and stir over low heat until chocolate melts and mixture is smooth. Serve in chafing dish over low flame. For dipping, use chunks of angel food cake, orange or tangerine slices, fresh whole strawberries, pineapple chunks or banana slices. Serves 8.

CARAMEL FONDUE

Over low heat melt 1 (15 ounce) bag caramels with ½ cup whipping cream. Stir in 2 Tablespoons brandy or rum. Serve from chafing dish using apple wedges, large marshmallows, pineapple chunks or stemmed maraschino cherries for dipping. Serves 8.

Mrs. Charles M. Head

Floating Islands

2 eggs, separated
2 egg yolks
1½ cups sugar, divided
¼ teaspoon salt

2 cups half and half cream,
  scalded
½ teaspoon vanilla
3 cups water

Beat the 4 egg yolks well. In top of double boiler combine eggs, ¼ cup sugar and salt. Slowly stir in scalded cream. Cook over boiling water until custard coats spoon. Cook 2 minutes more. Cool at once in sink of cold water, stirring several minutes. Stir in vanilla. Pour into individual bowls. Beat egg whites with a dash salt to soft peaks. Gradually add ¼ cup sugar. Beat to stiff peaks. In skillet heat water to a gentle boil. Drop egg whites, shaped in 6 puffs, into water. Poach 5 minutes, turning to poach each side. Drain on paper towels. Place 1 meringue puff on top of each bowl of custard. Caramelize remaining cup of sugar by stirring over low heat until sugar melts and forms a syrup. Immediately drizzle over meringue puffs and custard. Serve with shortbread cookies. Serves 6.

Mrs. Louis E. Ridgway, Jr.

Variation: For a rum-flavored custard add ¼ cup rum to cream before scalding. Almond extract may be used to flavor meringues.

Aunt Ruby's Apple Fritters

1½ cups flour
½ teaspoon salt
2 Tablespoons sugar
1 teaspoon baking powder
2 Tablespoons cooking oil
1 egg, beaten

1 Tablespoon milk
½ teaspoon vanilla
¼ teaspoon ground nutmeg
1 apple, peeled
Cooking oil for deep frying
Powdered sugar

Mix flour, salt, sugar and baking powder together. Make a well in the center of the mixture and add oil, egg and milk. Mix well. Add vanilla and nutmeg. Grate apple on large side of grater. Stir into batter and refrigerate overnight. Fry in deep oil by the heaping spoonfuls. Drain fritters on paper towels. Just before serving pour LEMON SAUCE over fritters and sprinkle with powdered sugar. Serves 6.

LEMON SAUCE

1 egg, beaten
4 Tablespoons butter
Juice of 2 lemons

1 cup sugar
½ cup water

Mix all ingredients. Cook in heavy saucepan over low heat until thicker and syrupy. Will keep in refrigerator 1 week. Makes 1½ cups sauce.

Mrs. Herbert A. Kroeze, Jr.

Special Techniques
for
Special Dishes

Soufflés

A soufflé is a dramatic production, but its basic ingredients are quite ordinary. It is essentially an egg dish with a base which often serves to stabilize the airy mixture. The ideal soufflé dish has straight sides and a flat bottom. For single portions an 8-ounce size is best. To prepare a soufflé dish, make a collar from a double layer of wax paper or foil. Use tasteless cooking oil to grease paper lightly on the inside so that it will peel off easily when the soufflé is set. Wrap band around dish so that it extends at least 1½ inches above it and attach it with a string. This should be done before beginning to combine ingredients.

INGREDIENTS   A perfectly smooth base is necessary for a successful hot soufflé. Careful cooking and constant stirring with a wire whisk over low heat can prevent lumps. The egg yolks give both lightness and thickening power to a soufflé. They may be added to the sauce in two ways. A portion of hot sauce may be blended into the thickly beaten egg yolks a little at a time to warm them and the mixture then stirred into the remaining sauce; or the sauce may be cooled for 10-15 minutes and the beaten egg yolks briskly stirred into it. An important step is the preparation and addition of the egg whites. They should be at room temperature. Cream of tartar added in the foamy stage of beating will increase volume and stability. Egg whites may be folded into sauce all at once or a portion may be stirred into the sauce until thoroughly blended and the remainder then folded in.

PROCEDURE   Preheat oven to specified temperature before placing soufflé in it. Sometimes the soufflé dish is placed in a pan of hot water to help hold the soufflé longer for serving. Do not peek at soufflé until 5 minutes before baking time is completed. Open oven and touch soufflé with finger to see if it springs back and is done. A hot soufflé must be served at peak of perfection, right out of the oven. To serve it quickly and easily, cut portions with a fork, then spoon them lightly onto the plate. The fork does less damage to the structure than a spoon would do in cutting it.

―――――――

A soufflé mixture can be prepared and placed in the soufflé dish up to 30 minutes before cooking. If soufflé is to be held for this length of time, place a bowl over it to keep it free from drafts.

Never Fail Cheese Soufflé

4 Tablespoons butter	1 cup shredded Cheddar cheese
6 Tablespoons flour	6 eggs, separated
1 cup evaporated milk	1 teaspoon salt

Wrap greased aluminum foil collar around edge of lightly greased 2-quart soufflé dish. Melt butter in saucepan; slowly stir in flour until smooth. Gradually stir in milk; simmer, stirring constantly, until thickened. Add cheese, well-beaten egg yolks and salt. Cook over low heat until cheese melts and the mixture is smooth. Cool about 30 minutes before folding in stiffly beaten egg whites. Pour into soufflé dish. Bake at 350°F for 30 minutes. Remove collar and serve at once. Serves 8.

Mrs. Nat Graham

Grand Marnier Soufflé

3 Tablespoons butter	5 egg yolks
2 Tablespoons flour	5 Tablespoons Grand Marnier
1 cup whipping cream	½ teaspoon cream of tartar
6 Tablespoons sugar	6 egg whites

Melt butter in top of double boiler and add the flour. Mix well and cook for a moment. Pour in cream, stirring constantly until mixture thickens; then add sugar. When sugar is dissolved, remove from heat and allow to cool. When cool, beat yolks and stir in along with Grand Marnier. Sprinkle cream of tartar over the egg whites while beating them into stiff, moist peaks. Take ⅓ of the beaten whites and mix vigorously into the Grand Marnier custard. Dribble custard over the remaining egg whites and fold together thoroughly and carefully. Butter sides and bottom of a 2-quart soufflé dish; then sprinkle thoroughly with sugar. Pour mixture into prepared dish and place in a preheated 350°F oven for about 25-30 minutes. Before removing from the oven, test to be sure soufflé is done by shaking to see if firm. Serve immediately, passing GRAND MARNIER SAUCE to spoon over individual servings. Serves 6.

GRAND MARNIER SAUCE

½ cup sugar	3 Tablespoons strong black
3 Tablespoons Grand Marnier	coffee

In a small, heavy iron skillet melt the sugar and stir until rich brown (be very careful not to burn). Remove from heat and stir in Grand Marnier and coffee. Return to heat for a moment and stir until blended. If caramelized sugar does not dissolve after a few minutes, add 1-2 Tablespoons water and stir over heat until it does dissolve. This sauce can be used hot, cold or lukewarm. Makes ¾ cup sauce.

Robert L. Abney

Caramelizing Sugar

CARAMELIZING SUGAR ALONE When a recipe calls for caramelizing a specified amount of sugar, measure sugar into a heavy-bottomed saucepan. Place over medium heat and allow sugar to melt, stirring if desired. When sugar has dissolved completely, continue cooking syrup until just golden in color. Do not overcook, as syrup will burn. Remove from heat and use as indicated in recipe.

CARAMELIZING SUGAR WITH WATER Place water and sugar in amounts called for in recipe in a heavy pan. As the liquid comes to a boil over moderate heat, swirl the pan by manipulating the handle. Do not stir. Continue to swirl the pan until liquid is clear and all sugar dissolved. Cover pan 2-3 minutes as the sugar boils to wash the side of the pan of sugar crystals. Uncover pan and swirl now and then until sugar is almost as brown as desired. Syrup will continue to brown after removal from heat. Use in recipe as indicated.

HANDLING CARAMELIZED SUGAR If recipe calls for water to be added to caramelized sugar, *heat* water and add it very slowly, stirring constantly. When adding caramelized sugar into a liquid, add it slowly to the *hot* liquid, stirring constantly. Do not scrape the bottom of the caramelizing pan or sugar crystals may be introduced into the liquid. Stir over low heat only until all the sugar is dissolved. Cover pan and let mixture simmer 3 minutes to dissolve any sugar crystals on the side of the pan. Remove cover and cook to the desired stage. If the liquid needs to be stirred, swirl it by the handle of the pan. When testing to determine the stage of the liquid, use a clean spoon or thermometer that is free from any sugar particles.

Southern Pecan Pralines

3 cups sugar, divided	Pinch baking soda
1 teaspoon salt	½ cup butter
1 (5.33 ounce) can	1 teaspoon vanilla
evaporated milk, rinsed with	1 quart pecans, toasted
a little water	

Combine 2 cups sugar with salt, milk and soda. Caramelize 1 cup sugar in an iron skillet over low heat. Pour caramelized sugar into milk mixture and stir until dissolved. Cook to soft ball stage on candy thermometer. Remove from heat and add butter and vanilla. Beat with spoon until shine has gone and it has cooled enough to drop on wax paper. Add pecans and drop on wax paper. If mixture gets too hard, place back on heat and add a little water. Makes 12 small pralines.

Mrs. Buford Yerger, Jr.

372

Caramel Icing

3½ cups sugar, divided
3 Tablespoons boiling water

1 cup whipping cream
3 Tablespoons butter, melted

Caramelize ½ cup sugar by melting it in a heavy saucepan until it becomes a golden brown syrup. Add boiling water slowly, stirring constantly. In a second saucepan stir together the remaining sugar, cream and butter. Warm cream mixture over low heat. Pour caramelized sugar into cream mixture and cook to the soft ball stage (240°F). Cool to 140°F. Beat to spreading consistency and spread on cooled cake. Icing is sufficient to ice a 2-layer 9-inch cake.

Mrs. Nat Graham

Flan
(Caramel Custard)

4 cups milk
1⅔ cups sugar, divided

4 eggs
1 teaspoon vanilla

Simmer milk and 1 cup sugar slowly for 5-6 minutes. Caramelize ⅔ cup sugar in a small pan until medium brown in color; pour a little in each mold. Let milk and sugar mixture cool. Beat eggs only enough to mix yolks and whites. Strain milk mixture into eggs. Blend; remove any foam. (Foam makes bubbles in custard.) Add vanilla. Fill molds and place them in a pan of cold water. Bake in preheated 400°F oven for 45 minutes. Custard is done when firm to the touch. Chill. When ready to serve unmold by running a knife around mold and inverting. May be prepared several days in advance. Makes 10 (6 ounce) molds.

Mrs. James R. Galyean, III

Caramel Pots de Crème

1 cup sugar, divided
2 cups milk, divided
3 Tablespoons flour
1/8 teaspoon salt
2 eggs, slightly beaten

1 teaspoon vanilla
Whipping cream, whipped
Chopped almonds, toasted
1 teaspoon brandy

Caramelize ½ cup sugar in a small heavy pan until light brown. Heat 1 cup milk in double boiler and slowly pour the caramelized sugar into it. Blend. Mix well the remaining sugar, flour and salt. Pour remaining milk over this mixture. Combine with the milk and caramel mixture. Allow mixture to cook a short while; then stir in the eggs, which have been mixed with a little of the hot mixture. Cook slowly, stirring, until mixture becomes the consistency of heavy cream. Add vanilla. Pour into pots de crème cups and chill. Serve topped with sweetened whipped cream to which almonds and brandy have been added. Serves 4.

Mrs. John Nicholson, Jr.

Puff Pastry

Basic Puff Pastry

2 cups butter (preferably
   unsalted)
4 cups sifted unbleached flour

½ teaspoon salt
1 Tablespoon lemon juice
1⅓ cups water, divided

Puff pastry is made by enclosing thin layers of butter between thin layers of dough. BUTTER: Use the best grade butter available. Flatten the cold butter by beating with a rolling pin. Dip hands in a bowl of ice and knead 1 stick butter at a time until waxy, pliable and no longer lumpy. Squeeze while kneading to remove water. Dip hands in ice from time to time to prevent butter from becoming oily. After each stick is kneaded, dry it on paper towels and set aside in a cool place. When all butter has been kneaded, form it together into a rough brick, wrap in wax paper and refrigerate. DOUGH: Set aside 3 Tablespoons flour. Place remaining flour in a pile on pastry board. Mix salt, lemon juice and 1 cup water in a small bowl. Make a well in the center of the flour and pour a little lemon water into it. Gather in enough flour to form a small rough ball. Continue to form balls until all the lemon water has been used. Add about ⅓ cup more water, sprinkling it over the remaining dry flour, and gather it with the small balls into 1 ball of dough which is sticky but firm. More or less water may be needed, depending on the flour. Knead the dough ball 15-20 minutes or until smooth and elastic. While kneading, dip fingers into some water to prevent dough from becoming too dry. Cover dough and let it rest in the refrigerator for 10 minutes. INCORPORATING BUTTER AND DOUGH: Remove the butter from the refrigerator and with a knife or pastry scraper form it into a 5-inch square brick. Coat the brick well with the reserved flour. Refrigerate until the resting period for the dough is over. Remove dough from refrigerator. Cut a crisscross in the top and spread it apart to form a 4-leaf clover shape. Roll out to flatten and extend the leaves. Place the butter brick in the center of the dough. Bring the leaves back on top of the butter, overlapping in the center. Seal leaves to enclose butter. Flour the package well, wrap in plastic wrap and refrigerate for 30 minutes. Flour pastry board and rolling pin well. Place dough, with the sealed leaf side up, in the center of the floured area. Roll the dough from the center to the end, stopping ½ inch from the end so the butter will not be expelled. Turn the dough and roll from the center to the opposite end. Continue rolling and turning dough until a rectangle 17 inches long, 8 inches wide and 3/8 inch thick has been formed. Roll over the short ends lightly in the opposite direction to flatten them to the same thickness as the rest. If at any time the butter breaks through, pat with a little flour and continue. TURNING: Brush the flour from the dough lightly. Fold dough back on itself to a point about ⅔ up the 17-inch side of the rectangle. Roll the folded part lightly to equalize it. Brush the flour from the top. Fold the top part of the dough (or the remaining ⅓ of the rectangle) over the first as in folding a business letter. One *turn* has now been completed. Wrap the dough in plastic wrap and chill for 15 or 20 minutes. Flour board and rolling pin well. Place dough with the short ends at the top and bottom and the open edge of the folded part facing left. Roll out from the center and fold as before to make a second *turn*, remembering to brush the flour off before folding the dough over that part. Make a 2-finger impression on the dough to signify the number of *turns* completed. Again wrap dough and chill 15 or 20 minutes. Complete 6 *turns* in all, chilling 15 or 20 minutes between *turns*. After the 6th *turn* has been completed, refrigerate the dough for at least 3 hours before forming. Puff pastry wrapped well can be kept in the refrigerator 3-4 days or frozen. Fresh puff pastry may be shaped, frozen and then baked up to 3 months later.

CROISSANTS DE PATISSERIE

Cut off a portion of puff pastry parallel to the short side. Roll the dough out in a long strip ¼ inch thick. Trim off the uncut edges. With a sharp knife cut the dough into 3 or 4-inch squares. Cut each square into 2 triangles. Brush the tops with an egg beaten with 1 teaspoon water. Roll up each triangle from the wide side going toward the point. Curve the rolled-up dough into a crescent with the point facing the inside center. Place on a baking pan with sides which has been rinsed with cold water. Place pan in freezer or the coldest spot of the refrigerator for 1 hour. Preheat oven to 375°F. Remove pan from freezer. Brush the tops of the croissants again with the egg wash. Do not let egg run down onto the pan or the croissants will not rise properly. Bake 30 minutes until puffy and brown. Croissants freeze well or may be kept in a plastic bag for several days. If frozen, heat in a 250°F oven for about 10 minutes or longer.

INDIVIDUAL PATTY SHELLS

Roll out pastry in a rectangle ¼ inch thick. Trim off all uncut edges to allow dough to rise properly. Cut rounds about 3 inches in diameter with a sharp cutter. Place ½ the rounds on a baking pan with sides which has been rinsed with cold water. Brush the tops with 1 egg beaten with 1 teaspoon water. Using a smaller cutter, cut a circle from the center of the remaining rounds, creating a ring about ½ inch wide. (Reserve small center rounds.) Place the rings on each large round on the baking pan and push into place. Mark the edges of the rounds with the dull side of a knife to form a tiny scallop pattern. Place reserved center rounds on pan and bake to use as tops for filled shells, if desired. Rounds will look almost flat but will rise up to 6 times the original size. Place pan in the freezer or the coldest spot of the refrigerator for 1 hour. Preheat oven to 425°F. Remove dough. Brush lightly with egg wash. Place 4 custard cups on the 4 corners of the pan and balance a wire rack on top of them. This will help keep the shells even as they bake. Bake for 15 minutes at 425°F. Turn heat down to 350°F and bake about 20 minutes longer, or until brown. Take shells from oven, remove from the centers any soggy unbaked pastry and return them to a turned-off oven to crisp. The shells may be frozen or stored in plastic bags. Crisp before using. Fill with creamed chicken or seafood.

Mrs. Herbert A. Kroeze, Jr.

Crêpes

COOKING CRÊPES   Heat 1 Tablespoon oil in a 5 or 7-inch crêpe pan or heavy skillet. Pour out oil. The little bit remaining in pan will be enough for cooking crêpes. Heat pan to a moderately high temperature. Select a spoon or ladle which holds enough batter to film the bottom of the pan. Pour a spoonful of batter into the pan and roll it around quickly until the base is completely covered. Tip out excess batter. As soon as the edges of the crêpe have begun to brown, use a spatula to flip it over. The second side will cook more quickly. Remove the first crêpe from the pan and throw it away, as it is used only to absorb the oil from the pan. The side which cooks first is the outside because it is more attractive. As each crêpe is made, place it in a stack on a clean tea towel. Continue making crêpes in this manner, thinning the batter with a little milk if it gets too thick. If the batter will not spread over the pan, the pan is too hot. Wave pan about in the air to cool it. Crêpes cooked at too high a heat are tough.

FILLING AND FOLDING CRÊPES   Place 2 Tablespoons filling on each small crêpe. Do not use more or it will leak out the ends. Usually 2-3 crêpes are served per person. Most crêpes are rolled jelly-roll fashion with filling in the middle. To fold crêpes into quarters (as for Crêpes Suzette), fold to a half-circle then in half once more, forming a fan shape. The envelope fold is used if the filling is juicy. Spoon filling into center of crêpe; fold sides in toward center. Next carefully roll up from the bottom, keeping sides tucked in. Crêpes will keep in refrigerator in a plastic bag for 2-3 days. They can be frozen either filled or unfilled with great success.

Basic Crêpe Batter

1 (13 ounce) can evaporated milk
¾ cup water
4 eggs
¼ cup butter, melted
½ teaspoon salt
1 Tablespoon sugar
1½ cups flour

2 Tablespoons minced parsley (optional)
1 Tablespoon chopped chives (optional)
2 Tablespoons toasted sesame seeds (optional)
1 teaspoon fresh dill (optional)

Blend first 7 ingredients in blender for 1½ minutes at medium speed. Stir in optional ingredients in any combination desired for crêpes with chicken or seafood fillings. Let sit covered in refrigerator at least 2 or 3 hours or overnight before making crêpes. Makes 24 crêpes.

Mrs. Alvin E. Brent, Jr.

―――――

For an easy dessert crêpe, fill crêpes with warmed pie filling or fruit preserves. Sprinkle rolled crêpes with powdered sugar and garnish with whipped or sour cream.

Lisbon Lemon Crêpes

8 crêpes
¾ cup sugar
2 teaspoons grated lemon rind
2 Tablespoons butter or
   margarine

SAUCE:
½ cup butter or margarine
¼ cup brandy
¼ cup orange-flavored liqueur
2 Tablespoons lemon juice

Prepare crêpes. Fold crêpes in half and arrange in a slightly overlapping layer in a buttered shallow flameproof dish. Sprinkle crêpes with sugar mixed with lemon rind and dot with butter. Broil crêpes about 5 inches from heat until sugar is melted and bubbling. While crêpes are broiling, make SAUCE. In saucepan melt butter and add brandy, liqueur and lemon juice. Stir until well blended. Serve crêpes immediately with SAUCE to spoon over them. Serves 4.

Mrs. Reuel May, Jr.

Almond Soufflé Crêpes

18 crêpes

PRALINE:
½ cup sugar
1 (4 ounce) package sliced
   almonds, divided

SOUFFLÉ:
8 eggs, separated

2 cups milk
1½ cups sugar, divided
1 Tablespoon cornstarch
½ cup flour
1 teaspoon vanilla
2 Tablespoons rum
1/8 teaspoon salt

Whipped cream (optional)

Prepare crêpes. *PRALINE:* In a heavy saucepan melt the sugar until caramelized; then add ½ the almonds and stir until well coated with caramelized sugar. Quickly pour onto a piece of aluminum foil or marble slab and let cool completely. When cool and hard, crush praline mixture with a hammer or in a food processor until quite fine. Set aside. *SOUFFLÉ:* In heavy saucepan combine egg yolks, milk, 1 cup sugar, cornstarch, flour and vanilla. Cook over moderate heat, stirring constantly with a wire whisk until very thick. Remove from heat, stir in rum and ½ the praline powder. Set aside to cool to room temperature. Beat egg whites with salt until frothy. Continue beating until stiff, gradually adding the remaining sugar. Stir ⅓ of the egg whites into the cooled custard to lighten it; then gently fold in the remaining whites. Butter 3 (8½ x 11 inch) Pyrex pans. Place ½ cup soufflé mixture in center of each crêpe and roll up. Place side by side in baking dish. Sprinkle with remaining praline powder and remaining almonds. Bake at 400°F for 12-15 minutes. Serve hot with almond flavored whipped cream, if desired. The crêpes may be made, covered and refrigerated up to 5 hours before serving. Bring to room temperature before baking. Serves 8-10.

Mrs. G. G. Mazzaferro

Crêpes Fruits de Mer

16 crêpes

2 Tablespoons each finely
chopped chives, parsley,
tarragon, divided

3 Tablespoons butter

2 Tablespoons finely chopped
shallots

⅓ cup dry white wine

1 cup finely diced cooked
lobster meat

1 cup finely diced cooked
shrimp

1 cup lump crab meat

Salt and freshly ground pepper
to taste

Butter, melted

Prepare crêpes, adding 1 Tablespoon each of chives, parsley and tarragon to the batter. Place butter in a saucepan and add the shallots. Cook briefly, stirring, and add wine. Cook to reduce by half. Add the remaining herbs and seafood and stir to blend. Sprinkle with salt and pepper and cook briefly, stirring, until thoroughly heated. Preheat oven to warm. Spoon equal portions of seafood mixture on the center of each crêpe and roll up. Arrange crêpes on a plate and brush with melted butter. Butter a sheet of wax paper and place it buttered side down over crêpes. Cover and place in the oven. Bake briefly just until heated. Serve on hot plates, spooning a little CURRY SAUCE on half of each crêpe and a little SAUCE PICANTE on the other half. Serves 8.

CURRY SAUCE

4½ Tablespoons butter,
divided

1 clove garlic, finely minced

⅓ cup finely chopped onion

⅓ cup finely chopped celery

3 Tablespoons chopped carrot

2 Tablespoons flour

2 Tablespoons curry powder

½ bay leaf

2 sprigs parsley, chopped

2 sprigs fresh thyme or
½ teaspoon dried

1¾ cups chicken broth

Salt and freshly ground pepper
to taste

Heat 3 Tablespoons butter in saucepan and add the garlic, onion, celery and carrot. Cook, stirring, until onion is wilted. Add flour and cook, stirring, about 3 minutes. Stir in the curry, bay leaf, parsley and thyme. Using a wire whisk, continue to stir briskly while adding the broth. Simmer covered about 30 minutes, stirring occasionally. Press the mixture, including vegetables, through a fine sieve using a wooden spoon. Add remaining butter to sauce and salt and pepper. Yields about 1½ cups sauce.

SAUCE PICANTE

2 Tablespoons Dijon mustard

3 Tablespoons Escoffier bottled
sauce Robert

4 Tablespoons Escoffier bottled
sauce Diable

¼ teaspoon Worcestershire
sauce

¼ teaspoon Tabasco

1¼ cups whipping cream

Salt and pepper

(Continued)

378

In a saucepan combine all ingredients. Simmer, stirring occasionally, about 10 minutes. Yields about 1½ cups sauce.

Mrs. Richard L. Redmont, Jr.

Crab Meat Crêpes with Sauce Parisienne

24 crêpes
14 Tablespoons butter, divided
½ cup plus 2 Tablespoons
  flour
2 teaspoons salt
1 quart milk
2 Tablespoons chopped onion
2 Tablespoons chopped green
  pepper
2 teaspoons lemon juice

Curry powder to taste (optional)
½ teaspoon Worcestershire
  sauce
¼ teaspoon pepper
Dash cayenne pepper
1 cup dry white wine
1½ pounds fresh crab meat
½ cup whipping cream
6 Tablespoons grated Parmesan
  cheese

Prepare crêpes. In a heavy 2-quart saucepan melt 10 Tablespoons butter. Remove from heat. Add flour and salt. Stir until smooth. Gradually add milk. Bring to boil, stirring; reduce heat. Simmer 5 minutes. Set aside. Reserve 1 cup white sauce for later use in SAUCE PARISIENNE. In remaining 4 Tablespoons butter, sauté onion and pepper for 1 minute. Stir in lemon juice, curry powder, if desired, Worcestershire sauce, pepper and cayenne pepper until smooth. Bring to a boil and remove from heat. Stir in remaining white sauce along with white wine. Fold in crab meat. Spread a little filling on bottom of baking dish. To assemble crêpes, spoon 2 Tablespoons filling into center of each and roll up. Arrange seam side down in prepared baking dish. Bake 20 minutes at 350°F. While crêpes are baking, prepare SAUCE PARISIENNE. Whip the cream and fold into it. Pour sauce over baked crêpes and sprinkle with Parmesan cheese. Place under broiler 4-6 inches from heat until nicely browned. Serves 12.

SAUCE PARISIENNE

2 egg yolks
¼ teaspoon salt
½ cup butter, melted

4 teaspoons lemon juice
1 cup white sauce

Beat egg yolks with salt until foamy. Gradually beat in half the butter. Combine remaining butter with lemon juice. Gradually beat into egg yolk mixture. Fold into white sauce. Makes 1½ cups sauce.

Mrs. G. Richard Greenlee

———

For a quick crêpe filling mix any diced leftover seafood with a can of cream of shrimp soup and season with lemon juice and sherry wine. Fill crêpes, sprinkle with grated Parmesan cheese and heat.

Tower of Crêpes with Crab Meat Sauce

24 (6 inch) crêpes

MORNAY SAUCE:
4 Tablespoons butter
5 Tablespoons flour
2¾ cups milk, warmed
¾ teaspoon salt
1/8 teaspoon white pepper
¼ cup whipping cream
¾ cup grated Swiss cheese

SPINACH FILLING:
1 Tablespoon minced green
   onion
2 Tablespoons butter
2 (10 ounce) packages frozen
   chopped spinach, cooked
   and drained
½ teaspoon salt

½ cup MORNAY SAUCE

MUSHROOM OR HAM
   FILLING:
4 ounces fresh mushrooms,
   finely minced, or 1 cup
   ground cooked ham
1 Tablespoon minced green
   onion
1 Tablespoon butter
½ Tablespoon cooking oil
1 (8 ounce) package cream
   cheese, softened
Salt and white pepper to taste
⅓ cup MORNAY SAUCE
1 egg, beaten
2 Tablespoons grated Swiss
   cheese
Butter

Prepare crêpes. *MORNAY SAUCE:* Melt butter. Stir in flour and cook, stirring, over low heat for several minutes. Take off heat and add milk and seasonings. Blend, return to heat and stir until thickened. Slowly stir in cream. Off the heat add cheese and stir until melted. *SPINACH FILLING:* Sauté onion in butter for a minute. Stir in spinach and salt and cook several minutes. Blend in *MORNAY SAUCE.* Set aside. *MUSHROOM OR HAM FILLING:* Sauté mushrooms and onion in butter and oil mixture 5 minutes. Beat cream cheese, salt and pepper. Stir in *MORNAY SAUCE,* egg and mushroom mixture. Set aside. Butter a baking dish that has a shallow rim (like a Pyrex pie pan). Begin with a crêpe placed in bottom of dish; spread it with a *very thin* layer of the first filling (about 2 Tablespoons). Top with a second crêpe; spread the second filling on it in a *very thin* layer. Repeat this sequence until all the crêpes are used, ending with a crêpe on top. Pour ¾ cup *MORNAY SAUCE* over the top of the tower. Sprinkle Swiss cheese on top and dot with butter. Warm the Tower in a preheated 350°F oven 20 minutes or until thoroughly heated. Cut into pie-shaped wedges and serve immediately. Pass CRAB MEAT SAUCE to spoon over the slices. Upon cutting, the 24 layers in alternating green and white make the Tower a spectacular looking luncheon entrée or equally as spectacular a first course for supper. Serves 12 as an entrée or 16 for a first course.

CRAB MEAT SAUCE

2 cups crab meat
3 Tablespoons dry vermouth

1½ cups MORNAY SAUCE
   (or amount remaining)

(Continued)

Sprinkle crab meat with vermouth and marinate for several hours in the refrigerator. Combine the crab meat and *MORNAY SAUCE* and heat thoroughly. Serve immediately. Makes 3½ cups sauce.

Mrs. Clyde Copeland, Jr.

Les Crêpes au Jambon

16 to 20 crêpes
¾ to 1 pound ham, thinly
  sliced (Smithfield or
  Prosciutto)

2 cups whipping cream
1 cup grated Gruyère or Swiss
  cheese
2 Tablespoons butter

Prepare crêpes. Fill them with the ham. Place crêpes in buttered flameproof serving dish. Pour cream over crêpes; sprinkle with cheese and dot with butter. Bake at 325°F for 15-20 minutes or until brown and bubbly. Serves 8-10.

Mrs. William B. Wilson

Chicken Curry Crêpes

36 crêpes
2 cups chopped celery
2 cups chopped onion
2 cups chopped green pepper
4 Tablespoons butter
4 Tablespoons flour
1 pint half and half cream
1 cup chicken stock

Milk for thinning
1 Tablespoon Worcestershire
  sauce
Salt and pepper to taste
1½ teaspoons mild curry
  powder
1 (5 pound) hen, cooked,
  deboned, chopped

Prepare crêpes. Sauté celery, onion and green pepper in melted butter. Stir in flour. Slowly add cream, chicken stock and milk to thin, if necessary. Add Worcestershire sauce, salt, pepper and curry powder. Stir in chicken. Additional milk may be added, if needed, but filling should be thick. Place a heaping Tablespoon of filling on each crêpe. Roll up and fasten with pick. Place crêpes in buttered baking dish and heat in oven at 300°F until hot. Remove picks before serving. Pass HOT FRUIT SAUCE in serving bowl for spooning over crêpes. Freezes well. Serves 12.

HOT FRUIT SAUCE

⅓ cup butter
1 (20 ounce) can crushed
  pineapple and juice

¾ cup brown sugar
4 apples, peeled and diced
½ (7 ounce) bag flaked coconut

Melt butter and add other ingredients. Stir and cook slowly on very low heat for about an hour.

Mrs. Howard L. McMillan, Jr.

Crêpes aux Fraises

12 crêpes	¼ teaspoon vanilla
2 (8 ounce) packages cream	1½ to 2 quarts fresh
cheese, softened	strawberries
5 Tablespoons powdered sugar	Sugar to taste
1⅓ cups sour cream	½ cup Cointreau

Prepare crêpes. Combine cream cheese with sugar, sour cream and vanilla. Spread a spoonful in the center of each crêpe. Roll up, arrange seam side down in a buttered shallow baking dish and sprinkle lightly with additional powdered sugar. Cover with foil. When ready to serve, heat for 15-20 minutes at 350°F. Slice and sugar strawberries. Barely warm them with the Cointreau in top of double boiler. Transfer crêpes to a warmed serving platter and pour sauce over. Sprinkle with additional powdered sugar and serve. Serves 12.

Mrs. Chick Warner, Vicksburg, Mississippi

Boning Poultry

Place raw dressed bird on a board; remove any trussing, wash and dry. Using a heavy cleaver, chop the ends off the drumsticks. Then chop off the outer 2 joints of the wings including the knobs of the little drumsticks. Chop off the tail. Place the bird breast side down. With a sharp boning knife, cut a slit to the bone down the center back. (This is the *only* time the skin is cut.) Boning only one side of the bird at a time, use the point of the knife to loosen the oyster (the pad of meat at the side of the back just above the point at which the thigh comes off the back). Edge knife up the center back and over the shoulder; then move down the ribs to free the breast section. Always be careful not to cut the skin. Work the knife through the joint joining the thigh and drumstick. Make a cut from the inside along the length of the thigh bone to expose it and cut the bone away from the meat with knife point. Pull the skin and meat from the thigh back from the drumstick. Cut and push the meat down and away from the drumstick. Slip the bone up and out like pulling one's arm from a sleeve. Pull the meat and skin away from the shoulder. Detach the wing joint with the knife tip. Work the wing bone away from the meat as done with the drumstick. Scrape the meat away from the shoulder blade and wishbone. One side is now boned with the meat attached only at the center breast. Bone the other side of the bird in the same manner. Last, hold the back and rib bones away from the meat. Be very careful near the center front of the breastbone as there is not much meat between bone and skin. Beginning at the top and continuing to the tip, cut across and down this bone, freeing the remaining meat. When this bone is removed, the chicken will lie flat except for small cylinders of meat from which the drumstick bones and wing bones were removed. Spread the boned bird flat, flesh side up, and stuff according to recipe.

Poulet Roulade

2 (3 pound) roasting chickens
Salt and pepper
Butter, melted
⅓ teaspoon each ground
    thyme, oregano, savory

POACHING STOCK:
Chicken bones, necks and
    giblets
Bouquet garni (¼ teaspoon
    thyme leaves, 4 sprigs
    parsley, 1 bay leaf tied in
    cheesecloth)
2 carrots, coarsely chopped
1 large onion, coarsely
    chopped

2 ribs celery, coarsely
    chopped

ZUCCHINI STUFFING:
1 pound small, firm zucchini
2 teaspoons salt
6 Tablespoons butter, divided
1 medium onion, finely
    chopped
½ cup ricotta cheese
Salt and pepper
Large pinch fresh marjoram,
    finely chopped
1 egg, slightly beaten
½ cup freshly grated Parmesan
    cheese

Debone the chickens. Leave in the drumsticks, if desired. Place the chickens skin side down. Salt, pepper and baste with melted butter. Sprinkle with the thyme, oregano and savory. The chickens are now ready for stuffing. *POACHING STOCK:* Place the chicken bones, necks and giblets (but not the livers) in a large pan and add the bouquet garni and the vegetables. Cover with water and simmer for 2 hours or more. Strain. *ZUCCHINI STUFFING:* Finely grate the zucchini; add salt and let sit for ½ hour. Squeeze out the zucchini, then place in a sieve and mash well to release all water. Sauté the zucchini in 2 Tablespoons butter for 7 minutes or until dry. Cool. Sauté the onion in 2 Tablespoons butter for 15 minutes without letting it color. Cool. Mash the ricotta cheese and the remaining 2 Tablespoons butter with the seasonings. Add the egg, onion, zucchini and Parmesan cheese. To assemble, divide the stuffing between the 2 chickens. Leave a ½-inch border around the edge of the chicken so the stuffing will not escape when it is rolled. Fold up the edges of the chicken, then fold the chicken in half to fully encase the stuffing. Roll the chicken tightly in a large length of cheesecloth. Twist and tie the ends with string; tie the entire roll at one-inch intervals. Place the chicken in the poaching stock and simmer for 1 hour. Remove from the liquid and let stand for 10 minutes before taking off the cheesecloth. Degrease the chicken stock and serve a little stock over each slice of chicken. Serves 8-10.

Mrs. Clarence H. Webb, Jr.

———

Bone a whole turkey and wrap it around any favorite dressing, enclosing dressing completely. Sew in place with trussing needles. Baste with butter and bake at 325°F for 2 hours or until done.

Pasta

All pasta is made of a flour and water dough that is kneaded and worked into a variety of shapes. Eggs are often added for richness. In making homemade pasta use ingredients of the highest quality, such as freshly grated Parmesan cheese and freshly ground pepper. Use sauces sparingly.

COOKING PROCEDURE   Bring a large pot of salted water to a boil (at least 2-3 quarts water for ½ pound pasta). Lower pasta into water. Long varieties like spaghetti will soften quickly so they can be curled into the pan. Bring the water back to a boil; stir the pasta with a wooden fork to separate the pieces and to prevent them from sticking to the bottom of the pot. Lower heat and simmer 8-12 minutes, stirring occasionally. Cook until slightly chewy or *al dente*. Strain the pasta at once into a colander and rinse with hot water to wash away the starch. Stock is sometimes used for boiling the noodles.

Homemade Pasta

4½ cups flour (preferably
unbleached)
3 eggs

3 egg whites
3 Tablespoons olive oil
3 teaspoons salt

Pour flour into a large mixing bowl or in a heap on a pastry board. Make a well in the center of the flour and in it place the eggs, egg whites, oil and salt. Mix together with a fork until the dough can be gathered into a rough ball. Moisten any remaining dry bits of flour with drops of water and press them into the ball. TO MAKE PASTA BY HAND: Knead the dough on a floured board, working in a little extra flour if the dough seems sticky. After about 10 minutes of kneading, the dough should be smooth, shiny and elastic. Wrap it in wax paper and let the dough rest for at least 10 minutes or more before rolling it. Divide the dough into 2 balls. Place 1 ball on a floured board, pastry cloth or dampened white cloth and flatten it with the palm of the hand into an oblong about 1 inch thick. Dust the top lightly with flour. Using a heavy rolling pin, start at one end of the oblong and roll it out lengthwise to within an inch of the farthest edge. Turn the dough crosswise and roll across its width. Repeat, turning and rolling the dough until it is paper thin. If at any time the dough begins to stick, lift it carefully and sprinkle more flour under it. Dust the rolled dough lightly with flour and let it rest for about 10 minutes. Gently roll the dough into a jelly-roll shape. With a sharp knife slice the roll crosswise into thin even strips 1/8 inch wide for tagliarini, ¼ inch wide for fettuccine or tagliatelle and ½-2 inches wide for lasagne. Unroll the strips and set them aside on wax paper. In the same fashion roll, shape and slice the second half of the dough. TO MAKE PASTA BY PASTA MACHINE: Pull off about a third of the dough at a time, set the smooth rolls of the pasta machine as far apart as possible and feed the piece of dough through them. Reroll this strip 2 or 3

(Continued)

more times folding under the ragged edges and dusting the dough lightly with flour if it feels sticky. When the dough is smooth, shiny and elastic and without any holes, it has been kneaded enough. Start rolling it out, setting the machine to the second notch and feeding the dough through with the rolls closer together. Set the machine at the third notch and roll the dough thinner. Repeat, if necessary, changing the notch after each rolling until the dough is about 1/16-1/32 inch thick. Feed through cutting blades for the desired size noodle. Homemade egg noodles may be cooked at once or covered with plastic wrap and refrigerated. Will keep for 24 hours. Can be dried by hanging over broom handles (or something similar) placed in parallel horizontal positions. Dries in about 24 hours. Store in tins. Serves 8.

James T. Canizaro

Pesto Sauce for Fettuccine

2 cups packed fresh basil leaves
½ cup olive oil
3 cloves garlic
½ teaspoon salt

½ cup grated Parmesan cheese
¼ cup pine nuts or walnuts
12 ounces fettuccine
½ cup butter (optional)

Place basil, oil, garlic and salt in a blender or food processor and purée. Add cheese and nuts and mix in. Toss cooked fettuccine with butter, then with pesto sauce and serve as a side dish with meats. Sauce may be prepared 2 days ahead. Freezes well. Makes 1¼ cups sauce serving 6-8.

Mrs. Henry H. Mounger

Seafood Sauce for Fettuccine

2 Tablespoons butter
1 bunch shallots, chopped
1 Tablespoon Worcestershire
   sauce
1 teaspoon basil
Salt and pepper

1 pint raw oysters
1 pound raw shrimp, peeled
1 pint sour cream
6 to 8 ounces fettuccine
Fresh parsley, chopped
Grated fresh Parmesan cheese

Melt butter in large skillet. Sauté shallots until soft. Add Worcestershire sauce, basil, salt and pepper. Add oysters and shrimp. Stir until shrimp are pink. Add sour cream and heat sauce thoroughly; *do not boil*. If sauce seems too thin (though it should be fairly thin), add a little flour dissolved in a little milk or cream. Serve at once over fettuccine which has been boiled in unsalted water. Garnish with parsley and Parmesan cheese. Serves 4.

Miss Charlotte Skelton

Fettuccine al Burro

½ cup butter, softened   ½ cup grated Parmesan cheese
¼ cup whipping cream   1 pound fettuccine noodles

Cream butter until light and fluffy. Blend in cream a little at a time. Blend in cheese. Cook fettuccine and drain. Toss with butter sauce and serve with extra cheese. Serves 8.

Mrs. Alexander Endy

Pâte à Choux

Basic Cream Puff Paste

½ cup butter   1 cup water
Salt   1 cup sifted flour
1 teaspoon sugar (for dessert   5 eggs
    puffs only)   1 teaspoon water

Combine butter, salt, (sugar) and 1 cup water in saucepan. (When making hors d'oeuvre puffs use 1 teaspoon salt and delete sugar. For dessert puffs use sugar and a pinch salt.) Bring to a boil, melting butter. Turn heat low and add flour. Beat until a ball forms in center of the pan. Remove from heat and beat in 4 eggs, one at a time. An electric mixer may be used. The last egg should be beaten with a fork and added a little at a time to lighten the paste until it is just stiff enough to stand in a peak. Beat the dough until it is very shiny. The dough may then be used immediately or kept in refrigerator in a well-covered bowl up to 2 days. To make small puffs, drop paste on a buttered baking sheet with a small teaspoon or with a pastry tube, placing 2 inches apart. For larger puffs, make mounds about 2 inches wide. Beat remaining egg with the teaspoon water and brush it lightly over tops of paste with pastry brush. Bake small or large puffs at 425°F for 20 minutes or until golden brown. Continue baking larger puffs at 375°F for 10-15 minutes more. Remove from oven and pierce side of each puff with knife. Return to oven, turn off heat and let sit with door ajar for 10 more minutes. Cool. Slice off tops and fill. Puffs freeze well after baking but need to be crisped in oven before filling. Yields 50-70 small or 25 medium puffs.

MINIATURE ÉCLAIRS

Fill small cream puffs with a custard filling; then garnish each top with a chocolate rosette made by beating together 1 Tablespoon softened butter, 2 Tablespoons cocoa, 2 Tablespoons milk and ½ cup powdered sugar until smooth, and piping mixture through a pastry tube. Chocolate icing can be spread instead of piped on top of puffs.

Shrimp Cream Puffs

50 small cream puffs
1 (8 ounce) package cream
 cheese, softened
1 teaspoon curry powder

Mayonnaise
1 pound shrimp, boiled, peeled,
 chopped

Make cream puffs by Basic Cream Puff Paste recipe. Cream the cheese with curry powder and enough mayonnaise to make the consistency of whipped cream. Fold in shrimp. Fill cream puffs only a few hours before serving. Makes 50 puffs.

Mrs. Charles Morris

Cream Puff Fillings

FRENCH CUSTARD

⅓ cup sugar
1 Tablespoon flour
1 Tablespoon cornstarch
¼ teaspoon salt
½ Tablespoon unflavored
 gelatin

1½ cups milk
1 egg, beaten
1½ teaspoons vanilla, divided
½ cup whipping cream
2 Tablespoons sugar

Mix together first 5 ingredients. Stir in milk. Cook mixture until thickened. Add a little hot mixture to egg. Return egg to custard and cook until thick. Add 1 teaspoon vanilla and cool. Before filling puffs whip cream with sugar and remaining vanilla and fold into custard. Fills 10 large or 50 small cream puffs.

CARAMEL CREAM

3 cups milk, divided
1½ cups sugar, divided
1/8 teaspoon salt

4½ Tablespoons cornstarch
6 Tablespoons butter
1½ teaspoons vanilla

Scald 2½ cups milk in top of double boiler. Caramelize 1 cup sugar until golden. Remove sugar from heat and slowly pour in the hot milk and remaining sugar. Cook until sugar is dissolved. Make a paste of the salt, cornstarch and remaining milk. Add this to caramel mixture. Cook until thick. Remove from heat. Stir in butter and vanilla. Chill. Fills 10 large or 50 small cream puffs.

Mrs. John McIntyre, Jr.

For quick hors d'oeuvres using leftover cream puff paste, beat 3-4 Tablespoons whipping cream into ½ cup warmed pâte à choux. Add several Tablespoons grated cheese or minced meat or seafood. Spread mixture on crackers or toast squares and bake in hot oven for 15 minutes.

Garnishes

Vegetable Garnishes

CARROT DAISIES   Cut carrot in 1/8-inch slices. Press out flower with truffle cutter. Remove center with end of a pencil with the eraser removed. Place a turnip disk on carrot center and spear with toothpick. Group daisies in a bouquet with bright parsley. If desired, spear carrot daisies into an orange for a base and twine toothpicks with parsley.

CUCUMBER TWISTS   Slice unpeeled cucumber very thinly. Cut cucumber slice on 1 side to the center and twist each end in opposite directions. Chill in ice water.

ONION MUMS   With sharp knife cut white or red onion into thin slivers from top to bottom, leaving bottom attached. Stop cuts about ½ to ¼ inch from bottom of onion. Soak in ice water to open petals. Mums may be colored by adding a few drops food coloring to ice water.

RADISH ROSES   Use rounded red radishes. Start at root end and cut thin strips of red peel through almost to stem. Place in ice water and petals will open.

TOMATO ROSES   Use a vegetable peeler or cut 1 long continuous piece of tomato peeling, beginning at stem end and peeling close to surface to prevent stretching or breaking strip. Wrap peel around finger and place on plate. Refrigerate.

TURNIP FLOWERS   Peel small white turnips. Cut into 1/16 to 1/8-inch slices. Cut small slice of carrot. Make hole in center of turnip slice the size of the carrot and insert carrot for center. Cut petals around edges in daisy design.

CELERY FANS   Cut celery rib into 3-inch lengths. Make parallel cuts forming narrow strips almost to the end, or cut each end of the celery almost to the center of each piece. Place in ice water and the slit ends will fan out and curl.

CARROT CURLS   Use medium or large carrots. Cut in half, lengthwise. Use a double-edge vegetable peeler to cut paper-thin lengthwise strips. Roll each strip into a curl and fasten tightly with a toothpick. Place in ice water for at least 1 hour. Remove toothpicks just before using.

RADISH FANS   Use oval-shaped radishes. With knife make thin cuts across the radish, cutting about ¾ of the way through. Leave at room temperature until slits spread easily. Chill in ice water at least 1 hour.

TOMATO FLOWERS   Select tiny or cherry tomatoes. Cut into sixths or eighths without cutting through the bottom. Separate carefully.

CUCUMBER WHEELS   Score the surface of a peeled or unpeeled cucumber by running tines of a fork along the lengthwise surface. Cut thin slices and crisp in ice water.

Fruit Garnishes

CITRUS BASKETS Slice orange, lemon or grapefruit in half and scoop fruit from shell. Cut a thin strip of peel from the top of each side of the shell. Leave peel connected on either side at center. Lift the 2 cut edges and tie together at center with ribbon. Use as dish for relish, salad or dessert.

LEMON BUTTERFLIES Cut a lemon in medium slices and cut each slice in half. Starting at the rind side, cut each slice almost to the center and force these cuts apart so the half slice forms wings. A piece of parsley placed in the center of the wings makes the butterfly's body.

MINT CUBES Place a sprig of mint and thin lemon segment in each ice cube square or in an ice ring before freezing. Use ice cubes in iced tea or minted fruit punch.

CRANBERRY CUTOUTS Slice a can of cranberry sauce into 1/8 to 1/4-inch slices. Use small cookie cutters or knife to cut decorative shapes for the appropriate season, such as stars and bells for Christmas.

STRAWBERRY FANS Wash berries and leave stem attached. Turn stem end down and, being careful not to cut through the stem, make cuts 1/8 inch apart. Separate carefully.

CITRUS CUPS Use a knife to make zigzag diagonal cuts around the middle of lemons, oranges or a grapefruit. Cut through to the center core. Separate halves of fruit. Serve fruit as is or remove pulp and fill with relish, fruit or salad. To keep cup level, remove a thin slice from bottom.

CITRUS CARTWHEELS With a sharp paring knife cut thin slices from limes, lemons or oranges. Cut notches in the rind of each slice. Dip edges in chopped parsley.

CITRUS TWISTS Cut lemon, lime or orange slices 1/8 inch thick. Start a cut almost at center of slice and extend cut through outside edge. Twist cut edges in opposite directions.

FRUIT KEBABS Place combination of 3 or 4 small pieces of fruit such as pineapple, orange, banana, apple and maraschino cherry on a wooden pick or skewer.

EASTER HAM DAISIES Cut 20 (1 inch) petals of candied orange peel and fasten each petal to ham with cloves. Center each daisy with a candied cherry half.

Chocolate Leaves

Melt 1 (8 ounce) package chocolate chips in double boiler. Arrange camellia or ivy leaves on sheet of wax paper. Spread chocolate on back side of each leaf with a spoon. Place immediately in freezer for 30 minutes to 1 hour. Peel away green leaf. Place hands in ice water to work with leaves.

Mrs. Alvin E. Brent, Jr.

Meringues

Basic Meringue

4 egg whites, at room
 temperature
¼ teaspoon cream of tartar or
 1 teaspoon vinegar

Pinch salt
1 teaspoon vanilla
1 cup sugar (preferably
 superfine)

Combine egg whites, cream of tartar, salt and vanilla in a large bowl. Beat at low speed until eggs begin to foam, then at medium speed until egg whites hold soft peaks. Gradually add ¾ cup sugar, 1 Tablespoon at a time, while beating on high speed. Beat until meringue is very stiff, dull and no longer grainy. Gently fold in remaining sugar. Meringues should be dried rather than baked to obtain the proper texture. Shape meringue according to recipe. Place in preheated 200°F oven for 1 hour. Turn heat off and let meringues remain in oven for at least 4 hours or overnight. When completely dry, meringues may be kept covered in a dry airy place for several weeks or frozen. If frozen, uncover to thaw and place in oven on very low heat if they feel moist in any way. Makes 12 tarts, 70 tartlets, 1 pie shell or 3 meringue discs.

For egg whites to mound their highest, no oil or grease should be on the bowl or beaters; the egg whites should be at room temperature; a little acid should be added in the form of cream of tartar, lemon juice or vinegar; the egg whites must be absolutely free from even a speck of egg yolk; the bowl should be slightly warm.

Lime Angel Pie

1 recipe Basic Meringue
4 egg yolks
1/8 teaspoon salt
½ cup sugar
4 Tablespoons lime juice

1 Tablespoon grated lime rind
Few drops green food coloring
 (optional)
1 pint whipping cream

Make meringue according to Basic Meringue recipe and shape into a pie shell in a greased 10-inch pie plate. Bake according to basic recipe instructions. Beat egg yolks until fluffy. Add all other ingredients except cream. Cook in top of double boiler until thick, about 8-10 minutes. Cool. Whip cream and fold half of it into the lime mixture. Pour into pie shell and spread remaining whipped cream on top. Sprinkle with additional grated lime rind. Chill at least 4 hours before serving. Preferably make a day ahead. Serves 8.

Mrs. Raymond Birchett

For an easy but pretty dessert, place a scoop of ice cream in a meringue tart shell and top with a dessert sauce.

Miniature Mushrooms

2 egg whites
1/8 teaspoon cream of tartar

½ teaspoon almond extract
⅔ cup sugar

Make meringue by instructions for Basic Meringue but use the above ingredients. With a plain round tip in a pastry bag or using wax paper rolled into a
funnel shape, press out meringue in 1½-inch rounds on a large cookie sheet
which has been greased and lightly floured. Smooth tops. To make stems, hold
bag upright and press out meringue, pulling straight back about 1½ inches.
Bake according to baking instructions for Basic Meringue. When cool, gently
puncture bottom of mushroom crown and insert stem. A dab of icing may be
used to attach it, if necessary. Brush mushroom tops with cocoa, if desired.
Use to garnish cakes or desserts. Makes about 30 mushrooms.

Mrs. Gus Primos

Meringue Cream Tartlets

1 recipe Basic Meringue
½ pint whipping cream
3 Tablespoons powdered sugar,
   or to taste
1 cup finely chopped fresh
   strawberries or
1 (10 ounce) box frozen
   raspberries, drained

1 teaspoon Cointreau
⅓ cup finely chopped toasted
   almonds
1 teaspoon sherry wine
1 teaspoon chopped
   crystallized ginger (optional)

Cover cookie sheet with a piece of heavy brown paper or greased foil. Make
meringue according to Basic Meringue recipe. Form into miniature meringue
shells by dropping meringue on prepared baking sheet with a teaspoon. Use
spoon to make a nest in the center. If desired, make larger tart shells by drawing around a cookie cutter with a pencil. Spread the meringue within the mark
or pipe it on using a pastry bag. If the shell is to be filled, pipe an additional
strip around the outside edge for a wall or shape it with a spoon. Bake either
shells according to basic recipe instructions. Whip cream and sweeten with
powdered sugar. Divide whipped cream into 2 equal parts. Add strawberries or
raspberries and Cointreau to 1 mixture. To the other mixture add almonds,
sherry and ginger, if desired. At serving time fill meringue shells with whipped
cream mixtures. Do not fill ahead of time. This is an ideal sweet to serve at
cocktail buffets at which finger food is appropriate. Makes 70 tartlets.

Mrs. John Nicholson, Jr.

———

*Make a quick caramel filling for meringue tartlets by boiling in water to cover
1 unopened (14 ounce) can Eagle Brand condensed milk for 3 hours. Cool 1
hour and open. Milk will be caramelized.*

Fillings for Meringue Tarts or Tartlets

CHOCOLATE FILLING

½ cup butter, softened
1 cup powdered sugar
2 (1 ounce) squares
  unsweetened chocolate

2 eggs
1 teaspoon vanilla
½ teaspoon dark rum

Cream together butter and sugar. Melt chocolate and beat in. Add eggs and beat 5 minutes. Add flavorings. Spoon into meringue shells. Fills 50 tartlets or 10 tarts.

LEMON FILLING

2 eggs
2 egg yolks
½ cup butter or part margarine

1 cup sugar
Juice and grated rind of
  2 lemons

Place eggs and egg yolks in top of double boiler. Beat gently until whites and yolks are mixed. Add rest of ingredients. Place over simmering water and stir with a wooden spoon until mixture is the consistency of mayonnaise. Store in covered jar in refrigerator until ready to use. Will keep for weeks. Fills 70 tartlets or 12 tarts.

Boccone Dolce

1 recipe Basic Meringue
6 (1 ounce) squares semisweet
  chocolate
3 Tablespoons water

2 cups whipping cream
⅓ cup sugar
1½ pints fresh strawberries

Prepare meringue according to Basic Meringue recipe. To shape into meringue discs, line a baking sheet with wax paper or foil. Trace 3 (8 inch) circles on the paper. Spread the meringue evenly over each circle about ¼ inch thick. Bake according to basic recipe instructions. After the meringues are dry, carefully peel off the wax paper and set discs aside. Melt chocolate with the water over hot water. Whip the cream until fairly stiff, gradually adding sugar. Slice strawberries in half if small and in slices if large. Save some of the prettiest whole ones to decorate top. Place a meringue disc on a serving plate, spread it with half the melted chocolate and with about a ½-inch layer whipped cream. Arrange the sliced strawberries on this with the pointed ends to the outside along the edge to make a pretty pattern. Repeat with second meringue disc, chocolate, whipped cream and strawberries. Place the third meringue disc on top and spread it with whipped cream. Decorate with whole strawberries and some whipped cream piped through a pastry bag. Frost the sides of the cake with whipped cream, if desired. Refrigerate for 2 hours. Serves 12-15.

Mrs. William B. Wilson

Rainy Days and Special Days

Men may conquer their mountains
And fly to the moon in their planes,
But none of their feats are equal
To being stuck with three kids when it rains!
    —Mrs. Ruth Stockett

This special section of craft ideas to do at home with things on hand has been designed to create activities for children of any age on any occasion. It could be a lifesaver for busy mothers, for baby-sitting grandmothers and for maiden aunts who want to be remembered for the fun activities the children are allowed to do. Hopefully the adults will enjoy the activities, too.

No-Cook Play Dough

1 cup salt
1 cup flour
1 Tablespoon salad oil

Food coloring, if desired
Water

Mix dry ingredients; add oil. Add food coloring to water. Slowly add water until desired consistency is reached.

Finger Paint

Mix together dry tempera colors with either liquid detergent or liquid starch and use as finger paint.

Creative Clay

1 (1 pound) package baking
    soda
1 cup cornstarch

1 ¼ cups cold water
Food coloring (optional)

Mix soda and cornstarch together; add water. Cook and stir over low heat until consistency of mashed potatoes. Remove from heat and cover with damp cloth until cool enough to handle. Use for play dough or jewelry shaping or roll it out to make ornamental cookies. Clay dries very hard. Store in plastic bag to keep from drying out. Clay may be colored with food coloring added to the water or painted with tempera when dry.

Soap Bubbles

2 cups warm water
2 Tablespoons liquid detergent

1 Tablespoon sugar
1 Tablespoon glycerin (optional)

Combine ingredients. Glycerin will make bubbles iridescent. Blow bubbles through wire loops or spools. To make lots of bubbles outdoors, place fly swatter in soapy water and swing it around.

Decorative Bread Dough

1 cup salt
4 cups flour

1 to 1¼ cups water

Mix ingredients and knead about 20 minutes, or until of desired consistency. Dough can be used in any creative way. Baskets may be made by weaving dough on back side of Pyrex baking dish. To make ornaments, roll dough and cut out shapes with cookie cutters. Prick to prevent air bubbles. Dampen to make pieces stick together. Bake at 300°F until golden brown. Paint with acrylic paint, if desired. Varnish and dry.

Soap Crayons

2 Tablespoons water
Ivory Flakes

Food coloring

Pour water into a 1-cup measuring cup. Fill the rest of the cup to the top with Ivory Flakes. With a spoon mix the water and soap flakes together until mixture becomes a thick soapy paste without any big lumps. Add about 30 or 40 drops of food coloring to the soap mixture and stir well until the soap has color. Scoop out some of the mixture and put it in one of the cube spaces of an ice cube tray. Press the soap paste down into the cube until it is filled to the top. Fill 1 or 2 more cubes with the remaining soap mixture. Dry cubes in a warm, dry place for 1 or 2 days until the soap paste gets hard (test by pressing with your finger). Pop the soap crayons out of the tray. Some colors will work better than others. Soap crayons are made from pure soap and food coloring, so whatever is drawn with them can be wiped off bathtubs, sinks, floors, windows, hands and faces. They are great for making disguises like a big moustache or a clown face.

Colored Coconut

Mix a few drops food coloring and 1 teaspoon water in a 1-pint jar. Fill with flaked or grated coconut. Seal jar and shake until coconut is the desired color. Use to decorate cupcakes or any desserts.

Old-Fashioned Pull Taffy

2 cups sugar
½ cup light Karo
½ cup water

¼ teaspoon cream of tartar
Food coloring, if desired
Flavoring desired

Combine sugar, Karo, water and cream of tartar. Place over heat. Stir until sugar dissolves. Cook, without stirring, to 265°F on candy thermometer. Remove from heat; add coloring and flavoring if desired. Pour on greased platter or pie pan. *Cool* until easily handled. Pull into ropes until chalky and porous. Break or cut into bite-size pieces with scissors.

This makes a mess but is a lot of fun for everyone involved. Greased hands make pulling easier.

Snow Ice Cream

1 (14 ounce) can condensed
   milk
1 (5.33 ounce) can evaporated
   milk

1 teaspoon vanilla
Snow

Mix milks and vanilla. Gradually beat in snow until ice cream is of desired consistency. Serves 5.

Since in the deep South it snows only enough to have snow ice cream about once a generation, the recipe must be handed down from parent to child anticipating the time when it will snow again.

"Look-In" Easter Eggs

1 drop food coloring, if desired
1 Tablespoon cold water
2 cups superfine sugar or
   granulated sugar, run in
   blender

ICING:
1 egg white
3 to 4 drops vinegar
1½ cups powdered sugar

Add coloring to water. Mix with sugar until it has the feel of sand. If sugar is sticky, add more sugar; if it is crumbly, add more water. Pack sugar firmly into plastic Easter eggs split end to end. Scoop out sugar, leaving a shell about ¼ inch thick. Place separate halves upside down on wax paper. Level off edges by pulling a piece of thread between edge of egg and wax paper. Leave eggs 6-8 hours to dry. When dry, lift off mold and carefully break off pointed end for peep hole. Beat *ICING* ingredients together. In the bottom half of sugar egg, decorate with flowers and figures, using *ICING* as a base. Place on top the remaining egg half, using the ICING to glue seams together. Decorate seam and top with icing squeezed through pastry tube and allow to dry. A school picture or baby picture is an innovative form of decoration.

Special Days

Not what we give, but what we share-
For the gift without the giver is bare.
—James Russell Lowell

Everyone likes to be unique in gift-giving. "Gifts in a Jar" may be used for teachers, the postman, neighbors or friends anytime during the year but especially at Christmas.

Christmas Odor Punch

1 fresh ginger root, split
3 pieces stick cinnamon
16 whole cloves
1 teaspoon ground allspice
1 to 2 Tablespoons pickling
    spice

Place dry ingredients in a jar or calico bag.

To mix, add dry ingredients to 1 quart water and simmer. This fills kitchen with a wonderful odor. THIS PUNCH IS NOT FOR CONSUMPTION.

Colored Sugar

Combine 1 cup sugar with a few drops food coloring. Shake in a jar until color is evenly distributed. Try placing several layers of different colored sugar in a glass jar for a gift.

Seasoned Salt

1 (26 ounce) box salt
1½ ounces black pepper
2 ounces red pepper
1 ounce garlic powder
1 ounce chili powder
1 ounce Accent

Combine ingredients and place in bottle or jar with tight-fitting lid. Makes 32 ounces.

Hot Mocha Mix

1 cup unsweetened cocoa
2½ cups sugar
2 cups dry non-dairy coffee
    creamer
2 cups nonfat dry milk powder
½ cup instant coffee
1 vanilla bean, cut into
    quarters

Combine ingredients in a large dry bowl; stir until well blended. Pack into jars, making sure a piece of vanilla bean is in each jar. Seal and label. Store in refrigerator at least a week before using to allow vanilla flavor to be absorbed into the mix. Makes 8 cups mocha mix.

Use 3 Tablespoons mocha mix for every ¾ cup boiling water. Top with a marshmallow or whipped cream.

Homemade Kahlúa

1 quart water
2½ cups sugar
3 Tablespoons instant coffee

1 Tablespoon vanilla
2½ cups vodka

Bring water, sugar and coffee to a boil in a saucepan. Simmer *very* slowly for 3 hours. Mixture will be very dark and syrupy. Cool. Add vanilla and vodka. Serve as an after-dinner liqueur or over vanilla ice cream. Bottle in carafes or decorative bottles for gifts. Makes 7 cups Kahlúa.

Cinnamon Sugar Butter

½ cup butter, softened
2 cups sugar

2 teaspoons ground cinnamon

Beat until thoroughly blended. Mixture will be crumbly. Store in jar in refrigerator. Makes 2½ cups butter.

To make cinnamon toast, sprinkle mixture liberally on bread. Toast in 400°F oven or broil.

Strawberry Butter

¾ cup frozen strawberries,
    thawed and drained
1 cup butter, softened

3 Tablespoons confectioners'
    sugar

Mix ingredients in blender until smooth. Delicious on hot homemade rolls. Yield: about 1 cup.

Buttermilk Dressing Mix

1 cup dry buttermilk powder
    (if unavailable, substitute
    nonfat dry milk powder in
    the mix and add 1 teaspoon
    lemon juice to the prepared
    dressing)
¼ cup sugar

4 teaspoons dried basil, crushed
4 teaspoons instant minced
    onion
2 teaspoons dry mustard
1 teaspoon garlic powder
1 teaspoon salt

Combine dry buttermilk powder, sugar and seasonings. Store in airtight container. Makes about 1 cup mix.

To make 1 recipe dressing, combine ¼ cup Buttermilk Dressing Mix with ½ cup cold water. Blend into ¾ cup mayonnaise or salad dressing. Shake well before serving. Makes about 1 cup dressing.

Fruited Rice Curry

1 cup raw long-grain rice	½ teaspoon salt
1 Tablespoon instant minced onion	¼ cup mixed dried fruits, chopped
2 teaspoons curry powder	2 Tablespoons golden raisins
2 beef bouillon cubes, crushed	¼ cup blanched slivered almonds

Combine all ingredients. Package in airtight container. Makes 2 cups rice mix.

To prepare rice curry, combine rice mix with 2½ cups water and 2 Table-spoons butter or margarine; cover tightly. Bring to boiling; reduce heat. Simmer 20 minutes. Do not lift cover. Makes 4 cups cooked rice.

Rice Mixes

LEMON DILL RICE:
1 Tablespoon dried grated
   lemon peel
1 teaspoon dried minced onion
4 chicken bouillon cubes or
   4 packets instant chicken
   broth
2 teaspoons dill weed
1 teaspoon salt
2 cups raw rice

VEGETABLE RICE:
4 packets instant vegetable
   broth or 4 vegetable
   bouillon cubes
1 teaspoon salt
2 teaspoons each celery seed,
   onion flakes, green pepper
   flakes, sweet pepper flakes
2 cups raw rice

Combine ingredients for either rice desired. Divide the mix used into 2 portions and store each portion in tightly closed containers. Each portion makes about 1¼ cups rice mix.

To cook, combine 1 portion rice mix with 2 cups water and 1 Tablespoon margarine in saucepan. Bring to a boil, cover tightly and cook over very low heat until liquid is absorbed (about 25 minutes). Each portion of mix makes 4-5 servings.

Spice Bags

ORANGE-ANISE SPICE BAGS   Spoon ½ teaspoon dried orange peel, ¼ teaspoon anise seed and 2 whole allspice in center of each 5-inch square, double-thickness piece of cheesecloth. Tie securely with cotton string. Give bags as gifts, noting to steep each in one 5 or 6-ounce cup hot apple juice.

CARDAMOM-CINNAMON SPICE BAGS   Spoon 2 whole cardamom, cracked, and 1 large stick cinnamon, broken, in center of each 5-inch square, double thickness piece of cheesecloth. Tie securely with a cotton string. Give bags as a gift, noting to steep each in one 5 or 6-ounce cup hot cranberry juice.

Seasoning Mixes

SALAD SEASONING

2 Tablespoons parsley flakes
1 Tablespoon seasoned salt
1 teaspoon seasoned pepper

1 Tablespoon each marjoram,
    basil, dried chives, celery
    seed, dill weed

Combine seasonings and sprinkle on salads or use in dressings as desired. Store in cool place in airtight container. Makes ¼ cup mix.

ITALIAN HERB SEASONING

Crushed dried marjoram
Basil
Oregano
Thyme
Rosemary
Savory

Sage
1 or 2 dried red chili peppers,
    crushed (seeds removed)
2 bay leaves, broken into small
    pieces

Mix equal amounts of the first 7 ingredients. Add chili peppers and bay leaves. Store in airtight container. Use to season a tossed salad.

POULTRY SEASONING

2 Tablespoons parsley flakes
1 teaspoon sage
1 teaspoon white pepper

1 Tablespoon each oregano,
    marjoram, thyme, rosemary,
    ground ginger, celery salt

Combine ingredients and store in container with tight-fitting lid. Use amount desired in cooking or frying poultry. Makes ⅓ cup mix.

FISH SEASONING

2 Tablespoons parsley flakes
1 Tablespoon each dried grated
    lemon rind, celery seed,
    savory, thyme, marjoram

1 teaspoon dried chives
1 bay leaf, broken into small
    pieces

Combine ingredients and store in container with tight-fitting lid. Use amount desired to season fish. Makes ⅓ cup mix.

CHILI SEASONING

1 Tablespoon chili powder
2 teaspoons ground cumin
1 teaspoon ground oregano
1 Tablespoon seasoned salt

1 dried chili pepper, crushed
    (seeds removed)
1 teaspoon instant minced onion
¼ teaspoon instant minced
    garlic

Combine ingredients and store in container with tight-fitting lid. Use as seasoning in any chili recipe using 1 pound hamburger meat. Makes ⅓ cup mix.

Table of Measurements and Equivalents in U.S. and Metric

U.S.	EQUIVALENTS	METRIC*
		volume-milliliters
Dash	Less than 1/8 teaspoon	
1 teaspoon	60 drops	5 ml.
1 tablespoon	3 teaspoons	15 ml.
2 tablespoons	1 fluid ounce	30 ml.
4 tablespoons	1/4 cup	60 ml.
5 1/3 tablespoons	1/3 cup	80 ml.
6 tablespoons	3/8 cup	90 ml.
8 tablespoons	1/2 cup	120 ml.
10 2/3 tablespoons	2/3 cup	160 ml.
12 tablespoons	3/4 cup	180 ml.
16 tablespoons	1 cup or 8 ounces	240 ml.
1 cup	1/2 pint or 8 fluid ounces	240 ml.
2 cups	1 pint	480 ml.
1 pint	16 ounces	480 ml. or .473 liter
1 quart	2 pints	960 ml. or .95 liter
2.1 pints	1.05 quarts or .26 gallons	1 liter
2 quarts	1/2 gallon	
4 quarts	1 gallon	3.8 liters
		weight-grams
1 ounce	16 drams	28 grams
1 pound	16 ounces	454 grams
1 pound	2 cups liquid	
1 kilo	2.20 pounds	

Temperature Conversion from Fahrenheit to Celsius*

FAHRENHEIT	200	225	250	275	300	325	350	375
CELSIUS	93	106	121	135	149	163	176	191

FAHRENHEIT	400	425	450	475	500	550
CELSIUS	205	218	231	246	260	288

*These are round figures. The important thing to remember in cooking is to use relative amounts in measuring.

Pan and Baking Dish Sizes

COMMON KITCHEN PANS TO USE AS CASSEROLES
WHEN THE RECIPE CALLS FOR

4-cup baking dish:
9-inch pie plate
8-inch layer cake pan
7 3/8 x 3 5/8-inch loaf pan

6-cup baking dish:
8 or 9-inch layer cake pan
10-inch pie plate
8½ x 3 5/8-inch loaf pan

8-cup baking dish:
8 x 8-inch square pan
11 x 7-inch baking pan
9 x 5-inch loaf pan

10-cup baking dish:
9 x 9-inch square pan
11¾ x 7½-inch baking pan
15 x 10-inch jelly-roll pan

12-cup baking dish and over:
13½ x 8½-inch glass baking pan   12 cups
13 x 9-inch metal baking pan   15 cups
14 x 10½-inch roasting pan   19 cups

TOTAL VOLUME OF SPECIAL BAKING PANS

Tube pans:
7½ x 3-inch bundt pan   6 cups
9 x 3½-inch kugelhupf tube or bundt pan   9 cups
9 x 3½-inch angel cake pan   12 cups
10 x 3¾-inch bundt pan   12 cups
10 x 4-inch kugelhupf tube pan   16 cups
10 x 4-inch angel cake pan   18 cups
Melon mold:
7 x 5½ x 4-inch mold   6 cups
Springform pans:
8 x 3-inch pan   12 cups
9 x 3-inch pan   16 cups
Ring molds:
8½ x 2¼-inch mold   4½ cups
9¼ x 2¾-inch mold   8 cups
Charlotte mold:
6 x 4¼-inch mold   7½ cups
Brioche pan:
9½ x 3¼-inch pan   8 cups

Index

INDEX

INDEX

INDEX

INDEX

Mail to:

Southern Sideboards
P. O. Box 4553
Jackson, Mississippi 39216

Please send me_____copies of *Southern Sideboards* at $11.95 per copy. I am including $1.55 each to cover postage and handling. (Mississippi residents add $.60 sales tax per book.) Also add $.25 for gift wrap.

Name: _____

Address: _____

City: _____State:_____Zip Code:_____

Charge to: ☐ Visa   ☐ Master Charge

Acct # _____Expiration date_____

Make checks payable to *Southern Sideboards*.

All proceeds will be used for community service projects sponsored by the Junior League of Jackson, Mississippi.

Mail to:

Southern Sideboards
P. O. Box 4553
Jackson, Mississippi 39216

Please send me_____copies of *Southern Sideboards* at $11.95 per copy. I am including $1.55 each to cover postage and handling. (Mississippi residents add $.60 sales tax per book.) Also add $.25 for gift wrap.

Name: _____

Address: _____

City: _____State:_____Zip Code:_____

Charge to: ☐ Visa   ☐Master Charge

Acct # _____Expiration date_____

Make checks payable to *Southern Sideboards*.

All proceeds will be used for community service projects sponsored by the Junior League of Jackson, Mississippi.

Mail to:

Southern Sideboards
P. O. Box 4553
Jackson, Mississippi 39216

Please send me_____copies of *Southern Sideboards* at $11.95 per copy. I am including $1.55 each to cover postage and handling. (Mississippi residents add $.60 sales tax per book.) Also add $.25 for gift wrap.

Name: _____

Address: _____

City: _____State:_____Zip Code:_____

Charge to: ☐ Visa   ☐Master Charge

Acct # _____Expiration date_____

Make checks payable to *Southern Sideboards*.

All proceeds will be used for community service projects sponsored by the Junior League of Jackson, Mississippi.